Research on Optimal Consumption Rate and Steady Economic Growth in China

Zhao Xincheng

Research on Optimal Consumption Rate and Steady Economic Growth in China

Translated by Ma Aoxue

PETER LANG
New York · Berlin · Bruxelles · Chennai · Lausanne · Oxford

Library of Congress Cataloging-in-Publication Data

Names: Zhao, Xincheng, author.
Title: Research on optimal consumption rate and steady economic growth in China / Zhao Xincheng.
Other titles: Zui you xiao fei lü yu Zhongguo jing ji wen ding zeng zhang yan jiu. English
Description: New York : Peter Lang, [2024] | Includes bibliographical references.
Identifiers: LCCN 2023005516 (print) | LCCN 2023005517 (ebook) |
ISBN 9781433197918 (hardback ; alk. paper) | ISBN 9781636672670 (ebook) |
ISBN 9781636672687 (epub)
Subjects: LCSH: Consumption (Economics)–China. | Economic development–China. |
China–Economic conditions–1949-
Classification: LCC HC430.C6 Z434813 2024–(print) | LCC HC430.C6–(ebook) |
DDC 339.4/70951–dc23/eng/20230215
LC record available at https://lccn.loc.gov/2023005516
LC ebook record available at https://lccn.loc.gov/2023005517
DOI 10.3726/b20708

Bibliographic information published by the Deutsche Nationalbibliothek.
The German National Library lists this publication in the German
National Bibliography; detailed bibliographic data is available
on the Internet at http://dnb.d-nb.de.

Cover design by Peter Lang Group AG

ISBN 9781433197918 (hardback)
ISBN 9781636672670 (ebook)
ISBN 9781636672687 (epub)
DOI 10.3726/b20708

Supported by a Grant from the Yunnan University Double First-Class Initiative

This edition is an authorized translation from the Chinese language edition
Published by arrangement with Social Sciences Academic Press (China)
All rights reserved

© 2024 Peter Lang Group AG, Lausanne
Published by Peter Lang Publishing Inc., New York, USA
info@peterlang.com - www.peterlang.com

All rights reserved.
All parts of this publication are protected by copyright.
Any utilization outside the strict limits of the copyright law, without the permission of the publisher, is forbidden and liable to prosecution.
This applies in particular to reproductions, translations, microfilming, and storage and processing in electronic retrieval systems.

This publication has been peer reviewed.

Contents

List of Figures ix
List of Tables xiii
Preface xvii

Chapter 1 Introduction 1
    1.1 Background and Some Basic Facts about the Research 1
    1.2 Approach and Methodology 7
    1.3 Definition and Literature Review 8
    1.4 Outline 26

Chapter 2 China's Consumption Rate and Economic Growth Steadiness: Stylized Facts 35
    2.1 Features of the Variation in China's Consumption Rate 36
    2.2 Features of the Steadiness of China's Economic Growth 47

	2.3	Factors Affecting China's Final Consumption Rate	49
	2.4	Summary	59
Chapter 3		Economic Dynamic Efficiency and Optimal Consumption Rate	63
	3.1	Economic Dynamic Efficiency and Its Evaluation Method	63
	3.2	Optimal Consumption Rate and Dynamic Efficiency: Theoretical Framework	65
	3.3	Optimal Consumption Rate and Dynamic Efficiency: Empirical Analysis	70
	3.4	Optimal Consumption Rate and Dynamic Efficiency: Analysis at the Provincial Level	90
	3.5	Conclusion and Policy Suggestions	100
Chapter 4		Optimal Consumption Rate in the Solow–Swan Model	109
	4.1	Theoretical Framework of Optimal Consumption Rate	110
	4.2	Measurement and Analysis of China's Optimal Consumption Rate	117
	4.3	China's Optimal Consumption Rate – Analysis Based on Capital-Output Ratio	121
	4.4	Summary and Policy Suggestions	128
Chapter 5		Optimal Consumption Rate in the Ramsey–Cass–Koopsman Model	133
	5.1	Analysis Framework for China's Optimal Consumption Rate: Theoretical Model	134
	5.2	Calculation of China's Optimal Consumption Rate Based on the Ramsey–Cass–Koopmans Model	145
	5.3	Summary and Policy Suggestions	153
Chapter 6		Optimal Consumption Rate in an Open Economy	157
	6.1	Determination of Optimal Consumption Rate in an Open Economy	159

	6.2	Numerical Simulation of the Optimal Consumption Rate in an Open Economy	168
	6.3	Summary	174
Chapter 7	Optimal Consumption Rate in the Dynamic Stochastic General Equilibrium (DSGE) Model		177
	7.1	Theoretical Framework of the DSGE Model	179
	7.2	Numerical Simulation and Dynamic Analysis	184
	7.3	Summary	194
Chapter 8	Evaluation of the Steadiness of China's Economic Growth and Analysis of the Factors Affecting It		197
	8.1	Demand Structure and Economic Growth Stability	199
	8.2	Industry Structure and Economic Growth Stability	209
	8.3	Factor Structure and Economic Growth Stability	218
	8.4	Ownership Structure and Economic Growth Stability	234
	8.5	Empirical Analysis of the Factors Affecting the Steadiness of China's Economic Growth	238
	8.6	Conclusion and Policy Suggestions	244
Chapter 9	Analysis of the Impact of Final Consumption Rate on Economic Growth and Its Steadiness		253
	9.1	Analysis of the Impact of Increase in Consumption Rate on Economic Growth – from the Perspective of National Accounts	255
	9.2	Impact of Variation in Consumption Rate on Economic Growth – Based on Input-Output Table	272
	9.3	Dynamic Analysis of the Impact of the Increase in Consumption Rate on China's Economic Growth	282

Chapter 10 Conclusion and Outlook 303
    10.1 Research Conclusions 303
    10.2 Policy Suggestions 313
    10.3 Deficiency and Outlook 320

Appendix 323

List of Figures

Figure 1-1	The Contribution Rates of Final Consumption, Gross Capital Formation and Net Export to China's Economic Growth	2
Figure 1-2	China's Economic Growth Driven by Final Consumption, Gross Capital Formation and Net Export	2
Figure 1-3	China's Final Consumption Rate, Household Consumption Rate and Government Consumption Rate	4
Figure 1-4	China's Rural Household Consumption Rate and Urban Household Consumption Rate	4
Figure 1-5	Simulation Curve of the Economic Growth Effect of Consumption Rate	17
Figure 2-1	Final Consumption Rates of the World and Countries with Different Income Levels	38
Figure 2-2	Evolution Trend of Final Consumption Rates of the Top Ten Countries in the GDP Ranking during 1960–2014	39
Figure 2-3	Evolution Trend of the Final Consumption Rates of the BRICS during 1960–2014	40

LIST OF FIGURES

Figure 2-4	Evolution Trend of China's Rural Household Consumption Rate and Urban Household Consumption Rate	44
Figure 2-5	Evolution Trend of China's Government Consumption Rate	45
Figure 2-6	Growth Rates of China's GDP, Final Consumption and Total Capital Formation	48
Figure 2-7	Growth Rates of China's GDP and the Three Industries since 1978	49
Figure 2-8	Kuznets Curve of Consumption	52
Figure 2-9	Evolution Path of China's Consumption Rate with the GDP Per Capita	53
Figure 3-1	Trend in China's Capital-Output Ratio during 1978–2016	73
Figure 3-2	China's Average Household Propensity to Consume and Proportion of Disposable Income in the GDP	80
Figure 3-3	Trend of China's Final Consumption Rate and Labour Income Ratio since 1992	81
Figure 3-4	AR Root Graph Testing the Stationarity of the VAR Model	83
Figure 3-5	Impulse Response Curve of *CR* and *LIR*	83
Figure 3-6	Relationship between Final Consumption Rate and Dynamic Efficiency	88
Figure 3-7	Impulse Response Curve of CR and DR	90
Figure 3-8	Average CR, LIR and Difference Ratio in 30 Provinces during 1993–2016	92
Figure 4-1	Steady State of the Solow Model	111
Figure 4-2	Impact of the Variation of CR on Steady State	112
Figure 4-3	Correspondence between Consumption Maximization and Golden-Rule Level of Capital Stock	114
Figure 4-4	Variation of China's Labour Income Ratio and Final Consumption Rate since 1992	117
Figure 4-5	Comparison between China's Final Consumption Rate and the Optimal Consumption Rate during 1978–2014	121
Figure 4-6	Consumption Maximization at the Steady State in the Solow Model	123
Figure 4-7	China's Optimal Consumption Rate, Final Consumption Rate and Capital-Output Ratio during 1978–2013	126
Figure 7-1	Impulse Response of Economic Variables to Technology Shocks	189

Figure 7-2	Impulse Response of Economic Variables to Government Consumption Shocks	190
Figure 8-1	Variation of China's Economic Growth Rate	198
Figure 8-2	Variation of the Stability of the Growth of China's GDP, Consumption, Investment and Net Export since the Reform and Opening-Up	202
Figure 8-3	Evolution of China's Demand Structure during 1978–2020	207
Figure 8-4	Growth Rates of China's GDP and the Three Demands	208
Figure 8-5	Variation of the Stability of China's GDP and the Three Industries since the Reform and Opening-Up	212
Figure 8-6	Evolution of China's Industry Structure during 1978–2020	216
Figure 8-7	Growth Rates of China's GDP and the Three Industries	217
Figure 8-8	China's Capital-labour Ratio during 1978–2013	219
Figure 8-9	Volatility Components of Output (Y), Capital stock (K), Labour force (L) and Factor Structure (S)	228
Figure 8-10	Estimated Time-Varying Parameters of the State-Space Model	230
Figure 8-11	Impulse Response of $\tilde{Y}$ to Shocks of $\tilde{K}$	232
Figure 8-12	Impulse Response of $\tilde{Y}$ to Shocks of $\tilde{L}$	233
Figure 8-13	Impulse Response of $\tilde{Y}$ to Shocks of $\tilde{S}$	233
Figure 8-14	Total Investment in Fixed Assets in China's Non-state-owned Economy and Its Proportion	237
Figure 8-15	Proportion of the Investment in Fixed Assets in the Non-state-Owned Economy and the Steadiness of the Economic Growth	237
Figure 8-16	China's Actual Growth Rate and Potential Growth Rate	238
Figure 8-17	China's Economic Growth Rate and Stability Index of Its Economic Growth	239
Figure 8-18	Stability Index and the Actual Growth Rate of Output	240
Figure 9-1	Estimated Variable Parameters of the Impact of Consumption and Investment on Economic Growth	259
Figure 9-2	China's Final Consumption Rate and Contribution Rate of Final Consumption since 1978	261
Figure 9-3	Fluctuation Components of China's Final Consumption Rate and Contribution Rate of Final Consumption	262

Figure 9-4	Trend Components of China's Final Consumption Rate and the Contribution Rate of Final Consumption	263
Figure 9-5	Variation Trend of the Steadiness of China's Economic Growth	265
Figure 9-6	GDP Growth Rates in Benchmark Scenario and Other Three Scenarios	267
Figure 9-7	Trend of the Rolling Standard Deviation of GDP Growth Rates in Benchmark Scenario and Other Three Scenarios	271
Figure 9-8	China's GDP Growth Rate, Final Consumption Rate and Capital Formation Rate during 1953–2020	283
Figure 9-9	Periodic Components of GDP Growth Rate, Final Consumption Rate and Capital Formation Rate	284
Figure 9-10	Trend Components of GDP Growth Rate, Final Consumption Rate and Capital Formation Rate	285
Figure 9-11	Unit Root Test on the VAR Model of Economic Growth Rate, Final Consumption Rate and Capital Formation Rate	289
Figure 9-12	Curve of Impulse Response of Economic Growth (GR) to Shocks of Itself, Final Consumption Rate (CR) and Capital Formation Rate (IR)	291
Figure 9-13	Curve of Impulse Response of Final Consumption Rate (CR) to Shocks of Economic Growth (GR), Itself and Capital Formation Rate (IR)	292
Figure 9-14	Curve of Impulse Response of Capital Formation Rate (IR) to Shocks of Economic Growth (GR), Final Consumption Rate (CR) and Itself	294

List of Tables

Table 2-1	Relationship between World Consumption Rate and Economic Development Processes during 1950–1970	37
Table 2-2	The Variations of China's Consumption Rate and Capital Formation Rate since 1978	42
Table 2-3	Fluctuation of China's Consumption Rate during 1978–2020	46
Table 2-4	Statistics of China's Consumption Rate and the Factors Affecting It during 1990–2016	56
Table 2-5	Result of Unit Root Test (ADF Test)	57
Table 2-6	Result of Johansen Cointegration Test	58
Table 3-1	Dynamic Efficiency of China's Economy during 1992–2016	71
Table 3-2	Relationship between Dynamic Efficiency and Consumption Rate	75
Table 3-3	Unit Root Test on *CR* and *LIR*	81
Table 3-4	Test on the Stationarity of the Residuals with EG Two-Step Approach	82
Table 3-5	Variance Decomposition of *CR* and *LIR*	86
Table 3-6	Granger Causality Test on *CR* and *LIR*	87
Table 3-7	Correlation Test on China's Final Consumption Rate and the Dynamic Efficiency	88

Table 3-8	Granger Causality Test on China's Consumption Rate and Dynamic Efficiency	89
Table 3-9	Relationship between Dynamic Efficiency and Optimal Consumption Rate at the Provincial Level in China's Eastern Region during 1993–2016	94
Table 3-10	Relationship between Dynamic Efficiency and Optimal Consumption Rate at the Provincial Level in China's Central Region during 1993–2016	97
Table 3-11	Relationship between Dynamic Efficiency and Optimal Consumption Rate at the Provincial Level in China's Western Region during 1993–2016	99
Table 4-1	China's Economic Statistics during 1978–2013	118
Table 4-2	Result of Unit Root Test (ADF Test)	119
Table 4-3	Result of Johansen Cointegration Test	120
Table 4-4	China's Optimal Consumption Rate and Relevant Statistics during 1978–2013	125
Table 4-5	Granger Causality Test on Capital-output Ratio and Optimal Consumption Rate	128
Table 5-1	Calibration Results of the Parameters Related to Optimal Consumption Rate	147
Table 5-2	Impact of Various Discount Rates on Optimal Consumption Rate	148
Table 5-3	Impact of Various Coefficient of Relative Risk Aversion on Optimal Consumption Rate	149
Table 5-4	Impact of Various Rates of Technological Progress on Optimal Consumption Rate	150
Table 5-5	Impact of Various Capital Flexibility of Output on Optimal Consumption Rate	151
Table 5-6	Impact of Various Population Growth Rates on Optimal Consumption Rate	152
Table 5-7	Impact of Various Depreciation Rates on Optimal Consumption Rate	153
Table 6-1	Equilibrium Consumption Rate in an Open Economy (Optimal Consumption Rate percent)	170
Table 7-1	Benchmark Values of Parameter Calibration in the Model	187
Table 7-2	Sensitivity Analysis of Steady-State Consumption Rate to Parameters	192
Table 8-1	Average Value, Standard Deviation and Coefficients of Standard Deviation of the Growth Rates of China's GDP and the Three Demands since the Reform and Opening-Up	203

LIST OF TABLES

Table 8-2	Growth Rates and the Variation of China's GDP and the Three Demands during 1978–2020	204
Table 8-3	Result of the Variance Decomposition of the GDP Volatility (Demand Structure)	209
Table 8-4	Average Value, Standard Deviation and Coefficients of Standard Deviation of the Growth Rates of China's GDP and the Three Industries since the Reform and Opening-Up	213
Table 8-5	Growth Rates and the Variation of China's GDP and the Three Industries during 1978–2020	214
Table 8-6	Result of the Variance Decomposition of the GDP Volatility (Industry Structure)	218
Table 8-7	Average Growth Rates of China's Factor Inputs in Various Periods	220
Table 8-8	Relevant Economic Statistics of China during 1978–2013	227
Table 8-9	Descriptive Statistics on Economic Fluctuation, Factor Shocks and Structural Variation	229
Table 8-10	Relevant Data of the Empirical Analysis of China's Economic Growth Stability	241
Table 8-11	Result of Unit Root Test (ADF Test)	242
Table 8-12	Result of Johansen Cointegration Test	243
Table 8-13	Result of the Empirical Analysis of the Factors Affecting Steadiness	243
Table 9-1	Estimation Result of the State-Space Model	258
Table 9-2	Growth Rates of the Three Demands since 1978	264
Table 9-3	Variation Trend of Final Consumption Rate in Benchmark Scenario and Other Three Scenarios	266
Table 9-4	GDP Growth Rates in Benchmark Scenario and Other Three Scenarios	268
Table 9-5	Standard Deviation and Average Value of GDP Growth Rate in Benchmark Scenario and Other Three Scenarios during Different Periods	269
Table 9-6	Standard Deviation and Average of the Growth Rates of China's Three Demands during Different Periods	270
Table 9-7	Non-competitive Input-Output Table	273
Table 9-8	Split Non-competitive Input-Output Table of 2012	276
Table 9-9	Final Products in China and the Increased Value Driven by Them in 2012	278
Table 9-10	Domestic Final Products and the Structure in Benchmark Scenario and Simulation Scenario	279

Table 9-11	Demand Structure in Benchmark Scenario and Simulation Scenario with Final Demand Ratio of Imports Taken into Consideration	280
Table 9-12	GDP and Its Structure in Benchmark Scenario and Simulation Scenario	281
Table 9-13	Correlation Coefficient of GDP Growth Rate (GR), Final Consumption Rate (CR) and Capital Formation Rate (IR)	285
Table 9-14	Result of Unit Root Test (ADF Test)	286
Table 9-15	Regression Result of the VAR Model of GR, CR and IR	287
Table 9-16	Variance Decomposition of GR	296
Table 9-17	Variance Decomposition of CR	297
Table 9-18	Variance Decomposition of IR	298

Preface

Since the start of reform and opening-up, China has maintained an annual GDP growth rate of 9.19 percent. Such rapid growth is known as "China's economic miracle"; meanwhile, the steadiness of economy growth has been progressively strengthened. According to the research carried out by Lin Jianhao and Wang Jinmei (2013), since 1996, China's economy has been out of the boom-bust cycle which refers to the alternating phases of economic growth and decline, and it has entered the Great Moderation where the waves of the economic cycle are becoming ripples. However, contrary to the rapid growth and the increasing economic steadiness, the proportion of consumption in GDP, which acts as the most significant indicator of the level of national economic welfare and lays the foundation for the steady economic growth, has been falling year by year with the final consumption rate decreasing from 61.4 percent in 1978 to 54.7 percent in 2020. Does the situation indicate a less impact of consumption on China's long-term economic growth? Is there an optimal consumption rate contributing to the steady economic growth? What is China's optimal consumption rate? How can the optimal consumption rate affect economic growth? These questions, both theoretical and practical, need to be figured out to maintain steady economic growth.

Since developed countries have never witnessed a relatively low consumption rate during their economic development, western economics evolved from the experience of developed countries barely has studies specifically on optimal consumption rate. Nevertheless there have been studies on optimal savings rate and optimal investment rate. For instance, Malthus (1798) argued that consumption and investment which are deemed as future productivity are the two sections of output. There must be an optimal ratio between them. Based on such optimal proportion, the sustainability of consumption and the productive capacity of economy need to be fully considered to achieve the greatest growth of wealth (economy); Phelps (1961) established the well-known golden rule of economic growth. When the economy achieved the golden-rule growth, consumer's level of consumption (utility) is maximized, and the consumption rate at this point is called the optimal consumption rate. Based on the previous research and theories on economic growth, this book uses different measures to obtain China's optimal consumption rate and analyses how the optimal consumption rate affects economic growth in both theoretical and practical ways. The outline of this book is as follows:

First, based on the previous research carried out by foreign and domestic scholars, this book looks into the issues related to optimal consumption rate within the five theoretical frameworks, namely the economic dynamic efficiency, the Solow–Swan model, the Ramsey–Cass–Koopmans model, the general equilibrium model in an open economy and the Dynamic Stochastic General Equilibrium (DSGE) model. By various methods such as comparative analysis of statistics, regression analysis and parameter calibration, China's optimal consumption rate can be calculated as follows: (i) Within the framework of the economic dynamic efficiency, the optimal consumption rate is about 55 percent. Though the number is far smaller than the average rate of the world as well as that of the middle-income countries during the corresponding period, the author believes it could be the best performance of the economic entity under the economic conditions during 1992–2016. Accordingly, China's final consumption rate is just "relatively" low. (ii)

Within the framework of the Solow–Swan model, the reasonable range of China's optimal consumption rate would be [64.9 percent, 67.7 percent], the median of which is about 66 percent, 11 percentage points higher than the optimal consumption rate (55 percent) calculated in the framework of the economic dynamic efficiency. Such difference can be explained by the fact that the Solow–Swan model emphasizes the long-term optimal economic growth while the economic dynamic efficiency stresses both the medium- and short-term growth and economic reality. (iii) Within the framework of the Ramsey–Cass–Koopmans model, China's optimal consumption rate is calculated to be 62.75 percent with parameter calibration. The impact of technological progress rate, discount rate and consumer's coefficient of relative risk aversion on optimal consumption rate is positive while that of capital elasticity of output, population growth rate and depreciation rate is negative. (iv) Within the framework of the general equilibrium model in an open economy, through numerical simulation with various parameters, the range of optimal consumption rate is calculated to be [51.1 percent, 80.8 percent]. Based on the premise that all parameters are set according to the economic reality, the median is calculated to be 66.0 percent. In other words, the optimal consumption rate in an open economy is 66.0 percent, which is close to the final consumption rates calculated based on the two long-run growth models: the Solow–Swan model and the Ramsey–Cass–Koopmans model. (v) Within the framework of the DSGE model, through numerical simulation with calibrated parameters, the optimal consumption rate is calculated to be 58.02 percent in a steady-state economy. The number equals to the final consumption rate, consisting of 43.02 percent household consumption rate and 15 percent calibrated government consumption rate. Given the fact that the average final consumption rate of China during 1978–2016 is 58.7 percent, the calculated result is close to China's actual final consumption rate.

The above calculations of China's optimal consumption rate based on the five models indicate the following: On the one hand, the dynamic efficiency model and the DSGE model accentuate the short-run character of China's economic reality and measure the level of final consumption (55 percent and 58.02 percent, respectively). The calculated result could be a short-term goal of demand structure adjustment in *The 13th Five-Year Plan*. The convergence from 53.6 percent in 2016 towards the optimal value helps motivate the consumption which is a driving force of economic growth and meanwhile strengthens the stability of economic growth to some extent. On the other hand, models of economic growth including the Solow–Swan model, the Ramsey–Cass–Koopmans model and the general equilibrium model in an open economy highlight the character of China's economic reality regarding the long-term optimal growth. Considering the result obtained based on the three models and judging from the point of view of long-run growth, the reasonable range of optimal consumption rate is [62.75 percent, 67.7 percent], which could be a long-term goal of China's demand structure adjustment.

Next, following the calculation of China's optimal consumption rate, this book assesses China's economic growth stability with empirical evidence and analyses the main factors affecting it. The conclusion is as follows: China's economic growth stability in both demand and supply is gradually improving, which is in line with the argument held by the domestic scholars in relevant field that China's economy has entered the Great Moderation; judging from the factors affecting economic growth stability, the evolution of demand structure has intensified economic volatility to some extent while adjustments in factor structure, industry structure and ownership structure increase economic growth stability to a certain degree.

Furthermore, this book offers statistics-based analysis of how the increase of final consumption rate affects economic growth and its steadiness from the following three aspects: (i) National accounts. Supposing the growth rate of consumption, investment and net export remains the same along with an increased consumption rate, a decreased investment rate and an unvarying net export rate, this book simulates the impact of changing final consumption rate on economic growth and its steadiness. The result shows that rise in consumption rate has much smaller impact on economic growth rate than it does on the stability of economic growth rate; (ii) Input and output. Supposing consumption rate goes up with a declining investment and a dropping net export rate, a rise in final consumption rate affects economic growth rate slightly; (iii) Vector Autoregression (VAR) model. The VAR model of final consumption rate, investment rate and economic growth rate based on the statistics in China from 1978 to 2016 is used to analyse the impact of varying consumption rate on economic growth and its steadiness. It can be concluded as follows: economic growth rate varies slightly to respond to a shock of final consumption rate; according to the result of the variance decomposition of economic growth rate and final consumption rate, the volatility of economic growth rate mainly comes from itself, which indicates variation in final consumption rate has minor impact on economic growth rate.

Finally, based on the research findings, this book puts forward the proposition that China's final consumption rate should converge towards the optimal value in order to maintain steady economic growth.

Chapter 1

Introduction

1.1 Background and Some Basic Facts about the Research

1.1.1 Background

Learning from the experience of developed countries, we can see that normally consumption rate accounts for about 70 percent in GDP. Such a high share indicates that consumption, as one of the "Troika" (investment, consumption and exports) that drives economic growth, contributes greatly to the steady economic growth of a country. Since the reform and opening-up, China has made astonishing economic achievements. According to Figure 1-1, during 1978–2020, the annual GDP growth reached 9.19 percent[1], and the average contribution rate of final consumption to economic growth touched 57.4 percent. Figure 1-2 demonstrates final consumption drives 5.30 percentage-point increase in economic growth on average annually. These statistics show that the stable final consumption lays the solid foundation for China's continuous and rapid economic growth.

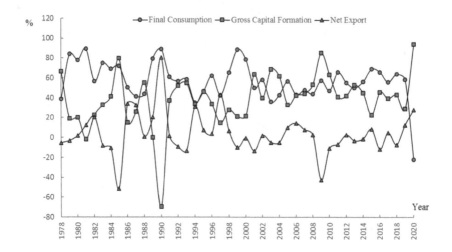

Figure 1-1 The Contribution Rates of Final Consumption, Gross Capital Formation and Net Export to China's Economic Growth
Source: Database of National Bureau of Statistics of China

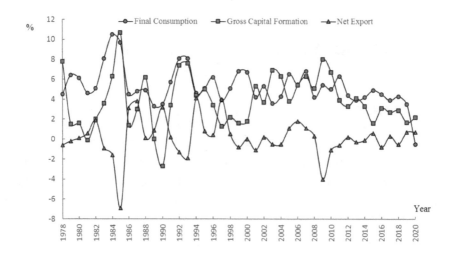

Figure 1-2 China's Economic Growth Driven by Final Consumption, Gross Capital Formation and Net Export
Source: Database of National Bureau of Statistics of China

However, while the economy has been growing rapidly, there still exists some problems in consumption. The most serious one among them is that the consumption level of China has been lower than that of the countries in the same development phase as well as world's average level, and the consumption rate keeps going down. Figure 1-3 demonstrates that China's final consumption rate moved up and down from 1978 to 2020. It rose from 61.9 percent in 1978 to 67.3 percent in 1983, and then it declined to 58.5 percent in 1994, followed by a rebound to 63.9 percent in 2000. Since 2000, it kept going down towards 54.3 percent in 2020. As for the two consisting parts of final consumption[2], the government consumption rate barely changed, maintaining around 14 percent whereas the household consumption rate shows a similar trend to the final consumption rate. As the government consumption rate almost remained the same, it is the decrease in the household consumption rate that causes the decline in the final consumption rate. The household consumption rate can be further divided into the rural household consumption rate and the urban household consumption rate: the former rose from 30.3 percent in 1978 to 33.7 percent in 1982 and then it fell back to 8.1 percent in 2020; the latter climbed from 18.5 percent in 1978 to 31.3 percent in 2000, and it went down to 26.5 percent in 2008, followed by a small rebound to 29.6 percent in 2020. Based on the above statistics, it can be deduced that the fall in the household consumption rate primarily results from the dive in the rural household consumption rate (see Figure 1-4).

Figure 1-3 China's Final Consumption Rate, Household Consumption Rate and Government Consumption Rate
Source: Database of National Bureau of Statistics of China

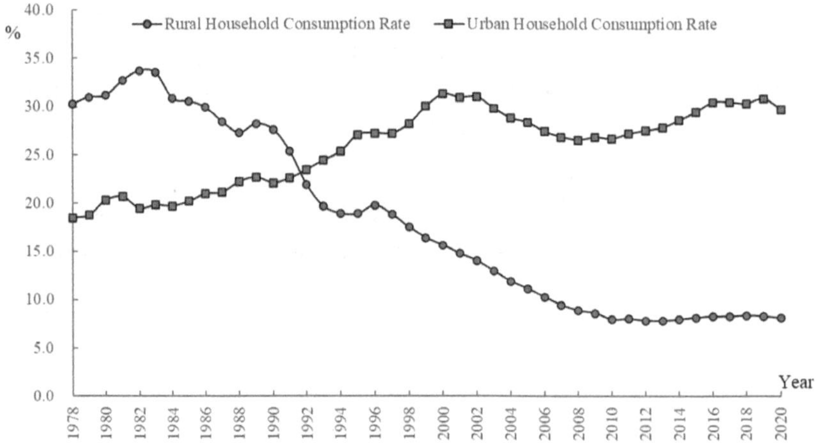

Figure 1-4 China's Rural Household Consumption Rate and Urban Household Consumption Rate
Source: Database of National Bureau of Statistics of China

1.1.2 Some Basic Facts about the Research

Faced with weak foreign demand, China prioritizes the need to propel domestic demand and stimulate consumption in its macroeconomic policy as a long-term goal. According to *The 13th Five-Year Plan for Economic and Social Development of the People's Republic of China*, China will "further coordinate development, and keep enhancing the contribution of consumption to economic growth." Consumption, as one of the "Troika" driving economic growth, plays a significant role in maintaining steady economic development. But China's low consumption has always been an obstacle to its stable economic growth (Yuan and Zhu, 2002[3]; Fang, 2009[4]). Why is China's policy in stimulating consumption not so effective? What is the "optimal" consumption rate in China? Is there a reasonable range of consumption rate? These are the theoretical and practical questions needed to be answered to keep stable economic growth.

Western economics has similar theories of optimal consumption rate. For instance, Malthus (1798)[5] argued that consumption and investment which is deemed as future productivity are the two sections of output. There must be an optimal proportion between them. Based on such optimal proportion, the sustainability of consumption and the productive capacity of economy need to be fully considered to achieve the greatest growth of wealth (economy); Phelps (1961)[6] established the well-known golden rule of economic growth. When the economy achieved the golden-rule growth, consumer's level of consumption (utility) is maximized, and the consumption rate at this point is called the optimal consumption rate. The Overlapping Generations Model shows when the economy reaches a steady state through market competition, capital overaccumulation may occur, which indicates the steady-state consumption rate is lower than the optimal consumption rate (Romer, 1999)[7]. As for domestic research on China's optimal consumption rate, Liu (2002)[8] and Yang (2005)[9] illustrate that the optimal consumption rate does exist in economy; Zeng (1997)[10] puts forward the concept of theoretical optimal consumption rate.

The previous studies show that countries of different levels of development all have their own reasonable ranges of consumption rate. According to the research carried out by Chenery and Syrquin (1975)[11], consumption rate is related to the level of development. In the agricultural society, consumption rate is relatively high because a large portion of income is spent on life necessities. In the industrial society, a large proportion of output is used for investment to meet a higher demand for capital and thus consumption rate declines. In the post-industrial society, the demand of market decides economic growth and consumption rate rebounds with the increasing household income. In a developed economy dominated by the service industry, the consumption rate becomes more stable as household income tends to be stable. How consumption rate varies with development processes can be illustrated by a U-shaped curve. Wen (2005)[12], based on the study of China's macroeconomics since 1990, argues that the appropriate range of China's consumption rate is [63 percent, 68 percent]. To achieve that, China's consumption needs to be further stimulated. Tian (2008)[13] learns from the Barro's idea of a natural condition for productive efficiency and uses Cobb-Douglas production function to calculate China's optimal consumption rate to be 66.46 percent. According to Wu (2011)[14], China's optimal consumption rate is 80.63 percent. But these three scholars merely calculate the optimal consumption rate without giving more thought to the steady-state economic models on optimal consumption rate and investment rate.

Since the world financial crisis, China's economic growth mainly depends on investment. But such long-term dependence on investment can result in overcapacity and declining consumption rate, which further leads to decreasing investment efficiency and weak growth in the long run. Therefore, it is urgent to raise China's consumption rate better to the optimal value so as to promote steady growth of national economy.

This book focuses on optimal consumption rate and discusses issues including the requirements an economy needs to meet to achieve optimal consumption rate, the possible evolutionary approach of consumption rate under economic development and the relationship between consumption rate in steady-state economy and optimal consumption rate. China's optimal consumption rate is calculated after the investigation into its relation with economic dynamic efficiency, and a more empirical analysis is given according to the statistics of China's 31 provinces. Solow–Swan model, Ramsey–Cass–Koopmans model, general equilibrium model in an open economy and DSGE model are used along with parameter calibration to simulate China's optimal consumption rate and the factors affecting it. With the relevant studies, the suggestion that China's consumption should be further stimulated is put forward.

1.2 Approach and Methodology

1.2.1 Research Approach

Though China has witnessed a rapid economic growth, its final consumption rate keeps falling every year. Therefore, in order to maintain stable economic growth, it is of great importance to study optimal consumption rate and the ways it affects stable economic growth. First, reviews are given on the literature related to optimal consumption rate, stable economic growth and the relationship between them. Due to the lack of relevant findings, this book is of research value. Second, through the study of the trend of China's final consumption rate since the reform and opening-up and the statistics of economic growth, a stylized fact about the evolution of final consumption rate and the stability of economic growth is observed. Third, based on the development processes of theories on economic growth, detailed analysis of optimal consumption rate and the ways that consumption exerts impact on stable economic growth are provided, and models used for investigating optimal consumption rate are decided. Fourth, according to China's statistics, the optimal consumption rate is calculated and analysis models are used to look into how optimal consumption rate promotes the stability of economic growth. Fifthl, through empirical analysis, the suggestion that China's final consumption rate should converge towards the optimal value to keep the stability of economic growth is put forward.

1.2.2 Research Methodology

Literature review. After reviewing the literature on economic growth, consumption economic, optimal consumption rate and other relevant fields, this book carries out the research into the relationship between stable economic growth and optimal consumption rate by applying economic growth models.

Theoretical deduction. This book looks into the issues around optimal consumption rate within the frameworks including economic dynamic efficiency, the Solow–Swan model and the Ramsey–Cass–Koopmans model.

Numerical simulation. Methods of parameter calibration and numerical simulation are used to analyse the impact of optimal consumption rate and the increase of final consumption rate on economic growth as well as its steadiness within the frameworks of the Ramsey–Cass–Koopmans model, the general equilibrium model in an open economy and DSGE model.

Econometric analysis. Based on China's statistics, statistical methods, regression analysis, VAR model and other approaches are implemented to study how optimal consumption rate affects the stability of economic growth.

1.3 Definition and Literature Review

1.3.1 Definition

Due to the differences in national accounts systems between China and Western countries and the reference to international comparison in the empirical analysis in this book, it is necessary to list the relevant definitions.

Final Consumption Expenditure[15]: It is the expenditure in both domestic and foreign economic territories by resident institutional units on goods or services that are used for the satisfaction of physical, cultural and mental needs (excluding the consumption expenditure of non-resident institutional units in domestic economic territory). It includes household final consumption expenditure and government final consumption expenditure. The annual final consumption expenditure in the expenditure-based GDP accounting is used in this book's calculation, consisting of household final consumption expenditure and government final consumption expenditure.

Final Consumption Rate: The proportion of final consumption expenditure in GDP by an economy in a certain period. Its calculation formula is as follows:

Final Consumption Rate (CR) = final consumption expenditure at current price/GDP at current price×100 percent.

Optimal Consumption Rate: The concept of optimal consumption rate in this book, corresponding to that of final consumption rate, is defined from two perspectives. The first perspective is dynamic efficiency. When an economy is at the balancing point between dynamic efficiency and inefficiency, the optimal consumption rate is reached: the consumption rate in a dynamically inefficient economy is lower than the optimal consumption rate, while it is higher in a dynamically efficient economy than the optimal consumption rate. The second perspective is the equilibrium of models. Since there is no economic dynamic inefficiency in models such as the Ramsey–Cass–Koopmans model, the consumption rate at the point where an economy is in equilibrium is defined as the optimal consumption rate in this book.

Economic Growth: During a certain period[16], it is the ratio of the incremental output of an economy to the total output during the last period. In national accounts, GDP is a measure of output. Let ΔY_t represent the incremental output during the present period, and let Y_t and Y_{t-1}, respectively, represent the total output during the last and current period. The calculation formula of g_Y is listed below[17]:

$$g_Y = \frac{Y_t - Y_{t-1}}{Y_t} \times 100\%$$

Economic growth can usually be measured in the aggregate or in per capita terms. Measured in the aggregate, economic growth refers to the increase in the production of final goods and services of an economy over a long period. In other words, it is the growth of total output. The macroeconomic statistics released by the National Bureau of Statistics of China are calculated based on the gross amount. For instance: "The result of the preliminary accounting shows that China's GDP in 2020 totaled RMB 10.15986 trillion, growing by 2.3 percent compared to the previous year." From the perspective of per capita index, economic growth equals the growth of GDP per capita. As the analysis in this book is on the relation among China's economic growth, final consumption rate and optimal consumption rate, the economic growth mentioned in the following refers to the gross GDP instead of per capita GDP.

Stability of Economic Growth: The existing research generally measures the Stability of economic growth based on the variation of economic growth rate with the following two kinds of index: the variation range of economic growth rate and the coefficient of (rolling) standard deviation. This book uses these two kinds of index as well.

In addition, regarding the variable symbols used in this book, due to many different kinds of models, formulas and mathematical symbols, the meanings of the mathematical symbols in every chapter may differ, unless otherwise noted.

1.3.2 Existing Domestic and Foreign Research

1.3.2.1. Research on China's Low Consumption Rate

In the late 1990s, because of China's weak foreign demand and the lack of driving force for economic growth caused by the financial crisis in Southeast Asia, China made active fiscal and monetary policies to propel domestic demand. Over this period, China's final consumption rate maintained around 60 percent, which was lower than the world's average level. Nevertheless, domestic scholars were not paying much attention to that problem because the final consumption rate was basically stable while the economic growth was quite slow. In such a situation, only a few scholars carried out the research on final consumption rate. For example, as Liu (1999[18], 2000a[19], 2000b[20]) points out, China's consumption rate fell to 56.09 percent in 1996, which was far lower than that of the countries at similar development level. The decline in consumption rate resulting from the decrease in the proportion of disposable income in national income leads to China's current weak demand for final consumption.

Since 2002, China's final consumption rate has decreased by 7.0 percentage points from 60.6 percent in 2002 to 53.6 percent in 2016. In the meantime, the rate of capital formation has increased by 7.3 percentage points from 36.9 percent in 2002 to 44.2 percent in 2016. Owing to the fact that the range of the decrease in consumption rate is close to that of the increase in the capital formation rate and China's economy has entered a new growth cycle since 2002, more domestic scholars began to study on the sustainability of the growth pattern of "high investment and low consumption". The analysis of China's low consumption rate is primarily from the following perspectives: The first is international comparison; the second is the sustainability of the growth pattern of "high investment and low consumption"; and the third is the underestimation in China's consumption rate. It is argued that based on accounting, China's consumption rate could be underestimated from its actual value.

(1) Studies on China's Low Consumption Rate Based on International Comparison

Two approaches are usually used to discuss China's low consumption rate based on international comparison. The first one is to learn from the empirical research carried out by Chenery et al. (1975)[21] on final consumption rates and capital formation rates in different development processes. Studies using such an approach include the following: Xiao (2004)[22] notes that China's consumption rate has long been deviating from Chenery's "Standard Structure" by nearly 20 percentage points, which is much lower than the world's average level. Comparing the variation of China's investment rate and consumption rate with Chenery's "Standard Structure", Wu (2006)[23] concludes that the ratio of investment to consumption in GDP is far from the "Standard Structure". China's investment rate is obviously higher than the standard value, while final consumption rate and national consumption rate are much lower; Chao and Wang (2009)[24] who revise Chenery's "Standard Structure" based on China's economic reality and make empirical analysis according to China's statistics of consumption rate conclude that China does have relatively low consumption rate. Ning and Tu (2010)[25] make international comparison between consumption rate and investment rate based on Chenery's general industrialization model and conclude that China's ratio of consumption to investment is far from "Standard Structure"; Fu (2011)[26] uses World Development Indicators (WDI) to verify Chenery's "Standard Structure" of consumption rate and suggests China should raise its consumption rate.

The second approach is to compare the statistics of the countries around the world, and compare the final consumption rates for countries at the same development level as China and that of the developed countries when they were at comparable development level. Through the comparison, it is concluded that China has relatively low consumption rate. Luo (2000)[27] points out it is not enough to measure the level of China's consumption rate through simple global horizontal comparison; Qiao (2005)[28] thinks that China's consumption rate is lower than the world average of 77.5 percent, which is bad for the macroeconomics operation. Jiang et al. (2009)[29], through comparative analysis of the world's statistics of consumption rate, conclude that China's consumption rate is far lower than the world average level, even lower than the levels of the upper income and lower-middle income countries. Lei (2009)[30] finds out that China's consumption rate is obviously low through international comparison on consumption rate and investment rate.

(2) Studies on the Reasons behind Low Consumption Rate from the Perspective of the Sustainability of the "High Investment and Low Consumption" Growth Pattern

In national accounts, if exports and imports are not taken into consideration, a high investment rate always indicates a low consumption rate. Therefore, many domestic scholars analyse China's low consumption rate from the perspective of the sustainability of the "high investment and low consumption" growth pattern, and most of them argue that such growth pattern is unsustainable. According to Luo's research, China's economy currently features high investment rate and low consumption rate. The consumption-investment structure cannot be simply explained by the result of international comparison as investment rate is essentially decided by consumption rate (Luo, 2004)[31]. The study of the Economic Growth Frontier Subject Team (2005)[32] shows that high investment rate is the cause of low consumption rate, and the latter can be raised through the increase of investment efficiency: Liang (2006)[33] points out that China's high investment rate and low consumption rate are closely related to its special transformation path of economy; Zhan (2006)[34] believes that the non-diminishing marginal product of capital and the progressive reform of interest rate liberalization are both essential to the long-term steady growth of China's economy with a high investment rate and a low consumption rate; Gong and Li (2013)[35] hold the view that the low consumption rate has been the main obstacle to the healthy growth of China's economy, and the decrease of consumption rate primarily results from a high proportion of the return to capital; Lv and Mao (2014)[36] investigate the fiscal foundation of high investment rate and low consumption rate which are the typical features of China's economy.

(3) Studies on the Underestimation in China's Consumption Rate from the Perspective of Accounting

To verify the proposition that China's economic growth typically features a high investment rate and a low consumption rate through national accounts and comparative analysis, many scholars believe that there can be an underestimation in China's consumption rate because of statistical omission. Gao (2014)[37] discusses the impact mechanism of hidden income on the underestimation of China's consumption rate and concludes that hidden income does cause the underestimation. Wang Qiushi and Wang Yinxin (2013[38], 2013[39]) conclude China's actual consumption rate is higher than the estimated value by using the main factors that affect consumption rate as indicators in international comparison. So is China's household consumption rate; the study carried out by Zhu and Zhang (2014)[40] shows that there is a large underestimation of China's consumption level in official statistics. China's actual consumption rate is higher by over 10 percentage points than the official statistics, which is 60 percent higher than GDP and extremely close to the consumption rate of the upper-income economies in East Asia during the period of their rapid growth. Kang (2014)[41] points out that China's consumption rate is underestimated because of the incompleteness of official statistics of service industry, the under-pricing of the service value of resident-owned housing, the substitution of employer paying for individual social consumption and the underestimation in household income and consumption caused by technical problems.

1.3.2.2. Research on Optimal Consumption Rate

Currently, only a few domestic scholars have directly studied China's optimal consumption rate. Most scholars discuss the reasonable range of consumption rate based on the ratio of investment to consumption. Thus the literature review in this book consists of the following two parts: the first part centres around the studies on the reasonable range of consumption rate, and the second part discusses the studies on optimal consumption rate.

(1) Studies on the Reasonable Range of Consumption Rate

Luo (1999[42], 2006[43]) discusses the range of consumption rate from the perspective of consumption-investment ratio. He argues that it is unreasonable to decide an optimal ratio and regard it as a policy goal. After analysing China's economic development processes, Wu (2006)[44] calculates the reasonable consumption rate to be 61 percent to 65 percent and the investment rate to be 35 percent to 38 percent through quantitative and qualitative analysis. With the study of the evolutionary path of China's investment and consumption as well as the economic growth model, Tan (2006)[45] points out that the moderate ranges of China's investment rate and consumption rate should, respectively, be 31.0–32.9 percent and 66.2–67.4 percent. He (2006)[46], learning from the result of historical comparison, international comparison and analysis of investment efficiency, holds the view that China's investment rate should be controlled at 30–35 percent, while consumption rate should be kept at 60–65 percent so as to maintain the long-term economic growth. Through international comparison, Cai and Wang (2010)[47] calculate the desired range of consumption rate and investment rate, respectively, to be 55–60 percent and 40–45 percent. Wu (2014)[48] learns from Chenery's approach to analyse the desired range of China's consumption rate. The result of the empirical analysis shows that over the five periods from 1982 to 2010, China's consumption rate has been lower than the desired level. Based on such a result, Wu predicts that the desired final consumption rate and household consumption rate during 2011–2016 are, respectively, 50.26 percent and 36.85 percent. Jing and Wang (2011)[49] derive a theoretical model of consumption rate based on Cobb-Douglas equation to calculate China's theoretical consumption rate and its reasonable range from 1991 to 2008. According to the calculation result, if net export is not taken into consideration, the reasonable range of the average consumption rate is [57.8 percent, 63.8 percent]. Otherwise, the range is [53.74 percent, 59.74 percent]. Chen (2014)[50] notes that the reasonable range of investment rate should be [35 percent, 40 percent], while that of household consumption rate should be [45 percent, 55 percent]. However, China's current investment-consumption structure strays away from the reasonable range. With the model of threshold cointegration, Ouyang (2016)[51] calculates the threshold of China's household consumption rate to be 53.6 percent and the threshold of final consumption rate is about 67.6 percent, equalling household consumption rate plus government consumption rate. Only when the final consumption rate reaches at least 67.6 percent will consumption have a different impact on economic growth[52].

(2) Studies on Optimal Consumption Rate

Studies on optimal consumption rate are based on the following two aspects: (1) direct research on optimal consumption rate; and (2) research on optimal savings rate (or optimal investment rate). Because national income equals consumption plus investment (saving), optimal consumption rate and optimal savings rate (or optimal investment rate) are like the two sides of a coin. The relevant theoretical studies include models of economic growth (Harrod-Domar model, Solow model, Ramsey model, and overlapping generation models), golden-rule growth, dynamic efficiency and the empirical research carried out by Chenery et al ...

Most studies on optimal consumption rate are carried out from two aspects, namely whether optimal consumption rate exists and the estimation of its value. Though Western scholars haven't directly put forward the concept of optimal consumption rate and conducted positive research on it, Phelps (1961)[53] did initiate the concept of "Golden

Rule Growth", which defines as the growth path with the highest consumption level of consumers[54]. As the optimal economic growth and the highest level of consumption can be achieved along the golden-rule growth path, the Golden-Rule theory indicates that the optimal consumption rate does exist. Through empirical research, Chenery and Syrquin (1988)[55] find out that the level of consumption rate is related to the economic development processes. The evolutionary path of the consumption rate over the economic development processes features a gentle U-shaped curve. Liu (2002)[56] and Yang (2005)[57] verify that the optimal consumption rate does exist in the economy. Zeng (1997)[58] puts forward the concept of the optimal consumption rate. Wu (2009)[59] also verifies its existence and sets the criterion for evaluation. Wu and Zhang (2011)[60] gives the method to calculate the optimal consumption rate from the perspective of economic dynamic efficiency. According to their calculation, China's optimal consumption rate is 80.6 percent. Ji (2013)[61] defines the steady-state consumption rate in the balanced growth path as the optimal consumption rate. Meanwhile, he looks into the relationship between China's consumption rate over the economic development processes and its economic growth. Mao et al. (2014)[62] use the intertemporal model to estimate the optimal household consumption rate through maximizing the utility of the representative households. The result shows that China's household consumption rate since 1991 has been lower than the optimal level. Lin (2016)[63] establishes a model with Cobb-Douglas production function to calculate China's optimal consumption rate since 1991 and estimates the reasonable range of consumption rate which avoids the "Middle Income Trap" from the perspective of upper-middle income. Liu and Wang (2016)[64] discuss the non-linear relationship between final consumption rate and economic growth based on Panel Smooth Transition Regression Model (PSTR Model). Their study shows that an inverted "V shape" can be used to describe the impact of final consumption rate on economic growth. According to the calculation of threshold, China's optimal consumption rate is 68.12 percent: (i) When the consumption rate is lower than 68.12 percent, consumption greatly promotes the economic growth; (ii) When it is higher than 68.12 percent, consumption makes less contribution to the economic growth.

Wang (2016)[65] adds more variables to the human capital growth model developed by Robert Lucas that include human capital, physical capital, R&D investment, market-oriented reform, the extent of opening-up, urbanization, government management costs, consumption rate and leverage ratio of debt. Based on growth accounting and regression analysis, Wang quantitatively measures the contribution of the variables to economic growth. The result of regression analysis shows that an inverted U-shaped curve can be used to illustrate the impact of final consumption rate (the proportion of final consumption in GDP) on the Total Factor Productivity (TFP) and economic growth (see Figure 1-5). The abscissa represents final consumption rate, and the ordinate represents economic growth effect. According to Figure 1-5, the critical value of economic growth effect of final consumption rate is 66.22 percent, which means a consumption rate higher or lower than 66.22 percent restricts the long-term economic growth. Wang empirically verifies the existence of optimal consumption rate and calculates China's optimal consumption rate to be 66.22 percent. China's consumption rate in 2016 was 53.6 percent, nearly 13 percentage points lower than 66.22 percent. It is suggested to lower the investment rate and increase the consumption rate with measures like structural adjustment and supply-side reform so as to promote the long-term economic growth.

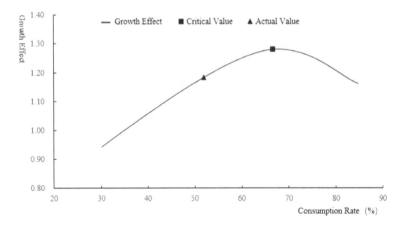

Figure 1-5 Simulation Curve of the Economic Growth Effect of Consumption Rate
Source: WANG Xiaolu, "Economic Structural Adjustments and A Forecast of China's Economic Growth," *Comparative Studies*, 2016 (5): 45–73.

Many domestic studies indicate that China's optimal savings rate is lower than the actual savings rate. In other words, its optimal consumption rate is higher than the actual consumption rate. According to the study carried out by Yuan and Song (2000)[66] on the age structure of population and pension system, China's current savings rate is higher than the optimal value, indicating that its current consumption rate is lower than the optimal value. Wan and Qiu (2005)[67] use the OLG model to analyse the optimal voluntary savings rate of China's urban residents based on the mixed pension system, concluding that China's current savings rate is indeed a bit high. Zhen (2008)[68] carries out the empirical analysis of various growth models after studying their developing processes. The study shows that China's current optimal savings rate is around 40 percent, and the consumption rate is lower than the optimal value. Ding (2014)[69], respectively, calculates the optimal savings rate based on the Harrod-Domar model and the Solow–Swan model to be 36.2 percent and 46.4 percent, determining that the range of China's optimal savings rate is [36.2 percent, 46.4 percent], and the corresponding range of the optimal consumption rate is [53.6 percent, 63.8 percent]. Learning from the "Golden Rule Level" developed by Phelps, Fan et al. (2014)[70] conclude that China's optimal savings rate has been lower than its actual savings rate for a long-term period. In other words, China's optimal consumption has been higher than the actual consumption rate for a long-term period.

Studies on optimal investment rate show that China's optimal investment rate is lower than the actual investment rate, which means its optimal consumption rate is higher than the actual consumption rate. Qiao and Pan (2005)[71] determine the model of reasonable investment rate for full employment and conclude from the empirical analysis that China's reasonable investment rate or savings rate should not be over 32.4 percent, indicating the corresponding consumption rate should not be lower than 67.6 percent. Gong (2010)[72] takes the factor of income distribution into consideration when Gong analyses the relationship between consumption, investment and economic growth. The study shows that when the Gini coefficient is between 0.2 and 0.3, the range of China's optimal investment rate is [31.8 percent, 35.2 percent]. From the perspective of welfare economics, Li et al. (2012)[73] look into the path of optimal investment rate towards the maximization of welfare through numerical simulation. The result shows that China's national investment rate has been obviously higher than the welfare-maximizing investment rate since 2002, and the gap is still widening. Currently, the national investment rate is about 15 percent higher.

1.3.2.3. Studies on the Evaluation of Economic Growth Stability

(1) Studies on the Evaluation Indications of Economic Growth Stability
At present domestic scholars mainly analyse economic growth stability from the following four aspects:

The first aspect is the traditional economic cycle. Since the reform and opening-up, the waves of China's economic cycle have been becoming ripples, indicating the economy has become steadier. To enhance its steadiness, in addition to taking full advantage of the fundamental functions of market mechanism, the coordination of macroeconomic should be strengthened (Liu, 2007[74]; Zhang, 2012[75]; Chen, 2010[76]).

The second aspect is the variation of economic growth rate. More specifically, two indexes can be used here: the variation range and the standard deviation of the growth rate. Mankiw (2006)[77] evaluates the steadiness of the U.S. economic growth based on the standard deviation of its economic growth, concluding that the U.S. economy has never been steadier since the 1990s. Li and Jin (2007)[78] measure economic growth stability based on the growth of economic growth rate. The study illustrates that the economic growth stability of Hebei Province has been gradually enhanced since the reform and opening-up. Lv (2002)[79] believes that the economic growth stability of Shanxi Province measured based on the variation of the growth rate is relatively poor. Liu (2004)[80] points out that since 1978, the economic growth stability of Shandong Province has strengthened, presenting a smaller volatility range and less frequency of volatility.

The third aspect is the indicators of economic growth stability. It is synthesized by a group of indexes of economic steadiness such as inflation rate, unemployment rate and economic volatility. Chao and Hui (2009)[81] carry out the Principal Component Analysis (PCA) based on indexes including inflation rate, unemployment rate and economic volatility and build the stability index of economic growth. They find that the steadiness of China's economic growth keeps going up despite the volatility. Using output fluctuation rate and price fluctuation rate as the main indexes of economic steadiness, Li and Feng (2016)[82] synthesize the index of economic growth stability with the entropy weight method, concluding that greater volatility is shown in the Stability of economic growth than in the sustainability and the coordination.

The fourth aspect is the time series modelling. Chen and Liu (2016)[83] measure the ability of the economic indicators to maintain the stability by using the sum of the Auto-Regression Coefficients of lagged variables (ARC) as the index in the dynamic time-varying Auto-Regressive (AR) process. Based on the ARC index of GDP growth rate and CPI growth rate, they build a measurement model regarding fluctuation term, intercept term and probability of structural break, finding out that China's economic growth has been presenting the "New Normal" features since 2010 including the increasing stability in the dynamic structure, the weakening volatility and the local stationariness.

In conclusion, to evaluate economic growth stability, besides the traditional method of measuring the distance "from wave wrest to wave wrest" or "from wave trough to wave trough" in the economic cycle, three main indexes are often used: (1) rolling standard deviation of economic growth rate or the standard deviation coefficient (Mankiw, 2006)[84]; (2) volatility range of economic growth rate, equalling the growth rate of economic growth rate (Li & Jin, 2007)[85] and (3) stability index of economic growth. Its calculation formula is as follows: the stability index of economic growth=100×(1-the absolute value of the deviation between the actual economic growth rate and the potential economic growth rate÷the potential economic growth rate) (Xiang, 2008)[86]. The above three indexes are used in this book to evaluate the steadiness of China's economic growth since the reform and opening-up.

(i) The Rolling Standard Deviation of Economic Growth Rate

The standard deviation coefficient is often used to describe the volatility of variables, but it can also be used to show the stability level of variables. Generally, the higher the standard deviation coefficient is, the greater the volatility of economic growth is (the poorer the steadiness is), and vice versa. The calculation formulas of the standard deviation coefficient and the standard deviation coefficient are as follows:

$$\boxed{\text{Standard deviation of economic growth rate}} — \delta = \left[\left(\frac{1}{n}\sum(g_t - \bar{g})\right)^2\right]^{\frac{1}{2}};$$

$$\boxed{\text{Average economic growth rate}} — \bar{g} = \frac{\sum g_t}{n}; \qquad (1\text{-}1)$$

$$\boxed{\text{Standard deviation coefficient of economic growth rate}} — V_\delta = \frac{\delta}{\bar{g}}$$

In the above formulas, δ represents the standard deviation; g_t represents the annual growth rates during the investigated period; t stands for the year; n represents the number of items (the number of years during the investigated period); $\bar{g}$ stands for the average growth rate; V_δ represents the standard deviation coefficient. In order to dismiss the implicit assumption contained in the single standard deviation coefficient of economic growth rate that the level of economic growth stability remains the same over the investigated period as well as to reflect the gradual variation of the level of economic growth stability, this book, learning from the studies of Blanchard and Simon (2001)[87], Mankiw (2006)[88] and Liu Jinquan and Liu Zhigang (2004)[89], uses the rolling standard deviation coefficient. That is to say, a standard deviation coefficient is calculated for each year based on the statistics of the previous 10 years (including this year).

(ii) The Variation Range of Economic Growth Rate
The calculation formula of the variation range of economic growth rate (i.e. the growth rate of economic growth rate) is as follows:

$$\eta_t = \frac{g_t - g_{t-1}}{g_{t-1}} \times 100\% \qquad (1\text{-}2)$$

In the above formula, g_t and g_{t-1}, respectively, stand for the economic rate of this year and the previous year; η_t represents the variation range of economic growth rate. Generally, a variation range of economic growth rate of [-30 percent, +30 percent] shows a relatively stable economic growth; a range of [-50 percent, -30 percent] or [30 percent, 50 percent] indicates a relatively volatile economic growth; a range higher than +50 percent or lower than -50 percent indicates the poor stability of economic growth.

(iii) The Stability Index of Economic Growth
The determination of the stability index of economic growth is primarily based on the deviation of the paths between the actual economic growth and the potential economic growth: when the actual economic growth equals the potential economic growth, the stability of economic growth is considered to achieve the optimal level; when the actual economic growth is higher or lower than the potential economic growth, the steadiness level is considered to be away from its optimal level. The calculation formula of the stability index of economic growth is as follows:

$$W_t = \left(1 - \frac{|g_t - g_{tp}|}{g_{tP}}\right) \times 100 \qquad (1\text{-}3)$$

In the above formula, W_t represents the stability index of economic growth; g_t represents the actual economic growth rate; and g_{tp} stands for the potential economic growth rate.

Therefore, there are two necessary steps to calculate the stability index of economic growth: first, the potential GDP needs to be calculated; second, the potential economic growth rate can be calculated based on the potential GDP. After these two steps, the stability index of economic growth can then be calculated based on the actual economic growth rate and the potential economic growth rate. Formula (1-3) shows that when W, the stability index of economic growth, achieves its optimal level, it equals 100. That is to say, the maximum value of W is 100. When the actual economic growth rate is higher or lower than the potential economic growth rate, W is lower than 100. Surely if classical fluctuations (decreases in the economic size) appear in the economy, or if the actual economic growth rate is about twice higher or lower than the potential economic growth rate, the value of W can be negative, indicating that the economic growth is highly volatile.

(2) Studies on Enhancing the Stability of Economic Growth
While the volatility in the output of the United States and the Group of Seven has greatly declined, the volatility of the main macroeconomic variables of China has also been decreasing. At present, scholars home and abroad carry out the studies on enhancing the stability of economic growth from the following two perspectives: (1) the Great Moderation; (2) the structures (demand structure and industry structure).

(i) Studies on the "Great Moderation" of the Economy
Research shows that as the economic cycle of growth occurs, countries with rapid and relatively steady growth have witnessed much lower volatility. The period with such characteristics are called the "Great Moderation". Since the 1980s, the variances of the main macroeconomic variables of the United States and the Group of Seven have decreased to different degrees[90]. Based on the research findings of Blanchard and Simon (2001)[91], Bernanke (2004)[92] points out that "the variability of quarterly growth in real output has declined by half since the mid-1980s, while the variability of quarterly inflation has declined by about two-thirds", and the United States has entered the "Great Moderation" since then. Additionally, many scholars look into the reasons behind U.S. Great Moderation. They find that economic policies, structural transformation, good luck (absence of the shocks) and technological progress may all result in the "Great Moderation" (Frankel & Orzsag, 2004[93]; Clark, 2009[94]). Lin and Wang (2013)[95] analyse the steadiness of China's economic growth and conclude that since the fourth quarter of 1995, China's economy has been out of the boom-bust cycle which refers to the alternating phases of economic growth and decline, and has entered the Great Moderation where the waves of the economic cycle are becoming ripples. Based on the statistics, they note that

investments in fixed assets and adjustments of monetary policy structure are the major reasons for China's "Great Moderation". Yang and Fan (2015)[96] discuss the influence of "Made in China", concluding that "Made in China" has greatly lowered the volatility of worldwide output growth and thus helped the global economy maintain a high level of growth with low volatility.

(ii) Transformation of the Economic Structure and the Stability of Economic Growth

Currently, the literature research on the transformation of the economic structure (industry structure and demand structure) and the stability of economic growth indicates that the structural transformation is a major reason for the improvement of economic growth stability. Based on the accounting statistics, Eggers and Ioannides (2006)[97] decompose the variance into structure effect, volatility effect and coupling effect from the perspective of demand structure and industry structure. Their empirical analysis shows that the adjustments in demand structure and industry structure in America since 1947 have a positive impact on its economic growth stability.

Domestic scholars believe that the transformation of the industry structure contributes to stabilizing the economy and carry out studies from the following two perspectives: (i) to verify whether the upgrading of industry structure helps stabilize the economy (Fang & Zhan, 2011[98]; Gan 2011[99]); (ii) to calculate the contribution rate of the adjustments in the industry structure to reducing the economic fluctuations with the model of variance decomposition developed by Eggers and Ioannides (2006) (Yang & Liu, 2011[100]; Li, 2012[101]; Li, 2010[102]).

According to the research on the impact of demand structure on economic growth stability, the development of China's demand structure contributes little to strengthening economic growth stability. Ji and Liu (2014)[103] analyse the impact of the demand structure on economic volatility through building the index of rationalization and optimization of demand structure. The result shows that the improvement in the levels of rationalization and optimization of demand structure helps suppress the economic volatility and thus enhance economic growth stability. Yang and Liu (2011)[104] decompose the variance into structure effect, volatility effect and coupling effect with the method developed by Eggers and Ioannides. They find that in terms of demand and supply, the adjustments in China's demand structure have no positive impact on the stable economic growth (the structure effect is -3.48 percent).

1.3.2.4. Research on Consumption Rate and Economic Growth Stability

Regarding the impact of the increase in the final consumption rate on China's economic growth and its steadiness, only a few scholars in China have carried out relevant studies, though not on this specific subject. For instance, Shen (2011)[105] analyses the influence of the changes in final demand on the transformation of industry structure with input-output tables. He points out that if the consumption rate increases by 5 percentage points with the rate of capital formation and exports, respectively, declining by 2.5 percentage points, the structural transformation of final demand barely affects GDP. Li (2003)[106] discusses the relationship between the consumption rate of China and its economic growth by figuring out the law of evolution of investment rate and consumption rate. He finds out that measures, including expanding investment scale, raising investment rate and stimulating investment to grow rapidly, have increasingly less influence on promoting rapid economic growth. Zhao (2015)[107] evaluates China's economic growth stability and investigates the factors affecting it, concluding the demand structure has a huge impact on economic growth stability.

1.3.3 Literature Review

This book makes a few conclusions based on the relevant literature: first, though China's final consumption rate is underestimated to some degree due to incomplete accounting statistics, it is indeed relatively low. Second, issues around optimal consumption rate concern the concepts related to the long-term economic growth rather than the short-term economic growth. Thus research on optimal consumption rate needs to be carried out within the theoretical frameworks of long-term economic growth. Current studies are mainly carried out within the frameworks such as the dynamic efficiency, the Solow–Swan model and the Ramsey–Cass–Koopmans model. But the results of these studies differ greatly from each other and are lack of linkage. Third, in terms of the studies on the stability of economic growth, most of them are qualitative studies, such as the research discussing the sustainability of economic growth from the aspect of "unsustainable high investment". Comparatively, quantitative studies are much fewer. A representative study among them is carried out by Lin and Wang (2013), illustrating that China's economy has entered the "Great Moderation". Therefore, how to quantitatively evaluate the steadiness of China's economic growth remains to be considered. Fourth, at present, scholars have not directly carried out studies on the relationship between consumption and economic growth stability. They have reached a consensus that as consumption is the most stable part of demand, raising its proportion in GDP (final consumption rate) contributes to enhancing the stability of economic growth. However, questions remain unsolved, including on what conditions the increase of final consumption rate helps strengthen economic growth stability, what weakens the steadiness and to what extent the steadiness is affected.

1.4 Outline

Based on the theories of economic growth, this book centres around optimal consumption rate, theoretically discusses the requirements an economy needs to meet for achieving optimal consumption rate, analyses the possible evolutionary path of consumption rate in relation with economic development and looks into the relationship between consumption rate and optimal consumption rate in a steady-state economy. Positive tests on China's optimal consumption rate since the reform and opening-up are made in the frameworks of dynamic efficiency, the Solow–Swan model, the Ramsey–Cass–Koopmans model and the VAR model. In addition, the suggestion to raise China's optimal consumption rate is given with the empirical analysis of the factors affecting it. This book first introduces the relevant theoretical studies, followed by the positive tests and the suggestion for countermeasures. The outline is as follows:

Based on theoretical and empirical analysis, Chapter 1 introduces the background of the research and some basic facts, talks about the thread and approach, and expounds on the definitions and existing domestic and foreign studies.

Chapter 2 analyses the stylized facts about the evolution of consumption rate and the stability of economic growth during China's economic development. Specifically speaking, it includes the illustration of the evolutionary characteristics, international comparison, direct evaluation of the stability of economic growth and the empirical analysis of the factors affecting final consumption rate.

Chapter 3 looks into the dynamic efficiency and optimal consumption rate within the framework of dynamic efficiency with empirical analysis of China's economic dynamic efficiency and its optimal consumption rate. In this chapter, the optimal consumption rate is defined as the consumption rate reached at the point where the economy achieves golden-rule growth. In that sense, the dynamic efficiency of economy helps illustrate the relationship between the actual consumption rate and the optimal consumption rate. The consumption rate in a dynamically inefficient economy is lower than the optimal consumption rate, while it is higher in a dynamically efficient economy than the optimal consumption rate.

Chapter 4 discusses how consumption rate affects economic growth and the requirements an economy needs to meet for achieving optimal consumption rate through using the theoretical Solow–Swan model and makes empirical analysis based on China's statistics from 1978 to 2013.

Chapter 5 analyses the issues around optimal consumption rate with the Ramsey–Cass–Koopmans model. First, it focuses on the optimal consumption rate in the Ramsey–Cass–Koopmans model. Next, it calculates China's optimal consumption rate through the calibration of the relevant parameters according to China's economic reality, followed by the simulation of the impact of the variation in parameters on the optimal consumption rate.

Chapter 6 addresses the optimal consumption rate in an open economy by establishing the general equilibrium model in an open economy. Due to the complexity of the general equilibrium model, it is hard to obtain the analytical solution. Thus numerical simulation is used to calculate the optimal consumption rate and analyse the factors affecting it.

Chapter 7 looks into consumption rate within the framework of the DSGE model. As the DSGE model is to analyse the optimization of an economic entity, this chapter defines the consumption rate reached at the point where the economy is at the steady state as the optimal consumption rate and investigates the response of optimal consumption rate and economic output to exogenous shocks.

Chapter 8 evaluates the steadiness of China's economic growth and analyses the factors affecting it. First, it discusses how the four structures including demand structure, industry structure, factor structure and ownership structure affect economic growth stability based on the relevant theories. Then it establishes an econometric model to make quantitative analysis of how much the factors affect the stability of economic growth within a framework. Finally, based on the research findings, it offers suggestions for enhancing the steadiness of China's economic growth.

Chapter 9 discusses the impact of the variation of consumption rate on economic growth and its steadiness from the following three perspectives: (1) National accounts (supposing the growth rate of consumption, investment and net export remains the same along with an increased consumption rate, a decreased investment rate and an unvarying net export rate); (2) Input and output (supposing consumption rate goes up with a declining investment and a dropping net export rate); (3) VAR model of final consumption rate, investment rate and economic growth rate (based on China's statistics from 1978 to 2020).

Summarizing the research findings, Chapter 10 puts forward the suggestion that China's final consumption rate should converge towards the optimal consumption rate.

Notes

1 Calculated by Geometric Means Method (GMM).
2 The expenditure-based GDP is the denominator in the calculation of the final consumption rate, household consumption rate, government consumption rate, rural household consumption rate and urban household consumption rate.

3 Yuan Zhigang,and Zhu Guolin, "Income Distribution and Aggregate Consumption in the Theory of Consumption: An Analysis of China's Low Consumption," *Social Sciences in China Press* 2 (2002).
4 Fang Fuqian, "An Inquiry into the Causes of Inadequate Household Consumption in China—An Analysis Based on Provincial Data of Urban and Rural China," *Social Sciences in China* 2 (2009).
5 Malthus T. R. *An Essay on the Principle of Population*, trans. Zhu Yang et al. (The Commercial Press, 1872).
6 Phelps. E.,"The Golden Rule of Accumulation: A Fable for Growthmen," *American Economic Review* 51, no. 4 (1961): 638–643.
7 Romer D., *Advanced Macroeconomics*, trans. Su Jian and Luo Tao (The Commercial Press, 1999).
8 Liu Yingqiu, "Secondary-High-Growth Economy of China," *China Social Sciences Press*, 2002.
9 Yang Shengming, "Yang Shengming Collection," *Shanghai Lexicographical Publishing House*, 2002.
10 Zeng Linghua, "On Theoretical Optimal Consumption Rate," *Seeker* 3 (1997).
11 Chenery H. and Syrquin M., *Patterns of Development1950–1970*, trans. Li Xinhua et al. (Economic Science Press, 1998).
12 Wen Qian, *Consumption Stimulating and Decomposition Mechanism of Income Growth* (China Financial & Economic Publishing House, 2005).
13 Tian Weimin, "Chinese Optimal Consumption Scale Based on Economic Growth:1978–2006," *Finance and Trade Research* 6 (2008).
14 Wu Zhongqun and Zhang Qunqun, "China's Optimal Consumption Rate and its Relevant Policies," *Research on Financial and Economic Issues* 3 (2011).
15 Source: the website of National Bureau of Statistics of China.
16 Normally it refers to a year or a quarter.
17 As percentage is widely used in the calculation of economic growth, the result is multiplied by 100%.
18 Liu Guoguang, "Views on China's Economy and Macro-economic Coordination Policy," *Economic Perspectives* 10 (1999).
19 LIU Guoguang, "Analysis of China' Economy," *Economic Research Journal*, 2000 (6).
20 LIU Guoguang, "Analysis and Forecast of China's Economy,"*Modern Economic Research*, 2000 (6).
21 Chenery H. and Syrquin M. *Patterns of Development1950–1970*, trans. Li Xinhua et al. (Economic Science Press, 1998).
22 Xiao Zequn, "Coordinating the Proportion of Investment to Consumption with Scientific Outlook on Development," *Social Sciences in Hunan* 5 (2004).
23 Wu Xianman, Cai Xiao, and Xu Chunming, "Comparative Research on the Relationship between Chinese and Foreign Investment and Consumption," *Forum of World Economics & Politics* 1 (2006).

24 Chao Gangling and Wang Lijuan, "The Criterion For the Reasonableness of China's Consumption Rate—Can Chenery Model Explaine that?" *Finance & Trade Economics* 4 (2009).
25 Ning Junming and Tu Dakun, "International Comparison on Investment Rate and Consumption Rate and Enlightenment—Based on Chenery's General Industrialization Model," *Journal of Henan Business College* 4 (2010).
26 Fu Lichun, "Study on China's Consumption Rate," Doctoral Thesis, Graduate School of Chinese Academy of Social Sciences, 2011.
27 Luo Yunyi, "Is China's Current Consumption Rate 'Relatively Low'?" *Macroeconomics* 5 (2005).
28 Qiao Weiguo, "The Reason behind China's High Investment Rate and Low Consumption Rate and the Countermeasures," *Macroeconomics* 8 (2005).
29 Jiang Lin, Ma Chunrong, and Kang Jun, "Comparative Analysis of Final Consumption Rate of China and Other Countries,"*Consumer Economics*, 2009(1).
30 Lei Hui, "International Comparison and Trend Analysis of China's Investment Rate and Consumption Rate Since the Reform and Opening-up," *Research on Development* 4 (2009).
31 Lu o Yunyi, "The Normality of China's Current Economy—Low Consumption Rate and High Investment Rate," *Macroeconomics* 5 (2004).
32 Economic Growth Frontier Subject Team, "High Growth of Investment, Macro-cost and the Sustainability of Economic Growth," *Economic Research Journal* 10 (2005).
33 Liang Dongli, "A Study of High Investment Rate and Low Consumption Rate of China's Economy," *Journal of Nanjing Normal University (Social Science Edition)* 1 (2006).
34 Zhan Minghua and XUu Yueli, Song Yang, "Sustainability of China's Economic Growth and Its Transformation Path," *The Journal of World Economy* 8 (2006).
35 Gong Min and Li Wenpu, "An Explanation for China's High Capital Share and Low Consumption Rate—Analysis and Calibration Based on a Dynamic General Equilibrium Growth Model," *Academic Monthly* 9 (2013).
36 Lv Bingyang and Mao Jie, "Fiscal Foundation of High Investment and Low Consumption in China," *Economic Research Journal* 5 (2014).
37 Gao Minxue, "Impact Mechanism of Hidden Income of on the Underestimation of China's Consumption Rate--A Discussion Based on Principles and Practices of the National Accounting," *Statistical Research* 7 (2014).
38 Wang Qiushi and Wang Yixin, "On the Underestimation of China's Consumption Rate: Discussion on High Demand for Investment in China," *Journal of Shandong University (Philosophy and Social Sciences)* 3 (2013).
39 Wang Qiushi and Wang Yixin, "Does China Actually Have Such Low Household Consumption Rate?--Research and Estimation of China's Actual Household Consumption Rate," *Economist* 8 (2013).

40 Zhu Tian and Zhang Jun, "To What Extent Is China's Consumption Rate Underestimated?" *China Journal of Economics* 2 (2014).
41 Kang Yuanzhi, "Is China's Consumption Insufficient or Underestimated?--Discussion on the Moderate Consumption in the Context of Propelling Domestic Demand," *Consumer Economics* 2 (2014).
42 Luo Yunyi, "A Review of the Theoretical Research on the Investment-Consumption Ratio," *Macroeconomics* 12 (1999).
43 Luo Yunyi, "On the Possibility of an Optimal Consumption-Investment Ratio," *Macroeconomics* 12 (2006).
44 Wu Zhongqun, "Consumption and Investment in Economic Growth in China," *Social Sciences in China* 3 (2002).
45 Tan Xiaofang, Wang Diming, and Zou Cunhui, "Positive Research on China's Reasonable Range of Investment-Consumption Structure," *Research on Financial and Economic Issues* 3 (2006).
46 He Keng, "A Research on the Investment, Consumption and Economic Development Strategy of China," *The Journal of Quantitative & Technical Economics* 5 (2006).
47 Cai Yuezhou and Wang Yuxia, "Factors Affecting Investment-Consumption Structure and the Desired Range of Investment and Consumption--International Comparison and Empirical analysis Based on Global Statistics," *Economic Theory and Business Management* 1 (2010).
48 Wu Zhenqiu, Wang Fang, and Zhou Yu, "The Research on Determining and Prognosticationof Desired Consumption Rate and Desired Household Consumption Rate in the Economic Development of China," *Journal of Central University If Finance & Economics* 11 (2014).
49 Jing Linbo and Wang Xuefeng, "Theoretical Model and Its Application to the Determination of Consumption Rate," *Economic Perspectives*, 11 (2011).
50 Chen Menggen, "Analysis of Optimal Structure for Investment and Consumption," *Finance and Trade Research* 2 (2014).
51 Ouyang Yao, Fu Yuanhai, and Wang Song, "The Scale Effect and Evolution Mechanism about Household ConsumptionDemand," *Economic Research Journal* 2 (2016).
52 The original text is as follows: "Specifically, when the household consumption rate is less than 0.539 and the long-term effects rises by 0.1, the second annual economic growth rate only increases by 0.077; when the household consumption rate is higher than 0.539 and the long-term effects rises by 0.1, the second annual economic growth rate only increases by 0.121."
53 Phelps. E., "The Golden Rule of Accumulation: A Fable for Growthmen," *American Economic Review* 51, no. 4 (1961): 638–643.
54 Specifically, the marginal product of capital equals the sum of the population growth, the rate of technological progress and the rate of depreciation. Please refer to Romer's *Advanced Macroeconomics* (2014).

55 Chenery H. and Syrquin M., *Patterns of Development1950–1970*, trans. Li Xinhua et al. (Economic Science Press, 1998).
56 Liu Yingqiu, "Secondary-High-Growth Economy of China," *China Social Sciences Press*, 2002.
57 Yang Shengming, "Yang Shengming Collection," *Shanghai Lexicographical Publishing House*, 2002.
58 Zeng Linghua, "On Theoretical Optimal Consumption Rate," *Seeker* 3 (1997).
59 Wu Zhongqun, "The Possible Existence of the Optimal Consumption Rate and Its Related Issues," *China Soft Science Magazine*, 2009 (S 1).
60 Wu Zhongqun and Zhang Qunqun, "The Optimal Consumption Rate in China and Its Policy Implications," *Research on Financial and Economic Issues* 3 (2011).
61 Ji Ming, Liu Zhibiao, and Cen Shutian, "The Steady-state of Consumption Rate, Evolution and Reality Choice of China's Sustained andBalanced Economic Growth—Based on the Analytical Framework of R-C-K Model," *Research on Economics and Management* 4 (2013).
62 Mao Zhonggen, Sun Hao, and Huang Rong, "An Estimation of China's Optimal Household Consumption Rate and Analysis of Its Variation Mechanism," *The Journal of Quantitative & Technical Economics* 3 (2014).
63 Lin Yanyu, "An Estimation of the Optimal Consumption Rate of China's Upper-middle Income Class," *Journal of Chengdu University (Social Science)* 3 (2016).
64 Liu Jinquan and Wang Qiaoru, "The Non-linear Relationship between Final Consumption Rate and Economic Growth--An International Empirical Analysis Based on PSTR Model," *International Economics and Trade Research* 3 (2017).
65 Wang Xiaolu, "Economic Structural Adjustments and A Forecast of China's Economic Growth," *Comparative Studies* 5 (2016).
66 Yuan Zhigang and Song Zheng, "On the Age Structure of Population, Pension System and Optimal Consumption Rate," *Economic Research Journal* 11 (2000).
67 Wan Chun and QIU Changrong, "The Welfare Analysis of Optimal Voluntary Saving Rate--Based on China's Pension System," *The Journal of Quantitative & Technical Economics* 12 (2015).
68 Zhen Chunxiong, "The Determination of China's Optimal Consumption Rate and Macroeconomics Effects," Doctoral Thesis, Party School of the Central Committee of the C.P.C, 2008.
69 Ding Haiyun, "Research on China's Optimal Consumption Rate for the Economic Growth," Thesis for Degree of Master, Capital University of Economics and Business (School of Economics), 2014.
70 Fan Zuojun, Chang Yali, and Hunag Liqun, "Optimal Saving Rate and Its Influencing Factors Measurement under the International Field of Vision," *Economic Research Journal*, 9 (2014).
71 Qiao Weiguo, Pan Bisheng, "Determination of the ReasonableCapital Formation Rate in Chinese Economic Growth," *China Soft Science Magazine* 7 (2005).

72 Gong Ge, "The Optimal Investment Rate and Its Realization," Thesis for Degree of Master, North China Electric Power University (Beijing), 2010.
73 Li Daokui, Xu Xin, and Jiang Hongping, "Analysis of China's National Investment Rate from the Perspective of Welfare Economics," *Economic Research Journal* 9 (2012).
74 Liu Shucheng, "On the Sound and Rapid Development," *Economic Research Journal* 6 (2007).
75 Zhang Jun, "Economic Growth and Transition with ChineseCharacteristics," *Study & Exploration* 3 (2012).
76 Chen Leyi, Li Yushuang, and Li Xing, "The Empirical Research on China Economic Growth and Fluctuation," *Economic Review Journal* 2 (2010).
77 Mankiw, N. G., *Macroeconomics (the 6th version)*, trans. Zhang Fan (China Renmin University Press, 2006).
78 Li Yanjun and Jin Hao, "Evaluation and Research on the Quality and Effect of the Economic Growth," *Journal of Industrial and Technological Economics*, 2 (2007).
79 Lv Xiaoning, Analysis of the Steadiness of the Economic Growth of Shanxi Province, *Productivity Research* 3 (2002).
80 Liu Huajun, Li Yunsheng, and N Ao, "A Empirical analysis of Stability and Sustainability ofShandong Economic Growth," *Journal of Shandong Institute of Light Industry* 3 (2004).
81 Chao Xiaojing and Hui Kang, "Measuring the Quality of Economic Growth of China," *The Journal of Quantitative & Technical Economics* 6 (2009).
82 Li Ping and Feng Mengli, "Impacts of the Interest Rate Marketization on China's EconomyGrowth Quality: A New Interpretation," *Economic Review* 2 (2016).
83 Chen Shoudong and Liu Yang, "Measuring the Steadiness of Economic Growth: An Empirical Analysis," *Journal of Shandong University(Philosophy and Social Sciences* 4 (2016).
84 Mankiw, N. G., *Macroeconomics (the 6th version)*, trans. Zhang Fan (China Renmin University Press, 2006).
85 Li Yanjun and Jin Hao, "Evaluation and Research on the Quality and Effect of the Economic Growth," *Journal of Industrial and Technological Economics* 2 (2007).
86 Xiang Aibao, "The Research on the Steadiness of China's Economic Growth Since the Reform and Opening-up," Thesis for Degree of Master, Hunan University, 2008.
87 Blanchard O and Simon J, "The Long and Large Decline in U.S.Output Volatility," *Brookings Papers on Economic Activity* 32, no. 1 (2001): 135–164.
88 Mankiw, N. G., *Macroeconomics (the 6th version)*, trans. Zhang Fan (China Renmin University Press, 2006).
89 Liu Jinquan and Liu Zhigang, "The Analysis of Dynamic Patterns and Resources of Output Volatilities in China's Business Cycles," *Economic Research Journal* 3 (2005).
90 Stock J.H. and Watson M.W., "Has the Business Cycle Changed and Why?" *NBER Macroeconomics Annual* 17, no. 1 (2002): 159–218.

91 Blanchard O. and Simon J., "The Long and Large Decline in U.S.Output Volatility," *Brookings Papers on Economic Activity* 32, no. 1 (2001): 135–164.
92 Bemanke B., "The Great Moderation," Remarks at the Meetings of the Eastern Economic Association, 2004.
93 Frankel J. A. and Orzsag P. R., *American economic policy in the 1990s*, trans. Xu Weiyu et al. (CITIC Press, 2004).
94 Clark Todd E., "Is the Great Moderation Over? An Empirical Analysis," *Economic Review-Federal Reserve Bank of Kansas City* 94（2009）: 5–42.
95 Lin Jianhao and Wang Meijin, "The Great Moderation of China's Macroeconomic Fluctuations: An InvestigationTiming and Potential Explanations," *China Economic Quarterly* 2 (2013).
96 Yang Jijun and Fan Conglai, "The Influence of 'Made in China' on the Great Moderation of the Global Economy: An Empirical Test Based on Value Chains," *Social Sciences in China* 10 (2015).
97 Eggers A. and Ioannides Y.M., "The Role of Output Composition in the Stabilization of U.S. Output Growth," *Discussion Papers* 28, no. 3 (2006): 585–595.
98 Fang Fuqian and Zhan Xinyu, "Empirical Analysis of the Stabilizing Effect of Industrial Structure Upgrading on the Economic Fluctuations in China," *Economic Theory and Business Management* 9 (2011).
99 Gan Chunhun, Zhen Ruogu,and YU Dianfan, "The Impact of China's Industry Structure Transformation on the Economic Growth and Fluctuation," *Economic Research Journal* 5 (2011).
100 Yang Tianyu and Liu Yunting, "Structural Transformation and Stabilization of China's Macroeconomy," *Economic Theory and Business Management* 7 (2011).
101 Li Qiang, "Industrial Structure Changes Aggravate or Restrain Economic Fluctuations?--Based on Analysis of China," *Research on Economics and Management* 7 (2012).
102 Li Meng, "Research on the Correlationship between Industry Structure and Economic Fluctuation," *Economic Review* 6 (2010).
103 Ji Ming and LIU Zhibiao, "The Impact of the Development of China's Demand Structure on the Economic Growth and Fluctuations," *Economic Science* 1 (2014).
104 Yang Tianyu and Liu Yunting, "Structural Transformation and Stabilization of China's Business Cycle," *Economic Theory and Business Management* 7 (2011).
105 Shen Lisheng, "How does the Change of Final Demand Structure Affect the Change of Industrial Structure?--Analysis Based on the Input-Output Model," *The Journal of Quantitative & Technical Economics* 12 (2011).
106 Li Jianwei, "The Law of Evolution of Investment Rate and Consumption Rate and Its Relationship with Economic Growth," *Economic Perspectives* 3 (2003).
107 Zhao Xincheng, "Economic Evaluation of the Steadiness of China's Growth and Its Influencing Factors," *Journal of Industrial and Technological Economics* 1 (2015).

Chapter 2

China's Consumption Rate and Economic Growth Steadiness: Stylized Facts

Studies show a stylized fact about China's consumption rate: though China's economic growth rate is much higher than the world average level, its consumption rate is going down year by year and is lower than the world average level. In this chapter, we discuss the stylized facts about China's consumption rate and the economic growth stability since the reform and opening-up. In 2.1, we horizontally compare the consumption rate of China with that of the major countries in the world to investigate whether it is relatively low. Moreover, we look into the evolution of China's consumption rate since the reform and opening-up. In 2.2, we analyse the variation of the steadiness of China's economic growth since the reform and opening-up based on the growth rate variations of the components of demand and supply. In 2.3, we discuss the factors affecting the final consumption rate, along with a rough empirical analysis based on the statistics for China.

2.1 Features of the Variation in China's Consumption Rate

2.1.1 International Comparison of Final Consumption Rates

The representative scholars including Rostow, Kuznets and Chenery, who carry out international studies on consumption rate, find out the law of how consumption rate varies with the economic development based on empirical statistics. Rostow (1962)[1] writes in his book titled *The Stages of Economic Growth: A Non-communist Manifesto* that the economic development of a country goes through five stages, namely "the traditional society, the preconditions for take-off, the take-off, the drive to maturity and the age of high mass-consumption"[2]. Rostow's theory indirectly shows how the consumption rate changes with the economic development: as economy develops, the consumption rate gradually falls before it progressively rises and finally reaches a steady level. Kuznets summarizes the growth pattern of various countries and common features of their economies in the 1950s from the perspective of national accounts in his paper series named "Quantitative Aspects of the Economic Growth of Nations". Though Kuznets's research concerns consumption and investment, his result has its limitations because the sample data he collected is incomparable. Chenery and Syrquin (1975)[3] study how consumption rate varies with the economic development level (GNP per capita) through regression analysis based on the statistics of 101 countries in their book titled *Patterns of Development 1950–1970*. When the GNP per capita (measured by the dollar's value in 1964) is lower than $100, the final consumption rate and the household consumption rate reach the highest level, respectively, to 89.8 percent and 77.9 percent. As the GNP per capita grows, the final consumption rate and the household consumption rate progressively decrease. When the GNP per capita is over $1000, the final consumption rate and the household consumption rate become more stable and even slightly increase. As for the government consumption rate, it follows a similar pattern: as the GNP per capita rises from $100 to $1000, the government consumption rate also gradually increases. When the GNP per capita is over $1000, the government consumption rate starts to fall (see Table 2-1).

Table 2-1 Relationship between World Consumption Rate and Economic Development Processes during 1950–1970

GNP per capita (dollar value in 1964)	<100	100	200	300	400	500	800	1000	>1000
Final Consumption Rate (%)	89.8	85.7	82	80.2	79	78.3	76.9	76.5	76.5
Household Consumption Rate (%)	77.9	72	68.6	66.7	65.4	64.5	62.5	61.7	62.4
Government Consumption Rate (%)	11.9	13.7	13.4	13.5	13.6	13.8	14.4	14.8	14.1

Source: CHENERY H, SYRQUIN M. "Patterns of Development 1950–1970," Translated by Li Xinhua et al., Economic Science Press, 1998.

Following Chenery's analytical paradigm, Fu (2011)[4] looks into the relationship between national consumption rate and economic development processes in countries of different income levels all over the world. The finding is similar to Chenery's conclusion. In 2.1.1, we try to reveal the average level of global consumption rate by illustrating the evolution trend of consumption rate in countries of different income levels across the globe. The top ten countries (the United States, China, Japan, Germany, the United Kingdom, France, Brazil, Italy, India and Russia) in the World GDP Ranking 2014 are taken as examples to show the evolution processes of major countries. The comparison among the BRICS who are at similar development level with China reflects the ranking of China's consumption level in the world. Since final consumption rate equals household consumption rate plus government consumption rate which is generally less volatile, final consumption rate and household consumption rate of a country share a similar variation trend. Therefore, we merely study the variation of final consumption rate. Furthermore, the statistics in 2.1.1 come from the World Development Indicators (WDI) of World Bank Databank.[5]

In Figure 2-1, the abscissa represents time periods, and the ordinate represents the final consumption rate of the world, the low-income countries, the middle-income countries and the high-income countries. The figure shows the evolution trend of the final consumption rates of the countries with different income levels across the globe. First, the world average final consumption rate rose slowly from 73.6 percent in 1970 to 77.7 percent in 2013. Over 40 years, it kept 2 percentage points above or below 75 percent. Second, the low-income countries had the highest final consumption rates, which averaged 93.0 percent during 1990–2013 and started to fall in volatility since 1990. Third, the final consumption rate of middle-income countries also kept falling. It was higher than the world average level until 1975 and was lower by 8 percentage points in 2013. Fourth, the final consumption rate of high-income countries shares a similar variation trend with the world average level and has been slightly higher than the latter since 2000. Fifth, the comparison among countries of different income levels shows that the final consumption rate of the low-income countries is the highest while that of the middle-income countries is the lowest. The final consumption rate of the high-income countries is basically the same as the world average level and tends to be stable (see Figure 2-1).

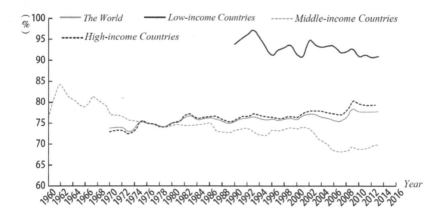

Figure 2-1 Final Consumption Rates of the World and Countries with Different Income Levels
Source: World Development Indicators (WDI) of World Bank Databank

Figure 2-2 shows the evolution trend of the top 10 countries in the 2014 GDP ranking: first, regarding the final consumption rates of the major countries, China's final consumption rate keeps falling in volatility and is lower than that of the other nine countries in most years. Especially it was lower by 34.0 percentage points than the highest level of the ten countries in 2013 and, respectively, lower by 28.1 percentage points and 20.1 percentage points than the world average level and that of the middle-income countries in the corresponding period. Second, the final consumption rates of the countries including the United States, the United Kingdom, Germany, France, Brazil and Italy are basically at steady state. Third, the final consumption rate of Japan which evolved from a middle-income country to a developed country in the 1970s keeps rising steadily and has reached the level of high-income countries. Fourth, Russia's final consumption rate is much more volatile and has basically reached the average level of middle-income countries. Fifth, India, whose final consumption rate keeps decreasing steadily and has reached the level of middle-income countries, shares a similar variation trend of final consumption rate with middle-income countries including China.

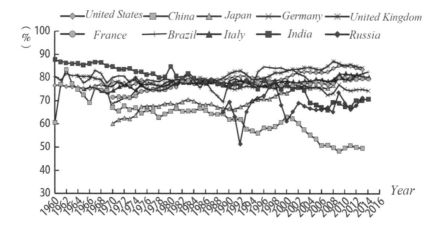

Figure 2-2 Evolution Trend of Final Consumption Rates of the Top Ten Countries in the GDP Ranking during 1960–2014
Source: World Development Indicators (WDI) of World Bank Databank

Figure 2-3 illustrates the final consumption rates of the BRICS which are at the same development stage[6]: first, only China and India have similar decreasing trend of final consumption rates with middle-income countries; next, the final consumption rates of South Africa and Brazil are around 80 percent, remaining steady; moreover, though Russia's final consumption rate is much more volatile, it basically reaches the average level of middle-income countries; finally, China's final consumption rate is lower than the other BRICS countries, respectively, lower by 32.1 percentage points, 32.6 percentage points, 20.9 percentage points and 21.7 percentage points than Brazil, South Africa, India and Russia.

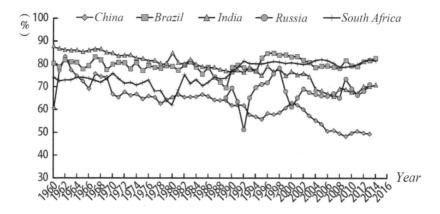

Figure 2-3 Evolution Trend of the Final Consumption Rates of the BRICS during 1960–2014
Source: World Development Indicators (WDI) of World Bank Databank

In conclusion, according to the statistics of WDI of World Bank Databank, during 1960-2014, China's final consumption rate kept falling and was lower than the world average level as well as the general level of both the middle-income countries and the BRICS.

2.1.2 Analysis of the Evolution of China's Consumption Rate

Since the reform and opening-up, the imbalance in China's demand structure has been more problematic as the economy rapidly grows. It can be shown by a spiralling investment rate, a year-by-year decreasing consumption rate, a greater dependence of economic growth on fixed asset investments and a year-by-year less contribution of consumption to economic growth. In section 2.1.2, we investigate the evolution trend of China's consumption rate and the reason behind it.

According to Database of National Bureau of Statistics of China (Table 2-2), under the development strategy of "high investment-high growth", China's final consumption rate and household consumption rate keep decreasing in volatility. Its evolution trend can be divided into four stages: up, down, then up again and then down again.

First stage (1978–1983): Since 1978, the final (household) consumption rate had been climbing for six consecutive years to 67.3 percent (53.4 percent) in 1983, 5.3 percentage points (4.6 percentage points) higher than it was in 1978. The reason behind it lies in the adjustment of the development strategy of encouraging accumulation and production but paying little attention to consumption and life quality. The measures implemented after the reform and opening-up such as raising wages as well as the prices of agricultural products help fix the long-lasting problems and improve the income level of the residents to some extent.

Second stage (1984–1983): The final (household) consumption rate fell by 6.3 percentage points (4.6 percentage points), from 65.7 percent (50.6 percent) in 1984 to 59.3 percent (46.0 percent) in 1995.

Third stage (1996–2001): The final consumption rate slightly rose, fluctuating around 61.6 percent (46.3 percent). Such increase can be explained by the following two facts: first, the policy of expanding domestic demand began to be implemented, including increasing investment and encouraging consumption; second, Asia was witnessing the financial crisis at that time, for which China implemented the policy to stimulate the economy and the consumption at the same time.

Fourth stage (2002 till now): China's final (household) consumption rate plummeted by 6.9 percentage points (7.3 percentage points), which results from the following facts: first, the changeable economic environment adds to the uncertainty faced by residents, bringing an increase in precautionary savings and a decrease in consumption. Thus the overall consumption rate dived; second, as the reform of commercial building kept being promoted, commercial building price has climbed sharply since 2002. Therefore, a huge slice of residents' income is spent on housing, leaving less for consumption; third, with the development of higher education marketization, a large proportion of household income is spent on children's education, resulting in less income available for consumption; fourth, from the perspective of income distribution, the proportion of household income in national income has been falling year by year, explaining the decline of China's final consumption rate and household consumption rate.

Table 2-2 The Variations of China's Consumption Rate and Capital Formation Rate since 1978

Unit: %

Year	Final Consumption Rate	Household Consumption Rate	Rural Household Consumption Rate	Urban Household Consumption Rate	Government Consumption Rate
1978	61.9	48.8	30.3	18.5	13.2
1979	63.7	49.8	31.0	18.8	14.0
1980	65.4	51.5	31.2	20.3	13.9
1981	66.6	53.4	32.7	20.7	13.2
1982	66.4	53.2	33.7	19.5	13.2
1983	67.3	53.4	33.5	19.8	13.9
1984	65.7	50.6	30.9	19.7	15.0
1985	65.0	50.8	30.6	20.2	14.2
1986	64.8	50.9	30.0	21.0	13.8
1987	62.7	49.6	28.5	21.1	13.1
1988	62.0	49.5	27.3	22.2	12.5
1989	64.0	50.9	28.2	22.7	13.1
1990	63.3	49.7	27.6	22.1	13.6
1991	61.9	47.9	25.3	22.6	14.0
1992	59.8	45.4	21.9	23.5	14.5
1993	58.5	44.1	19.7	24.4	14.4
1994	58.5	44.3	18.9	25.3	14.2
1995	59.3	46.0	18.9	27.1	13.4
1996	60.3	47.0	19.8	27.2	13.2
1997	59.9	46.1	18.8	27.2	13.8
1998	60.7	45.7	17.5	28.2	15.0
1999	62.9	46.4	16.4	30.0	16.5
2000	63.9	47.0	15.6	31.3	16.9
2001	62.2	45.7	14.8	31.0	16.5
2002	61.2	45.1	14.0	31.0	16.1

Table 2-2 Continued

Year	Final Consumption Rate	Household Consumption Rate	Rural Household Consumption Rate	Urban Household Consumption Rate	Government Consumption Rate
2003	58.1	42.8	13.0	29.8	15.3
2004	55.4	40.7	11.9	28.8	14.7
2005	54.3	39.5	11.1	28.4	14.8
2006	52.5	37.7	10.3	27.4	14.8
2007	50.9	36.3	9.5	26.9	14.6
2008	50.0	35.4	8.9	26.5	14.5
2009	50.2	35.4	8.6	26.8	14.8
2010	49.3	34.6	8.0	26.7	14.7
2011	50.6	35.2	8.1	27.1	15.4
2012	51.1	35.4	7.9	27.4	15.7
2013	51.4	35.6	7.9	27.7	15.8
2014	52.3	36.5	8.1	28.4	15.7
2015	53.7	37.6	8.2	29.4	16.1
2016	55.1	38.7	8.3	30.4	16.4
2017	55.1	38.7	8.3	30.4	16.4
2018	55.3	38.7	8.4	30.2	16.6
2019	55.8	39.1	8.3	30.8	16.7
2020	54.3	37.7	8.1	29.6	16.6

Note: GDP is the denominator in the calculation of consumption rates here.

Source: Database of National Bureau of Statistics of China

2.1.3 Variations of China's Urban Household Consumption Rate and Rural Household Consumption Rate

Considering the typical urban-rural dual structure in China, household consumption consists of urban consumption and rural consumption. In this way, household consumption rate equals rural household consumption rate plus urban household consumption rate. Figure 2-4 illustrates the evolution of China's rural household consumption rate and urban household consumption rate since the reform and opening-up: we can tell that 1992 was the turning point. Prior to 1992, China's rural household consumption rate was higher than urban household consumption rate. Since 1992, the former has been lower than the latter.

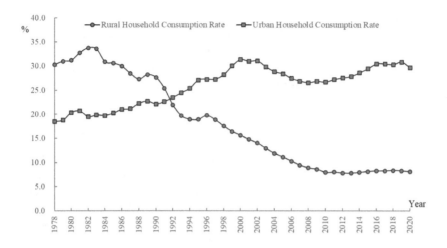

Figure 2-4 Evolution Trend of China's Rural Household Consumption Rate and Urban Household Consumption Rate

The evolution of the rural household consumption rate has gone through two stages: in the first stage (1978–1983), it rose from 30.3 percent in 1978 to 33.5 percent in 1983, higher by 3.2 percentage points within five years. On average it climbed by 0.64 percentage points yearly. At the beginning of the reform and opening-up, due to the implementation of the Household Contract Responsibility System and the government policies to encourage agriculture, the net income per capita of farmers rose, bringing an increase in the rural household consumption rate. In the second stage (1984 till now), the rural household consumption rate has been falling year by year, from 30.9 percent in 1984 to 8.1 percent in 2020. Overall it decreased by 22.5 percentage points. During this period, such decrease can be explained from the following two aspects: first, the growth rate of rural residents' income has long been lower than the economic growth rate, which causes the fall of the proportion of rural residents' income in national income; second, the gap between China's urban income and rural income keeps widening.

The evolution of the urban household consumption rate has also experienced two stages: in the first stage (1978–2002), it went up year by year, from 18.5 percent in 1978 to 31.0 percent in 2002. Overall it increased by 12.5 percentage points, going up by about 0.52 percentage points every year. Compared with the decreasing trend of the rural household consumption rate during the same period, the urban household consumption rate kept climbing, thanks to the emphasis on urban construction in the government policies and thus urban residents enjoyed more benefits brought by economic growth than rural residents did. In the second stage (2002 till now), the urban household consumption rate has been slightly going down because of the increase of housing price and the higher education marketization.

2.1.4 Variations of China's Government Consumption Rate

Relatively speaking, China's government consumption rate has a far narrower fluctuation range than the final consumption rate and household consumption rate do, fluctuating around its average of 14.8 percent since the reform and opening-up within the range between 12.5 percent in 1988 and 16.9 percent in 2000 (see Figure 2-5). Generally, fluctuation in government consumption rate is caused by the changes of fiscal policies. For instance, in certain years, measures such as rising expenses on infrastructure contributed to the increase in government consumption rate. Based on the above data along with the analysis in 2.1.3, we can conclude that China's government consumption rate is at the level of middle-income countries, and no lower than the average level of the countries in the same development stage.

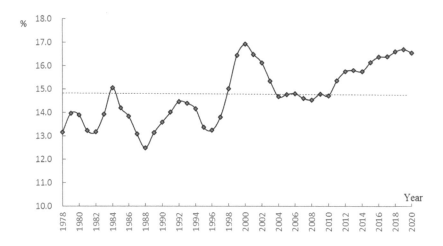

Figure 2-5 Evolution Trend of China's Government Consumption Rate

2.1.5 Fluctuation of China's Consumption Rate

According to the theories related to the stages of economic development, the fluctuation of final consumption rate and household consumption rate normally shows the following features: at the beginning of the economic development, both final consumption rate and household consumption rate were relatively high. During the stage of the preconditions for take-off and the take-off, they fell because of the demand for capital accumulation. When the economic development reached a certain point, the consumption rate progressively rose due to the more attention paid to life quality: (i) As the economy keeps growing, the consumption rate tends to be more stable; (ii) As for the government consumption rate, it has been relatively stable, fluctuating between 10 percent and 20 percent. Table 2-2 shows that China's final consumption rate and household consumption rate reached the lowest point around 2010 and are currently in a rising trend (see Chapter 2.3). But the government consumption rate has been fluctuating around 14.8 percent within the range between 12.5 percent and 16.9 percent. The statistical analysis indicates that during 1978–2020, China's average final consumption rate, household consumption rate and government consumption rate were, respectively, 58.68 percent, 43.92 percent and 14.76 percent. Their respective standard deviations were 5.422 percent, 6.060 percent and 1.223 percent with coefficients of standard deviation of 0.092, 0.138 and 0.083. Judging from that, we can see that the household consumption rate is the most volatile followed by the final consumption rate, while the government consumption rate is the most stable (see Table 2-3).

Table 2-3 Fluctuation of China's Consumption Rate during 1978–2020

	Average (%)	Standard Deviation (%)	Coefficient of Standard Deviation
Final Consumption Rate	58.68	5.422	0.092
Household Consumption Rate	43.92	6.060	0.138
Government Consumption Rate	14.76	1.223	0.083

Source: The calculation is based on the statistics from Database of National Bureau of Statistics of China

2.2 Features of the Steadiness of China's Economic Growth

In section 2.2, we roughly discuss the evolution trend of China's economic growth stability since the reform and opening-up based on the variations of the growth rates of different consisting parts of the demand and supply. The result shows that the fluctuation ranges of all macroeconomic variables are becoming narrower, which straightforwardly reflects the improvement in China's economic growth stability.

2.2.1 Demand Analysis of China's Economic Growth Stability

In terms of the demand, the GDP consists of final consumption expenditure, total capital formation and net exports. Figure 2-6 presents the respective growth rates of China's GDP, final consumption and capital formation since 1978. First, there have been two stages in the variations of the growth rates of China's GDP: final consumption and capital formation. In the first stage (1978–1991), the fluctuation ranges of all variables were relatively greater. Typically while the growth rate of total capital formation touched 27.4 percent in 1985, it fell to -7.9 percent in 1990. In the second stage (1992–till now), the fluctuation ranges of all variables became narrower. Next, the growth rate of total capital formation is the most volatile, followed by the growth rate of final consumption expenditure. Comparatively, the GDP growth rate is most stable. Finally, the growth rate of net exports is more volatile than that of final consumption expenditure and total capital formation. But since the proportion of net exports is relatively small in the GDP, its growth rate does not affect much on economic growth stability.

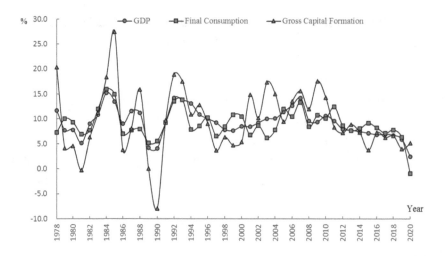

Figure 2-6 Growth Rates of China's GDP, Final Consumption and Total Capital Formation

2.2.2 Supply Analysis of China's Economic Growth Stability

In terms of the supply, the GDP consists of the added value of the primary industry, the secondary industry and the tertiary industry. Figure 2-7 shows the respective growth rates of China's GDP and the three industries since 1978. First, the variation of China's GDP and the three industries has gone through two stages: in the first stage (1978–1991), the promotion of marketization reform just began. As the reform in system as well as various external shocks has a great impact on economy, the growth rates of the GDP and the three industries were relatively volatile. In the second stage (1992–till now), their fluctuation ranges become narrower. Next, the growth rate of the secondary industry is most volatile while that of the tertiary industry is most stable. Finally, since 1992, the growth rates of the three industries synchronously have been varying with the GDP growth rate.

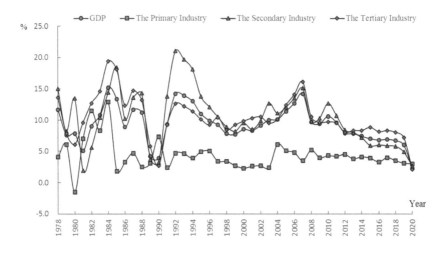

Figure 2-7 Growth Rates of China's GDP and the Three Industries since 1978

2.3 Factors Affecting China's Final Consumption Rate

2.3.1 Preliminaries

As the largest as well as the most stable item of expenditure in the Troika, the consumption lays a foundation for the steady and healthy growth of economy. As for the final consumption rate, it measures how much the total consumption contributes to the GDP. A higher final consumption rate indicates a greater contribution it makes to the GDP, and vice versa[7]. But since 2000, China's final consumption rate has kept decreasing from 63.9 percent in 2000 to 49.3 percent in 2010. After the policy that encourages consumption came out, the rate slightly bounced back to 54.3 percent in 2020. Since 2007, the weak consumption has resulted in the decrease of the economic growth rate which fell from 14.2 percent in 2007 to 6.0 percent in 2019. Such continuous decrease badly affects the steadiness and sustainability of China's economic growth. What affects the final consumption rate? Whether the adjustments in these factors can help slow down the fall of the final consumption rate in order to promote the stable economic growth? The answers to the above questions are key to the sustainable and steady growth of China's economy in the future.

Currently there hasn't been much literature directly studying on the influencing factors of consumption rate. Since national income equals consumption plus investment (savings), studying on consumption rate and studying on savings rate (or optimal investment rate) are like the two sides of a coin. Most scholars choose to carry out the research from the perspective of the influencing factors of China's high savings rate, so there is much relevant literature. Here we merely look into the literature that directly studies the factors affecting consumption rate. Wu (2017)[8] builds a theoretical model that integrates the "driving force" and the "propelling force" of consumption demand, and further analyses the impact of label income share, relative total factor productivity, household consumption price index, urbanization rate, Gini coefficient, interest rate of household savings deposit and financing constraints on household consumption. According to the study result, Gini coefficient, interest rate of household savings deposit and financing constraints have a negative impact while the other factors have a positive impact on household consumption. Yi and Yang (2015)[9] discuss the factors affecting household consumption rate based on international panel data, taking 17 variables into the econometric model including GDP per capita, economic structure, extent of opening-up, cultural factors, urbanization rate and social security expenditure. They find that household consumption rates of the countries across the globe are greatly influenced by cultural factors, growth rate of GDP per capita, inflation rate, government consumption rate, economic structure and social security expenditure. Zhou (2016)[10] builds a VAR model to analyse the impact of population, land, natural resources, capital, system and innovation on China's household consumption rate. The result indicates that elderly dependency ratio, income gap between urban and rural residents and turnover tax revenue hold back the increase of the household consumption rate. The increase of netizen numbers helps raise the household consumption rate. Cai and Yuan (2009)[11] point out that the level of export orientation, economic development stage, economic system, income level of residents, urbanization and other factors affect the consumption rate of a country. Specifically speaking, as the GDP per capita rises, the consumption rate goes down before it climbs and then becomes stable. It has a negative correlation with the level of export orientation.

Additionally, the improvement in urbanization raises the consumption rate. Li and He (2010)[12] carry out a grey relational analysis of the factors affecting the final consumption rate, concluding that gap between the rich and the poor has the biggest impact on the final consumption rate, followed by industrial structure. Comparatively, capital formation rate has the least impact. Moreover, the influence of industrial structure is increasingly greater. Han (2015)[13] believes that China's household consumption rate is mainly affected by factors including consumption habits, level of regional economic development, government's fiscal expenditure on people's livelihood, level of urbanization, urban-rural income gap, price level and population structure. Xu (2015)[14] builds a VAR model to analyse the impact of the factors including willingness to consume (propensity to consume), income distribution, price index and marketization index on the consumption rate. The average propensity to consume has a bigger influence on the consumption rate than the impact of Gini coefficient, price index and level of marketization.

In section 2.3, to provide some suggestions for the policies propelling consumption, we investigate every influencing factor of final consumption rate and carry out an empirical analysis to answer the questions including which factors mainly contribute to the decrease of China's final consumption rate since 2000, and which factors help slow down the decrease.

2.3.2 Factors Affecting Final Consumption Rate

It is generally believed that final consumption rate is affected by many factors, such as GDP per capita, label income share, income gap, economic transition, level of economic openness, population structure and cultural factors.

Economic development stage (GDP per capita). According to the study carried out by Chenery and Syrquin (1975)[15], how the consumption rate evolves with development processes can be illustrated by a U-shaped curve. As the GDP per capita increases, the consumption rate goes down before rising. Gong (2012)[16] further makes an empirical analysis based on the statistics of Organization for Economic Cooperation and Development (OECD) countries during 1950–2004, illustrating the

U-shaped evolution path of the consumption rate as a Kuznets curve of consumption (how the proportion of consumption in the GDP varies with the GDP per capita) (see Figure 2-8). Converting the GDP per capita into constant price in 2000, Figure 2-9 shows a scatter plot and fitting curve which indicates the evolution path of China's consumption rate fits in with the U-shaped curve developed by Chenery and Gong. Furthermore, it is straightforward to calculate the inflection point of the curve: When the GDP per capita touched 21,000 yuan, the consumption rate is 49 percent, reaching its lowest point. In China's economic reality, the consumption rate in around 2010 reached the inflection point of the Kuznets curve of consumption.

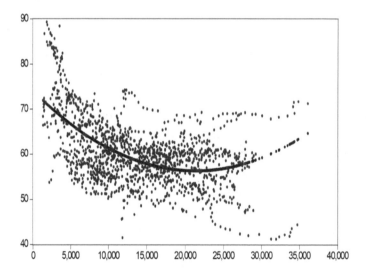

Figure 2-8 Kuznets Curve of Consumption
Note: Figure 2-8 is quoted from Gong, Yang (2013) and Gong (2012).

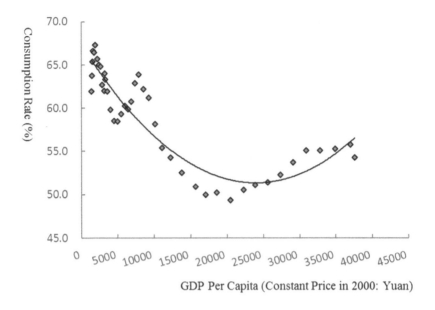

Figure 2-9 Evolution Path of China's Consumption Rate with the GDP Per Capita

Labour income share. Among the few studies on the relationship between labour income share and consumption rate, most of them are empirical. Liu and Shen (2017)[17] discuss the mechanism of how labour income share affects consumption rate. Their study shows that the variation of labour income share has an impact on consuming capacity (scale of consumption) by changing the proportion of every sector in the primary distribution of national income, and it also influences the consumption demand (GDP) by affecting the social propensity to consume. If labour income share shows a positive impact on the scale of household consumption and has little influence on the GDP, it must present a positive impact on household consumption rate. In addition, according to the empirical research based on China's statistics, the rise of labour income share is the main reason for the rebound of China's consumption rate in recent years, but the influence of labour income share on the consumption rate is caused by the negative impact of labour income share on the GDP. Zou and Yu (2011)[18] analyse the relationship between labour income share and China's household consumption from another perspective. They point out the impact of labour income share includes direct and indirect effects resulting from the influence of the changing labour income share on income gap. Gao (2014)[19] carries out an empirical study based on the inter-provincial panel data and finds out that every 1 percentage-point increase of labour income share will result in a 0.2658 percentage-point rise of household consumption rate. Liu and Li (2010)[20] believe that the fall of labour income share leads to the continuous decrease in China's consumption rate.

Income gap. The marginal propensity to consume is much greater of the poor than that of the rich, and the widening income gap between them explains why the increase of the final consumption is lower than that of the GDP. These factors finally cause the fall of the final consumption rate (Zhu et al.[21], 2002; Yang, Zhu[22], 2007). Chen (2012)[23] illustrates the mechanism of the impact of widening income gap on consumption rate through building a life cycle model. Moreover, he makes an empirical analysis based on inter-provincial panel data, concluding that every unit of increase in urban-rural income gap leads to a 6.5 percentage-point decrease in the household consumption rate. Such widening income gap results in a 3.42 percentage-point fall of the household consumption rate during 2000–2008, responsible for 30.8 percent of the decrease of the household consumption rate over this period. Therefore, income gap is a major reason for the variation of final consumption rate. In the follow-up empirical analysis, the income gap is reflected by urban-rural income ratio (annual disposable income per capita of urban residents/ annual net income per capita of rural resident).

Level of economic openness. Since the reform and opening-up, China's level of opening-up has been improving year by year, judging by the fact that China's degree of dependence on foreign trade which is an indicator of openness level has achieved 70 percent. According to the theory of comparative advantage, developing countries promote the development of their labour-intensive industries, which further brings an increase in labour income share and consumption rate. Thus level of economic openness is expected to be positively correlated with consumption rate.

Population structure. In the relevant literature, the study on the impact of population structure on consumption rate usually uses the two indicators: the child dependency ratio and the elderly dependency ratio (Wang, Huang, 2015[24]; Li, Qiu, 2012[25]). Liu Kaihao[26] and Liu Yulin

(2014)[27] build an overall consumption model based on expanded overlapping generation model to look into the influence of the changes in population structure on household consumption. Their study shows that the child dependency ratio obviously has a positive impact on China's household consumption rate, while the elderly dependency ratio has a greatly negative impact. In section 2.3, we also use the above two indicators to discuss the impact of population structure on consumption rate.

2.3.3 Empirical Analysis of the Factors Affecting Final Consumption Rate

2.3.3.1. Building of Model

Based on the analysis of the impact of the factors including economic development stage, labour income share, income gap, population structure and urbanization on the consumption rate, we here make a quantitative study to discuss the degree of impact by building a simple linear regression model. The model is as follows:

$$CR = \beta_0 + \beta_1 LNGDP + \beta_2 LNGDP \wedge 2 + \beta_3 LIR + \beta_4 CDR + \beta_5 EDR + \beta_6 IG + \beta_7 MY + \mu \quad (2\text{-}1)$$

In Formula 2-1, CR represents consumption rate; LNGDP represents the logarithm of the GDP per capita; LIR stands for labour income ratio; CDR stands for child dependency ratio; EDG means elderly dependency ratio; IG means income gap; and MY represents degree of dependence on foreign trade. To verify whether the evolution path of final consumption rate with the transition of economic development stages fits in with the Kuznets curve of consumption, we add the quadratic term of LNGDP to the model. All statistics come from the database of the National Bureau of Statistics and China's Statistics Yearbooks (see Table 2-4).

Table 2-4 Statistics of China's Consumption Rate and the Factors Affecting It during 1990–2016

Year	Final Consumption Rate	LIR	IG	MY	CDR	EDR	LNGDP (Constant Price in 2000)
1990	62.94	53.10	2.20	29.46	41.49	8.35	8.09
1991	61.54	51.80	2.40	32.84	41.79	9.03	8.17
1992	59.36	51.70	2.58	33.53	41.67	9.30	8.29
1993	57.93	48.40	2.80	31.60	40.70	9.22	8.41
1994	57.91	49.40	2.86	41.91	40.52	9.54	8.52
1995	58.82	49.90	2.71	38.31	39.58	9.23	8.61
1996	59.76	49.20	2.51	33.61	39.27	9.54	8.70
1997	59.37	50.10	2.47	33.83	38.46	9.69	8.78
1998	60.20	49.60	2.51	31.52	38.02	9.91	8.84
1999	62.34	49.70	2.65	33.01	37.52	10.20	8.91
2000	63.30	47.50	2.79	39.16	32.64	9.92	8.98
2001	61.61	46.60	2.90	38.05	31.96	10.09	9.05
2002	60.57	47.40	3.11	42.21	31.86	10.38	9.13
2003	57.49	46.10	3.23	51.29	31.39	10.65	9.22
2004	54.74	47.60	3.21	59.03	30.32	10.69	9.31
2005	53.62	47.10	3.22	62.42	28.14	10.67	9.42
2006	51.86	45.90	3.28	64.24	27.31	10.96	9.53
2007	50.14	44.80	3.33	61.77	26.78	11.10	9.66
2008	49.22	44.80	3.31	56.31	26.03	11.33	9.74
2009	49.37	45.60	3.33	43.16	25.30	11.60	9.83
2010	48.45	44.30	3.23	48.84	22.30	11.90	9.93
2011	49.59	43.60	3.13	48.31	22.10	12.25	10.01
2012	50.11	45.40	3.10	45.18	22.20	12.66	10.08
2013	50.31	48.20	3.03	43.37	22.20	13.08	10.15
2014	50.73	46.51	2.97	41.03	22.45	13.69	10.22
2015	51.82	47.89	2.95	35.63	22.63	14.33	10.28
2016	53.62	47.46	2.85	32.71	22.90	15.00	10.34

Note: After 2017, China's Statistical Yearbook will no longer publish the GDP of the income method, so the data will only be available in 2016.

2.3.3.2. Data Stationarity and Cointegration Test

Table 2-5 shows the result of an Augmented Dickey-Fuller test (ADF) for the data stationarity. Conducting an ADF test on the level value and the first-order difference of seven variables including CR, LIR, IG, MY,

CDR, EDR and LNGDP, we see that at the significance level of 1 percent, the level values of the seven variables are non-stationary. However, at the significance level of 5 percent, the first-order difference series of the seven variables are stationary. In other words, the seven variables series are integrated of order one.

Table 2-5 Result of Unit Root Test (ADF Test)

Variable	ADF	Critical Value at 1%	Critical Value at 5%	Critical Value at 10%	Condition (G,T,N)	Result
CR	-1.69908	-3.72407	-2.98623	-2.6326	(G,0,1)	Non-stationary
△CR	-2.11304	-2.66072	-1.95502	-1.60907	(0,0,1)	Stationary
LNGDP	1.139049	-2.66072	-1.95502	-1.60907	(0,0,1)	Non-stationary
△LNGDP	-4.2611	-4.37431	-3.6032	-3.23805	(G,T,1)	Stationary
LIR	-2.50153	-3.71146	-2.98104	-2.62991	(G,0,0)	Non-stationary
△LIR	-5.99697	-3.72407	-2.98623	-2.6326	(G,0,1)	Stationary
CDR	-1.41319	-4.35607	-3.59503	-3.23346	(G,T,0)	Non-stationary
△CDR	-4.48752	-4.37431	-3.6032	-3.23805	(G,T,1)	Stationary
EDR	-0.60225	-2.67974	-1.95809	-1.60783	(G,0,5)	Non-stationary
△EDR	-2.75128	-2.66485	-1.95568	-1.60879	(0,0,1)	Stationary
MY	-0.65412	-4.35607	-3.59503	-3.23346	(G,T,0)	Non-stationary
△MY	-4.10942	-4.37431	-3.6032	-3.23805	(C,T,1)	Stationary
IG	-1.92227	-4.37431	-3.6032	-3.23805	(G,T,1)	Non-stationary
△IG	-2.36797	-2.66072	-1.95502	-1.60907	(0,0,1)	Stationary

Notes: C, T and N, respectively, represent "with constant term", "with time trend" and "with difference lag order". The Schwarz Information Criterion (SIC) is used in the selection of lag order.

Though non-stationary, the seven variables including CR, LIR, IG, MY, CDR, EDR and LNGDP are all integrated of order one and meet the premises of a cointegration test. The Johansen cointegration test is adopted here to verify whether there exists a long-term equilibrium relation among the variables. The test result (Table 2-6) indicates that at the significance level of 5 percent, there exists a cointegration relation among the seven variables.

Table 2-6 Result of Johansen Cointegration Test

Null Hypothesis	Characteristic Value	Trace Statistics	Critical Value at 5%	Probability	Maximum Characteristic Value	Critical Value at 5%	Value of P
None*	0.956684	240.5661	125.6154	0.0000	78.48084	46.23142	0.0000
At most 1*	0.869113	162.0852	95.75366	0.0000	50.83548	40.07757	0.0022
At most 2*	0.795753	111.2497	69.81889	0.0000	39.71068	33.87687	0.0090
At most 3*	0.770164	71.53906	47.85613	0.0001	36.75970	27.58434	0.0025
At most 4*	0.527329	34.77936	29.79707	0.0123	18.73389	21.13162	0.1048
At most 5*	0.405555	16.04547	15.49471	0.0413	13.00319	14.26460	0.0783
At most 6	0.114578	3.042278	3.841466	0.0811	3.042278	3.841466	0.0811

2.3.3.3. Empirical Analysis

Regressing the Equation 2-1 based on the statistics in Table 2-4, we obtain:

$$CR = -646.0270 - 177.2493 \times LNGDP + 11.1690 \times LNGDP \wedge 2 + 0.2920 \times LIR + 1.2438 \times CDR$$

$$(-10.87) \quad (-14.00) \quad\quad\quad (14.89) \quad\quad\quad\quad (2.94) \quad\quad (1.68)$$

$$-6.0492 \times EDR - 2.9920 \times IE - 0.2014 \times MY + \left[AR(1) = 0.3894, AR(2) = -0.5368 \right]$$

$$(-0.89) \quad\quad\quad (-1.98) \quad\quad (-5.32) \quad\quad\quad\quad (2.04) \quad\quad\quad\quad\quad (-3.53)$$

$$R^2 = 0.9832, \ D.W = 2.4353, \ F = 93.6347 \quad\quad\quad\quad (2\text{-}2)$$

Table 2-2 shows that the t-statistics of regression parameters of all the variables except CDR and EDR are higher than the critical value at the significance level of 5 percent. The goodness of fit after adjustment is higher than 0.9832 with the Durbin-Watson (DW) statistic of 2.4353, indicating that the model has no autocorrelation and is well set.

We can tell from Equation 2-2 that how China's final consumption rate varies with the GDP per capita fits in with the U-shaped Kuznets curve of consumption. In other words, as the GDP per capita grows, China's consumption rate decreases before going up. Labour income share has a positive impact on final consumption rate. For every 1 percentage-point increase in labour income share, the consumption rate rises by 0.2920 percentage points. Such a result is similar to the study finding of Gao (2014)[28], showing that labour income share is a major factor influencing final consumption rate. For every 1 unit expanded in the urban-rural income gap (when the income of urban resident is doubled relative to that of rural residents), the final consumption rate goes down by about 3 percentage points. The finding is consistent with China's actual situation over the recent years. Figure 2-4 indicates that the decrease in China's rural consumption rate over the recent years is the main reason for the fall of its final consumption rate; the final consumption rate is in negative correlation with the degree of dependence on foreign trade. For every 1 percentage-point rise of the degree of dependence on foreign trade, the final consumption rate falls by 0.20 percentage points. Therefore, the uncertainty of the economic opening-up has a negative impact on the consumption rate.[29] The impact of the child dependency ratio on the final consumption rate is positive while that of the elderly dependency ratio is negative. But since their t-statistics fail the test, both of them have little impact on the final consumption rate.

2.4 Summary

In this chapter, we roughly analyse the stylized facts of the variations of China's final consumption rate and economic growth stability based on statistics. We can arrive at the following conclusions:

First, judging from the international comparison, China's final consumption rate is lower than the world average level as well as the average level of the countries in the similar development stage.

Second, the decrease of China's final consumption rate mainly results from the fall of its household consumption rate. We investigate the impact of final consumption rate on economic growth and its steadiness in the follow-up analysis rather than discussing why China has such a low final consumption rate.

Third, from the perspectives of both demand and supply, it is an important fact that the steadiness of China's economic growth is progressively improving.

Fourth, the analysis of the factors affecting final consumption rate indicates that the evolution path of China's final consumption rate with the variation of the GDP per capita fits in with the U-shaped Kuznets curve of consumption. It means that as the GDP per capita grows, China's consumption rate decreases before rising. Labour income share and income gap are the major factors affecting final consumption rate.

Notes

1 Rostow W.W., *The Stages of Economic Growth: A Non-communist Manifesto*, trans. Editorial Office of *The Journal of International Relations* (The Commercial Press, 1962).
2 According to Rostow, the features of the six stages of development are as follows: (i) The traditional society dominated by agriculture has a low level of consumption; (ii) In the stage of the preconditions for take-off, the dominate industry is usually the primary industry or the labour-intensive manufacturing. For the purpose of capital accumulation which is necessary for development, there is less room for consumption, leading to a relatively low consumption rate; (iii) In the stage of the take-off, labour force shifts greatly from the primary industry to manufacturing, which results in an increase of foreign investment. Thus the investment rate further rises and the consumption rate remains relatively low; (iv) In the stage of the drive to maturity, the focus of investment shifts from labour-intensive industries to capital-intensive industries. As there is huge improvement in national welfare, transportation and communication facilities, the level of consumption is strengthened; (v) In the age of high mass-consumption, people spend more on leisure, education, national security and social security. Accordingly, the level of consumption is relatively steady with a stable consumption rate.
3 Chenery H. and Syrquin M. *Patterns of Development 1950–1970*, trans. Li Xinhua et al. (Economic Science Press, 1998).
4 Fu Lichun, "Study on China's Consumption Rate," Doctoral Thesis, Graduate School of Chinese Academy of Social Sciences, 2011.
5 The statistical calibre of WDI on consumption rate has changed after 2015, For example, households consumption expenditure (% of GDP) has replaced with households and NPISHs consumption expenditure (% of GDP).
6 BRICS countries are all middle-income countries.
7 It should be noted that the consumption's contribution to economy can be measured from the following two perspectives: first, its contribution to the GDP; second, its contribution to the economic growth. The former is usually measured by final consumption rate which is the proportion of final consumption in the GDP and reflects the contribution of total consumption to the GDP by expenditure

approach. The contribution of consumption increment to the GDP by expenditure approach can be measured by consumption's contribution rate. The corelationship between final consumption rate and final consumption's contribution rate is as follows: they have the same variation trend. Generally, when final consumption's contribution rate rises, final consumption rate also rises, and vice versa. Therefore, final consumption rate can indirectly present how consumption drives economic growth.

8　Wu Zhenqiu, "Expanding China's National Consumption: Theoretical Models and Empirical Research," *Study and Practice* 9 (2017).

9　Yi Xingjian and Yang Biyun, "An Empirical Test of the Determinants of the National Consumption Rate in Countries across the Globe," *The Journal of World Economy* 1 (2015).

10　Zhou Ling, "An Empirical Research on the Factors Affecting China's Household Consumption Rate under the Supply-side Structural Reform," *Commercial Times* 24 (2016).

11　Cai Yuezhou and Yuan Jing, "Factors Affecting Consumption Rate and Suggestions on Promoting Household Consumption," *China Economic & Trade Herald* 23 (2009).

12　Li Lihui and He Hui, "A Grey Relational Analysis of China's Final Consumption Rate and Its Influencing Factors," *Knowledge Economy* 5 (2010).

13　Han Jinrong, "An Empirical Analysis of the Change of the Consumption Rate in China and Its Influencing Factors-Based on Provincial Panel Data," Thesis for the Master Degree, Huazhong University of Science & Technology, 2015.

14　Xu Rujia, "A Research on the Influencing Factors of China's Consumption Rate in the Context of Middle-income Countries," Thesis for the Master Degree, Hunan Normal University, 2015.

15　Chenery H, and Syrquin M., *Patterns of Development1950–1970*, trans. Li Xinhua et al. (Economic Science Press, 1998).

16　Gong Gang, *Contemporary Chinese Economy* (Routledge Press, 2012).

17　Liu Donghuang and Shen Kunrong, "Labour Income Ratio and Household Consumption Rate: Mechanism and China's Experience," *Social Science Research* 1 (2017).

18　Zou Hong and Yu Kaizhi, "Labour Income Share, Urban-Rural Income Gap and Household Consumption in China," *Economic Theory and Economic Management* 3 (2011).

19　Gao Fan, "Share of labour Remuneration, Urban-rural Income Distribution and Chinese Household Consumption Rate-An Empirical Study Based on the Inter Provincial Panel Data,"*Academic Monthly* 11 (2014).

20　Liu Dujian and Li Zhenming, "Discussion of Purpose to Promote labour Share on Expanding Consumption Strategy," *Shanghai Economic Review* 2 (2010).

21　Zhu Guolin, Fan Jianyong, and Yan Yan, "On China's Consumption Sag and Income Distribution," *Economic Research Journal* 5 (2002).

22 Yang Rudai and Zhu Shie, "Can Equity and Efficiency Coexist: Study on the Marginal Propensity to Consume in China," *Economic Research Journal* 12 (2007).
23 Chen Binkai, "Income Inequality and Consumption Demand: Theory and Evidence from China," *Nankai Economic Studies* 1 (2012).
24 Wang Huan and Huang Jianyuan, "An Empirical Study on the Relationship between Population Age Structure and Household Consumption in Urban and Rural China," *Population & Economics* 2 (2015).
25 Li Chengzheng and Qiu Junjie, "Research on Demographic Structure and Household Consumption in Rural China," *Population & Economics* 1 (2012).
26 Liu Kaihao, "The Differential Effects of Demographic Changes on Urban and Rural Consumption Rates: Evidence from Chinese Provincial Panel Data," *Population Research* 2 (2016).
27 Liu Kaihao and Liu Yulin, "Theoretical Mechanism and Empirical Test on China's Household Consumption Growth: An Explanation from the Perspective of Population Structure Changes," *Studies in labour Economics* 2 (2014).
28 Gao Fan, "Share of labour Remuneration, Urban-rural Income Distribution and Chinese Household Consumption Rate-An Empirical Study Based on the Inter Provincial Panel Data," *Academic Monthly* 11 (2014).
29 Yi and Yang (2015) take net export ratio as a factor affecting household consumption rate. Their study based on international statistics shows that both the short-term and long-term effects of net export ratio on the household consumption rate are negative. Thus foreign demand has a great substitution effect on domestic demand.

Chapter 3

Economic Dynamic Efficiency and Optimal Consumption Rate

In Chapter 3, we define the optimal consumption rate from the perspective of economic dynamic efficiency as the consumption rate reached at the point where the economy achieves the golden-rule growth. We discuss the relationship between dynamic efficiency and optimal consumption rate: when the economy is dynamically inefficient, the actual consumption rate is lower than the optimal consumption rate; when the economy is dynamically efficient, the actual consumption rate is higher than the optimal consumption rate. With theoretical analysis, we carry out empirical research on optimal consumption rate and dynamic efficiency based on national and regional statistics.

3.1 Economic Dynamic Efficiency and Its Evaluation Method

3.1.1 Dynamic Efficiency and Golden-Rule Capital Stock

Dynamic efficiency of an economy concerns the optimal capital accumulation. Specifically speaking, it is related to judging whether the capital stock of an economy is consistent with the capital stock necessary for achieving the optimal growth[1]. Phelps (1961)[2] proposed the Golden Rule of capital accumulation[3] based on the Solow Model and is the first one to look into the dynamic efficiency of an economy. If the capital stock of an economy exceeds the Golden-Rule capital stock, then the economy is dynamically inefficient: capital over accumulation occurs. At this point, the current and future resource allocation fails to achieve Pareto optimality, leaving room for Pareto improvement. Adjustment can be made when the economy deviates from the path of optimal growth to make it converge towards the path. In fact, when the economy meets the condition that labourers consume with their earnings and capital owners invest with their earnings, the golden-rule of economic growth can be achieved. In other words, aggregate consumption equals labour income and aggregate investment equals capital gain[4].

3.1.2 Approach to Evaluate Dynamic Efficiency

Theoretically speaking, there are three approaches to evaluate the dynamic efficiency of an economy: (1) comparing the capital stock in actual economy with the golden-rule capital stock. If the former exceeds the latter, the economy is dynamically inefficient; (2) comparing the marginal productivity of capital or profit rate with the economic growth rate. If the former is lower than the latter, the economy is dynamically inefficient; (3) the AMSZ cash flow criterion: if the net capital gain is lower than 0, the economy is dynamically inefficient. When there is no uncertainty in the economy, the above three approaches are equivalent, but when there exists uncertainty, the AMSZ cash flow criterion is the best approach among them[5].

In China's economic transition, the fast accumulation of capital has been a major drive for the rapid economic growth. During 1978–2016, China's average capital formation rate was 39.6 percent, way higher than the world average level in the same period. With such fast capital accumulation over more than three decades, whether there has been overaccumulation in China's economy has been concerning domestic and foreign scholars. They evaluate the dynamic efficiency of China's economy with various approaches: most scholars evaluate based on the

AMSZ criterion. But due to the difference in the statistics they use, their results differ from each other. At the beginning most results showed dynamic inefficiency, but over recent years dynamic efficiency tends to be the result in more studies because of improvement in data collection (Shi & Du, 2001[6]; Shi & Qi, 2002[7]; Yuan & He, 2003[8]; Liu, 2004[9]; Xiang, 2008[10]; Huang, 2007[11]; Meng & Yan, 2008[12]; Pu & Wang, 2008[13]). Other scholars assess the dynamic efficiency through comparing the marginal productivity of capital or profit rate with the economic growth rate. Yuan and He (2003), and Wang Xiaofang and Wang Weihua (2007)[14] conclude that China's economy is dynamically inefficient, while Lv (2008)[15] concludes that the capital accumulation is dynamically efficient because the national marginal productivity rate of capital is much higher than the economic growth rate.

3.2 Optimal Consumption Rate and Dynamic Efficiency: Theoretical Framework

In empirical research, the AMSZ cash flow criterion is widely applied to evaluate the economic dynamic efficiency. Thus the same criterion and its extensions developed by Abel et al. (1989)[16] are applied in this chapter to analyse the relationship between dynamic efficiency and optimal consumption rate.

3.2.1 AMSZ Cash Flow Criterion and Its Extensions

To evaluate the dynamic efficiency of capital accumulation in China's economy, we apply the AMSZ cash flow criterion developed by Able et al. (1989). We assume each individual lives for two periods and maximizes a von Neumann–Morgenstern utility function:

$$MaxU = u(c_{1t}) + E_t v(c_{2t+1}) \quad (3\text{-}1)$$

c_{1t} is the consumption of individuals in the cohort born in period t; c_{2t+1} is the consumption in period $t+1$, and Et is the expectation conditional on information available at time t. There are N_t individuals in the cohort born at time t. The young supply their labour inelastically, gaining wage which is represented by w_t, and do not work in his old age. So N_t is also the labour supply in period t. An individual consumes some of the return of the first period and saves the rest for the consumption in retirement in the second period. He therefore faces the following budget constraint:

$$c_{1t} = w_t - V_t s_t \qquad (3\text{-}2)$$

$$c_{2t+1} = (D_{t+1} + V_{t+1}) s_t \qquad (3\text{-}3)$$

w_t is the wage, s_t is his share of the market portfolio, V_t is the total value of the market portfolio ex dividend, and D_t is the total dividend. Letting R_{t+1} denote the return on any asset between period t and period $t+1$, then the standard first-order condition for capital asset pricing is:

$$E_t \left[\frac{v'(c_{2t+1}) R_{t+1}}{u'(c_{1t})} \right] = 1 \qquad (3\text{-}4)$$

Equation (3-4) also holds for the return on the market portfolio, for which $R_{t+1} = R^M_{t+1} = (D_{t+1} + V_{t+1}) / V_t$.

According to the above analysis, Aggregate consumption equals the consumption of the young and the old in the certain period: $C_t = N_t c_{1t} + N_{t-1} c_{2t}$, and $N_t s_t = 1$. Equations (3-2) and (3-3) therefore imply that consumption is labour income plus the dividend:

$$C_t = w_t N_t + D_t \qquad (3\text{-}5)$$

Let Y_t be gross output, $\pi_t = Y_t - w_t N_t$ be profit, and $I_t = Y_t - C_t$ be investment. Equation (3-5) implies:

$$D_t = \pi_t - I_t \qquad (3\text{-}6)$$

The dividend as we define it equals profit less investment. (Equivalently, the dividend equals consumption less labour income.) Note the difference between the dividend here and what it represents in the general sense. A repurchase of shares by firms is represented here as a dividend payment. Similarly, a new equity issue is a negative dividend. The dividend thus represents the net flow of goods from firms to households (except for labour income).

Firms produce output from capital and labour. We assume that the production technology is:

$$Y_t = F(I_{t-1}, I_{t-2}, \cdots, I_{t-n}; N_t, \theta_t) \tag{3-7}$$

I_t is the gross investment in period t, and θ_t, which includes the current and previous shocks, and is the state of nature in period t. Under the common assumption that capital fully depreciates each period, each period's investment equals next period's capital stock, so $Y_t = F(I_{t-1}, I_{t-2}, \cdots, I_{t-n}; N_t, \theta_t)$. A dependence of output on past investment, however, arises if there are costs of adjustment of capital. Note that the technology expressed in equation (3-7) is very general. It also arises if, as is plausible, capital does not fully depreciate each period and the type of capital built each period varies because of changes in the available technology. We assume that the technology has constant returns to scale. That is, F(.) is homogeneous of degree one in past investment and current labour supply. The competitive wage is therefore:

$$w_t = \partial F(I_{t-1}, I_{t-2}, \cdots, I_{t-n}; N_t, \theta_t) / \partial N_t \tag{3-8}$$

The total return to capital is:

$$\pi_t = \sum_{i=1}^{\infty} F_t^i I_{t-i} \tag{3-9}$$

F_t^i indicates the partial derivative of $\partial F(I_{t-1}, I_{t-2}, \cdots, I_{t-n}; N_t, \theta_t) / \partial I_{t-i}$ with respect to vintage t-i investment. We assume that $F_t^i \geq 0$, the specification in Equation (3-7) implies that $F_t^i = 0$ for $i > n$. Equation (3-9) says that profits are composed of return to capital of all vintages.

Let $\xi(\theta_t)$ be the ex-ante utility of generation t given that this generation is born in state of nature θ_t. That is: $\xi(\theta_t) = u[c_{1t}(\theta_t)] + E_t v[c_{2t+1}(\theta_{t+1}) | \theta_t]$

We call an initial equilibrium dynamically efficient if it is impossible to reallocate resources to increase $\xi(\theta_t)$ for some θ_s in $\{\theta_t\}$ without decreasing any other $\xi(\theta_t)$ for any other θ_s. Otherwise equilibrium is dynamically inefficient. Hence we obtain the AMSZ cash flow criterion.

AMSZ cash flow criterion: if $D_t/V_t \geq \varepsilon > 0$ in all periods and all states of nature, then the equilibrium is dynamically efficient, and if $D_t/V_t \leq -\varepsilon < 0$ in all periods and all states of nature, then the equilibrium is dynamically inefficient.

The criterion for dynamic efficiency depends on whether the cash flow goes into or comes out of an economy's production sector. If the amount of the cash flow going into the production sector is greater than that of the cash flow coming out, then the economy is dynamically inefficient.

Considering that much of the previous literature on dynamic efficiency expresses the relevant conditions accessing dynamic efficiency in terms of rate of return and growth rate, Abel et al. (1989) made some extensions based on the AMSZ cash flow criterion so as to ensure the comparability with the previous studies.

Recall the rate of return on the market portfolio: $R_{t+1}^M = (D_{t+1} + V_{t+1})/V_t$.

Defining $G_{t+1} = V_{t+1}/V_t$ as the growth rate of the value of the market portfolio, we obtain:

$$R_{t+1}^M / G_{t+1} = 1 + D_{t+1}/V_t \qquad (3\text{-}10)$$

Equation (3-10) immediately implies the following corollary.

Corollary 1: If $R_t^M / G_t \geq 1 + \varepsilon > 1$ in all periods and all states of nature, then the equilibrium is dynamically efficient. If $R_t^M / G_t \leq 1 - \varepsilon < 1$ in all periods and all states of nature, then the equilibrium is dynamically inefficient.

Corollary 1 states that the rate of return on capital can be used in assessing whether the economy is dynamically efficient because in a steady state the growth rate of the capital stock equals economic growth rate. In fact, a more general result is also available for assessing dynamic efficiency. The competitive rate of return on any other asset can also be potentially useful in determining whether the economy is dynamically efficient or inefficient. Let R_{t+i} be the competitive rate of return between period t and period t+i on an arbitrary asset, and we obtain Proposition 1:

Proposition 1: If there is some asset with rate of return R_t, such that $R_t/G_t \geq 1+\varepsilon > 0$ in all periods and all states of nature, then the equilibrium is dynamically efficient. If there is some asset with rate of return R, such that $R_t/G_t \leq 1-\varepsilon < 0$ in all periods and all states of nature, then the equilibrium is dynamically inefficient.

Due to the difficulty in collecting the statistics of China's return on assets necessary for evaluating the dynamic efficiency of rate of return and the difference between the accounting system in China and Western countries, we make some extensions on Proposition 1 proposed by Abel et al. Equation (3-5) implies: $D_t=C_t-w_tN_t=C_t-L_t$, and $L_t=w_tN_t$. Based on that, we obtain Proposition 2.

Proposition 2: If $C_t/L_t \geq 1+\varepsilon > 1$ 1in all periods and all states of nature, then the equilibrium is dynamically efficient. If $C_t/L_t \leq 1-\varepsilon < 1$ in all periods and all states of nature, then the equilibrium is dynamically inefficient.

Proposition 2 states that dynamic efficiency can be evaluated through the comparison between consumption and labour income: if consumption exceeds labour income, the exceeding part, defined as dividend (profit less investment) in the AMSZ cash flow criterion, must come from capital gains. If profit exceeds investment (the exceeding part is called net capital gain) and thus consumption is more than labour income, then the equilibrium is dynamically efficient. Since GDP by expenditure and income approaches are both applied in China's accounting system, Proposition 2 is more consistent with China's economic situation than the AMSZ cash flow criterion when we evaluate dynamic efficiency.

3.2.2 Relationship between Optimal Consumption Rate and Dynamic Efficiency

When the economy is at the critical point between dynamic efficiency and dynamic inefficiency, the optimal consumption rate can be achieved.

If the investment is increased which decreases consumption and thus brings about a lower consumption rate, then the economy is about to be dynamically inefficient; if the investment is reduced which increases consumption and thus raises the consumption rate, then the economy is about to be dynamically efficient. According to the AMSZ cash flow criterion and Proposition 2, if $D_t/V_t \geq \varepsilon > 0$ (or $C_t/L_t \geq 1+\varepsilon > 1$), the economy is dynamically efficient. At this point, the insufficient investment causes a gap between the capital stock and the golden-rule capital stock. The consumption rate exceeds the optimal consumption rate, and the difference between them is in positive correlation with ε; if $D_t/V_t \leq -\varepsilon < 0$ (or $C_t/L_t \leq 1-\varepsilon < 1$), the economy is dynamically inefficient. At this point, the over-investment results in the higher capital stock than the golden-rule capital stock. The consumption rate is lower than the optimal consumption rate, and the difference is in positive correlation with ε.

Assessing economic dynamic efficiency can indirectly show the relationship between consumption rate and optimal consumption rate in actual economy: when the economy is dynamically inefficient, the actual consumption rate is lower than the optimal consumption rate and the difference is positively correlated with ε; when the economy is dynamically efficient, the consumption rate in the actual economy is higher than the optimal consumption rate and the difference is also positively correlated with ε.

3.3 Optimal Consumption Rate and Dynamic Efficiency: Empirical Analysis[17]

3.3.1 Assessment of China's Economic Dynamic Efficiency

3.3.1.1. Source and Processing of the Statistics
As mentioned before, the AMSZ cash flow criterion is equivalent to Proposition 2. That is to say, the dynamic efficiency of an economy can be evaluated through comparing aggregate consumption and labour income: (i) If consumption exceeds labour income, the exceeding part, defined as dividend (profit less investment) in the AMSZ cash flow criterion, must come from capital gains. (ii) If profit exceeds investment (the exceeding part is called net capital gain) and thus consumption

is more than labour income, then the equilibrium is dynamically efficient.

The statistics of aggregate consumption come from the final consumption consisting of household consumption and government consumption in China's accounting by expenditure approach. Labour income is generally constituted by labourer wage and labour tax revenue[18]. But due to the difficulty in collecting the statistics of labour tax revenue, we process the relevant statistics as follows: According to the statistics in the study carried out by Huang (2010)[19], during 1985–2005, the labour tax revenue accounts for 5 percent on average in labour income with the standard deviation of 2.5 percent. Therefore, all of the labour tax revenue (national and provincial) mentioned in this book is calculated as 5 percent of labour income. The statistics of labourer wage come from the flows-of-funds table (physical transaction). Since China's statistics of labour income that is based on the flows-of-funds table (physical transaction) start from 1992, we select the statistics of final consumption rate and labourer income during 1992–2016 to assess the dynamic efficiency of China's economy (see Table 3-1).

Table 3-1 Dynamic Efficiency of China's Economy during 1992–2016
Unit: 100 million Yuan, %

Year	Aggregate Consumption	Labour Income	Difference between Aggregate Consumption and Labour Income	Ratio of the Difference in the GDP	Dynamic Efficiency
1992	16246.10	15431.54	814.56	2.99	Dynamically Efficient
1993	20826.90	19082.07	1744.83	4.88	Dynamically Efficient
1994	28305.90	26466.30	1839.60	3.78	Dynamically Efficient
1995	36225.70	33691.77	2533.93	4.13	Dynamically Efficient
1996	43117.60	38940.09	4177.51	5.81	Dynamically Efficient
1997	47556.70	43963.92	3592.78	4.51	Dynamically Efficient
1998	51509.80	46536.42	4973.38	5.84	Dynamically Efficient
1999	56681.90	49491.33	7190.57	7.95	Dynamically Efficient
2000	63729.20	52520.58	11208.62	11.20	Dynamically Efficient
2001	68617.20	57093.02	11524.19	10.41	Dynamically Efficient
2002	74171.70	63686.91	10484.79	8.62	Dynamically Efficient
2003	79641.50	70173.81	9467.69	6.89	Dynamically Efficient

(Continued)

Table 3-1 Continued

Year	Aggregate Consumption	Labour Income	Difference between Aggregate Consumption and Labour Income	Ratio of the Difference in the GDP	Dynamic Efficiency
2004	89224.80	84998.31	4226.49	2.62	Dynamically Efficient
2005	101604.20	97805.39	3798.81	2.02	Dynamically Efficient
2006	114894.90	111687.45	3207.45	1.46	Dynamically Efficient
2007	136438.70	134314.87	2123.83	0.79	Dynamically Efficient
2008	157746.30	158037.33	-291.03	-0.09	Dynamically Inefficient
2009	173093.00	175305.84	-2212.84	-0.64	Dynamically Inefficient
2010	199508.40	200412.94	-904.54	-0.22	Dynamically Inefficient
2011	241579.10	233545.03	8034.07	1.67	Dynamically Efficient
2012	271718.60	269392.13	2326.47	0.44	Dynamically Efficient
2013	301008.40	313914.40	-12906.00	-2.19	Dynamically Inefficient
2014	328312.61	334171.00	-5858.39	-0.91	Dynamically Inefficient
2015	362266.51	363467.43	-1200.92	-0.17	Dynamically Inefficient
2016	399910.10	388735.54	11174.56	1.50	Dynamically Efficient

Source: Wind-Economic Database. The aggregate consumption corresponds to the final consumption rate in the accounting by expenditure. Labour income equals labourer wage plus labour tax revenue. Specifically, the statistics of labour income come from the flows-of-funds table (physical transaction). The labour tax revenue is calculated as 5 percent of the labourer wage according to the study of Huang (2010). The GDP in the calculation of the ratio of the difference is measured by expenditure.

Note: After 2017, China's Statistical Yearbook will no longer publish the GDP of the income method, so the data will only be available in 2016.

Table 3-1 shows that there were six years where China's aggregate consumption was lower than its labour income during 1992–2016, indicating the dynamic inefficiency of the economy. Thus we can tell that China's economy fails to meet the sufficient condition to be dynamically efficient. The evolution of China's dynamic efficiency can be roughly divided into two stages: in the first stage (1992–2007), the economy was dynamically efficient. The aggregate consumption exceeded the labour income with a difference accounting for 5.2 percent in the GDP on average. The surplus of capital gain after depreciation and new investment was used for consumption. Accordingly the capital gain over this period was higher than the capital cost. In the second stage (2008–till now), there were three years (2011, 2012, 2016) where the economy was dynamically efficient. But compared with the last period, the dynamic efficiency was in a decreasing trend. During 2008–2010, 2013–2015, the economy was dynamically inefficient. In these six years, the aggregate consumption was lower than the labour income with a difference accounting for -0.61 percent in the GDP on average. The capital gains were not sufficient for depreciation and new investment, and thus labour income was used to make up for the insufficient part. As a result, the capital gain during this period was lower than the capital cost. The variation in China's investment efficiency since 1992 can illustrate the evolution of its dynamic efficiency. Such variation can be reflected by capital-output ratio (see Figure 3-1). From the 1970s to the 1980s, China's capital-output ratio was basically stable, fluctuating around 1.5. Since the 1990s, it started to rise slowly while the investment efficiency slowly went down. Since the global financial crisis in 2008, the capital-output ratio rapidly went up, leading to a decrease in the investment efficiency. Thus the capital gain was lower than the investment cost, and the economy began to be dynamically inefficient. According to the relevant economic theories, the fall of the capital investment efficiency raises the cost of future consumption in intertemporal consumption. At this point, the current consumption should be increased. However, China implemented investment-stimulating measures to ensure its economic growth, resulting in the dynamic inefficiency and over-investment.

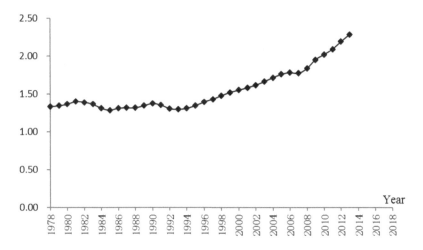

Figure 3-1 Trend in China's Capital-Output Ratio during 1978–2016
Note: The capital stock, whose statistics come from the study of Shan (2008) and are extended to 2016, and the actual GDP, whose statistics come from the National Bureau of Statistics of China, are both calculated with the constant price in 1978.

3.3.2 Relationship between Actual Consumption Rate and Optimal Consumption Rate from the Perspective of Economic Dynamic Efficiency

According to Proposition 2, dynamic efficiency can be assessed through comparing aggregate consumption with labour income. If these two variables are both divided by the GDP of the same year, the dynamic efficiency can also be evaluated by final consumption rate and labour income ratio[20]: specifically, if final consumption rate is greater than labour income ratio, then the economy is dynamically efficient. The gap between them results from the increase in consumption rate driven by capital gain. In other words, capital gain raises final consumption rate. At this point, the consumption rate in actual economy exceeds the optimal consumption rate and the difference between them is positively correlated with the difference between final consumption rate and labour income ratio. On the contrary, if final consumption rate is smaller than labour income ratio, then the economy is dynamically inefficient. The gap is caused by the increase in investment rate driven by labour income. In other words, labour income increases investment rate. At this point, the consumption rate in actual economy is lower than the optimal consumption rate and the difference is also positively correlated with the difference between final consumption rate and labour income ratio.

Table 3-2 shows the relationship between dynamic efficiency and consumption rate through the comparison between final consumption rate and labour income ratio.

Table 3-2 Relationship between Dynamic Efficiency and Consumption Rate
Unit: %

Year	Final Consumption Rate	Labour Income Ratio in GDP	Difference between the Proportion of Consumption Rate and Labour Income	Dynamic Efficiency	Increase in Consumption Rate Driven by Capital Gain	Comparison between the Actual Consumption Rate and the Optimal Consumption Rate
1992	59.7	56.7	2.99	Dynamically Efficient	2.99	The final consumption rate is higher than the optimal consumption rate.
1993	58.3	53.4	4.88	Dynamically Efficient	4.88	The final consumption rate is higher than the optimal consumption rate.
1994	58.2	54.4	3.78	Dynamically Efficient	3.78	The final consumption rate is higher than the optimal consumption rate.
1995	59.1	54.9	4.13	Dynamically Efficient	4.13	The final consumption rate is higher than the optimal consumption rate.
1996	60.0	54.2	5.81	Dynamically Efficient	5.81	The final consumption rate is higher than the optimal consumption rate.
1997	59.6	55.1	4.51	Dynamically Efficient	4.51	The final consumption rate is higher than the optimal consumption rate.
1998	60.5	54.6	5.84	Dynamically Efficient	5.84	The final consumption rate is higher than the optimal consumption rate.
1999	62.7	54.7	7.95	Dynamically Efficient	7.95	The final consumption rate is higher than the optimal consumption rate.
2000	63.7	52.5	11.20	Dynamically Efficient	11.20	The final consumption rate is higher than the optimal consumption rate.
2001	62.0	51.6	10.41	Dynamically Efficient	10.41	The final consumption rate is higher than the optimal consumption rate.

(*Continued*)

Table 3-2 Continued

Year	Final Consumption Rate	Labour Income Ratio in GDP	Difference between the Proportion of Consumption Rate and Labour Income	Dynamic Efficiency	Increase in Consumption Rate Driven by Capital Gain	Comparison between the Actual Consumption Rate and the Optimal Consumption Rate
2002	61.0	52.4	8.62	Dynamically Efficient	8.62	The final consumption rate is higher than the optimal consumption rate.
2003	57.9	51.1	6.89	Dynamically Efficient	6.89	The final consumption rate is higher than the optimal consumption rate.
2004	55.2	52.6	2.62	Dynamically Efficient	2.62	The final consumption rate is higher than the optimal consumption rate.
2005	54.1	52.1	2.02	Dynamically Efficient	2.02	The final consumption rate is higher than the optimal consumption rate.
2006	52.4	50.9	1.46	Dynamically Efficient	1.46	The final consumption rate is higher than the optimal consumption rate.
2007	50.6	49.8	0.79	Dynamically Inefficient	0.79	The final consumption rate is higher than the optimal consumption rate.
2008	49.7	49.8	-0.09	Dynamically Inefficient	-0.09	The final consumption rate is lower than the optimal consumption rate.
2009	50.0	50.6	-0.64	Dynamically Inefficient	-0.64	The final consumption rate is lower than the optimal consumption rate.
2010	49.1	49.3	-0.22	Dynamically Inefficient	-0.22	The final consumption rate is lower than the optimal consumption rate.
2011	50.2	48.6	1.67	Dynamically Efficient	1.67	The final consumption rate is higher than the optimal consumption rate.
2012	50.8	50.4	0.44	Dynamically Efficient	0.44	The final consumption rate is higher than the optimal consumption rate.

2013	51.0	53.2	-2.19	Dynamically Inefficient	-2.19	The final consumption rate is lower than the optimal consumption rate.
2014	50.7	51.6	-0.91	Dynamically Inefficient	-0.91	The final consumption rate is lower than the optimal consumption rate.
2015	51.8	52.0	-0.17	Dynamically Inefficient	-0.17	The final consumption rate is lower than the optimal consumption rate.
2016	53.6	52.1	1.50	Dynamically Efficient	1.50	The final consumption rate is higher than the optimal consumption rate.

Note: After 2017, China's Statistical Yearbook will no longer publish the GDP of the income method, so the data will only be available in 2016.

Table 3-2 tells us that in 1992–2007, 2011, 2012 and 2016, China's economy was dynamically efficient, indicating the aggregate consumption exceeded the labour income. In addition to make up for capital investment, capital gain was also used for consumption, and thus the final consumption rate was higher than labour income ratio. For instance, in 2003, capital gain raised the final consumption rate by 6.89 percentage points. In 2008–2010 and 2013–2015, China's economy was dynamically inefficient, indicating the aggregate consumption was lower than the labour income. Capital gain was insufficient to cover capital investment, and part of consumption went into the capital sector to be used for investment. As a result, the final consumption rate was lower than the labour income ratio. For instance, in 2013, capital gain lowered the final consumption rate by 2.19 percentage points.

In fact, dynamic efficiency reflects the relationship between actual economic efficiency and optimal consumption rate. During 1992–2007, the evolution of China's final consumption rate and the labour income ratio has gone through three stages: in the first stage (1992 to 2002), the final consumption rate fluctuated around 60 percent in a slightly increasing trend, while the labour income ratio in the same period fluctuated around 54 percent in a slightly decreasing trend. In the second stage (2003 to 2007), the final consumption rate fell from 57.9 percent in 2003 to 50.6 percent in 2007, while the labour income ratio decreased from 51.1 percent in 2003 to 49.8 percent in 2007. Overall China's final consumption rate exceeded the labour income ratio over this period. The economy was dynamically efficient with the actual final consumption rate higher than the optimal consumption rate. However, judging from the criterion of the golden-rule growth, there existed overconsumption to some extent. In the third stage (2008 till now), China's final consumption rate was basically stable around 50 percent while the labour income ratio declined a bit, fluctuating around 50 percent. Overall, over this period, China's final consumption rate was lower than the labour income ratio. The economy was dynamically inefficient with the actual final consumption rate lower than the optimal consumption rate. Judging from the criterion of the golden-rule growth, there existed under-consumption to some extent.

3.3.3. The Determination of China's Optimal Consumption Rate from the Perspective of Dynamic Efficiency

Table 3-2 shows that China's economy was dynamically efficient prior to 2008, indicating the final consumption rate was higher than the optimal consumption rate. During 2008–2016, China's economy was dynamically inefficient with the final consumption rate lower than the optimal consumption rate. Over this period, China's final consumption rate fluctuated within the range between 49.7 percent and 63.7 percent. China's economy evolved to be dynamically efficient. According to the variation law of the ratio of the difference between final consumption rate and the labour income ratio in the GDP, it can be roughly deduced that China's optimal consumption rate was about 55 percent during 1992–2016, respectively lower by 21.5 percentage points and 16 percentage points than the world average level (76.5 percent) and the level of middle-income countries (71.5 percent)[21]. Such situation can be explained from the following two aspects. On one hand, due to $CR = \frac{C}{GDP} = \frac{C}{Y} \times \frac{Y}{GDP}$, in which CR, C, Y and GDP, respectively, represent consumption rate, final consumption, disposable income and gross domestic product, $\frac{C}{Y}$ is the average propensity to consume and $\frac{Y}{GDP}$ is the proportion of disposable income[22]. That is to say, the final consumption rate equals the average propensity to consume times disposable income. According to the study carried out by Pan (2010)[23], China's average household consumption rate rose from 0.69 in 1992 to 0.75 in 2001 while the proportion of disposable income in the same period basically maintained around 65 percent (see Figure 3-2). Affected by both of them, the final consumption rate went up from 59.4 percent in 1992 to 61.6 percent in 2001. Since 2001, due to the increasing uncertainty faced by consumers, the average propensity to consume showed an obvious decreasing trend[24]. Meanwhile, the proportion of disposable income also presented a decreasing trend. As a result, China's final consumption rate fell by 8.4 percentage points from 62.0 percent in 2001 to 53.6 percent in 2016. On the other hand, China is the country most influenced by Confucianism in the world. Yi and Yang (2015)[25] find out that the final consumption rate of Confucian countries is lower by 5.5 percentage points than other countries. That may explain why China's consumption rate is lower than the world average level and the level of middle-income countries.

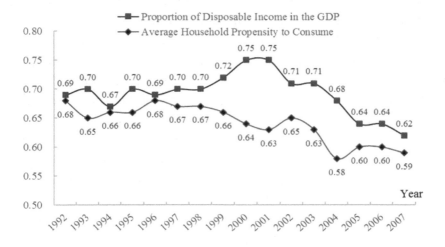

Figure 3-2 China's Average Household Propensity to Consume and Proportion of Disposable Income in the GDP
Source: PAN Chunyang, DU Li, CAI Jingzi, "Uncover the Mystery of Consumption Rate Declining in China: An Analysis of Funds Flow Account(1992~2007),"*Shanghai Economic Review*, 2010 (7).

Therefore, based on Proposition 2 and the principle that labourers consume with their earnings and capital owners invest with their earnings, we can say that labour income decides aggregate consumption and thus the evolution trend of labour income decides that of aggregate consumption (see Figure 3-3). Moreover, the evolution trend of labour income also decides that of final consumption rate. We will further discuss the relationship between final consumption rate and labour income ratio in the following part.

ECONOMIC DYNAMIC EFFICIENCY AND OPTIMAL CONSUMPTION RATE

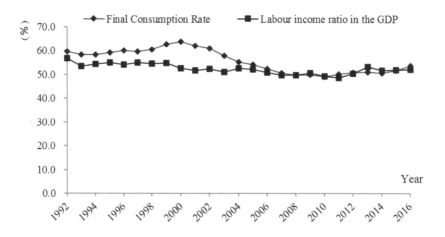

Figure 3-3 Trend of China's Final Consumption Rate and Labour Income Ratio since 1992

3.3.4 Test on the Relationship between Final Consumption Rate and Labour Income Ratio

3.3.4.1. Building of VAR Model

Conducting a unit root test with ADF on final consumption rate (CR) and labour income ratio (LIR), we have the result as Table 3-3 shows. Both CR and LIR are non-stationary variables while the first-order differences of them which are significant at the significance level of 5 percent are both stationary. Accordingly, CR and LIR are integrated of order one, meeting the premises of a cointegration test.

Table 3-3 Unit Root Test on CR and LIR

Variable	ADF	Critical Value at 10%	Critical Value at 5%	Critical Value at 1%	Condition (G,T,N)	Prob.	Result
CR	-1.009928	-2.650413	-3.020686	-3.808546	(G,0,1)	0.7289	Non-stationary
$\triangle CR$	-2.307855	-1.607456	-1.959071	-2.685718	(0,0,1)	0.0237	Stationary
LIR	-0.617855	-1.607830	-1.958088	-2.679735	(G,0,0)	0.4375	Non-stationary
$\triangle LIR$	-4.801417	-1.607456	-1.959071	-2.685718	(0,0,1)	0.0001	Stationary

Note: C, T and N, respectively, represent "with constant term", "with time trend" and "with difference lag order". The Schwarz Information Criterion (SIC) is used in the selection of lag order.

Since both CR and LIR are integrated of order one, we conduct a cointegration test with Engle-Granger (EG) two-step approach on CR and LIR. Taking CR as dependent variable and LIR as independent variable to perform an OLS regression, we obtain the following regression equation:

$$CR = 1.07277 LIR + \mu_t$$
$$(73.24) \qquad\qquad (3\text{-}11)$$
$$R^2 = 0.459744, \text{D.W} = 1.72$$

If CR is not cointegrated with LIR, then the calculation result should show stationarity and an ADF test is carried out on the residual series. It should be noted that the DF test or the ADF test here is performed on the residual series calculated based on cointegration regression rather than the actual model error μ_t. Since the Ordinary Least Squares (OLS) principle estimates that the sum of squared residuals is the minimum, the estimated coefficient of the model is underestimated, leading to a greater possibility of a Type I error. Thus the critical value of DF and ADF for stationarity test should be smaller than that of ordinary DF and ADF. Mackinnon (1991) obtained the critical value in the cointegration test through simulation. Table 3-4 shows the critical value at 1 percent, 5 percent and 10 percent. The residual series are significant at the significance level of 5 percent, indicating that the residual series are stationary and CR is cointegrated with LIR. The model of CR and LIR built in this chapter is efficient. Though the variation of LIR will cause CR to deviate from equilibrium in the short term, it will drive CR towards equilibrium in the long run which contributes to the stable economic growth.

Table 3-4 Test on the Stationarity of the Residuals with EG Two-Step Approach

ADF	Critical Value $\alpha=1\%$	Critical Value $\alpha=5\%$	Critical Value $\alpha=10\%$
-3.723857	-2.6819	-2.08682	-1.62422

ECONOMIC DYNAMIC EFFICIENCY AND OPTIMAL CONSUMPTION RATE

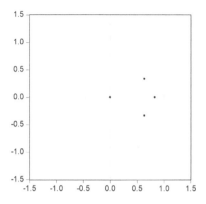

Figure 3-4 AR Root Graph Testing the Stationarity of the VAR Model

According to the above analysis, CR is cointegrated with LIR, which can be further illustrated with impulse response function. But the stationarity of the VAR model needs to be tested before analysing with impulse response function. Only when the reciprocals of the characteristic roots of the model lie inside the unit circle can the impulse response function analysis be carried out because the result indicates the VAR model is stationary. Figure 3-4 shows all of the reciprocals of the roots lie inside the unit circle, revealing a high goodness of fit. Therefore, we carry out the follow-up impulse response function analysis.

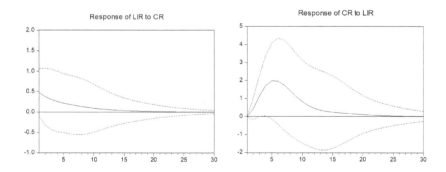

Figure 3-5 Impulse Response Curve of CR and LIR

3.3.4.2. Impulse Response Function Analysis

The impulse response function reflects the dynamic impact of random disturbances on the corresponding variables in the system in response to one standard deviation innovation shock. We use the impulse response function to analyse the response of CR and LIR to one standard deviation innovation shock and further reflect the process of their dynamic response. Based on the VAR model, we use orthogonal method and Cholesky decomposition technique to obtain the impulse response function of CR and LIR (see Figure 3-5). In Figure 3-5, the solid line in the middle illustrates the impulse response curve with the abscissa representing the lag period of shocks and the ordinate representing the positive-negative response of variables to an innovation shock.

Figure 3-5 demonstrates that when CR gives a positive shock to LIR, LIR experiences a positive fluctuation and reaches the peak of the fluctuation in the first period. In other words, in the early period, the rise of CR leads to the increase of LIR. That may be because under capital overaccumulation, the increase of consumption rate will cause the decrease of overall economic accumulation with an improvement in investment efficiency. In this way, the overall economic output climbs with less capital income and higher labour income ratio. Such effect weakens as time goes by and the impact of CR shock on LIR finally disappears in the eighteenth period.

When LIR gives a positive shock to CR, CR constantly experiences positive fluctuations with a rapid short-term growth and reaches the peak of the fluctuation in the fifth period. In other words, as LIR climbs in the early period, CR also goes up. That may be because the rise of LIR motivates labourers, thus speeding up the economic growth and bringing about higher income of consumers. As consumers are constrained by liquidity, consumption increases with a higher consumption rate. After the fifth period, the positive fluctuation progressively declines and the impact of LIR on CR eventually disappears in the twentieth period. Since then, both CR and LIR are in equilibrium.

3.3.4.3. Variance Decomposition Analysis

As the impulse response function cannot compare the extent of impact of various shocks on a specific variable, we use Cholesky technique to conduct a dynamic variance decomposition of *CR* and *LIR* so as to further discuss their interaction process. During the variation trend of *LIR* (see Table 3-5), the contribution rate reached 12 percent in the first period due to the variation caused by itself. The contribution rate of the variation of *LIR* to its variance gradually goes up to 13 percent in the eighteenth period with the self-contribution rate rising to 13 percent. During the process, the contribution rate of *CR* to *LIR* progressively falls, which indicates that the impact of *CR* on the variation of *LIR* becomes stable with the relationship between *CR* and *LIR* in equilibrium. In the variation process of *CR*, *LIR* greatly drives the variation of *CR* variance with the contribution rate falling from 100 percent in the first period to 37 percent in the seventeenth period. Since then, the extent of impact progressively declines, showing that the economic response to the rise of *LIR* becomes stable as time goes by and the relationship between *CR* and *LIR* tends to be in equilibrium. The self-contribution rate of *CR* rises from 0 in the first period to 63 percent in the seventeenth period, showing a slow-down trend of decreasing speed. According to the above analysis, during the early period after the shock, the contribution rate of *LIR* to *CR* variance is higher than that of *CR* itself to its variance. Moreover, as time goes by, such contribution converges towards 36 percent instead of 0, demonstrating that LIR has a lasting impact on *CR*. Such conclusion is basically consistent with the result of the impulse response function analysis.

Table 3-5 Variance Decomposition of CR and LIR

Period	Variance Decomposition of LIR			Variance Decomposition of CR		
	S.E.	LIR	CR	S.E.	LIR	CR
1	1.358584	12.04512	87.95488	1.058062	100	0
2	1.737774	12.0345	87.9655	1.921741	94.59606	5.403942
3	1.939854	12.1568	87.8432	2.786513	80.36946	19.63054
4	2.059437	12.33472	87.66528	3.605297	65.66314	34.33686
5	2.134902	12.51597	87.48403	4.297454	54.52548	45.47452
6	2.184878	12.67139	87.32861	4.817426	47.14213	52.85787
7	2.219118	12.78984	87.21016	5.168185	42.60634	57.39366
8	2.243041	12.87198	87.12802	5.383615	39.98762	60.01238
9	2.259868	12.92459	87.07541	5.506374	38.56139	61.43861
10	2.271674	12.95617	87.04383	5.573183	37.82208	62.17792
11	2.279891	12.97431	87.02569	5.609434	37.44969	62.55031
12	2.285553	12.98458	87.01542	5.630099	37.26130	62.73870
13	2.289419	12.99058	87.00942	5.642992	37.16121	62.83879
14	2.292042	12.99435	87.00565	5.651855	37.10235	62.89765
15	2.293818	12.99692	87.00308	5.658381	37.06260	62.93740
16	2.295020	12.99879	87.00121	5.663331	37.03235	62.96765
17	2.295837	13.00019	86.99981	5.667076	37.00804	62.99196
18	2.296395	13.00123	86.99877	5.669846	36.98862	63.01138
19	2.296777	13.00200	86.99800	5.671833	36.97371	63.02629
20	2.297040	13.00254	86.99746	5.673213	36.96282	63.03718
21	2.297221	13.00292	86.99708	5.674148	36.95522	63.04478
22	2.297346	13.00317	86.99683	5.674770	36.95011	63.04989
23	2.297432	13.00335	86.99665	5.675180	36.94675	63.05325
24	2.297491	13.00346	86.99654	5.675453	36.94457	63.05543
25	2.297532	13.00354	86.99646	5.675635	36.94314	63.05686
26	2.29756	13.00359	86.99641	5.675758	36.94219	63.05781
27	2.297579	13.00362	86.99638	5.675843	36.94155	63.05845
28	2.297592	13.00365	86.99635	5.675902	36.94112	63.05888
29	2.297601	13.00366	86.99634	5.675943	36.94081	63.05919
30	2.297607	13.00367				

3.3.4.4. Causality Test

The above analysis demonstrates that *CR* is clearly correlated with *LIR*. In this chapter, we statistically carry out the Granger causality test on the variables of *CR* and *LIR*. Table 3-6 shows the following result: at the significance level of 5 percent, the probability of making a type I error to reject the null hypothesis that *LIR* is not the Granger-cause for *CR* is 0.0387. Such a result indicates at least at the confidence level of 95 percent, we can say *LIR* is the Granger-cause for *CR*. In other words, the variation of *LIR* is the main reason behind the variation of *CR*. It can also be told from the OLS analysis mentioned above: as *LIR* changes by 1 percentage point, *CR* changes by 1.07 percentage points. The fact that *CR* is not the Granger-cause for *LIR* is relatively consistent with the economic reality that the change of income leads to the change of consumption and the change of *LIR* causes the change of *CR*.

Table 3-6 Granger Causality Test on *CR* and *LIR*

Null Hypothesis H_o	Sample Size	F-statistic	Probability	Result
LIR is not the Granger-cause for *CR*	24	10.8823	0.0040	Reject
CR is not the Granger-cause for *LIR*	24	0.34848	0.5623	Accept
LIR is not the Granger-cause for *CR*	23	3.72526	0.0387	Reject
CR is not the Granger-cause for *LIR*	23	0.00369	0.9963	Accept

3.3.5 Relationship between China's Final Consumption Rate and Economic Dynamic Efficiency

Theoretically speaking, capital overaccumulation will result in a decrease in investment efficiency, and dynamic efficiency will fall as final consumption rate goes down (see Figure 3-6). The fundamental logic behind this process is as follows: the increase of capital formation rate causes capital overaccumulation, which then leads to the fall of dynamic efficiency. On the contrary, capital overaccumulation brings about a decrease in consumption rate which further results in the fall of dynamic efficiency. In addition, dynamic efficiency that indirectly reflects whether consumption achieves its optimal level also has a relatively big impact on the variation of final consumption rate. Therefore, there may theoretically exist a close statistical relationship between final consumption rate and dynamic efficiency.[26]

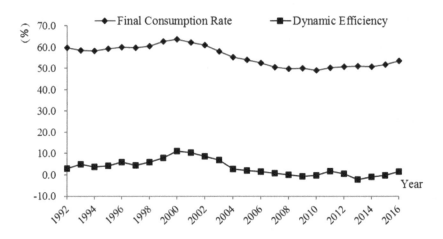

Figure 3-6 Relationship between Final Consumption Rate and Dynamic Efficiency
Note: Here we use the difference between CR and LIR as a quantitative measure of dynamic efficiency.

3.3.5.1. Positive CorRelationship between Final Consumption Rate and Economic Dynamic Efficiency

During 1992–2000, China's final consumption rate rose from 59.7 percent to 63.7 percent, while the dynamic efficiency went up from 2.99 percent to 11.2 percent; during 2001–2016, the final consumption rate fell from 62.0 percent to 53.6 percent while the dynamic efficiency decreased from 10.41 percent to 1.5 percent. According to the Pearson correlation test, during 1992–2016, China's final consumption rate was positively correlated with the dynamic efficiency, which can also be shown in Table 3-7: their correlation coefficient reaches 0.91 with the probability of 0.0000. That is to say, the significant level is above 1 percent.

Table 3-7 Correlation Test on China's Final Consumption Rate and the Dynamic Efficiency

Period	Degree of Freedom	Correlation Coefficient	T-statistic	Probability
1992~2016	25	0.908463	9.720353	0.0000

3.3.5.2. One-Way Causality between Final Consumption Rate and Dynamic Efficiency

Table 3-8 demonstrates the result of the Granger Causality Test on China's final consumption rate and dynamic efficiency at lag order of 1–3. We can tell that the hypothesis that CR is not the Granger-cause for DR is rejected by all in the test model,[27] while the hypothesis that DR is not the Granger-cause for CR is accepted by all. In other words, the change of CR is the Granger-cause for the change of DR, while the change of DR is not the Granger-cause for the change of CR. Accordingly, judging from the statistical result, the year-by-year decrease in China's final consumption rate causes the fall of China's dynamic efficiency. The fundamental logic behind it is that the fall of final consumption rate brings about the increase of investment rate, and the decrease of investment efficiency leads to the decline of economic dynamic efficiency.

Table 3-8 Granger Causality Test on China's Consumption Rate and Dynamic Efficiency

Null Hypothesis H_0	Sample Size	F-statistic	Probability	Result
CR is not the Granger-cause for DR	24	10.8823	0.0040	Reject
DR is not the Granger-cause for CR	24	2.88696	0.1065	Accept
CR is not the Granger-cause for DR	23	5.63815	0.0149	Reject
DR is not the Granger-cause for CR	23	3.02526	0.0787	Accept
CR is not the Granger-cause for DR	22	3.48387	0.0502	Reject
DR is not the Granger-cause for CR	22	2.65846	0.0957	Accept

3.3.5.3. Impulse Response Analysis of Final Consumption Rate and Dynamic Efficiency

Since 1992, China's final consumption rate is highly correlated with the dynamic efficiency. To look into the interaction between them, we carry out the following impulse response analysis.

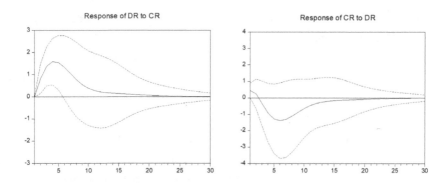

Figure 3-7 Impulse Response Curve of CR and DR

Figure 3-7 shows that when CR gives a positive shock to DR, DR experiences positive fluctuations and reaches the peak of the fluctuation in the fifth period. In other words, as CR rises in the early period, DR also increases. That is because as investment rate is constantly high and investment efficiency declines year by year, the rise of CR causes the decrease of overall economic accumulation, further leading to an increase of investment efficiency. As a result, the overall economic output goes up with an improvement in DR. But such effect gradually declines as time goes by and the impact of CR eventually disappears in the twentieth period.

When DR gives a positive shock to CR, CR experiences positive fluctuations in the first three periods, which means the rise of DR brings about the increase of capital investment efficiency. Thus the economic growth speeds up and the income of consumers is raised. As consumers are constrained by liquidity, consumption increases with a higher consumption rate. Since the third period, CR began to experience negative fluctuations and reaches the peak after the seventh period. The impact of DR on CR progressively disappears in the twentieth period. Since then, both DR and CR are in equilibrium.

3.4 Optimal Consumption Rate and Dynamic Efficiency: Analysis at the Provincial Level

In section 3.3, we discussed the relationship between optimal consumption rate and dynamic efficiency at the national level and further carry out the empirical research. In section 3.4, based on the statistics of 30 provinces (excluding Tibet) in China, we look into the relationship between optimal consumption rate and dynamic efficiency at the provincial level and compare the statistics of various regions so as to get a full understanding of this topic.

3.4.1 Source and Processing of the Statistics

As mentioned before, the AMSZ cash flow criterion is equivalent to Proposition 2, which indicates that the dynamic efficiency of an economy can be accessed from the comparison between aggregate consumption and labour income: if consumption exceeds labour income, the exceeding part, defined as dividend (profit less investment) in the AMSZ cash flow criterion, must come from capital gains. If profit exceeds investment (the exceeding part is called net capital gain) and thus consumption is more than labour income, then the equilibrium is dynamically efficient.

The provincial statistics of aggregate consumption come from the final consumption data in the provincial accounting by expenditure approach, including household consumption and government consumption. Generally speaking, labour income consists of labourer wage and labour tax revenue. To be consistent with the analysis at the national level, the provincial labour tax revenue mentioned in this book is calculated as 5 percent of labour income. The statistics of labour income come from the data in the provincial accounting by income approach. Since the statistics of labour income in most provincial accounting by income approach start from 1003, we select the statistics of final consumption and labour income during 1993–2016 to assess the dynamic efficiency of different provinces. In Figure 3-8, we analyse the relationship between dynamic efficiency and optimal consumption rate at the provincial level based on CR, LIR and the average of their difference ratio in the GDP during 1993–2016. See Addendum Table 1-30 for the relationship between dynamic efficiency and optimal consumption rate in specific years at the provincial level.

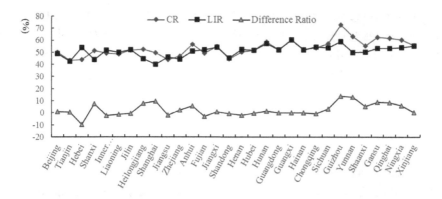

Figure 3-8 Average CR, LIR and Difference Ratio in 30 Provinces during 1993–2016
Note: Difference Ratio represents the ratio of the difference between CR and LIR in the GDP

3.4.2 Overall Assessment on the Provincial Dynamic Efficiency and Optimal Consumption Rate

Overall, during 1993–2016, in 13 provinces including Hebei, Liaoning, Jiangsu, Fujian, Shandong, Guangdong, Hainan, Jilin, Henan, Hubei, Guangxi, Inner Mongolia and Chongqing, final consumption expenditure was lower than labour income and the ratio of the difference between them in the GDP was below 0. Thus the capital gains were not sufficient for depreciation and new investment, and thus labour income was used to make up for the insufficient part. As a result, the capital gain during this period was lower than the capital cost. The economy at this point was dynamically inefficient. The final consumption rate in these provinces was lower than the labour income ratio, indicating that the economy was dynamically inefficient with the actual consumption rate lower than the optimal consumption rate. Judging from the criterion of the golden-rule growth, there existed under-consumption to some extent.

In 17 provinces including Beijing, Tianjin, Shanghai, Zhejiang, Shanxi, Heilongjiang, Anhui, Jiangxi, Hunan, Sichuan, Guizhou, Yunnan, Shaanxi, Gansu, Qinghai, Ningxia and Xinjiang, the final consumption expenditure exceeded the labour income and the ratio of the difference between them in the GDP was above 0. The surplus of capital gain after depreciation and new investment was used for consumption.

Therefore, over this period, the capital gain was higher than the capital cost. The economy at this point was dynamically efficient. The final consumption rate in these provinces was higher than the labour income ratio, showing that the economy was dynamically efficient with the actual consumption rate higher than the optimal consumption rate. Judging from the criterion of the golden-rule growth, there existed over-consumption to some extent.

Judging from the dynamic efficiency in China's eastern, central and western regions, the conclusion we make in this book is contrary to the relevant studies. We find out that in the eastern region, the economy is dynamically inefficient to a mild extent; in the central region, the economy is dynamically efficient; and in the western region, the dynamic efficiency is the highest. Judging from the relationship between the actual consumption rate and optimal consumption rate, in the central and western regions, the final consumption rate is higher than the optimal consumption rate which indicates over-consumption (insufficient accumulation) while in the eastern region, the final consumption rate is lower than the optimal consumption rate which shows overaccumulation (insufficient consumption). Such situation can be explained from the following two aspects: first, according to the variation of the regional final consumption rates, during 1993–2016, the average final consumption rates in the eastern, central and western regions were, respectively, 47.59 percent, 53.41 percent and 59.48 percent. Dynamic efficiency is mainly decided by final consumption rate. If the other conditions are the same, the western region has the highest dynamic efficiency, followed by the central region. The eastern region has the lowest. Moreover, according to the variation of the regional labour income ratios, during 1993–2016, the average labour income ratios in the eastern, central and western regions were, respectively, 47.99 percent, 50.88 percent and 54.29 percent. The ranking remains the same.

In conclusion, the final consumption rates of China's central and western regions with relatively lower economic development level are higher than that of the eastern region with higher economic development level. The consumption is relatively over-sufficient in the central and western regions and relatively insufficient in the eastern region. This may be a major reason for the fact that the economic development level of the eastern region is higher than that of the central and western regions. The eastern region has more capital accumulation which brings about more output. Though more output does not necessarily lead to a faster growth speed, it definitely results in a higher economic development level.

3.4.3 Relationship between Dynamic Efficiency and Optimal Consumption Rate at the Provincial Level in China's Eastern Region

Table 3-9 demonstrates the relationship between dynamic efficiency and optimal consumption rate at the provincial level in China's eastern region during 1993–2016. In terms of the overall situation in the eastern region, the average final consumption rate and labour income ratio were, respectively, 47.59 percent and 47.99 percent. That is to say, the final consumption rate was lower by 0.40 percent than the labour income ratio, indicating that the economy was dynamically inefficient to a mild extent with the actual final consumption rate lower than the optimal consumption rate. Judging from the criterion of the golden-rule growth, there existed under-consumption to some extent in the eastern region.

Table 3-9 Relationship between Dynamic Efficiency and Optimal Consumption Rate at the Provincial Level in China's Eastern Region during 1993–2016

Region	CR (%)	LIR (%)	Difference Ratio (%)	Dynamic Efficiency	Comparison between the Actual Consumption Rate and the Optimal Consumption Rate
Beijing	49.84 (10.48)	48.88 (5.32)	0.96 (7.98)	Dynamically Efficient	Higher
Tianjin	43.14 (4.23)	42.53 (6.53)	0.61 (5.46)	Dynamically Efficient	Higher
Hebei	43.97 (2.63)	53.72 (4.12)	-9.75 (4.69)	Dynamically Inefficient	Lower
Liaoning	48.41 (6.45)	49.79 (3.38)	-1.37 (7.83)	Dynamically Inefficient	Lower

Table 3-9 Continued

Region	Average & Standard Deviation during 1993–2016			Dynamic Efficiency	Comparison between the Actual Consumption Rate and the Optimal Consumption Rate
	CR (%)	LIR (%)	Difference Ratio (%)		
Shanghai	49.72 (5.73)	40.21 (3.07)	9.51 (3.42)	Dynamically Efficient	Higher
Jiangsu	43.81 (2.64)	45.92 (2.81)	-2.12 (2.92)	Dynamically Inefficient	Lower
Zhejiang	46.64 (2.58)	44.34 (2.72)	2.30 (3.56)	Dynamically Efficient	Higher
Fujian	49.13 (7.12)	52.23 (3.68)	-3.10 (7.90)	Dynamically Inefficient	Lower
Shandong	44.71 (4.28)	45.36 (3.85)	-0.64 (3.29)	Dynamically Inefficient	Higher
Guangdong	51.81 (3.23)	51.91 (3.86)	-0.10 (2.09)	Dynamically Inefficient	Higher
Hainan	52.34 (4.25)	52.04 (3.78)	-0.69 (5.22)	Dynamically Inefficient	Lower
Average	47.59 (3.31)	47.99 (4.59)	-0.4 (4.55)	Dynamically inefficient in seven provinces; Dynamically efficient in four provinces	Lower in seven provinces; Higher in four provinces

Note: Inside the brackets is the standard deviation of the corresponding variable. "Higher" means the consumption rate is higher than the optimal consumption rate and "Lower" represents the consumption rate is lower than the optimal consumption rate.

Comparing the average of the indicators of the 11 provinces in the eastern region during 1993–2016, we can see that in the seven provinces including Hebei, Liaoning, Jiangsu, Fujian, Shandong, Guangdong and Hainan, the final consumption expenditure was lower than the labour income and the ratio of the difference between them in the GDP was below 0. The capital gain was not sufficient for depreciation and new investment, and thus labour income was used to make up for the shortfall. As a result, capital gains during this period were lower than capital costs. The economy at this point was dynamically inefficient. The final consumption rate in these provinces was lower than the labour income ratio, indicating that the economy was dynamically inefficient with the actual consumption rate lower than the optimal consumption rate. Judging from the criterion of the golden-rule growth, there existed under-consumption to some extent.

In the four provinces including Beijing, Tianjin, Shanghai and Zhejiang, the final consumption expenditure was higher than the labour income and the ratio of the difference between them in the GDP was above 0. The surplus of capital gain after depreciation and new investment was used for consumption, indicating the economy at this point was dynamically efficient. The final consumption rate in these provinces was higher than the labour income ratio. Thus the economy was dynamically efficient with the actual consumption rate higher than the optimal consumption rate. Judging from the criterion of the golden-rule growth, there existed over-consumption to some extent.

3.4.4 Relationship between Dynamic Efficiency and Optimal Consumption Rate at the Provincial Level in China's Central Region

Table 3-10 shows the relationship between dynamic efficiency and optimal consumption rate at the provincial level in China's central region during 1993–2016. In terms of the overall situation in the central region, the average final consumption rate and labour income ratio were, respectively, 53.41 percent and 50.88 percent. That is to say, the final consumption rate was higher by 2.53 percent than the labour income ratio, indicating that the economy was dynamically efficient with the actual final consumption rate higher than the optimal consumption rate. Judging from the criterion of the golden-rule growth, there existed over-consumption to some extent in the central region.

Table 3-10 Relationship between Dynamic Efficiency and Optimal Consumption Rate at the Provincial Level in China's Central Region during 1993–2016

Region	CR (%)	LIR (%)	Difference Ratio (%)	Dynamic Efficiency	Comparison between the Actual Consumption Rate and the Optimal Consumption Rate
Shanxi	51.19 (5.26)	43.79 (3.85)	7.39 (5.31)	Dynamically Efficient	Higher
Jinlin	51.58 (10.78)	52.15 (12.79)	-0.57 (4.60)	Dynamically Inefficient	Lower
Heilongjiang	52.38 (3.72)	44.61 (4.87)	7.77 (5.03)	Dynamically Efficient	Higher
Anhui	56.52 (5.57)	50.84 (3.65)	5.68 (6.52)	Dynamically Efficient	Higher
Jiangxi	55.01 (6.97)	54.34 (9.24)	0.67 (3.44)	Dynamically Efficient	Higher
Henan	50.38 (4.18)	52.49 (5.49)	-2.11 (6.10)	Dynamically Inefficient	Lower
Hubei	51.56 (5.18)	51.60 (5.43)	-0.04 (5.95)	Dynamically Inefficient	Lower
Hunan	58.64 (8.66)	57.22 (4.97)	1.42 (5.85)	Dynamically Efficient	Higher
Average	53.41 (2.96)	50.88 (4.57)	2.53 (3.84)	Dynamically inefficient in three provinces; Dynamically efficient in five provinces	Lower in three provinces; Higher in five provinces

Note: Inside the brackets is the standard deviation of the corresponding variable. "Higher" means the consumption rate is higher than the optimal consumption rate, and "Lower" represents the consumption rate is lower than the optimal consumption rate.

Comparing the average of the indicators of the eight provinces in the central region during 1993–2016, we can tell that in the three provinces including Jilin, Henan and Hubei, the final consumption expenditure was lower than the labour income and the ratio of the difference between them in the GDP was below 0. The capital gain was not sufficient for depreciation and new investment, and thus labour income was used to make up for the insufficient part. The economy at this point was dynamically inefficient. The final consumption rate in these provinces was lower than the labour income ratio, indicating that the economy was dynamically inefficient with the actual consumption rate lower than the optimal consumption rate. Judging from the criterion of the golden-rule growth, there existed under-consumption to some extent.

In the five provinces including Shanxi, Heilongjiang, Anhui, Jiangxi and Hunan, the final consumption expenditure exceeded the labour income and the ratio of the difference between them in the GDP was above 0. The surplus of capital gain after depreciation and new investment was used for consumption, indicating the economy at this point was dynamically efficient. The final consumption rate in these provinces was higher than the labour income ratio. Thus the economy was dynamically efficient with the actual consumption rate higher than the optimal consumption rate. Judging from the criterion of the golden-rule growth, there existed over-consumption to some extent.

3.4.5 Relationship between Dynamic Efficiency and Optimal Consumption Rate at the Provincial Level in China's Western Region

Table 3-11 demonstrates the relationship between dynamic efficiency and optimal consumption rate at the provincial level in China's western region during 1993–2016. In terms of the overall situation in the western region, the average final consumption rate and labour income ratio were, respectively, 59.48 percent and 54.29 percent. That is to say, the final consumption rate was higher by 5.19 percent than the labour income ratio, indicating that the economy was dynamically efficient with the actual final consumption rate higher than the optimal consumption rate. Judging from the criterion of the golden-rule growth, there existed over-consumption to some extent in the western region.

Table 3-11 Relationship between Dynamic Efficiency and Optimal Consumption Rate at the Provincial Level in China's Western Region during 1993–2016

Region	CR (%)	LIR (%)	Difference Ratio (%)	Dynamic Efficiency	Comparison between the Actual Consumption Rate and the Optimal Consumption Rate
Guangxi	60.70 (7.50)	60.72 (4.66)	-0.02 (6.97)	Dynamically Inefficient	Lower
Inner Mongolia	49.14 (8.63)	51.58 (8.67)	-2.44 (5.88)	Dynamically Inefficient	Lower
Chongqin	53.84 (6.09)	54.48 (7.22)	-0.64 (5.68)	Dynamically Inefficient	Lower
Sichuan	57.49 (5.89)	54.00 (5.75)	3.49 (2.80)	Dynamically Efficient	Higher
Guizhou	72.95 (11.10)	59.14 (6.02)	13.81 (11.21)	Dynamically Efficient	Higher
Yunnan	63.39 (4.45)	50.05 (2.29)	13.34 (5.42)	Dynamically Efficient	Higher
Shaanxi	55.68 (9.67)	50.38 (8.74)	5.30 (4.95)	Dynamically Efficient	Higher
Gansu	62.61 (3.78)	53.62 (4.05)	9.00 (4.88)	Dynamically Efficient	Higher
Qinghai	61.93 (6.19)	53.45 (4.56)	8.48 (5.16)	Dynamically Efficient	Higher
Ningxia	60.57 (7.15)	54.34 (2.71)	6.23 (8.09)	Dynamically Efficient	Higher
Xinjiang	56.03 (4.95)	55.47 (3.95)	0.57 (3.14)	Dynamically Efficient	Higher
Average	59.48 (6.20)	54.29 (3.29)	5.19 (5.57)	Dynamically inefficient in three provinces; Dynamically efficient in eight provinces	Lower in three provinces; Higher in eight provinces

Note: Inside the brackets is the standard deviation of the corresponding variable. "Higher" means the consumption rate is higher than the optimal consumption rate, and "Lower" represents the consumption rate is lower than the optimal consumption rate.

Comparing the average of the indicators of the 11 provinces in the western region during 1993–2016, we can tell that in the three provinces including Guangxi, Inner Mongolia and Chongqing, the final consumption expenditure was lower than the labour income and the ratio of the difference between them in the GDP was below 0. The capital gain was not sufficient for depreciation and new investment, and thus labour income was used to make up for the insufficient part. The economy at this point was dynamically inefficient. The final consumption rate in these provinces was lower than the labour income ratio, indicating that the economy was dynamically inefficient with the actual consumption rate lower than the optimal consumption rate. Judging from the criterion of the golden-rule growth, there existed under-consumption to some extent.

In the eight provinces including Guizhou, Yunnan, Sichuan, Shaanxi, Gansu, Qinghai, Ningxia and Xinjiang, the final consumption expenditure exceeded the labour income and the ratio of the difference between them in the GDP was above 0. The surplus of capital gain after depreciation and new investment was used for consumption, indicating the economy at this point was dynamically efficient. The final consumption rate in these provinces was higher than the labour income ratio. Thus the economy was dynamically efficient with the actual consumption rate higher than the optimal consumption rate. Judging from the criterion of the golden-rule growth, there existed over-consumption to some extent.

3.5 Conclusion and Policy Suggestions

In this chapter, we define the optimal consumption from the perspective of economic dynamic efficiency as the consumption rate reached at the point where the economy achieves the golden-rule growth. Furthermore, we discuss the relationship between dynamic efficiency and optimal consumption rate: When the economy is dynamically inefficient, the actual consumption rate is lower than the optimal consumption rate; when the economy is dynamically efficient, the actual consumption rate is higher than the optimal consumption rate. Based on the statistics from 1992 to 2016, we investigate China's dynamic efficiency and further look into the issue around China's optimal consumption rate. Our conclusions are as follows:

(1) According to Proposition 2 derived from the expanded AMSZ cash flow criterion, the dynamic efficiency of an economy can be assessed from the comparison between aggregate consumption and labour income: if consumption exceeds labour income, the exceeding part, defined as dividend (profit less investment) in the AMSZ cash flow criterion, must come from capital gains. If profit exceeds investment (the exceeding part is called net capital gain) and thus consumption is more than labour income, then the equilibrium is dynamically efficient.

(2) Assessing China's dynamic efficiency based on Proposition 2, we can tell that in 1992–2007, 2011, 2012 and 2016, China's economy was dynamically efficient, indicating the aggregate consumption exceeded the labour income. In addition to make up for capital investment, capital gain is also used for consumption, and thus the final consumption rate was higher than labour income ratio. In 2008–2010, and 2013–2015, China's economy was dynamically inefficient, indicating the aggregate consumption was lower than the labour income. Capital gain was insufficient to cover capital investment, and part of consumption went into the capital sector to be used for investment. As a result, the final consumption rate was lower than labour income ratio.

(3) In 1992–2007, 2011, 2012 and 2016, China's economy was dynamically efficient with the final consumption rate higher than the optimal consumption rate. In 2008–2010, 2013–2015, China's economy was dynamically inefficient with the final consumption rate lower than the optimal consumption rate. Over this period, China's final consumption rate fluctuated within the range between 49.7 percent and 63.7 percent. Thus China's economy evolved to be dynamically efficient. According to the variation law of the ratio of the difference between final consumption rate and the labour income ratio in the GDP, it can be roughly deduced that China's optimal consumption rate was about 55 percent during 1992–2016.

(4) During 1992–2016, China's optimal consumption rate was around 55 percent. Though it was much lower than the world average level and the level of middle-income countries, we believe that it could be the optimal response of an economy under the economic conditions over this period. In that case, China's final consumption rate is just "relatively" low.

(5) The decomposition of final consumption rate indicates that final consumption rate depends on labour income ratio and average household propensity. How these two variables vary basically explains the evolution trend of China's final consumption rate during 1992–2016.

(6) Based on VAR model, we analyse the relationship between final consumption rate and labour income ratio. It turns out there exists a one-way causality between them. Labour income ratio is the Granger-cause for final consumption rate, while final consumption rate is not the Granger-cause for labour income ratio. The increase of labour income ratio greatly contributes to the rise of final consumption rate.

(7) Judging from the final consumption rate at the provincial level, we see that China's final consumption rate was negatively correlated with economic development level during 1993–2016. Among the three regions, the eastern region with the highest level of economic development has the lowest final consumption rate. The central region with the moderate level of economic development has the moderate final consumption rate. The western region with the lowest level of economic development has the highest final consumption rate; Judging from the dynamic efficiency at the provincial level, we obtain the contrary conclusion to the existing findings: Overall, the economy is dynamically inefficient in the eastern region, while it is dynamically efficient in the central and western regions. Judging from the relationship between final consumption rate and optimal consumption rate, the final consumption rate in the eastern region is overall lower than optimal consumption rate, reflecting the under-consumption in the region. The final consumption rate in the central and western regions is overall higher than the

optimal consumption rate, reflecting the over-consumption in the regions.

The above analysis shows that the increase of final consumption rate is critical to the long-term stability of economic growth, and the improvement in consumer welfare and final consumption rate depends on labour income ratio and average household propensity. Accordingly, we put forward the following suggestions for raising China's final consumption rate and the optimal consumption rate[28]: first, the income distribution system of China should be further reformed through raising the income share of labourers in primary distribution and redistribution, because the rise of income share will directly increase the final consumption rate at the macro level. Next, the household income should be raised in many ways, including helping the unemployed in urban and the rural-to-urban migrant workers find jobs and providing employment training for college students. According to the classic theory of consumption, consumption is a function of income. That is to say, an increase of income will lead to a rise of consumption, which further causes a rise of final consumption rate at the macro level. Finally, the social security system should be improved. Currently, the reform in all areas is increasingly deepened, which adds the uncertainty faced by residents. Though the household income goes up, the increased income is more used as precautionary saving instead of consumption spending to overcome the uncertainty. The establishment of the social security system that combines individual counts with social pooling should be speeded up to solve the problems for residents in housing, education, medical care, pension and unemployment relief. Thus the average household propensity can progressively goes up, eventually resulting in the rise of final consumption rate.

Addendum

To prove the theory that when labourers consume with their earnings and capital owners invest with their earnings, the economy converges to the balanced growth path and achieves the golden-rule growth, we assume that capital and labour gains from marginal product with all capital income saved for investment and all labour income used for consumption. Then we obtain:

$$\dot{K} = [\partial F(K, AL)/\partial K]K - \delta K$$

(1) Proving that the economy can converge to the balanced growth path

With k=K/AL, we differentiate both sides of the equation with respect to time, and obtain:

$$\dot{k} = \frac{\dot{K}(AL) - K[\dot{L}A + A\dot{L}]}{(AL)^2} = \frac{\dot{K}}{AL} - \frac{K}{AL}\left[\frac{\dot{L}A + A\dot{L}}{AL}\right] = \frac{\dot{K}}{AL} - k\left(\frac{\dot{L}}{L} + \frac{\dot{A}}{A}\right) \quad (3\text{-}12)$$

Substituting $\dot{K} = [\partial F(K, AL)/\partial K]K - \delta K, \frac{\dot{L}}{L} = n, \frac{\dot{A}}{A} = g$ into Equation(3-12), we obtain:

$$\dot{k} = \frac{[\partial F(K, AL)/\partial K]K - \delta K}{AL} - (n+g)k = \frac{\partial F(K, AL)}{\partial K}k - (n+g+\delta)k \quad (3\text{-}13)$$

Substituting $[\partial F(K, AL)/\partial K] = f'(k)$ into Equation (3-13), we obtain:

$$\dot{k} = [f'(k) - (n+g+\delta)]k \quad (3\text{-}14)$$

When $\dot{k} = 0$, the average capital stock per unit of effective labour (k) remains the same. With k=K/AL, since k remains unchanged when the economy reaches a steady state, capital stock (K) grows at the same rate of "n+g" as effective labour (AL) does. As the return to scale of production function remains the same, output (Y) in the balanced growth path also grows at the rate of "n+g". The above analysis indicates that all the variables grow at constant rates.

Now we analyse how the economy converges to the balanced growth path: when k=k* and $f'(k)-(n+g+\delta)=0$, the economy is on the balanced growth path. If k>k* and k*<0 because of f''(k)<0, then the economy deviates downwards from the balanced growth path. On the contrary, if k<k* and k*>0, then the economy deviates upwards from the balanced growth path. In conclusion, whether the initial value is higher or lower than k*, the economy will eventually converge to the balanced growth path.

(2) Proving that the economy achieves the golden-rule growth on the balanced growth path

The golden-rule level of the capital stock is the capital level that maximizes consumption per unit of effective labour. That is to say, $f'(k_{GR})=(n+g+\delta)$. At this point, the slope of production function equals that of break-even investment line and k reaches the exact level where the economy converges to the balanced growth path. All capital income is saved, while all labour income is used for consumption. In this model, the contribution of capital (marginal products of capital times the amount of capital) is saved. If the contribution of capital exceeds break-even investment, indicating $kf'(k)>(n+g+\delta)k$, then k rises. On the contrary, if $kf'(k)<(n+g+\delta)k$, then k decreases. Therefore, the economy converges to $k^*f'(k^*)=(n+g+\delta)k^*$, which means $f'(k^*)=(n+g+\delta)$. Then it can be deduced that k*=k_{GR}. In this way, we can say that the economy achieves the golden-rule growth on the balanced growth path.

In conclusion, when labourers consume with their earnings and capital owners invest with their earnings, the economy can achieve the golden-rule growth.

Notes

1 Yuan Zhigang and He Zhangyong, "Dynamic Inefficiency in China's Economy Since 1990s," *Economic Research Journal* 7 (2003).
2 Phelps E., "The Golden Rule of Accumulation: A Fable for Growthmen," *American Economic Review*, 51, no. 4 (1961): 638–643.

3 As Robert J. Barro and Xavier Sala-i-Martin noted in Economic Growth, the source of the golden rule of capital accumulation "is the biblical Golden Rule, which states, 'Do unto others as you would have others do unto you.' In economic terms, the golden-rule result can be interpreted as: If we provide the same amount of consumption to members of each current and future generation—that is, if we do not provide less to future generations than to ourselves."
4 See the Appendix of this chapter for the verification of this proposition.
5 Ta Xin and Zhao Xincheng, "Research Review on Economic Dynamic Efficiency," *Journal of Yunnan University of Finance and Economics* 4 (2011).
6 Shi Yongdong and Du Liangsheng, "The Impact of Asset Pricing Bubble on Economy," *Economic Research Journal* 10 (2001).
7 Shi Yongdong and Qi Yingfei, "Dynamic Efficiency of China's Economy," *The Journal of World Economy* 8 (2006).
8 Yuan Zhigang and He Zhangyong, "Dynamic Inefficiency in China's Economy since 1990s," *Economic Research Journal* 7 (2003).
9 Liu Xian, "Is There Capital Overaccumulation in China's Economy?" *Journal of Finance and Economics* 10 (2004).
10 Xiang Benwu, "Assessing Dynamic Efficiency in China's Economy: 1992–2003," *The Journal of Quantitative & Technical Economics* 2 (2008).
11 Hang Weili and Sui Guangjun, "The Dynamic Efficiency of China's Economy-A Study Based on Improved Golden Rule," *Journal of Shanxi University of Finance & Economics* 3 (2007).
12 Meng Xiangzhong, Yan Fashan, and Wang Xiao, "Empirical Research on the Dynamic Efficiency of Chinese Economic Growth," *World Economic Papers* 5 (2008).
13 Pu Yanping and Wang Weiqun, "Dynamic Efficiency and Regional Differences of China's Capital Investment: 1952–2006," *Inquiry into Economic Issues*, 4 (2009).
14 Wang Xiaofang and Wang Weihua, "The Dynamic Efficiency of China's Economy-An Empirical Assessment Based on Household Saving-Consumption Mechanism," *Journal of Shanxi University of Finance & Economics* 8 (2007).
15 Lv Bingyang,"The Dynamic Efficiency of China's Capital Accumulation:1978—2005," *China Economic Quarterly* 1 (2008).
16 Abela., Mankiw N.G., Summers L.H., and Zeckhauser R.J., "Assessing Dynamic Efficiency: Theory and Evidence," *Review of Economic Studies*, 56 no. 1 (1989): 1–20.
17 To avoid confusion, a few concepts need to be clarified: in the analysis of optimal consumption rate in terms of dynamic efficiency, the aggregate consumption in the model corresponds to China's consumption rate. That is to say, the aggregate consumption mentioned in this chapter is equivalent to the final consumption, and the final consumption rate is equivalent to the consumption rate in the actual economy. In the model analysis, the terms of aggregate consumption and consumption rate in the actual economy are used while the terms of final consumption and final consumption rate are used in the empirical analysis. To be consistent

with the previous part, the terms of aggregate consumption and consumption rate in the actual economy are still used in the headers of Table 3-1 and Table 3-2.
18 Liu Rongcang and Ma Shuanyou, "On Taxation and Economic Growth --The Effects of Taxation Imposed on labour, Capital and Consumption," *Social Sciences in China* 1 (2002).
19 Huang Feiming, "Assessing Chinese Economy's Dynamic Efficiency Based on the Perspective of Consumption-Income," *The Journal of Quantitative & Technical Economics* 4 (2010).
20 "The labour income ratio in the GDP" is abbreviated to "the labour income ratio".
21 The statistics come from the World Development Indicators (WDI) database of World Bank.
22 As the property income of residents in China is relatively low, we regard the proportion of disposable income as the equivalent of the labour income ratio.
23 Pan Chunyang, Du Li, and Cai Jingzi, "Uncover the Mystery of Consumption Rate Declining in China: An Analysis of Funds Flow Account(1992~2007)," *Shanghai Economic Review* 7 (2010).
24 Since 2001, factors including the industrialization of higher education, reform of medical system and commercial housing system have caused the increase in uncertain spending of consumers, and thus consumers add their precautionary savings with decreasing propensity to consume.
25 Yi Xingjian and Yang Biyun, "An Empirical Test on the Deciding Factors of Household Consumption Rate in Countries (Regions) All over the World," *The Journal of World Economy* 1 (2015): 3–24.
26 Here we use the difference between CR and LIR as a quantitative measure of dynamic efficiency.
27 Here CR represents final consumption, and DR stands for dynamic efficiency.
28 The suggestions here are based on Proposition 2 that demonstrates dynamic efficiency is decided by aggregate consumption rate and labour income ratio. Moreover, the model indicates that the optimal consumption rate is equivalent to labour income ratio. Thus an increase of labour income ratio is indeed an increase of the optimal consumption rate.

Chapter 4

Optimal Consumption Rate in the Solow–Swan Model

In Chapter 4, we carry out empirical analysis of how consumption rate affects the economic growth and the requirements an economy needs to meet for achieving optimal consumption rate through analysing the theoretical Solow–Swan model, and make positive analysis based on China's statistics from 1978. The outline of this chapter is as follows: in section 4.1, we discuss the relationship between optimal consumption rate and traditional golden-rule capital stock along with theoretical analysis based on the Solow model; in section 4.2, we build an econometric model to investigate China's optimal consumption rate based on its economic statistics; in section 4.3, we define optimal consumption rate from the perspective of capital-output ratio and further conduct quantitative analysis; and in section 4.4, we put forward the suggestions on the policies regarding optimal consumption rate based on relevant theories and empirical conclusions.

4.1 Theoretical Framework of Optimal Consumption Rate

In fact, the Solow model divides output into consumption and investment. Meanwhile, it analyses the issue around optimal investment, which concludes that the investment achieved at the point where the economy has the golden-rule capital stock is optimal. Such conclusion could be enlightenment on the study on optimal consumption rate. In the framework of Solow model, we define optimal consumption rate as the consumption rate corresponding to the golden-rule capital stock. When optimal consumption rate is achieved, the economic growth reaches its optimal level, which means the economy grows at the highest and the most sustainable rate and the level of resident (household) welfare is maximized.

4.1.1 Solow Model

Supposing the production function is presented as follows:

$$Y_t = F(K(t), A(t)L(t)) \tag{4-1}$$

Here Y (t), K(t), A(t) and L(t), respectively, represent output, capital stock, technology progress and labour. The production function satisfies the following conditions: (1) Decreasing marginal output: $\partial F/\partial K > 0$, $\partial^2 F/\partial K^2 < 0$; $\partial F/\partial AL > 0$, $\partial^2 F/\partial (AL)^2 < 0$; (2) Constant returns to scale: $F(\lambda K(t), \lambda A(t) L(t)) = \lambda F(K(t), A(t) L(t))$; (3) Inada Conditions: $\lim_{K \to 0} F_K = \lim_{AL \to 0} F_{AL} = \infty$, $\lim_{K \to \infty} F_K = \lim_{AL \to \infty} F_{AL} = \infty$.

In addition, the dynamic path of Y (t), K(t), A(t) and L(t) is assumed as follows: the equation of motion of K(t) is: $\dot{K}(t) = (1 - CR)Y(t) - \delta K(t)$. Here CR represents consumption rate[1]; technology progress and labour, respectively, grow at the rate of g and n: $\dot{A}(t) = gA(t), \dot{L}(t) = nL(t)$

Because the return to scale of the production function is assumed to be constant, it can be converted to a dense form:

OPTIMAL CONSUMPTION RATE IN THE SOLOW-SWAN MODEL 111

$$y(t) = f(k) \quad (4\text{-}2)$$

Here the output per unit of effective labour is as follows: y (t) = Y (t) / A(t) L(t). The capital stock per unit of effective labour is as follows: k (t) = K (t) / A(t) L(t). Accordingly the equation of motion of the capital stock per unit of effective labour is as follows:

$$\dot{k}(t) = (1 - CR) f(k) - (n + g + \delta) k(t) \quad (4\text{-}3)$$

The average capital stock per unit of effective labour equals the difference between the average actual investment per unit of effective labour (1-CR) f (k) and the break-even investment per unit of effective labour (n+g+δ) k (t). If the average actual investment per unit of effective labour is lower than the necessary break-even investment, then k(t) decreases. If the former is higher than the latter, then k(t) increases; if the former equals the latter, then k(t) remains unchanged. According to what a steady-state economic growth suggests (see Figure 4-1), no matter how the economy was going, it will eventually converge to the steady state in the model. When the variables in the model are at the steady state, they all grow at constant rates.

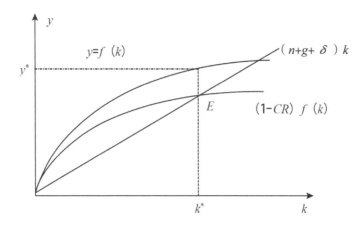

Figure 4-1 Steady State of the Solow Model

4.1.2 Mechanism of the Impact of Consumption Rate on Economic Growth

4.1.2.1. Analysis of the Effect of Variations in Consumption Rate on Economic Growth

Government can affect household consumption with fiscal policies and further change the consumption rate of the overall economy. Supposing CR experiences a permanent decrease, the impact of such variation on economic growth and steady state of the model is shown in Figure 4-2:

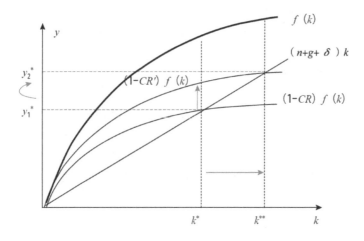

Figure 4-2 Impact of the Variation of CR on Steady State

The fall of consumption rate from CR to CR' leads to the rise of actual investment line, which further makes the steady-state value of the capital stock per unit of effective labour rise from k* to k**. Specifically speaking, at the beginning of the fall of CR, k equals k*. At this level, the actual investment exceeds the break-even investment and thus $\dot{K}$ is positive. When k starts to rise to the new steady-state value k**, k remains unchanged. In terms of the average yield of labour (Y/L), Y/L = Af (k). That is to say, Y/L increases as A and K rise. During the decreasing of CR, since $\dot{k} > 0$, the growth rate of Y/L exceeds g. When k rises to k**, the growth rate of Y/L goes back to g.

Therefore, the fall of CR results in the rise of Y/L with the same growth rate when the economy enters its new path of steady-state growth. In other words, the variation of CR has a level effect rather than a growth effect on Y/L, which means when CR varies, it only changes the level of Y/L without affecting the growth rate of Y/L at the steady-state.

4.1.2.2. The Impact of Variations in Consumption Rate on the Level of Consumption

In the Solow model, the average consumption level per unit of effective labour represents the household welfare level, equalling the output per unit of effective labour f (k) times CR which is the proportion used for consumption in the output. Accordingly, the discontinuous changes of CR at the beginning lead to a sharp decrease in the average consumption level per unit of effective labour. Then as k rises, consumption will progressively climb. But whether the consumption level at the new steady-state k** will exceed the original level remains uncertain. Letting c* represent the average consumption level per unit of effective labour, we obtain c*=f (k*) - (1-CR) f (k*). Additionally, we have (1-CR) f (k*) = (n+g+δ) k*. Thus c*= f (k*) - (n+g+δ) k*. Since k* depends on the parameters of the model including CR, n, g and δ, it can be deduced that

$$\frac{\partial c^*}{\partial CR} = \left[f'(k^*(CR,n,g,\delta)) - (n+g+\delta) \right] \frac{\partial k^*(CR,n,g,\delta)}{\partial CR}$$

According to the above analysis, the decrease in CR will raise the average capital per unit of effective labour (k*). As a result, the question whether the decrease in CR will improve the consumption level in the long run depends on if the marginal product of capital f' (k*) is higher or lower than n+g+δ (see Figure 4-3). The fall of CR will increase the capital stock (k) and in order to maintain such increasing trend, the f' (k*) which is gained from the additional investment has to offset n+g+δ which stands for the consumption of capital stock. If f' (k*) < n+g+δ, it implies the gain from the additional capital is insufficient to offset the consumption of capital. To maintain the capital stock at a relatively high level, the consumption level has to fall. If f' (k*) > n+g+δ, it indicates that the gain from the additional capital exceeds the consumption of capital and the exceeding part can be used for consumption. Thus the consumption level rises. If f' (k*) = n+g+δ, it implies that the gain from the additional capital just offsets the consumption of capital. Thus the consumption level remains the same. At this point, k* is the golden-rule level of capital stock k_{GR}.

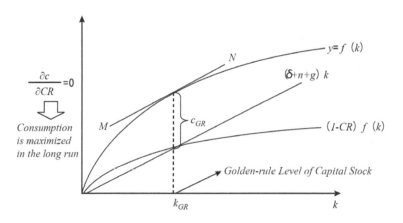

Figure 4-3 Correspondence between Consumption Maximization and Golden-Rule Level of Capital Stock

4.1.3 Determination of Optimal Consumption Rate in the Economic Growth

To obtain the explicit solution of optimal consumption rate in the Solow model, we assume the production function to be Cobb-Douglas production function. Then the capital, output and consumption per unit of effective labour at the steady-state of economy are, respectively, as follows:

$$k(t)^* = [(1-CR)/(n+g+\delta)]^{1/(1-\alpha)} \tag{4-4}$$

$$y(t)^* = [(1-CR)/(n+g+\delta)]^{\alpha/(1-\alpha)} \tag{4-5}$$

$$c(t)^* = CR[(1-CR)/(n+g+\delta)]^{\alpha/(1-\alpha)} \tag{4-6}$$

The so-called golden-rule level of capital stock refers to the capital stock reached when the consumption level per unit of effective labour is maximized. The meaning of the assessment of this indicator lies in the evaluation of social welfare level, which is the core of all the analysis in economics and is more valuable than the assessment of economic variables including capital and output.

CR can be obtained from Equation (4-4):

$$CR = 1 - (n + g + \delta)k(t)^{*(1-\alpha)} \tag{4-7}$$

Substituting Equation (4-7) into Equation (4-6) and simplifying the equation:

$$c(t)^* = k(t)^{*\alpha} - (n + g + \delta)k(t)^* \tag{4-8}$$

In other words, the consumption per unit of effective labour equals the output per unit of effective labour minus the actual investment per unit of effective labour which equals the break-even investment per unit of effective labour.

The optimization of c* with respect to k* can be deduced from Equation (4-8):

$$\partial c^* / \partial k^* = \alpha k^{*\alpha-1} - (n + g + \delta) = 0 \tag{4-9}$$

Then it can be simplified as: $\alpha k^{*\alpha-1} = (n + g + \delta)$

Equation (4-9) implies the level of the golden-rule level of capital stock, as the equation f'(k*) = (n+g+δ) indicates the slope of production function equals that of break-even investment line.

Thus the golden-rule optimal capital level can be deduced according to Equation (4-9):

$$k_{GR}^* = \left[\alpha / (n + g + \delta)\right]^{1/(1-a)} \tag{4-10}$$

Substituting Equation (4-10) into Equation (4-7), we obtain the golden-rule level of consumption rate, that is, the optimal consumption rate: $CR_{GR} = 1 - (n+g+\delta)[\alpha/(n+g+\delta)]^{1-\alpha/(1-\alpha)}$, which can be further simplified as:

$$CR_{GR} = 1 - \alpha \qquad (4\text{-}11)$$

Equation (4-11) shows that regarding Cobb-Douglas production function, optimal consumption rate equals labour flexibility of output (also output share of labour) (Sorensen, Whitta-Jacobsen, 2012[1]; Luo, 2014[2]). We believe such conclusion accords with China's actual economic situation. On one hand, China's capital market and other financial markets are not completely developed. As a result, property income only accounts for a small proportion in disposable income of a household[3], which indicates that household consumption mainly comes from labour income. On the other hand, the features shown in China's macroeconomic statistics also implies labour income ratio is the most important factor affecting China's consumption rate (Li, 2011)[4]. China's labour income ratio fell from 56.7 percent in 1992 to its minimum value of 48.6 percent in 2011 and slightly rebounded to 52.1 percent in 2016. Meanwhile, final consumption rate declined by 6.1 percentage points over 14 years, from 59.7 percent in 1992 to 53.6 percent in 2016. According to Figure 4-4, China's final consumption rate is highly correlated with labour income ratio, sharing a similar variation curve where final consumption progressively decreases as labour income share falls.

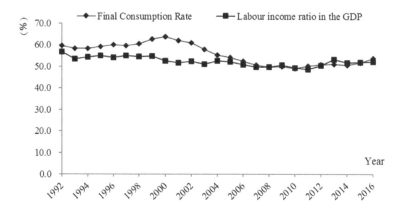

Figure 4-4 Variation of China's Labour Income Ratio and Final Consumption Rate since 1992

4.2 Measurement and Analysis of China's Optimal Consumption Rate

4.2.1 Settings of the Model and Notes on Statistics

4.2.1.1. Settings of the Model

Supposing the production function is Cobb-Douglas production function with input factors including labour and capital, we obtain the labour flexibility and capital flexibility through regression analysis and take the labour flexibility of output as a measure of China's optimal consumption rate. The production function is presented as follows:

$$Y(t) = K(t)^\alpha \left[A(t)L(t) \right]^\beta e^\mu \qquad (4\text{-}12)$$

Taking the log of both sides of Equation (4-12), we obtain:

$$\ln(Y(t)) = \alpha_0 + \alpha \ln(K(t)) + \beta \ln L(t) + \mu \qquad (4\text{-}13)$$

Here $\alpha_0 = \beta \ln A(t)$. Equation (4-13) is used as the model to calculate China's optimal consumption rate. The statistics necessary for the calculation include output of the actual economy, capital stock and labour force.

4.2.1.2. Source of the Statistics

The statistics necessary for the analysis here include three indicators: China's output of the actual economy, capital stock and labour force. The notes on these three indicators are as follows: in terms of output, we take the GDP as a measure of output and convert the GDP index into the constant price in 1978; in terms of labour force, we directly take the number of China's employed people as labour input. Regarding the accounting of capital stock, the statistics from 1978 to 2008 come from the study carried out by Shan (2008) on the provincial statistics of capital stock which are converted into the constant price in 1978; the statistics from 1978 to 2008 is calculated by perpetual inventory method with the constant price in 1978. Considering the availability, we select the statistics from 1978 to 2013 (see Table 4-1) which mainly come from *Comprehensive Statistical Data and Materials on 50 Years of New China* and *China Statistical Yearbook-2014*.

Table 4-1 China's Economic Statistics during 1978–2013

Year	Actual GDP (Y): 100 Million yuan	Capital Stock (K): 100 Million yuan	Labour Force (L): 10 Thousand People	Year	Actual GDP (Y): 100 Million yuan	Capital Stock (K): 100 Million yuan	Labour Force (L): 10 Thousand People
1978	3650.2	5686.6	40152.0	1996	20239.5	32973.6	68950.0
1979	3927.6	6172.4	41024.0	1997	22101.6	36979.0	69820.0
1980	4237.9	6764.7	42361.0	1998	23825.5	41202.3	70637.0
1981	4454.0	7288.0	43725.0	1999	25636.2	45612.8	71394.0
1982	4854.9	7888.1	45295.0	2000	27789.7	50386.8	72085.0
1983	5379.2	8583.1	46436.0	2001	30096.2	55710.4	72797.0
1984	6196.9	9492.8	48197.0	2002	32835.0	62089.8	73280.0
1985	7033.4	10573.3	49873.0	2003	36118.5	70274.8	73736.0
1986	7659.4	11749.4	51282.0	2004	39766.4	79723.6	74264.0
1987	8555.6	13156.4	52783.0	2005	44260.0	90985.7	74647.0
1988	9522.3	14649.0	54334.0	2006	49881.1	103908.4	74978.0
1989	9922.3	15589.6	55329.0	2007	56964.2	118048.1	75321.0
1990	10309.3	16554.6	64749.0	2008	62432.8	133948.3	75564.0
1991	11268.0	17821.4	65491.0	2009	68176.6	155492.7	75828.0
1992	12879.3	19672.1	66152.0	2010	75403.3	177905.5	76105.0
1993	14669.6	22253.6	66808.0	2011	82566.6	201660.4	76420.0
1994	16591.3	25404.5	67455.0	2012	88924.2	227430.1	76704.0
1995	18416.3	28986.2	68065.0	2013	95771.4	255468.4	76977.0

4.2.2 Empirical Analysis

4.2.2.1. Data Stationarity and Cointegration Test

Due to the non-stationarity of the statistics, spurious regression tends to occur when time-series data are used. Thus we test for the data stationarity before regression. Table 4-2 shows the result of an ADF test for the data stationarity. Conducting an ADF test on the level value and the first-order difference of three variables including log GDP (lnY), log capital stock (lnK) and log labour input (lnL), we see that at the significance level of 1 percent, the level values of the three variables are non-stationary; at the significance level of 1 percent, the first-order difference series of the three variables are stationary. In other words, the three variables series are integrated of order one.

Table 4-2 Result of Unit Root Test (ADF Test)

Variable	ADF	Critical Value at 10%	Critical Value at 5%	Critical Value at 1%	Condition (G,T,N)	Result
lnY	-0.302511	-2.619160	-2.960411	-3.661661	(G,0,4)	Non-stationary
△lnY	-3.751911	-2.619160	-2.960411	-3.661661	(C,0,3)	Stationary
lnK	2.495819	-2.615817	-2.954021	-3.646342	(G,0,2)	Non-stationary
△lnY	-3.881637	-3.209642	-3.552973	-4.262735	(G,T,2)	Stationary
lnY	-0.738643	-3.204699	-3.544284	-4.243644	(G,T,0)	Non-stationary
△lnY	-4.926406	-2.614300	-2.951125	-3.639407	(G,0,1)	Stationary

Notes: C, T and N, respectively, represent "with constant term", "with time trend" and "with difference lag order". The Schwarz Information Criterion (SIC) is used in the selection of lag order.

Though non-stationary, the three variables including lnY, lnK and lnL are all integrated of order one and meet the premises of a cointegration test.

Since time trends are shown in most macroeconomic statistics, presenting the feature of non-stationarity, direct regression analysis tends to cause spurious regression. To avoid that, we carry out Johansen

Cointegration test for the data stationarity and cointegration relation. According to the result, trace statistics and maximum characteristic value reject null hypothesis at the significance level of 5 percent, which indicates there at least exists one cointegration relation among lnY (t), lnK (t) and lnL (t).

Table 4-3 Result of Johansen Cointegration Test

Null Hypothesis	Characteristic Value	Trace Statistics	Critical Value at 5%	Probability	Maximum Characteristic Value	Critical Value at 5%	Value of P
None	0.492038	36.15968	24.27596	0.0010	22.35250	17.79730	0.0096
At most 1	0.337002	13.80719	12.32090	0.0280	13.56244	11.22480	0.0191
At most 2	0.007389	0.244749	4.129906	0.6797	0.244749	4.129906	0.6797

4.2.2.2. Result Analysis

Regressing the Equation (4-13) with the software Eviews 6, we obtain:

$$\ln Y = -5.4846 + 0.7535 \ln K + 0.6765 \ln L \qquad (4\text{-}14)$$

$$(10.17) \quad (70.27) \quad (11.71)$$

$$R^2 = 0.9991 \ AdjR^2 = 0.9991 \ F = 17776.30$$

The result of regression shows that all coefficients of the variables pass the significance test at the significance level of 1 percent. The equation passes the F test, and the model has no autocorrelation.

Equation (4-14) shows that labour flexibility of output was 67.6 percent, which means China's optimal consumption rate was 67.6 percent during 1978–2013, close to the consumption level of middle-income countries. Figure 4-5 illustrates the comparison between the optimal consumption rate and the actual final consumption rate. It can be told that China's final consumption rate had always been lower than the optimal level: it was lower than 60 percent in most periods except the 1980s when it was above 60 percent and relatively close to the optimal level.

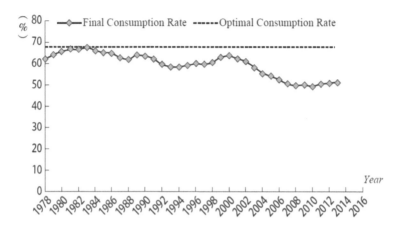

Figure 4-5 Comparison between China's Final Consumption Rate and the Optimal Consumption Rate during 1978–2014

The regression analysis shows that China's optimal consumption rate was 67.6 percent during 1978–2013, higher by 12.6 percentage points than the optimal consumption rate which was 55 percent from the perspective of dynamic efficiency. Such a result can be explained from the following two aspects for which the perspectives to evaluate are different: on one hand, from the perspective of dynamic efficiency of economy, the optimal consumption rate is obtained through the comparison between aggregate consumption and labour income. Specifically, the consumption rate achieved when aggregate consumption equals labour income is the optimal consumption rate while in the Solow model, labour flexibility of output equals the optimal consumption. On the other hand, from the perspective of dynamic efficiency, the optimal consumption rate is calculated based on the annual consumption and labour income while in the Solow model, the optimal consumption rate presents the consumption-output ratio over a certain period.

4.3 China's Optimal Consumption Rate – Analysis Based on Capital-Output Ratio

In section 4.3, we, respectively, calculate China's annual optimal consumption rates from 1978 to 2013 based on capital-output ratio and further compare them with the actual annual consumption rates, along with the detailed explanation on the differences between them. The analysis of optimal consumption rate in terms of capital-output ratio is mainly based on the study carried out by Fan et al. (2014)[5].

4.3.1 China's Optimal Consumption Rate Based on Capital-Output Ratio

According to the previous analysis, when economy is at the steady state, $\dot{k}(t) = (1-CR)f(k) - (n+g+\delta)k(t) = 0$. The equation implies: the variation of the average capital stock per unit of effective labour equals the difference between the average actual investment per unit of effective labour (1-CR) f ($k_{(t)}$) and the break-even investment per unit of effective labour (n+g+δ) k (t). If the average actual investment per unit of effective labour equals the break-even investment, then k remains unchanged, indicating the economic growth is at the steady state (see Figure 4-6). According to what a steady-state economic growth suggests, no matter how the economy was going, it will eventually converge to the steady state in the model. When the variables in the model are at the steady state, they all grow at constant rates.

In Figure 4-6, k^*_{GR} represents the golden-rule level of capital stock corresponding to the maximized consumption per capita. The consumption rate at this point is the optimal consumption rate mentioned in 4.3. Considering the consistence with what is mentioned before and the fact that China is at the acceleration period of capital accumulation, we assume that when China's economy is at the steady state, it achieves the golden-rule growth. The consumption rate in Figure 4-6 equals the optimal consumption rate (CR$_{GR}$), which means the slope of the production function is n+g+δ. That is $CR_{GR} = 1 - (n+g+\delta)\dfrac{k}{f(k)} = 1 - (n+g+\delta)\dfrac{K}{F(K,AL)} = 1 - (n+g+\delta)\dfrac{K}{Y}$, that is to say CRGR equals [1- (n+g+δ)] times the capital-output ratio. During the convergence of economy towards its steady state, growth rate of output per capita equals growth rate per unit of effective labour. Thus we suppose the actual GDP equals growth rate of population plus rate of technology progress rate. Letting the actual GDP be g'=n+g, we obtain the theoretical model of optimal consumption rate:

$$CR_{GR} = 1 - (g' + \delta)\frac{K}{Y} \qquad (4\text{-}15)$$

4.3.2 Source of the Statistics and Selection of Indicators

According to Equation (4-15), the necessary indicators for the calculation of China's optimal consumption rate include the following four variables: actual economic growth rate, capital depreciation rate, capital stock and output level.

In terms of actual economic growth rate, we deduct 100 from the GDP index (which was 100 in the last year) recorded in *China Statistical Yearbook-2015* to obtain the annual economic growth rates from 1978 to 2013.

In terms of capital depreciation rate, it is generally assumed to be [0.05, 0.08] in the world. For instance, Perkins (1988)[6], Wang and Yao (2001)[7] all assume depreciation rate to be 5 percent while Hall and Jones (1999)[8] and Young (2003)[9] both assume it to be 6 percent. Given the fact that China is a developing country, capital depreciates faster than the developed countries and representative scholars in China generally assume capital depreciation rate to be 9.6 percent (Zhang et al., 2000)[10], we also assume it to be 9.6 percent in this book.

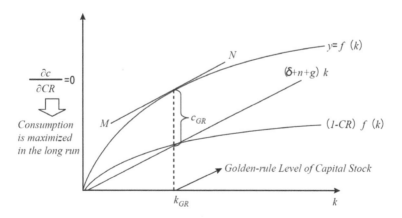

Figure 4-6 Consumption Maximization at the Steady State in the Solow Model

In terms of the accounting of capital stock, the statistics from 1991 to 2008 (constant price in 1952) come from the study carried out by Shan (2008)[11] on the provincial statistics of capital stock which are converted into the constant price in 1978; capital stocks from 2009 to 2013 are calculated by perpetual inventory method with the constant price in 1978.

In terms of output level, we take the GDP as an indicator and convert the GDP index into the constant price in 1978.

4.3.3 Calculation of China's Optimal Consumption Rate

With the statistics of the four variables including actual economic growth rate, capital depreciation rate, capital stock and output level, we calculate the annual optimal consumption rates from 1978 t0 2013 based on Equation (4-15) (see Table 4-4). Table 4-4 shows that during 1978–2013, China's final consumption rate had been lower than its optimal level (except in 1984). Judging from their averages: during 1978–2013, the average optimal consumption rate was 64.9 percent, higher by 5.5 percentage points than the average final consumption rate which was 59.4 percent; during 2000–2013, the average final consumption rate was 58.1 percent, higher by 4.0 percentage points than the average final consumption rate which was 54.1 percent. Since the optimal consumption rate is calculated based on China's actual economic statistics during 1978–2013, the variation of the optimal consumption rate can reflect that of the economic situation. According to the theory of consumption, economic output is divided into consumption and investment and capital stock is accumulated by investment. Thus as investment increases, capital stock rises with consumption decreasing, which eventually leads to a decline in final consumption rate. Following that logic, we can conclude that capital-output ratio is negatively correlated with optimal consumption rate (Figure 4-7): when capital-output ratio rises (which causes capital investment efficiency to fall), optimal consumption rate decreases, and vice versa.

Table 4-4 China's Optimal Consumption Rate and Relevant Statistics during 1978–2013

Year	Output (100 Million yuan)	Capital Stock (100 Million yuan)	Actual GDP Growth Rate(%)	Depreciation Rate (%)	Optimal Consumption Rate (%)	Final Consumption Rate (%)
1978	3650.2	5686.6	11.60	9.60	67.0	61.4
1979	3927.6	6172.4	7.60	9.60	73.0	63.9
1980	4237.9	6764.7	7.90	9.60	72.1	65.5
1981	4454.0	7288.0	5.10	9.60	75.9	66.7
1982	4854.9	7888.1	9.00	9.60	69.8	66.5
1983	5379.2	8583.1	10.80	9.60	67.4	67.4
1984	6196.9	9492.8	15.20	9.60	62.0	65.8
1985	7033.4	10573.3	13.50	9.60	65.3	65.0
1986	7659.4	11749.4	8.90	9.60	71.6	64.8
1987	8555.6	13156.4	11.70	9.60	67.2	62.6
1988	9522.3	14649.0	11.30	9.60	67.8	61.8
1989	9922.3	15589.6	4.20	9.60	78.3	63.9
1990	10309.3	16554.6	3.90	9.60	78.3	63.3
1991	11268.0	17821.4	9.30	9.60	70.1	61.9
1992	12879.3	19672.1	14.30	9.60	63.5	59.7
1993	14669.6	22253.6	13.90	9.60	64.4	58.3
1994	16591.3	25404.5	13.10	9.60	65.2	58.2
1995	18416.3	28986.2	11.00	9.60	67.6	59.1
1996	20239.5	32973.6	9.90	9.60	68.2	60.0
1997	22101.6	36979.0	9.20	9.60	68.5	59.6
1998	23825.5	41202.3	7.80	9.60	69.9	60.5
1999	25636.2	45612.8	7.60	9.60	69.4	62.7
2000	27789.7	50386.8	8.40	9.60	67.4	63.7
2001	30096.2	55710.4	8.30	9.60	66.9	62.0
2002	32835.0	62089.8	9.10	9.60	64.6	61.0
2003	36118.5	70274.8	10.00	9.60	61.9	57.9
2004	39766.4	79723.6	10.10	9.60	60.5	55.2
2005	44260.0	90985.7	11.30	9.60	57.0	54.1
2006	49881.1	103908.4	12.70	9.60	53.5	52.4
2007	56964.2	118048.1	14.20	9.60	50.7	50.6
2008	62432.8	133948.3	9.60	9.60	58.8	49.7

(*Continued*)

Table 4-4 Continued

Year	Output (100 Million yuan)	Capital Stock (100 Million yuan)	Actual GDP Growth Rate(%)	Depreciation Rate (%)	Optimal Consumption Rate (%)	Final Consumption Rate (%)
2009	68176.6	155492.7	9.20	9.60	57.1	50.0
2010	75403.3	177905.5	10.60	9.60	52.3	49.1
2011	82566.6	201660.4	9.50	9.60	53.4	50.2
2012	88924.2	227430.1	7.70	9.60	55.8	50.8
2013	95771.4	255468.4	7.70	9.60	53.9	51.0
Average during 1978–2013					64.9	59.4

Source: *China Statistical Yearbook-2015* and Author's calculation

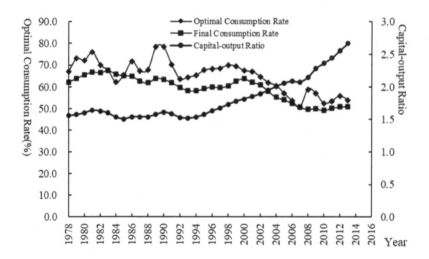

Figure 4-7 China's Optimal Consumption Rate, Final Consumption Rate and Capital-Output Ratio during 1978–2013

Since the reform and opening-up, the evolution of China's capital-output ratio can be divided into the following two stages (see Figure 4-7): in the first stage (1978–2000), the capital-output ratio basically fluctuated around 1.6 while the optimal consumption rate (final consumption rate) fluctuated around 69.2 percent (62.7 percent); in the second stage (2001 till 2016), the capital-output ratio was in an increasing trend, climbing from 1.85 in 2001 to 2.67 in 2013. Meanwhile, the optimal consumption rate (final consumption rate) dramatically declined from 66.9 percent (62.0 percent) in 2001 to 53.9 percent (51.0 percent) in 2013. The variation of the capital-output ratio reflects the relationship between the variation trend of capital growth and that of output growth: when the growth rate of capital stock exceeds that of output, the capital-output ratio rises; when the growth rate of capital stock was lower than that of output, the capital-output ratio decreases. Since 2001, the rapid growth of China's capital-output ratio indicates the growth rate of capital is higher than that of output. As China's labour growth rate is relatively stable, the high growth rate of capital implies the capital deepening is gradually enhanced which is no good for the improvement of China's consumption rate.

Ding (2015)[12] analyses the relationship between China's consumption rate and capital deepening through building a theoretical model, concluding that the impact of capital deepening on consumption rate depends on elasticity of factor substitution: when elasticity of factor substitution is below 1, capital deepening will raise labour income share and further increases consumption rate; when elasticity of factor substitution is above 1, capital deepening will lower labour income share which further decreases consumption rate. According to the calculation, China's elasticity of factor substitution is higher than 1 and thus the capital deepening inhibits the consumption rate from rising.

To figure out the relationship between China's capital-output ratio and the optimal consumption rate, we carry out the Granger causality test to verify the argument that the increase of capital-output ratio causes the optimal consumption rate to fall. As Table 4-5 shows, at the significance level of 1 percent, the probability of making a type I error to reject the null hypothesis that capital-output ratio is not the Granger-cause for optimal consumption rate is 0.0028. Such a result indicates that at least at the confidence level of 95 percent, we can say capital-output ratio is the Granger-cause for optimal consumption rate. In other words, the variation of capital-output ratio is the main cause for the variation of optimal consumption rate.

Table 4-5 Granger Causality Test on Capital-output Ratio and Optimal Consumption Rate

Null Hypothesis	Obs	F-statistic	Probability
Capital-output ratio is the Granger-cause for optimal consumption rate	35	10.5188	0.0028
Optimal consumption rate is the Granger-cause for capital-output ratio	35	0.09164	0.7641

To further clarify the quantitative relationship between capital-output ratio and optimal consumption rate, we carry out regression analysis with optimal consumption rate (CR_{GR}) as explained variable and capital-output ratio (cor) as explanatory variables and obtain:

$$CR_{GR} = 91.76 - 14.76 * cor + [AR(1) = 0.563] \qquad (4\text{-}16)$$

$$(11.5) \quad (-3.49) \qquad\qquad (3.76)$$

$$R^2 = 0.726,\ F = 42.35,\ D.W = 1.50$$

The result shows that in terms of the critical value of the t-statistic of every variable at the significance of 5 percent, D.W=1.50. Therefore, there exists no autocorrelation. Cor is obviously in negative correlation with CR_{GR}. For every 1 increased by cor, CR_{GR} fall by 14.76 percentage points, which is consistent with the result illustrated by Figure 4-7. For instance, when Cor rose from 1.57 in 1995 to 2.67 in 2013, CR_{GR} fell from 67.3 percent in 1995 to 53.9 percent in 2013.

4.4 Summary and Policy Suggestions

In Chapter 4, we look into China's optimal consumption rate based on the Solow model from the following two perspectives: first, the golden-rule capital stock. It is deduced that optimal consumption rate equals labour flexibility of output. According to the empirical research, China's optimal consumption rate is 67.7 percent; second, the capital-output ratio. We calculate China's average optimal consumption rate from 1978 to 2013 since the reform and opening-up to be 64.9 percent. Accordingly, based on the Solow model, the reasonable range of China's optimal consumption rate is [64.9 percent, 67.7 percent].

Judging from the analysis based on the model in this chapter along with the fact that China's current consumption rate is relatively low, we put forward the following suggestion for measures to promote consumption and thus increase consumption rate towards the optimal consumption rate in the hope of eventually realizing the sustainable growth of China's economy.

First, adjustments in income distribution should be made to raise the proportion of labour income in the primary distribution. Our analysis indicates that if property income occupies a smaller proportion in disposable income, optimal consumption rate equals labour income share and thus the rise of labour income share can help raise consumption. In addition, increasing labour income share contributes to the improvement of household consumption level and marginal propensity to consume of total income. Generally speaking, compared with capital income and other property income, labour income has the greatest marginal propensity to consume. Therefore, judging from all the factors, raising labour income share has the most direct and obvious impact on realizing the sustainable growth of China's economy.

Next, the improvement of social security system should be accelerated to promote China's household consumption. Currently, there is much room for the improvement. A large part of household income is saved for child education, housing, medication and unemployment. If the social security is improved, then such part can be used for consumption. In this way, the consumption propensity of residents will be greatly strengthened and thus the macroeconomic consumption rate will also be raised.

Furthermore, the investment structure needs adjusting to enhance investment efficiency. Since the reform and opening-up, due to the relatively fast growth speed of investment, capital makes the greatest contribution to China's economic growth compared with other factors, which further enhances China's capital deepening and rapidly increases the capital-output ratio. Yet such growth pattern driven by high investment is unsustainable in the long run. Accordingly, there is little probability to drive China's economic growth with investment in a certain period in the future. We have to improve investment efficiency through adjusting the investment structure and eliminating ineffective capacity to weaken capital deepening and lower the capital-output ratio, which finally helps the final consumption rate converge towards the optimal consumption rate.

Finally, the household property income should be increased in many ways. The main source of income of most households in China is labour. For example, the rise of property income will bring increase in disposable income. According to the consumption function, consumption level and consumption rate will also be strengthened.

Notes

1 Sorensen P. B. and Whitta-Jacobsen H. J., *Introducing Advanced Macroeconomics: Growth and Business Cycles(2nd Edition)*, trans. Wang Wenping et al. (China Renmin University Press, 2012).
2 Romer D. *Advanced Macroeconomics (4th Edition)*, trans. Wu Huabin & Gong Guan (Shanghai University of Finance and Economics, 2014).
3 From 1992 to 2005, China's household property income increased by 2.79 times from 121.838 billion yuan to 461.28 billion yuan, while its contribution to household disposable income progressively fell from 6.59 percent to 4.17 percent. The relative scale of property income, compared with that of returns from labour, also decreased. The ratio of them gradually declined from 1: 13.9 in 1992 to 1: 20.1 with the proportion of property income gradually dropping.
4 Li Daokui, Xu Xiang, "Reseach on the Adjustments in China's Economic Structure and Its Dynamics," *New Finance* 6 (2013).
5 Fan Zuojun, Chang Yali, and Huang Liqun, "Optimal Saving Rate and Its Influencing Factors Measurement under the International Vision—Based on the Solow Growth Model," *Economic Research Journal* 9 (2014).
6 Perkins D.H., "Reforming China's Economic System," *Journal of Economic Literature* 26, no. 2 (1988): 601–645.
7 Wang Yan and Yao Yudong, "Sources of China's Economic Growth 1952–1999: Incorporating Human Capital Accumulation," *World Bank Working Paper* 1 (2001).
8 Hall Robert E. and Jones Charles I., "Why do Some Countries Produce So Much More Output per Worker than Others?" *Quarterly Journal of Economics* 114, no. 1 (1999): 83–116.

9 Young Alwyn, "Gold into Base Metals: Productivity Growth in the People's Republic of China during the Reform Period," *Journal of Political Economy*, 111, no. 6 (2003): 1220–1260.
10 Zhang Jun, Wu Guiying, and Zhang Jipeng, "The Estimation of China's provincial capital stock: 1952–2000," *Economic Research Journal* 10 (2004).
11 Shan, "Reestimating the Capital Stock of China: 1952~2006," *The Journal of Quantitative & Technical Economics* 10 (2008).
12 Ding Jianxun, "The Relationship between Capital Deepening and Consumption Rate in China," *Shanghai Journal of Economics* 9 (2015).

Chapter 5

Optimal Consumption Rate in the Ramsey–Cass–Koopsman Model

As a typical model for analysing intertemporal optimal consumption and savings strategy, the Ramsey model is named after Frank Ramsey, a British mathematician and a logician at Cambridge University, who wrote *A Mathematical Theory of Saving*[1] published in the *Economic Journal* in December of 1982 to study on resource allocation from the perspective of intertemporality. Improved by Cass (1955)[2] and Koopsman (1965)[3], it gradually developed to be the Ramsey–Cass–Koopsman model in today's macroeconomics courses[4]. In Chapter 5, we discuss optimal consumption rate based on the Ramsey model: in section 5.1, we look into the determination of optimal consumption rate in the Ramsey model; in section 5.2, we calculate China's optimal consumption rate through calibrating exogenous parameters based on China's actual economic situation and further simulate the impact of the variation of various exogenous parameters on the optimal consumption rate; and in section 5.3, we summarize the previous analysis and put forward suggestion.

5.1 Analysis Framework for China's Optimal Consumption Rate: Theoretical Model[5]

5.1.1 Production Function and Behaviour of Firms

In terms of economic output, we assume all firms in the economy are homogeneous and then we abstract a representative firm which decides its labour and capital through maximizing profits. The production function is of labour-augmenting technological progress:

$$Y(t) = F(K(t), A(t)L(t)) \tag{5-1}$$

Here Y (t), K(t), A(t) and L(t), respectively, represent output, capital stock, technology progress and labour. Supposing the production function has constant returns to scale, decreasing marginal output with all factors of production and is second-order continuously differentiable on the interval [0, +∞). Meanwhile, it satisfies the Inada Conditions of a strictly concave function. Thus it can be shown as follows:

$$F(\lambda K, \lambda AL) = \lambda F(K, AL), \lambda > 0 \tag{5-2}$$

$$F_K > 0, F_{KK} < 0, F_{AL} > 0, F_{(AL)(AL)} < 0 \tag{5-3}$$

$$F(0, AL) = F(K, 0) = 0, \lim_{K \to 0} F_K = \lim_{AL \to 0} F_{AL} = \infty, \lim_{K \to \infty} F_K = \lim_{AL \to \infty} F_{AL} = 0 \tag{5-4}$$

Supposing technological progress is exogenously determined, we have:

$$A(t) = A(0)e^{gt} \tag{5-5}$$

Here A (0) represents the technological level at the economic beginning (Period 0) and is standardized to 1. Then we obtain: A (t) = e^{gt}. Since the return to scale of the production function is assumed to be constant, it can be converted to a dense form:

$$y(t) = \frac{Y}{AL} = F\left(\frac{K}{AL}, 1\right) = f(k) \qquad (5\text{-}6)$$

Here y (t) = Y (t) / A(t) L(t) is the output per unit of effective labour while k (t) = K (t) / A(t) L(t) is the capital stock per unit of effective labour. In this way, we present the output per unit of effective labour with the function of the capital stock per unit of effective labour. According to the assumption of the aggregate production function, the dense production function meets the following condition:

$$f(0) = 0, f'(k) > 0, f''(k) < 0, \lim_{k \to 0} f'(k) = +\infty, \lim_{k \to \infty} f'(k) = 0 \qquad (5\text{-}7)$$

Firms hire labour and capital for production. Its cost at every period includes wage cost (wL) and interest on capital (rK). Additionally, we assume capital depreciation rate is δ. Therefore, the total cost for firms to hire L and K is wL+ (r+δ) K, and the profit of the representative firm is:

$$\Pi = F(K, AL) - (r + \delta)K - wL$$

$$= ALf(k) - AL(r + \delta)k - wL \qquad (5\text{-}8)$$

Supposing that commodity market and factor market are perfectly competitive and firms can adjust the level of hiring of labour and capital to maximize their profits at every period, we obtain:

$$\Pi = \max_{K,L} F(K, AL) - (r + \delta)K - wL$$

$$= \max_{K,L} ALf(k) - AL(r + \delta)k - wL \qquad (5\text{-}9)$$

The first-order condition of the optimization problem of firms is presented as follows:

$$r(t) = f'(k) - \delta, w(t) = Af(k) - Akf'(k) \qquad (5\text{-}10)$$

5.1.2 Utility Function and Behaviour of Consumers

In terms of consumers, we assume the following: a household is engaged in economy as a whole, and the household income which comes from providing labour and gaining interests through renting capital to firms is used for household consumption and saving/investment activities to maximize household utility; each household includes at least one person (determined by initial population and population growth rate). When the household is making decisions, the decision-maker takes into consideration the welfare level of both the current household population and the future generation as well as resource constraints. Supposing the individual in a household has infinite lifespan, we look into the activities of optimal consumption and saving of a household within a certain period of time.

5.1.2.1. Utility Function

Supposing the current decision-maker of a household can precisely foresee the population growth rate which is represented by n and the population is standardized to be 1 at Period 0, then the total population at any time (t) is: L (t) = e^{nt}. C (t) represents the aggregate consumption of a household at t and c' (t)=C (t)/L (t) stands for the consumption level per capita. Accordingly, the utility level of a household at t is L (t) u (c' (t)) where u (·) represents individual instantaneous utility function which is a concave function with positive and decreasing marginal utility. The function satisfies the following conditions:

$$u(c') > 0, u'(c') > 0, u''(c') < 0, \forall c' > 0$$

Supposing u (·) meets the Inada Conditions, we obtain:

$$\lim_{c' \to 0} u'(c') = +\infty, \lim_{c' \to \infty} u'(c') = 0$$

For the convenience, the coefficient of relative risk aversion is assumed to be constant in the instantaneous utility function in Chapter 5:

$$u(c') = \frac{c'^{1-\theta}}{1-\theta} \qquad (5\text{-}11)$$

Here θ represents the coefficient of relative risk aversion.

We assume the time discount rate is 0<ρ<1, which indicates decision-maker of a household always believes the present is more important than the future. The utility level of 1 unit at t in the future equals that of $e^{-\rho t}$ at present. The household utility function considered by the decision-maker at 0 is the discounted sum of the utility level of all family members at all periods in both the present and the future:

$$U = \int_0^\infty e^{-(\rho-n)t} u(c'(t)) dt \qquad (5\text{-}12)$$

The decision-maker of a household maximizes the total household utility (Equation 5-12) at all periods through deciding the level of consumption and saving per capita (c' (t)). To ensure the convergence of the total household utility function, we assume ρ-n- (1-θ) g>0. Here g represents rate of technological progress; n represents population growth rate; and θ stands for the coefficient of relative risk aversion.

5.1.2.2. Budget Constraint

A household can hold its assets in deposits, stocks, bonds and any other forms and also hold negative assets in the form of loans and liabilities. Supposing the economy we discuss here is closed without uncertainty and assets such as deposits, stocks and bonds are substitutable, then they must have the same real rate of return r (t). W (t) represents the actual total assets of a household while ā (t) = W (t)/L (t) stands for the actual net asset per capital in a household. We assume that every family member inelastically provide 1 unit of labour at any t period with average wage level of w(t). Thus the total household income equals labour income plus asset income, that is to say, W (t) L (t) + r (t) W (t). Then the household budget constraint is as follows:

$$\dot{W}(t) = r(t)W(t) + w(t)L(t) - C(t) \qquad (5\text{-}13)$$

Here $\dot{W}$ represents the derivative of the variable with respect to time and the budget constraint per capita[6] is:

$$\dot{\bar{a}}(t) = r(t)\bar{a}(t) + w(t) - c'(t) - n\bar{a}(t) \qquad (5\text{-}14)$$

In addition, a non-Ponzi Game condition needs to be imposed on household activities. The present value of assets of a household cannot be below 0 at infinity time, which means a household cannot have negative assets at infinity time in the future.

$$\lim_{t \to 0}\left\{W(t)\exp\left[-\int_0^t r(s)ds\right]\right\} = \lim_{t \to 0}\bar{a}(t)\exp\left\{-\int_0^t [r(s) - n]ds\right\} > 0 \qquad (5\text{-}15)$$

5.1.2.3. Optimizing Behaviour of Households

According to the above assumptions, the problem in decision-making of a household is to maximize the lifetime utility function (U) of a household while the budget constraint and the non-Ponzi Game condition are satisfied, given the initial asset per capita. Therefore, the optimization problem of a household can be summarized as:

$$\max_{c'(t)} \int_0^\infty e^{-(\rho-n)t} \frac{c'(t)^{1-\theta}}{1-\theta} dt$$

$$\text{s.t.} \dot{\bar{a}}(t) = r(t)\bar{a}(t) + w(t) - c'(t) - n\bar{a}(t) \qquad (5\text{-}16)$$

$$\lim_{t \to 0}\bar{a}(t)\exp\left\{-\int_0^t [r(s) - n]ds\right\} > 0$$

Given ā (t) with c' (t)≥0

5.1.3 Market Equilibrium and Balanced Growth Path

Since we generally analyse the dynamic evolution of the economic variables in per unit of effective labour, we let c (t)=c' (t) /A (t) and a (t)= ā (t)/A (t) to analyse the activities of optimal consumption and saving in per unit of effective labour, and rewrite Equation (5-16) into the following form which is in per unit of effective labour:

$$\max_{c(t)} \int_0^\infty e^{-[\rho-n-(1-\theta)g]t} \frac{c(t)^{1-\theta}}{1-\theta} dt$$

$$s.t. \dot{a}(t) = r(t)a(t) + w(t) - c(t) - na(t) - ga(t) \tag{5-17}$$

$$\lim_{t \to 0} a(t) \exp\left\{-\int_0^t [r(s) - n - g] ds\right\} > 0$$

Given a (0) with c (t)≥0

Considering the first-order condition of optimization problem of firms:

$$r(t) = f'(k) - \delta, w(t) = Af(k) - Akf'(k) \tag{5-18}$$

When the economy is at its steady state, both product market and factor market are cleared. Meanwhile, there only exists one sort of net asset in the economy, which is the capital, and the sum of inter-household liabilities is 0. As a result, when the capital market achieves equilibrium, a (t), which is the asset per unit of effective labour, equals k (t), the capital per unit of social effective labour. Considering such condition and substituting Equation (5-18) into Equation (5-17), we convert the optimization problem into:

$$\max_{c(t)} \int_0^\infty e^{-[\rho-n-(1-\theta)g]t} \frac{c(t)^{1-\theta}}{1-\theta} dt$$

$$s.t. \dot{k}(t) = f(k) - c(t) - (n+g+\delta)k \tag{5-19}$$

$$\lim_{t \to 0} k(t) \exp\left\{-\int_0^t [f(k(s)) - \delta - n - g] ds\right\} > 0$$

Given k (0) with c(t) ≥0

Solving Equation (5-18) with Hamiltonian method, we obtain the household dynamic adjustment path of average consumption per unit of effective labour:

$$\frac{\dot{c}(t)}{c(t)} = \frac{(f'(k) - \rho - \theta g)}{\theta} \tag{5-20}$$

Given the dynamic adjustment path per unit of effective labour

$$\dot{k}(t) = f(k) - c(t) - (n + g + \delta)k \tag{5-21}$$

Equation (5-20) and Equation (5-21) form a dynamic system where the economy reaches steady state when the average capital and consumption per unit of effective labour no longer changes (the growth rate is 0). According to Equation (5-20), when the economy is at the steady state, we have the following equation:

$$f'(k^*) = \rho + \theta g \tag{5-22}$$

It presents the average capital stock per unit of effective labour when the economy reaches the steady state. Supposing the production function is Cobb-Douglas production function, we have: $Y(t) = F(K(t), A(t)L(t)) = K(t)^\alpha (A(t)L(t))^{1-\alpha}$, $y(t) = f(k) = k^\alpha$.

Thus when the economy reaches the steady state, the steady-state interest rate is as follows:

$$f'(k^*) = \alpha k^{*\alpha-1} = \rho + \theta g \tag{5-23}$$

Simplifying Equation (5-23) to obtain the average capital stock per unit of effective labour with the economy at its steady state:

$$k^* = \left(\frac{\alpha}{\rho + \theta g}\right)^{\frac{1}{1-\alpha}} \tag{5-24}$$

5.1.4 Optimal Consumption Rate and Steady State of Economy

When the economy is at the steady state, the average capital stock per unit of effective labour becomes constant, that is $\dot{k}(t) = 0$. Accordingly, based on Equation (5-21), we have:

$$f(k^*) - c^*(t) - (n + g + \delta)k^* = 0 \qquad (5\text{-}25)$$

Dividing both sides of Equation (5-25) by f (k*), substituting Equation (5-24) and simplifying the equation, we have:

$$CR^* = \frac{\rho + \theta g - \alpha(n + g + \delta)}{\rho + \theta g} \qquad (5\text{-}26)$$

As we define optimal consumption rate as the consumption rate achieved when the economy reaches the steady state, it can be said from Equation (5-26) that optimal consumption rate depends on discount rate (ρ), the coefficient of relative risk aversion (θ), technological progress (g), capital flexibility of output (α), population growth rate (n), depreciation rate (δ) and other exogenous parameters.

5.1.4.1. Discount Rate and Optimal Consumption Rate

Taking the partial derivatives of the both sides of Equation (5-26) with respect to ρ, we obtain:

$$\frac{\partial CR^*}{\partial \rho} = \frac{\alpha(n + g + \delta)}{(\rho + \theta g)^2} \qquad (5\text{-}27)$$

Equation (5-27) shows that discount rate has a positive impact on optimal consumption rate, which means the rise of discount rate results in the increase of optimal consumption rate. Generally speaking, discount rate measures the patience of consumers. The greater the discount rate is, the little patience consumers have. In other words, consumers prefer present consumption to future consumption, which helps raise present consumption rate; the lower the discount rate is, the greater patience consumers have. That is to say, consumers are willing to sacrifice present consumption for higher consumption in the future, resulting in the decrease of present consumption rate.

5.1.4.2. Coefficient of Relative Risk Aversion

Taking the partial derivatives of the both sides of Equation (5-25) with respect to θ, we obtain:

$$\frac{\partial CR^*}{\partial \theta} = \frac{\alpha g(n+g+\delta)}{(\rho+\theta g)^2} \qquad (5\text{-}28)$$

Equation (5-28) indicates that the coefficient of relative risk aversion has a positive impact on optimal consumption rate. In other words, the increase of the coefficient of relative risk aversion leads to the rise of optimal consumption rate. Generally speaking, the coefficient of relative risk aversion measures the extent of consumers' aversion to risk. Since the reciprocal of the coefficient of relative risk aversion is the elasticity of intertemporal substitution, the coefficient of relative risk aversion reflects consumers' preference of consumption in different periods. A higher coefficient of relative risk aversion (smaller elasticity of substitution) indicates that consumers are more willing to make average consumption in every period; a lower coefficient of relative risk aversion (greater elasticity of substitution) shows that consumers are more willing to maximize utility through inter-period consumption substitution, incentivized by different returns on assets.

5.1.4.3. Rate of Technological Progress and Optimal Consumption Rate

Taking the partial derivatives of the both sides of Equation (5-25) with respect to g, we obtain:

$$\frac{\partial CR^*}{\partial g} = -\frac{\alpha[\rho-\theta(n+\delta)]}{(\rho+\theta g)^2} \qquad (5\text{-}29)$$

Equation (5-29) shows that rate of technological progress has an uncertain impact on optimal consumption rate when other parameters are unknown. With $\rho > \theta$ $(n+\delta)$, the rise of rate of technological progress causes the decrease of optimal consumption rate; with $\rho < \theta$ $(n+\delta)$, the rise of rate of technological progress leads to the increase of optimal consumption rate. Generally speaking, the increase of rate of technological progress will permanently raise the level of economic output when factors including labour and capital remain the same. According to modern theories of consumption (permanent income hypothesis and life cycle theory), the rise of permanent income of consumers will further raise the consumption level, having an uncertain impact on consumption rate. If the capital stock is far lower than the golden-rule level, then the improvement in rate of technological progress causes the increase of output level. A relatively large proportion in the incremented output is used for capital accumulation, which results in the fall of consumption rate. On the contrary, if the capital stock is higher than the golden-rule level, then the rise of rate of technological progress leads to the improvement in output level. A relatively large proportion in the incremented output is used for consumption, which results in the rise of consumption rate.

5.1.4.4. Capital Elasticity of Output and Optimal Consumption Rate

Taking the partial derivatives of the both sides of Equation (5-25) with respect to α, we obtain:

$$\frac{\partial CR^*}{\partial \alpha} = -\frac{n+g+\delta}{\rho+\theta g} \tag{5-30}$$

Equation (5-30) shows that the increase of capital elasticity of output causes the fall of optimal consumption rate. Judging from the perspective of transmission mechanism, capital elasticity of output represents the incremented percentage of output caused by the increase of 1 percent in capital input. When we adopt Cobb-Douglas production function, $Y(t) = F(K(t), A(t)L(t)) = K(t)^\alpha (A(t)L(t))^{1-\alpha}$. The marginal output of capital is $\alpha Y/K$, which indicates that the rise of α results in the increase of marginal output. Therefore, the rise of capital elasticity of output reflects the increase of capital efficiency which will permanently raise the economic output level with factors including labour and capital remaining unchanged. A relatively large proportion in the incremented output is used for capital accumulation, which leads to the fall of consumption rate.

5.1.4.5. Population Growth Rate and Optimal Consumption Rate

Taking the partial derivatives of the both sides of Equation (5-25) with respect to n, we obtain:

$$\frac{\partial CR^*}{\partial n} = -\frac{\alpha}{\rho + \theta g} \qquad (5\text{-}31)$$

Equation (5-31) indicates that the increase of population growth rate results in the fall of optimal consumption rate. Judging from the perspective of transmission mechanism, with other conditions remaining unchanged, the rise of population growth rate has an impact on the following two aspects: on one hand, as population growth rate goes up, the proportion of average capital used to maintain the labour per unit increases, which causes a smaller proportion used for consumption. Therefore, the optimal consumption rate achieved when the economy is at the steady-state declines; on the other hand, when the population growth rate rises, the incremented population also consumes, further leading to the decrease of consumption rate with output and aggregate consumption remaining the same.

5.1.4.6. Depreciation Rate and Optimal Consumption Rate

Taking the partial derivatives of the both sides of Equation (5-25) with respect to δ, we obtain:

$$\frac{\partial CR^*}{\partial \delta} = -\frac{\alpha}{\rho + \theta g} \qquad (5\text{-}32)$$

Equation (5-31) shows that the increase of depreciation rate leads to the fall of optimal consumption rate. Judging from the perspective of transmission mechanism, with other conditions remaining unchanged, when depreciation rate goes up, more savings are needed to maintain the steady-state capital stock at the same level. When output and aggregate consumption remain the same, the rise of proportion of savings will result in the decline of proportion of consumption. In other words, when the economy re-achieves the steady state, consumption rate falls.

5.2 Calculation of China's Optimal Consumption Rate Based on the Ramsey–Cass–Koopmans Model

5.2.1 Economic Development Stages and Optimal Consumption Rate

According to the previous analysis in 5.1, optimal consumption rate depends on discount rate (ρ), the coefficient of relative risk aversion (θ), technological progress (g), capital flexibility of output (α), population growth rate (n), depreciation rate (δ) and other exogenous parameters. Among these parameters, capital flexibility of output is closely related to economic development stages. In accordance with the features of economic development in various stages, the comparative advantage of the economy generally evolves from resource-intensive development to labour-intensive development and eventually to capital-technology-intensive development. During such process, due to the adjustment in the economic structure and the alternation of industries, capital flexibility of output goes up before going down and then tends to be stable. According to the previous analysis in section 5.1, capital flexibility of output is in negative correlation with consumption rate in steady-state economy. As a result, consumption rate in steady-state economy may decrease before climbing and eventually become stable.

5.2.2 Calibration of Parameters

Since the consumption rate in steady-state economy equals $CR^* = \dfrac{\rho + \theta g - \alpha(n + g + \delta)}{\rho + \theta g}$, we can calculate China's optimal consumption rate based on the reasonable evaluation of discount rate (ρ), the coefficient of relative risk aversion (θ), technological progress (g), capital flexibility of output (α), population growth rate (n), depreciation rate (δ) and other exogenous parameters, given China's actual economic situation.

In terms of discount rate (ρ), domestic and foreign scholars normally carry out studies from the perspective of discount factor. The relationship between discount factor and discount rate can be shown by the following equation: β=1/(1+ρ). In empirical research, the range of discount factor is [0.95, 0.98]. When discount factor is at 0.95 which is the minimum value, the corresponding discount rate is 5.26 percent.

In terms of the coefficient of relative risk aversion (θ), Gu and Xiao (2004)[7] calculate China's coefficient of relative risk aversion during 1985–2002 with Keynes-Ramsey Rule and Arrow-Pratt Measures of Risk Aversion. The respective results are 3.169 and 3.916 on average. Gu et al. (2013)[8] improve the model of intertemporal substitution elasticity of consumption as well as the method, and further estimate China's household coefficient of relative risk aversion to be 3.2 on average during 2000–2008 with chronological recursion. Yao (2010)[9] calculates the coefficient of relative risk aversion of Hebei Province to be 2.32 through building an autoregressive distributed lag dynamic model. Considering the study object is the whole country, we assume the number to be 3.5 which is the median value of the calculation results in the study.

In terms of rate of technological progress (g), we assume g=0.12, based on the studies carried out by Ji (2013),[10] Wang & Gong (2007)[11] and Gu & Xiao (2007)[12].

In terms of capital flexibility of output (α), we assume α=0.75, based on the conclusion made in Chapter 3.

In terms of population growth rate (n), it is assumed in the Solow model and the Ramsey model that perfect competition is intensified and labour force is fully employed. Thus growth rate of population equals that of labour force. According to Table 3-1, China's growth rate of labour force during 1978–2013 is: n=1.87 percent.

In terms of depreciation rate (δ), [0.05, 0.08] is generally the assumed range in the world. For instance, Perkins (1988)[13], Wang & Yao (2001)[14],

Hall & Jones (1999)[15] and Young (2003)[16] all assume the number to be 6 percent. To be consistent with the previous analysis, we assume it to be 9.6 percent.

All the calibration results of the parameters are demonstrated in Table 5-1. According to Table 5-1 and Equation (5-26), China's optimal consumption rate in steady-state economy is 62.75 percent.

Table 5-1 Calibration Results of the Parameters Related to Optimal Consumption Rate

Parameter	P	θ	g	α	n	δ
Calibration Value	5.26%	3.5	0.12	0.75	1.87%	9.6%

5.2.3 Impact of Exogenous Parameters on China's Optimal Consumption Rate

5.2.3.1. Impact of Discount Rate on Optimal Consumption Rate

As Table 5-2 shows, to analyse the impact of discount rate on China's optimal consumption rate, we compare the impact of different discount rates on the optimal consumption rate, taking 5.26 percent as the benchmark discount rate, while other parameters remain unchanged. The result demonstrates that discount rate has a positive impact on optimal consumption rate. In other words, the increase of discount rate causes the rise of optimal consumption rate. Specifically speaking, when discount rate progressively rises from 3.26 percent to 4.26 percent, 5.26 percent, 6.26 percent and 7.26 percent, optimal consumption rate goes up by 0.84 percentage points, 0.80 percentage points, 0.77 percentage points and 0.75 percentage points. As discount rate gradually climbs, consumption rate goes down, which indicates that raising discount rate has a decreasing marginal effect on optimal consumption rate.

Table 5-2 Impact of Various Discount Rates on Optimal Consumption Rate

Parameter	ρ(%)	θ	g	α	n (%)	δ (%)	CR* (%)	Various of CR*caused by the 1 percentage-point increase of ρ (per percentage point)
Case 1	3.26	3.5	0.12	0.75	1.87	9.6	61.11	—
Case 2	4.26	3.5	0.12	0.75	1.87	9.6	61.95	0.84
Benchmark	5.26	3.5	0.12	0.75	1.87	9.6	62.75	0.80
Case 3	6.26	3.5	0.12	0.75	1.87	9.6	63.52	0.77
Case 4	7.26	3.5	0.12	0.75	1.87	9.6	64.27	0.75

5.2.3.2. Impact of the Coefficient of Relative Risk Aversion on Optimal Consumption Rate

As Table 5-3 demonstrates, to analyse the impact of the coefficient of relative risk aversion on China's optimal consumption rate, we compare the impact of different coefficients of relative risk aversion on the optimal consumption rate, taking 3.5 as the benchmark coefficient of relative risk aversion, while other parameters remain unchanged. The result shows that the coefficient of relative risk aversion has a positive impact on optimal consumption rate. In other words, the increase of the coefficient of relative risk aversion results in the rise of optimal consumption rate. Specifically speaking, when the coefficient of relative risk aversion progressively rises from 1.5 to 2.5, 3.5, 4.5 and 5.5, optimal consumption rate goes up by 25.76 percentage points, 12.68 percentage points, 7.54 percentage points and 5.00 percentage points. As the coefficient of relative risk aversion gradually goes up, consumption rate goes down, which indicates that increasing the coefficient of relative risk aversion has a decreasing marginal effect on optimal consumption rate.

Table 5-3 Impact of Various Coefficient of Relative Risk Aversion on Optimal Consumption Rate

Parameter	ρ(%)	θ	g	α	n (%)	δ (%)	CR* (%)	Changes of CR* caused by the 1-unit increase of θ (per percentage point)
Case 1	5.26	1.5	0.12	0.75	1.87	9.6	24.32	—
Case 2	5.26	2.5	0.12	0.75	1.87	9.6	50.08	25.76
Benchmark	5.26	3.5	0.12	0.75	1.87	9.6	62.75	12.68
Case 3	5.26	4.5	0.12	0.75	1.87	9.6	70.30	7.54
Case 4	5.26	5.5	0.12	0.75	1.87	9.6	75.30	5.00

5.2.3.3. Impact of Rate of Technological Progress on Optimal Consumption Rate

As Table 5-4 shows, to analyse the impact of rate of technological progress on China's optimal consumption rate, we compare the impact of different rates of technological progress on the optimal consumption rate and meanwhile compare ρ with θ (n+δ) based on Equation (5-29), taking 0.12 as the benchmark rate of technological progress, while other parameters remain unchanged. With 0.0526<0.40145, we conclude that rate of technological progress has a positive impact on optimal consumption rate. In other words, the increase of rate of technological progress results in the rise of optimal consumption rate. Specifically speaking, when rate of technological progress rises from 0.10 to 0.11, 0.12, 0.13 and 0.14, optimal consumption rate goes up by 1.49 percentage points, 1.27 percentage points, 1.09 percentage points and 0.95 percentage points. As rate of technological progress gradually climbs, consumption rate goes down, which indicates that raising rate of technological progress has a decreasing marginal effect on optimal consumption rate.

Table 5-4 Impact of Various Rates of Technological Progress on Optimal Consumption Rate

Parameter	ρ(%)	θ	g	α	n (%)	Δ (%)	CR* (%)	Variation of CR* caused by 1 percentage-point increase in g (per percentage point)
Case 1	5.26	1.5	0.10	0.75	1.87	9.6	60.00	—
Case 2	5.26	2.5	0.11	0.75	1.87	9.6	61.49	1.49
Benchmark	5.26	3.5	0.12	0.75	1.87	9.6	62.75	1.27
Case 3	5.26	4.5	0.13	0.75	1.87	9.6	63.84	1.09
Case 4	5.26	5.5	0.14	0.75	1.87	9.6	64.79	0.95

5.2.3.4. Impact of Capital Flexibility of Output on Optimal Consumption Rate

As Table 5-5 demonstrates, to analyse the impact of capital flexibility of output on China's optimal consumption rate, we compare the impact of different capital flexibility of output on the optimal consumption rate, taking 0.75 as the benchmark capital flexibility of output, while other parameters remain unchanged. We can see from Equation (5-30) that capital flexibility of output has a negative impact on optimal consumption rate. In other words, the increase of capital flexibility of output leads to the fall of optimal consumption rate. Specifically speaking, when capital flexibility of output progressively climbs from 0.65 to 0.70, 0.75, 0.80 and 0.85, optimal consumption rate, respectively, goes down by 2.48 percentage points. As capital flexibility of output gradually rises, consumption rate remains the same, which indicates that improving capital flexibility of output has a constant marginal effect on optimal consumption rate.

Table 5-5 Impact of Various Capital Flexibility of Output on Optimal Consumption Rate

Parameter	ρ(%)	θ	g	α	n (%)	Δ (%)	CR* (%)	Changes of CR* caused by the 5 percentage-point increase of α (per percentage point)
Case 1	5.26	1.5	0.12	0.65	1.87	9.6	67.72	—
Case 2	5.26	2.5	0.12	0.70	1.87	9.6	65.24	-2.48
Benchmark	5.26	3.5	0.12	0.75	1.87	9.6	62.75	-2.48
Case 3	5.26	4.5	0.12	0.80	1.87	9.6	60.27	-2.48
Case 4	5.26	5.5	0.12	0.85	1.87	9.6	57.79	-2.48

5.2.3.5. Impact of Population Growth Rate on Optimal Consumption Rate

As Table 5-6 shows, to analyse the impact of population growth rate on China's optimal consumption rate, we compare the impact of different population growth rates of output on the optimal consumption rate, taking 1.87 percent as the benchmark population growth rate, while other parameters remain unchanged. We can see from Equation (5-31) that population growth rate has a negative impact on optimal consumption rate. In other words, the increase of population growth rate causes the decline of optimal consumption rate. Specifically speaking, when population growth rate progressively rises from -0.13 percent to 0.87 percent, 1.87 percent, 2.87 percent and 3.87 percent, optimal consumption rate, respectively, decreases by 1.59 percentage points. As population growth rate gradually rises, consumption rate remains the same, which indicates that raising population growth rate has a constant marginal effect on optimal consumption rate.

Table 5-6 Impact of Various Population Growth Rates on Optimal Consumption Rate

Parameter	ρ(%)	θ	g	α	n (%)	δ (%)	CR* (%)	Changes of CR* caused by the 1 percentage-point increase of n (per percentage point)
Case 1	5.26	1.5	0.12	0.65	-0.13	9.6	65.93	—
Case 2	5.26	2.5	0.12	0.70	0.87	9.6	64.34	-1.59
Benchmark	5.26	3.5	0.12	0.75	1.87	9.6	62.75	-1.59
Case 3	5.26	4.5	0.12	0.80	2.87	9.6	61.17	-1.59
Case 4	5.26	5.5	0.12	0.85	3.87	9.6	59.58	-1.59

5.2.3.6. Impact of Depreciation Rate on Optimal Consumption Rate

As Table 5-7 shows, to analyse the impact of depreciation rate on China's optimal consumption rate, we compare the impact of different depreciation rates of output on the optimal consumption rate, taking 9.6 percent as the benchmark depreciation rate, while other parameters remain unchanged. We can see from Equation (5-32) that depreciation rate has a negative impact on optimal consumption rate. In other words, the rise of depreciation rate results in the decrease of optimal consumption rate. Specifically speaking, when depreciation rate progressively rises from 7.6 percent to 8.6 percent, 9.6 percent, 10.6 percent and 11.6 percent, optimal consumption rate, respectively, decreases by 1.59 percentage points. As depreciation rate gradually goes up, consumption rate remains the same, which indicates that raising depreciation rate has a constant marginal effect on optimal consumption rate.

Table 5-7 Impact of Various Depreciation Rates on Optimal Consumption Rate

Parameter	ρ(%)	θ	g	α	n (%)	δ (%)	CR* (%)	Changes of CR* caused by the 1 percentage-point increase of δ (per percentage point)
Case 1	5.26	1.5	0.12	0.65	-0.13	7.6	65.93	—
Case 2	5.26	2.5	0.12	0.70	0.87	8.6	64.34	-1.59
Benchmark	5.26	3.5	0.12	0.75	1.87	9.6	62.75	-1.59
Case 3	5.26	4.5	0.12	0.80	2.87	10.6	61.17	-1.59
Case 4	5.26	5.5	0.12	0.85	3.87	11.6	59.58	-1.59

5.3 Summary and Policy Suggestions

In Chapter 5, we analyse the explicit solution of optimal consumption rate within the framework of the Ramsey model with endogenous saving-consumption under the condition that optimal consumption rate is defined as the consumption rate achieved when the economy reaches the steady state. In addition, we discuss how the changes of exogenous parameters affect optimal consumption rate and simulate the extent of impact of various parameters. Based on the model analysis and the numerical simulation result, we make the following conclusions:

First, optimal consumption rate depends on discount rate (ρ), the coefficient of relative risk aversion (θ), technological progress (g), capital flexibility of output (α), population growth rate (n), depreciation rate (δ) and other exogenous parameters. Through calibrating the parameters based on China's actual economic situation and the previous research carried out by domestic and foreign scholars, we conclude that China's optimal consumption rate is 62.75 percent since the reform and opening-up.

Next, according to the explicit solution of optimal consumption rate, discount rate (ρ), the coefficient of relative risk aversion (θ) and technological progress (g) have a positive impact on optimal consumption rate; technological progress (g) has an uncertain impact; capital flexibility of output (α), population growth rate (n) and depreciation rate (δ) have a negative impact.

Furthermore, the numerical simulation result shows that capital flexibility of output (α), population growth rate (n) and depreciation rate (δ) all have a constant marginal effect on optimal consumption rate: (i) When capital flexibility of output (α) rises by 5 percentage points, optimal consumption rate falls by 2.48 percentage points; (ii) When population growth rate (n) and depreciation rate (δ) increase by 1 percentage point, optimal consumption rate decreases by 1.59 percentage points. Since the condition that ρ<θ (n+δ) is met, the rise of rate of technological progress will result in the increase of optimal consumption rate and discount rate (ρ), the coefficient of relative risk aversion (θ) and technological progress (g) have a decreasing marginal effect on optimal consumption rate.

Finally, among the six exogenous parameters including discount rate (ρ), the coefficient of relative risk aversion (θ), technological progress (g), capital flexibility of output (α), population growth rate (n) and depreciation rate (δ), the coefficient of relative risk aversion (θ) has the largest impact on optimal consumption rate. The impact of one-unit change of θ is ten times larger than that of other parameters.

Given the fact that China's consumption rate is relatively low compared to the world level, we believe that we can make consumption rate converge towards its optimal value through adjusting the above exogenous parameters. Specifically we put forward the following suggestion for measures:

First, continuity and coherence of the economic policies should be ensured to reduce the economic volatility because high volatility in inflation rate, economic growth rate and interest rate will affect the preference of consumers, especially the discount rate and the coefficient of relative risk aversion: when inflation rate and interest rate are high, the discount rate of consumers will be accordingly raised. Though such rise helps increase the optimal consumption rate, a high consumption rate is not necessarily good for economy. It should adapt to the current economic development stage; when inflation rate, economic growth rate, and interest rate are highly volatile, the uncertainty faced by consumers are increased, which leads to the deviation of consumption rate from its optimal level.

Second, the input into research and development should be increased. Our numerical simulation result shows that the rise of rate of technological progress will cause the increase of optimal consumption rate. Therefore, accelerating technology progress helps consumption rate converge towards its optimal value. After 40 years of development, the gap between the technology level of China and that of developed countries keeps narrowing. Since there is little room for improving the level of production technology through technology introduction, we should level up the input into independent research and development.

Third, capital flexibility of output should be reduced. High capital flexibility of output will cause the following problems: on one hand, high capital flexibility of output indicates low output elasticity of labour and also low labour income share. Relevant studies show that marginal propensity to consume of labour income is far greater than that of capital income, and low labour income share is bad for the continuous increase of consumption; on the other hand, high capital flexibility of output results in continuous high investment, eventually leading to capital overaccumulation and dynamic inefficiency of the economy.

Fourth, population should grow at a moderate rate. According to the simulation result, as population growth rate goes up, optimal consumption rate goes down. Though population growth contributes to economic growth, it takes long time to achieve such effect and will lead to the constant negative effect – aging of population.

Fifth, capital depreciation in some fields should be reduced, and the reduced part can be used for consumption to raise consumption rate. Many buildings in China are demolished shortly after they were built, which is a great waste of capital. Though the GDP rises, national welfare is not much improved. Thus proper plans should be made before capital investment to raise the efficiency of capital use.

Notes

1 Ramseyf. P., "A Mathematical Theory of Saving," *The Economic Journal* 38, no. 152 (December 1928): 543–559.
2 Cass David, "Optimum Growth in an Aggregative Model of Capital Accumulation," *Review of Economic Studies* 32, no. 3 (July 1965): 223–240.

3 Koopmans Tjalling C., *On the Concept of Optimal Economic Growth: In the Economic Approach to Development Planning* (Amsterdam: Elsvier, 1965).
4 Romer D., *Advanced Macroeconomics*, trans. Wu Huabin & Gong Guan (Shanghai University of Finance and Economics, 2014).
5 The setting of the parameters and the analysis here are based on the study of Ji et al. (2013). Ji Ming, Liu Shubiao, and Cen Shutian, "The Steady -state of Consumption Rate, Evolution and Reality Choice of China's Sustained and Balanced Economic Growth-Based on the Analytical Framework of R - C - K Model," *Economy and Management* 4 (2013).
6 $\bar{a}(t) = \dfrac{W(t)}{L(t)}$
7 Gu Liubao and Xiao Hongye, "Two Statistical Methods to Estimate Intertemporal Substitution Elasticity of Consumption of China," *Statistical Research* 9 (2004).
8 Gu Liubao, Yao Hailiang, and Chen Bofei, " Research on the Estimation of China's Household Intertemporal Substitution Elasticity of Consumption with Chronological Recursion," *China Economic Quarterly* 4 (2013).
9 Yao Hailiang, "A Research on Econometric Models of Consumer Behavior of Residents in Hebei Province," Thesis for the Master Degree, Hebei University, 2010.
10 Ji Ming, Liu Shubiao, and Cen Shutian, "The Steady-state of Consumption Rate, Evolution and Reality Choice of China's Sustained and Balanced Economic Growth-Based on the Analytical Framework of R - C - K Model," *Economy and Management* 4 (2013).
11 Wang Dihai and Gong Liutang, "On the Consumption and Savings in a Persisted-growth Economy," *Journal of Financial Research* 12 (2007).
12 Gu Liubao and Xiao Hongye, "Two Statistical Methods to Estimate Intertemporal Substitution Elasticity of Consumption of China," *Statistical Research* 9 (2004).
13 Perkins D.H., "Reforming China's Economic System," *Journal of Economic Literature* 26, no. 2 (1988): 601–645.
14 Wang Yang and Yao Yudong Yao, "Sources of China's Economic Growth 1952–1999: Incorporating Human Capital Accumulation," *World Bank Working Paper*, 2001.
15 Hall Robert E. and Jones Charles I., "Why do Some Countries Produce So Much More Output per Worker than Others?" *Quarterly Journal of Economics* 114, no. 1 (1999): 83–116.
16 Young Alwyn, "Gold into Base Metals: Productivity Growth in the People's Republic of China during the Reform Period," *Journal of Political Economy* 111, no. 6 (2003): 1220–1260.

Chapter 6

Optimal Consumption Rate in an Open Economy

Compared with a closed economy, an open economy offers more options for consumption and investment, which brings more complicated factors affecting aggregate consumption and consumption rate. In an open economy, the resources necessary for economic activities are not constrained by domestic resource endowment, and meanwhile, consumption and investment of commodities are not limited by domestic output. In other words, factor flow and commodity flow provide more options for the activities of production and consumption of an economy. For example, when the saving of a nation is quite sufficient (savings rate is relatively high), along with a domestic capital stock close to or even higher than the golden-rule level, then capital overaccumulation and decrease of capital efficiency caused by domestic investment can be avoided by engaging in foreign productive investment projects or granting loans to overseas borrowers. Therefore, it can be deduced that an open economy contributes to the stability of the national consumption, but economic openness has an uncertain impact on consumption rate: on one hand, currently there lacks literature on the impact of economic openness on consumption rate from the theoretical perspective[1]. Moreover, it is hard to define economic openness and deduce the relationship between them in an economic model; on the other hand, from the perspective of empirical research, studies that are carried out from different perspectives show different results regarding the impact of economic openness on consumption rate: Chen (2012)[2] points out that an open economy helps demonstrate the comparative advantage (labour-intensive production) of developing countries, which is beneficial for the increase of labour income share and household consumption rate; Yi and Yang (2015)[3] study on the factors affecting household consumption rate, using net export ratio to reflect economic openness. Their empirical research shows that the short-term effect of net export ratio on household consumption rate is -0.281 while the long-term effect is -0.915. Accordingly, there exists strong substitutability between domestic and foreign demand, which means economic openness has a negative impact on household consumption rate.

Currently, there is little literature on optimal consumption rate in an open economy, and the concept of optimal consumption rate has never been directly mentioned. Most of the studies analyse the existence of "golden rule" in an open economy. Sorensen and Whitta-Jacobsen (2012)[4] find out that there exists no such level of savings that maximizes consumption per capital (there exists no golden rule) in the Solow model of a small open economy, implying the non-existence of optimal consumption rate. Sun and Shou (2006)[5] deduce the optimal consumption path in an open economy and give the reasons behind the insufficiency of China's consumption as well as the corresponding measures. Song (2003)[6] discusses whether golden rule exists in an open economy in a general sense and compares the difference between a closed economy and an open economy in terms of the transition from non-golden-rule steady state to golden-rule steady state. Jing and Wang (2011)[7] use Cobb-Douglas equation to deduce the theoretical model determining consumption rate, respectively, in a closed economy and an open economy. The result shows that the theoretical consumption rates, respectively, in a closed economy and an open economy merely differ in net export rate. Furthermore, they use such model to project China's optimal consumption rates corresponding to various economic growth rates during *The 13th Five-Year Plan* period. For instance, when the economic growth rate is 7 percent, the theoretical optimal consumption rate in a closed economy is 65.51 percent while it is 64.11 percent in an open economy.

Given the fact that there lacks literature that directly studies on the impact of economic openness in final consumption rate from both theoretical and empirical perspectives, and this book does not centre around this topic, here we build a general equilibrium under the condition of open economy to discuss the determination of optimal consumption rate in an open economy. Since it is difficult to obtain the analytic solution due to the complexity of the model, we obtain the optimal consumption rate and analyse the factors affecting it through numerical simulation. The outline of this chapter is as follows: in section 6.1, we build the model to determine the optimal consumption rate under the condition of open economy based on the model built by Obstfeld and Rogoff (2010)[8]; in section 6.2, we calculate China's optimal consumption rate and the growth rate of consumption through numerical simulation.

6.1 Determination of Optimal Consumption Rate in an Open Economy

The model of open economy involves three kinds of markets, namely capital market, labour force market and commodity market. Among them, the first two markets are open markets while labour force market is a relatively closed market. In other words, capital and commodity can flow freely whereas labour force can't. The free flow of capital can be shown by the fact that residents can freely purchase the shares of domestic and foreign firms, which causes the domestic and foreign rates of return on capital to be equal after some factors such as risk premium are excluded. As for the free flow of commodity, it can be reflected by the current account condition in the national income accounts which further evolves to be the constraints on residents and firms. The labour demand of firms can only be satisfied by the labour supply from national residents. Consumers and firms are the two representative behavioural agents in the model. The former maximizes its utility through supplying labour and leasing capital, while the latter maximizes the profits through leasing capital and hiring labour force.

6.1.1 Consumer Behaviour

Consumers participate in the economy through providing factors to firms and purchasing products of firms. They maximize household utility through household consumption and saving/investment with income gaining from wages as well as interests and dividends of shares of firms[9]. Supposing the individual in a household has infinite life, we discuss the activities of optimal consumption and saving of an infinite-lived household.

6.1.1.1. Utility Function

Let's suppose the utility of consumers depends on the consumption level (C) of consumers and the level of leisure ($\bar{L}$-L). Specifically, the consuming product C includes both domestic products and imported trade products, and the level of leisure ($\bar{L}$-L) is the difference between the total time spent by consumers in each period and the time (L) spent on producing activities. Here u (C,$\bar{L}$-L) represents the instantaneous utility function of consumers which is a concave function with positive and decreasing marginal utility. The function satisfies the following conditions:

$$u_C > 0, u_{\bar{L}-L} > 0, u_{CC} < 0, u_{(\bar{L}-L)(\bar{L}-L)} < 0, u_{C(\bar{L}-L)} > 0$$

Supposing u (·) meets the Inada Conditions, we obtain:

$$\lim_{C \to 0} u_C = +\infty, \lim_{C \to \infty} u_c = 0, \lim_{(\bar{L}-L) \to 0} u_{(\bar{L}-L)} = \infty, \lim_{(\bar{L}-L) \to \infty} u_{(\bar{L}-L)} = 0$$

For convenience, the coefficient of relative risk aversion is assumed to be constant in the instantaneous utility function in this chapter:

$$u(C, \bar{L}-L) = \frac{1}{(1-1/\sigma)} \left[C^{\gamma} (\bar{L}-L)^{1-\gamma} \right]^{(1-1/\sigma)}$$

Here σ represents the elasticity of intertemporal substitution and γ stands for the relative share between consumption and leisure. We obtain the utility function of representative consumers as follows:

$$U_t = \sum_{s=t}^{\infty} \beta^{s-t} \frac{1}{(1-1/\sigma)} \left[C_s^\gamma (\bar{L} - L_s)^{1-\gamma} \right]^{(1-1/\sigma)}$$

Here β stands for discount factor, and ρ represents discount rate: $\beta = 1/(1+\rho)$.

6.1.1.2. Budget Constraint

x_{s+1} represents the shares of domestic firms possessed by consumers at the end of Period s, and d_s stands for the dividends paid by firms during Period s. When entering a period, an individual possesses the foreign assets and domestic shares purchased during the previous periods. He/she will gain interests and dividends from these assets with capital gains and capital loss from the possessed shares. In addition, he/she obtains labour income and then consumes. Savings are divided between the increment in foreign asset and the increment in value of shares and further kept in the next period. Therefore, the budget constraint of consumers is as follows:

$$B_{s+1} - B_s + V_s x_{s+1} - V_{s-1} x_s = rB_s + d_s x_s + (V_s - V_{s-1}) x_s + w_s L - C_s \quad (6\text{-}1)$$

Here B_{s+1} represents the foreign asset at the end of Period s, and V_s stands for the market price of domestic shares. Under perfect expectation, supposing the total rate of return on stocks equals the total interest rate, we assume that the foreign asset and domestic shares are no different in terms of margin:

$$1 + r = \frac{d_{s+1} + V_{s+1}}{V_s} \quad (6\text{-}2)$$

Based on the above assumption, we can illustrate the budget constraint in another way, in which Q_{s+1} represents the value of individual financial wealth at the end of the period, equalling the sum of foreign assets and value of domestic shares:

$$Q_{s+1} = B_{s+1} + V_s x_{s+1}$$

The above equation is always true under perfect expectation, which indicates:

$$d_s x_s + (V_s - V_{s-1})x_s = rV_{s-1}x_s \quad (6\text{-}3)$$

Equation (6-1) indicates a period of lag. Accordingly, when s>t, we simplify Equation (6-1) as follows:

$$Q_{s+1} - Q_s = rQ_s + w_s L - C_s$$

Such restriction is only true when there is no unexpected shock. As for s=t, we should apply Equation (6-1) here, and then obtain:

$$Q_{t+1} = (1+r)B_t + d_t x_t + V_t x_t + w_t L - C_t \quad (6\text{-}4)$$

We apply forward iterative method on Equation (6-4) to obtain intertemporal budget constraint:

$$\sum_{s=t}^{\infty} (\frac{1}{1+r})^{s-t} C_s = (1+r)B_t + d_t x_t + V_t x_t + \sum_{s=t}^{\infty} (\frac{1}{1+r})^{s-t} w_s L_s$$

$$= (1+r)B_t + (1+r)V_{t-1}x_t + \sum_{s=t}^{\infty} (\frac{1}{1+r})^{s-t} w_s L_s$$

$$= (1+r)Q_t + \sum_{s=t}^{\infty} (\frac{1}{1+r})^{s-t} w_s L_s \quad (6\text{-}5)$$

Such constraint restricts the consumption of consumers to be the sum of financial wealth at the initial period and present value of after-tax labour income. Additionally, a non-Ponzi Game condition needs to be imposed on household activities:

$$\lim_{T\to\infty}(\frac{1}{1+r})^T Q_{t+T+1} = 0$$

The present value of the assets of consumers cannot be below 0 at infinity time, which means consumers cannot have negative assets at infinity time in the future.

6.1.1.3. Optimization of Consumers Behaviour

According to the above assumptions, the problem in decision-making of consumers is to maximize the lifetime utility function (U) of consumers while the budget constraint and the non-Ponzi Game condition are satisfied, given the initial financial wealth (Q_t). Therefore, the optimization problem of representative consumers can be summarized as:

$$MaxU_t = \sum_{s=t}^{\infty} \beta^{s-t} \frac{1}{(1-1/\sigma)} \left[C_s^\gamma (\bar{L} - L_s)^{1-\gamma} \right]^{(1-1/\sigma)}$$

Constrained by the following equation, the utility is maximized:

$$\sum_{s=t}^{\infty} \beta^{s-t} (\frac{1}{1+r})^{s-t} C_s = (1+r)q_t + \sum_{s=t}^{\infty} \beta^{s-t} (\frac{1}{1+r})^{s-t} w_s L_s$$

6.1.2 Firm Behaviour

6.1.2.1. Market Value of Firm Stocks

Equation (6-2) shows that during Period t, we have:

$$V_t = \frac{d_{t+1}}{1+r} + \frac{V_{t+1}}{1+r} \tag{6-6}$$

Applying backward iterative method on Equation (6-4), we obtain:

$$V_t = \sum_{s=t+1}^{\infty} (\frac{1}{1+r})^{s-t} d_s \tag{6-7}$$

Supposing the condition that excludes self-fulfilling speculative asset price bubble is true, we have:

$$\lim_{T \to \infty} (\frac{1}{1+r})^T V_{t+T} = 0 \qquad (6\text{-}8)$$

Given the hypothesis in Equation (6-8), Equation (6-7) indicates that with t+1 as the initial Period, the market value of a firm in Period t equals the discounted value of the dividends that the firm will pay to shareholders in the future. Thus V_t is sometimes called the market value of a firm after payment of dividends.

6.1.2.2. Firm Behaviour

The dividend paid by a firm in a period is its spot profit, equalling the return ($Y_s - w_s L_s$) minus investment expenditure. Accordingly, Equation (6-7) implies:

$$V_t = \sum_{s=t+1}^{\infty} \left(\frac{1}{1+r}\right)^{s-t} [A_s F(K_s, L_s) - w_s L_s - (K_{s+1} - K_s)] \qquad (6\text{-}9)$$

Firms make the policies of employment and investment for the current period to maximize the present value of dividends in the current and future periods to equal $d_t + V_t$. Given K_t, we obtain:

$$d_s + V_t = \sum_{s=t}^{\infty} (\frac{1}{1+r})^{s-t} [A_s F(K_s, L_s) - w_s L_s - (K_{s+1} - K_s)]$$

Deriving the last expression, we can tell that (with s>t) for a firm, capital and labour force share similar first-order maximization condition:

$$A_s F_K(K_s, L_s) = r \qquad (6\text{-}10)$$

$$A_s F_L(K_s, L_s) = w_s \qquad (6\text{-}11)$$

Furthermore, as capital can only be adjusted after a period, an unexpected shock in a period may cause the difference between $A_s F_K (K_s, L_s)$ and r^{10}. However, the input in labour force can soon be adjusted. Thus the first-order condition of labour force is true in the initial Period t exactly after the shock. Assuming capital freely flows in an open economy, we deduce that the marginal return of domestic capital will eventually converge towards r; additionally, factor of labour is unable to flow freely among nations. In this way, w, which is the function with respect to technological level (A) and international interest rate (r), is affected by A (as well as r).

According to Euler's theorem, $AF(K, L) = AF_K K + AF_L K = rK + wL$. Substituting the equation into Equation (6-9), we obtain:

$$V_t = \sum_{s=t+1}^{\infty} (\frac{1}{1+r})^{s-t} [rK_s - (K_{s+1} - K_s)]$$

$$= \sum_{s=t+1}^{\infty} (\frac{1}{1+r})^{s-t} [(1+r)K_s - K_{s+1})] = K_{t+1} \qquad (6\text{-}12)$$

Therefore, the maximized market value of a firm after the payment of dividends exactly equals the capital inputted in production in the next period. Under equilibrium, Q=B+K: the financial wealth of a nation at the end of a period is equal to the sum of its net foreign assets and capital. With Equation (6-8) and the first equation in Equation (6-4), we obtain the budget constraint of representative consumers:

$$\sum_{s=1}^{\infty} (\frac{1}{1+r})^{s-t} C_s = [(1+r)B_t + (1+r)K_t] + \sum_{s=t}^{\infty} (\frac{1}{1+r})^{s-t} w_s L_s$$

$$= (1+r)Q_t + \sum_{s=t}^{\infty} (\frac{1}{1+r})^{s-t} w_s L_s \qquad (6\text{-}13)$$

Equation (6-13) shows that the present value of consumption of representative consumers equals the return on assets in the current period plus the present value of labour force in the future periods.

6.1.3 Market Equilibrium

The optimization problem of representative consumers can be summarized as:

$$MaxU_t = \sum_{s=t}^{\infty} \beta^{s-t} \frac{1}{(1-1/\sigma)} \left[C_s^{\gamma} (\bar{L} - L_s)^{1-\gamma} \right]^{(1-1/\sigma)}$$

$$s.t. \sum_{s=t}^{\infty} \beta^{s-t} (\frac{1}{1+r})^{s-t} C_s = (1+r)Q_t + \sum_{s=t}^{\infty} (\frac{1}{1+r})^{s-t} w_s L_s \qquad (6\text{-}14)$$

Considering the first-order condition of optimization problem of firms:

$$A_s F_K(K_s, L_s) = r \qquad (6\text{-}10)$$

$$A_s F_L(K_s, L_s) = w_s \qquad (6\text{-}11)$$

When the economy achieves equilibrium, markets of capital, product and factor are cleared at the same time. It is worth-noted that in the capital market, the return on domestic assets (stocks of firms) equals the return on foreign assets deducting risk premium, while the supply of both domestic and foreign assets are equal to the demand ($V_t x_{t+1} = K_{t+1}$). The clearing of labour force market implies that labour supply is equal to labour demand and the equilibrium in product market shows that output equals the sum of consumption and investment. These conditions can be expressed by Equation (6-10) and (6-14)[11].

According to the optimal solver (Obstfeld & Rogoff, 1996), the following first-order optimal conditions can be obtained after Equation (6-14) of utility maximization is solved:

$$u_{\bar{L}-L}(C_s, \bar{L} - L_s) = u_C(C_s, \bar{L} - L_s) w_s \Rightarrow \bar{L} - L = \frac{1-\gamma}{\gamma w_s} C_s \qquad (6\text{-}15)$$

$$u_C(C_s, \bar{L} - L_s) = (1+r)\beta u_C(C_{s+1}, \bar{L} - L_{s+1}) \Rightarrow C_{s+1} = (\frac{w_{s+1}}{w_s})^{(1-\gamma)(1-\sigma)} (1+r)^{\sigma} \beta^{\sigma} C_s \qquad (6\text{-}16)$$

Equation (6-15) shows that based on the distribution of time in every period s between work and leisure, the marginal utility of leisure equals the marginal consumption by wages. Equation (6-16) is an Euler equation, indicating that the substitution relationship between current consumption and future consumption depends on growth of wages, interest rate and discount factor[12].

Converting Equation (6-16), we obtain the growth rate of consumption and the expression of international interest rate (r):

$$g_c^* = \frac{C_{s+1}}{C_s} - 1 = (\frac{w_{s+1}}{w_s})^{(1-\gamma)(1-\sigma)}(1+r)^\sigma \beta^\sigma - 1 \qquad (6\text{-}17)$$

$$r = (1+g_c^*)^{1/\sigma} / \left[\beta(w_{s+1}/w_s)^{(1-\gamma)(1-\sigma)}\right] - 1 \qquad (6\text{-}18)$$

Combining the Euler Equation (6-14) with budget constraint, we have the optimal consumption of representative consumers:

$$C^* = \frac{(1+r)Q_t + \sum_{s=t}^{\infty} \beta^{s-t}(\frac{1}{1+r})^{s-t} w_s L_s}{\sum_{s=t}^{\infty}\left[(1+r)^{\sigma-1}\beta^\sigma\right]^{s-t}(w_s/w_t)^{(1-\gamma)(1-\sigma)}} \qquad (6\text{-}19)$$

Equation (6-19) implies that the optimal consumption of representative consumers depends on two factors: domestic and foreign return on assets and discount value of labour income.

Combining Equation (6-10) with Equation (6-18) and using Cobb-Douglas production function, we can then obtain the optimal growth rate of consumption per capita (g_C^*). By calibrating discount factor β, the coefficient of relative risk aversion σ, proportion of consumption in the utility function γ and wages w (A, r), we obtain the numerical solution of the optimal growth rate of consumption. Since consumption plus saving equals total income, output and capital stock need to grow at the same rate as consumption on the balanced path of the economy to keep the economic balance. In that sense, the optimal economic growth rate is also g_C^*.

6.1.4 Current Account and Optimal Consumption

In an open economy, issues around optimal consumption and optimal consumption rate always concern the dynamic equilibrium of current account. In the intertemporal analysis, current account is defined as the inter-period changes of net foreign assets, that is to say, $CA_t = B_{t+1} - B_t = Y_t + rB_t - C_t - I_t$. When the current account of a nation achieves equilibrium ($CA_t = 0$), then the nation reaches external equilibrium. But in the intertemporal research on open economy, the maximization of welfare (utility) rather than the equilibrium of current account is the ultimate economic goal of a nation. Accordingly, the equilibrium of current account is not the normal state of the economy. When a national income fails to cover the optimal consumption resulted from a short-term decrease due to external shocks, the nation can borrow foreign loans to avoid the deviation of consumption from its optimal path. In this way, the current account deficit happen. On the contrary, when the consumption demand of a nation is insufficient, resulting in the deviation of consumption from its optimal path, the nation has to make it up with export demand, causing the current account surplus. Furthermore, current account is also dynamically influenced by the deviation of output (Y_t), government purchase (G_t) and Investment (I_t) from their respective optimal path.

6.2 Numerical Simulation of the Optimal Consumption Rate in an Open Economy

6.2.1 Parameter Calibration

Regarding optimal consumption as well as optimal consumption rate, optimal consumption and optimal output need to be calculated first. Equation (6-19) indicates that the equation of optimal consumption is a non-linear equation with respect to related variables. Thus we apply numerical simulation to solve the equation, which is the same method used to obtain the optimal output in a steady-state economy. For convenience, the consumption rate achieved when the economy is at its steady state is defined as the ratio of the optimal consumption to the optimal output and also the optimal consumption rate in an open economy.

Equation (6-19) shows that as long as the exogenous parameters are valued within reasonable ranges based on China's actual economic development, including discount factor(β), the elasticity of intertemporal substitution (σ), the relative share between consumption and leisure (γ), the elasticity of output capital (α), the coefficient of productivity (A) and the growth rate of wages (w_{s+1}/w_s), the simulated value of optimal consumption rate can be obtained through numerical simulation.

As for discount factor (β), in empirical research, its general range is [0.95, 0.98]. Considering that numerical simulation is applied to analyse the relationship between discount factor and optimal consumption rate, we, respectively, take 0.85, 0.90 and 0.95 as the values of discount factor. As for the elasticity of intertemporal substitution (σ), we take 1, 3 and 5; for the relative share between consumption and leisure (γ), we take 0.75; and for the elasticity of output capital (α), based on the previous conclusions made in Chapter 3, we take 0.25, 0.50 and 0.75 to, respectively, denote the various stages of economic development. As for the coefficient of productivity (A), we assume A_1 to be $0.5^{-\alpha}$ and A_2 to be 1.05 percent A_1. In other words, the rate of technological progress is 5 percent. As for the growth rate of wages (w_{s+1}/w_s), since wages vary with A, we assume $w_{s+1}/w_s = 1.05$.

6.2.2 Numerical Simulation and Result Analysis

Based on the above parameters and the constraint conditions in Equation (6-17), (6-18) and (6-19), we obtain the equilibrium value of the variables including consumption, investment and financial wealth. As we mainly look into the equilibrium consumption rate in an open economy, we divide equilibrium consumption by equilibrium output after having the equilibrium solution to obtain equilibrium consumption rate (see the optimal consumption rates in Table 6-1).

Table 6-1 Equilibrium Consumption Rate in an Open Economy (Optimal Consumption Rate percent)

Optimal Consumption Rate	σ=1			σ=3			σ=5		
	β=0.85	β=0.90	β=0.95	β=0.85	β=0.90	β=0.95	β=0.85	β=0.90	β=0.95
α=0.25	75.7	73.4	67.6	72.5	64.7	51.1	68.6	61.9	52.4
α=0.50	77.8	76.2	73.6	77.3	76.2	71.6	78.7	72.8	68.5
α=0.75	79.1	78.5	76.4	80.4	78.3	75.8	80.8	78.7	75.7

Table 6-1 shows the impact of the two parameters that reflect consumption behaviour of households on equilibrium consumption rate: (i) When other parameters are given, discount factor is inversely proportional to equilibrium consumption rate. In other words, a higher discount factor implies greater patience consumers have to postpone consumption in the future, thus leading to a lower equilibrium consumption rate. (ii) When other parameters are given, elasticity of substitution is in negative correlation with equilibrium consumption rate. Higher elasticity of intertemporal substitution indicates a lower equilibrium consumption rate, which means consumers are more willing to substitute current consumption between future periods.

The range of equilibrium consumption rate with different parameters is [51.1 percent, 80.8 percent]. With all parameters in line with actual economic conditions, we take the median of 66.0 percent. In other words, the optimal consumption rate in an open economy is determined to be 66.0 percent. Such a result is close to that of the Solow model and the Ramsey model, which can be explained from the following two aspects: on one hand, the model of consumption in an open economy is essentially a long-term model where the representative behavioural agents (consumers and firms) are assumed to have infinite lives and thus their consumption behaviour differ little from each other in different long-term growth models; on the other hand, the major difference between model of open economy and model of closed economy lies in that the former can use external resources to balance consumption. But except those high-income countries with high-tech advantages which can export production factors such as technology and capital to raise national income and further increase consumption rate[13], most countries differ little from each other in consumption behaviour and closed economy.

The equilibrium consumption rate calculated through the model of intertemporal equilibrium in an open economy is close to the world average level as well as the level of consumption rate of developed countries (high-income countries). Such a result explains the consumption behaviour of these countries. But this number is far from China's level of consumption rate, which is higher by 16.4 percentage points than China's final consumption rate in 2016 (53.6 percent). In that sense, is this model suitable for illustrating China's consumption behaviour?

In a model of open economy, complete market economy and completely open economy are assumed, which is contrary to China's incomplete marketization[14] and incompletely open economy. Therefore, the setting of parameters in the numerical simulation might not accord with China's actual circumstance. First, the variable of wage in the model is assumed to be endogenous, which means a household is assumed to independently supply based on its economic circumstance. But in China, due to excess supply of labour force in the dual economy, the variable of wage is exogenously given, indicating that the household decision on labour supply is slightly affected by wage. However, with the coming of Lewis Turning Point over recent years, the demographic dividend resulted from excess supply of labour force has been gradually disappearing (Wang & Zhang, 2014)[15], and wage has an increasingly obvious impact on adjusting the supply and demand of labour force. Next, the variable of interest rate in the model is assumed to be decided by financial market and equal to the world interest rate. In China, the interest rate is controlled by the monetary policies of the People's Bank of China. But as China has been increasingly opening up, the interaction of interest rate between China and other countries in the world is increasingly strengthened. Furthermore, since the reform and opening-up, measured from the aspect of both trade and investment, the extent of China' opening-up has continuously improved. Finally, the variable of technology in the model is assumed to be 5 percent. As a latecomer, China can promote technological progress through technology introduction. Yet as China gets closer to the frontier of technology, China needs to drive technological progress through independent research, which is the reason why China implements the innovation-driven development strategy.

In conclusion, the equilibrium model of open economy can explain China's consumption behaviour. Comparing with China's actual economic circumstance and the evolution path of the optimal consumption rate, we find out that in the Solow model, the Ramsey model and the model of open economy, China's final consumption rates are all much lower than its optimal consumption rate. The result implies that China's economic development deviates from its optimal development path.

First, as the reform is progressively advanced, the uncertainty faced by households keeps increasing, causing household propensity to consume to continuously decrease while household income remains rising[16]. The previous model analysis shows that the two parameters including discount factor and elasticity of intertemporal substitution are inversely proportional to propensity to consume. During the first stage of China's reform (1978–1991), the process of reform went relatively slowly and just a few areas were involved. As a result, household consumption behaviour was just slightly influenced and household propensity to consume moderately decreased despite a little volatility. When the reform entered the second stage (1992 till now), especially after 2002, household propensity to consume sharply fell. Though the income of residents kept rising, it grew at a lower rate than the GDP did. Moreover, the decrease of propensity to consume resulted in the fall of the proportion of consumption in China's GDP, which was directly reflected by the decrease of China's final consumption rate. The changes in household consumption behaviour might be explained from the following aspects: (i) As the reform was further promoted, the employees in state-owned enterprises no longer have a permanent job. The resettlement of laid-off workers made households raise their savings to deal with uncertainty. (ii) The marketization of higher education have made households to increase their savings to cover the high expense of college education. Prior to the reform of education, college students did not have to pay for the tuition fees and the nation guaranteed job assignments for college graduates. After the reform, in addition to the high tuition fees, they may face unemployment after graduation. Thus households make savings for both the tuition fees and the potential unemployment of the offspring. (iii) The reform of medial system largely increases household expenses of medical service. With an uncertain outlook for the reform, the uncertainty faced by households increases, leading to the increase of both patience and willingness to substitute during household consumption.

Next, the high housing price resulting from China's housing monetization reform consumes most of the household disposable income, which further leaves little room for household consumption. In the national accounting system, household purchase of house is considered as investment (residential Investment) rather than consumption, which is mainly because of the following two characteristics of housing: (i) It is the long life service of housing. The service life of China's commodity housing reaches 70 years; (ii) The huge expense on housing due to the high housing price can exhaust household savings and even overdraw future income. From the beginning of purchase of housing to the end of mortgage loan, a major portion of income is used to repay the loan. Given the household income level and the growth rate, the increase of expenses on housing causes the decrease of expenses on purchase on other consumer goods and services, which further results in the weak consumption. The study carried out by Tan (2010)[17] indicates that after 2005, the rapid rise of housing price results in the continuous growth of Gini coefficient which measures the wealth gap and the number has exceeded 40 percent of the international alarm level. The rapid growth of housing price and the resulting bubbles lead to the crowding-out effect on consumption, and such effect has become increasingly obvious.

Finally, in an open economy, when the consumption is too weak to stay on its optimal path, the nation needs to make it up with export demand, resulting in current account surplus. Since the reform and opening-up, investment makes far greater contribution to economic growth than consumption and export do. When the weak external demand leads to slow economic growth, the rapid economic growth can only be maintained by stimulating domestic demand. Since China has kept stimulating investment to promote economic growth, the room for consumption growth is occupied to some extent, which results in some severe economic problems such as overcapacity.

6.3 Summary

In Chapter 6, we build a model of intertemporal general equilibrium. With calibration of parameters in the model, we discuss the determination and factors affecting optimal consumption rate in an open economy through numerical simulation and make the following conclusions:

First, the equilibrium model of open economy can explain China's consumption behaviour. Comparing with China's actual economic circumstance and the evolution path of the optimal consumption rate, we find out that in the Solow model, the Ramsey model and the model of open economy, China's final consumption rates are all much lower than its optimal consumption rate. The result implies that China's economic development deviates from its optimal development path.

Next, the range of optimal consumption rate in an open economy with different parameters is [51.1 percent, 80.8 percent]. With all parameters in line with actual economic conditions, we take the median of 66.0 percent. In other words, the optimal consumption rate in an open economy is determined to be 66.0 percent. Such a result is close to that of the Solow model and the Ramsey model.

Finally, the impact of the two parameters which reflect household consumption behaviour on equilibrium consumption is as follows: (i) When other parameters are given, discount factor is inversely proportional to equilibrium consumption rate. In other words, a higher discount factor implies greater patience consumers have to postpone consumption in the future, thus causing a lower equilibrium consumption rate. (ii) When other parameters are given, elasticity of substitution is in negative correlation with equilibrium consumption rate. Higher elasticity of intertemporal substitution indicates a lower equilibrium consumption rate, which means consumers are more willing to substitute current consumption between future periods.

Notes

1 Many scholars decompose China's current account into smoothed current account and tilted current account in order to analyse the impact of economic openness on

final (household) consumption. Yet there is little literature discussing such topic from theoretical perspective.

2 Chen Binkai, "Income Inequality and Consumption Demand: Theory and Evidence from China," *Nankai Economic Studies* 1 (2012).
3 Yi Xingjian and Yang Biyun, "An Empirical Test on the Deciding Factors of Household Consumption Rate in Countries (Regions) All over the World," *The Journal of World Economy* 1 (2015): 3–24.
4 Sorensen P. B. and Whitta-Jacobsen H. J., *Introducing Advanced Macroeconomics: Growth and Business Cycles (2nd Edition)*, trans. Wang Wenping et al. (China Renmin University Press, 2012).
5 Sun Feng and Shou Weigunag, "Optimal Consumption, Economic Growth and Dynamics of Current Account-Reflecting on China's Open-economy from the Angle of Intertemporal," *The Study of Finance and Economics* 5 (2001).
6 Song Jinyu, "Study on Gold Rule of Capital under Open Economy," *Journal of Yunnan University of Finance and Economics* 4 (2003).
7 Jing Linbo and Wang Xuefeng, "Theoretical Model and Its Application to the Determination of Consumption Rate," *Economic Perspectives* 11 (2011).
8 Obstfeld Maurice and Rogoff Kenneth, *Foundations of international Macroeconomics*, trans. Liu Hongzhong (China Financial Publishing House, 2010).
9 V_t represents the price of ownership of future firm's full profits (since Period t+1) during Period t.
10 Here r represents the level of international interest rate which is not affected by the economic conditions of a nation.
11 Generally, the variables of supply and demand should be distinguished in the model with the superscript of s denoting supply and the superscript of d representing demand. For example, supply of labour in the utility function is denoted as L^s, while demand of labour in the production function is denoted as L_d. For convenience, the two variables are not distinguished in this book.
12 Since we *endogenize the labor force* in the model, we add the item of growth rate of wages in Equation (6–14): $\left(\dfrac{W_s}{W_{s+1}}\right)^{(1-\gamma)(\sigma-1)}$.
13 In an open economy, the export of high technology and the domestic overcapitalization contribute to the increase of national income and consumption rate. The main reason behind this is that the denominator in the formula for calculating consumption rate is the GDP rather than the GNP.
14 The research on marketization index carried out by Wang Xiaolu and other Chinese scholars annually publishes the national as well as the provincial marketization index, which shows that China's marketization keeps being promoted, yet far from the level of marketization of Western countries.

15 Wang Bida and Zhang Zhongjie, "International Industrial Capital Influx and Emergence of Lewis Turning Point," *Economist* 7 (2014).
16 At the beginning of the reform and opening-up, China's final consumption rate was nearly 70 percent, which was close to the world average level.
17 Tan Zhengxun: "Theoretical and empirical researches on housing bubbles and their influence on resident consumption in China," *Economist* 3 (2010).

Chapter 7

Optimal Consumption Rate in the Dynamic Stochastic General Equilibrium (DSGE) Model

As a significant tool in the "Macroeconomics Lab", the Dynamic Stochastic General Equilibrium (DSGE) model is widely applied in the analysis of modern macroeconomics to investigate how economic agents respond to the changes of the environment within the theoretical framework of dynamic general equilibrium, where all endogenous economic variables are simultaneously determined and microeconomics lays a foundation. Such a tool is generally used by academic circles, central banks and other public economic institutions to analyse macroeconomic issues.

Currently, most literature analysing China's consumption with the DSGE model focuses on the impact of various exogenous shocks on household consumption rate and government consumption as well as the relationship between them (Huang, 2005[1]; Jia & Guo, 2012[2]; Wang & Xiao, 2015[3]; Mao et al., 2013[4]). The main literature studying consumption rate includes the following: Gong and Li (2013)[5] build the model of dynamic general equilibrium to re-explain the continuous fall of the consumption rate during China's economic development.

They conclude that the high proportion of capital return is a major reason for the decrease of China's consumption rate and further propose that the proportion of capital return should be lowered so as to suppress the fall of the consumption rate. Wu and Chao (2014)[6] discuss the impact of structure of fiscal expenditure on household consumption rate and its transmission mechanism within the framework of dynamic general equilibrium. The results demonstrate that among the variables including government consumption expenditure, government transfer payment, government investment expenditure and government service expenditure, government consumption expenditure has a crowding-out effect which lowers household consumption while the rest variables all have a crowding-in effect that raises household consumption. Wu et al. (2014)[7] involve the characteristics of household consumption including uncertainty, credit constraints and habit formation in the DSGE model to study on the influencing mechanism of credit constraints and habit formation on China's macroeconomic fluctuation and household consumption rate. They find that habit formation effectively helps smooth household consumption, further weakening the impact of uncertainty on household consumption rate and savings rate.

At present, since there lacks literature that studies consumption rate as well as optimal consumption rate with the DSGE model and a unified analysis paradigm, we try to build a DSGE model to look into consumption rate. Considering that the DSGE model is based on the optimization of economic agents, we define the consumption rate in a steady-state economy as the optimal consumption rate for convenience to further analyse how optimal consumption rate and economic output respond to various exogenous shocks. The outline of Chapter 7 is as follows. In section 7.1, we build a dynamic general equilibrium model of optimal consumption rate based on optimized behaviour of three economic agents including household, firm and government; in section 7.2, we calculate China's optimal consumption rate through parameter calibration and impulse response analysis and investigate the response of optimal consumption rate to various exogenous shocks.

7.1 Theoretical Framework of the DSGE Model

With a dynamic general equilibrium model based on the economic behaviour of household, firm and government, we calculate China's optimal consumption rate through parameter calibration and impulse response analysis to study on the response of output and optimal consumption rate to various exogenous shocks.

7.1.1. Model Assumptions

7.1.1.1 Representative Consumers

Supposing that there are numerous homogeneous consumers and each one of them has infinite life, we extract a representative consumer. Also, supposing the utility level of consumers depends on the level of leisure and consumption, consumers have one unit of time endowment and it is allocated to labour supply (L_t) and leisure (1-L_t); based on the method developed by Ludger Linneman (2005)[8] and Li (2012)[9], we include consumption habits in the utility function. Accordingly, the consumption function of consumers can be demonstrated as: $C_t^* = (1-\phi) C_t + \phi (C_t - C_{t-1}) = C_t - \phi C_{t-1}$. Here ϕ represents the coefficient reflecting continuity of habit. If $\phi=0$, then consumption is barely affected by consumption (consumption function degenerates to general form); if $\phi=1$, the previous consumption level has a relatively large impact on consumption in the current period[10]. Representative consumers maximize the lifetime expected utility through adjusting the decisions on consumption and saving and labour supply in every period:

$$MaxE_0 \left\{ \sum_{t=0}^{\infty} \beta^t \frac{C_t^{*1-\theta} L_t^{1+\sigma}}{1-\theta} \right\} \qquad (7\text{-}1)$$

Here E_0 represents conditional expectation operator based on the information in Period 0; β represents intertemporal discount factor[11]; $\phi>0$ stands for the coefficient reflecting continuity of habit; θ stands for the coefficient of relative risk aversion of representative consumers; σ

represents labour preference elasticity; C_t represents the consumption level of representative consumers in Period t.

The budget constraint of representative consumers is as follows:

$$C_t + S_t + T_t = W_t L_t^s + (1+R_t)K_t^s \qquad (7\text{-}2)$$

Here S_t represents the savings in Period t; T_t denotes the lump-sum tax consumers paid to the government in Period t; W_t represents the labour remuneration (wage rate) in Period t-1; K^s_t and L^s_t, respectively, stand for the capital stock and labour force consumers supply in Period t; R_t stands for the rental rate in Period t. Budget constraint implies that the sum of consumption, saving and tax expenditure of consumers should not exceed the sum of consumers' factor income of both labour supply and capital supply.

7.1.1.2. Representative Firms

Firms need to obtain the optimal value that maximizes the utility of labour force and capital. The production of ultimate output Y requires service of labour force and capital. When factor price is given to firms, capital and labour force are hired in Period t to maximize profits. The applied technology comes from the Cobb-Douglas production function with constant returns to scale:

$$Y_t = A_t (K_t^d)^a (L_t^d)^{1-a}, 0 \le a \le 1 \qquad (7\text{-}3)$$

Here Y_t represents the output in Period t; A_t denotes the total factor productivity in Period t; K^d_t and L^d_t stand for the demand of capital and labour; ε^A_t stands for the technological shock in Period t. Supposing it obeys the first-order autoregressive process (AR (1) process), then we obtain:

$$\log A_t = (1-\rho_A)\log \overline{A} + \rho_A \log A_{t-1} + \varepsilon_t^A, \varepsilon_t^A \sim N(0, \sigma_A^2) \qquad (7\text{-}4)$$

Here $\bar{A}$ represents the steady-state value of A_t and $\{\varepsilon^A_t\}_{t=0}^{\infty}$ represents independent and identically distributed random variables. Additionally, capital stock is computed with perpetual inventory method:

$$K_t = (1-\delta)K_{t-1} + I_t \tag{7-5}$$

The static maximization problem of firms is as follows:

$$Max\ \Pi = A_t(K_t^d)^{\alpha}(L_t^d)^{1-\alpha} - R_t K_t^d - W_t L_t^d \tag{7-6}$$

$$\text{s.t.}\ Y_t = A_t(K_t^d)^{\alpha}(L_t^d)^{1-\alpha}$$

$$K_t = (1-\delta)K_{t-1} + I_t$$

7.1.1.3. Government

Finally, we consider the function of the government as a taxation entity and a provider of commodity and service. We assume the lump-sum tax T_t imposed by the government on consumers is the expenditure G_t. Meanwhile the government budget in every period is balanced ($T_t=G_t$), along with G_t as an exogenous variable whose variation is dominated by the following equation:

$$\log G_t = (1-\rho_G)\log \bar{G} + \rho_G \log G_{t-1} + \varepsilon_1^G, \varepsilon_t^G \sim N(0, \sigma_G^2) \tag{7-7}$$

Here $\bar{G}$ represents the steady-state value of G_t and $\{\varepsilon_t^G\}_{t=0}^{\infty}$ represents independent and identically distributed random variables.

7.1.2 Model Equilibrium and First-Order Condition

Once the optimal decision of representative consumers and firms is obtained, we then look into the economic equilibrium of the model, which requires us to overall consider the decisions of the economic agent. On one hand, given the price of production factor, consumers make decisions to maximize the lifetime expected utility based on the amount of consumption C_t, the amount of savings (investment) S_t and the length of working time. On the other hand, given the price of production factor, the ultimate quantity of products produced by firms depends on their decisions on the amount of capital K_t and labour force L_t. Moreover, the government imposes tax, consumes and makes transfer payments based on budget constraint.

Competitive Equilibrium: The competitive equilibrium of economy is related to the sequences of consumption, leisure, saving (investment) of representative consumers $\{C_t, I-L_t, S_t\}_{t=0}^{\infty}$, and the capital and labour force used by firms $\{K_t, L_t\}_{t=0}^{\infty}$. Given the sequence of price $\{W_t, R_t\}_{t=0}^{\infty}$, the following conditions are satisfied:

(i) The optimization problem of consumers is solved.
(ii) Given the price of capital and labour force, the first-order condition on capital and labour force of firms is satisfied.
(iii) The feasibility constraint in the economy is satisfied.

The competitive equilibrium requires the markets of labour force, capital and commodity to be cleared. In other words, when equilibrium is achieved, $K^d_t = K^s_t$ (capital market is cleared), $L^d_t = L^s_t$ (labour force market is cleared) and $Y_t = C_t + I_t + G_t$ (labour force market is cleared).

Under the hypothesis of perfect competition, though sharing the same result with decentralized equilibrium, central planning equilibrium is much easier to solve. Therefore, it is optimal to solve the model with central planning:

$$MaxE_0 \left\{ \sum_{t=0}^{\infty} \beta^t \frac{C_t^{*1-\theta} L_t^{1+\sigma}}{1-\theta} \right\} \qquad (7\text{-}8)$$

$$s.t. C_t + K_{t+1} - (1-\delta)K_t + G_t = A_t K_t^{\alpha} L_t^{1-\alpha} = Y_t$$

$$\log A_t = (1-\rho_A)\log \overline{A} + \rho_A \log A_{t-1} + \varepsilon_t^A$$

$$\log G_t = (1-\rho_G)\log \overline{G} + \rho_G \log G_{t-1} + \varepsilon_t^G$$

We construct a Lagrangian function to solve the above optimal problem:

$$L = E_0 \left\{ \sum_{t=0}^{\infty} \beta^t \frac{C_t^{*1-\theta} L_t^{1+\sigma}}{1-\theta} \right\} + \lambda_t \beta^t \left[A_t K_t^\alpha L_t^{1-\alpha} - C_t - K_{t+1} + (1-\delta)K_t - C_t \right] \quad (7\text{-}9)$$

Taking the partial derivatives of Equation (7-9) with respect to C_t, N_t and K_{t+1} and letting the partial derivative be 0, we obtain:

$$\frac{\partial L}{\partial C_t} = 0 \Rightarrow C_t^{*-\theta} L_t^{1+\sigma} - \beta\phi C_{t+1}^* L_{t+1}^{1+\sigma} = \lambda_t \quad (7\text{-}10)$$

$$\frac{\partial L}{\partial L_t} = 0 \Rightarrow \frac{C_t^{*1-\theta}}{\theta-1}(1+\sigma)L_t^\sigma = \lambda_t(1-\alpha)\frac{Y_t}{L_t} \quad (7\text{-}11)$$

$$\frac{\partial L}{\partial K_{t+1}} = 0 \Rightarrow \lambda_t = \beta E_t \lambda_{t+1} (\alpha \frac{Y_{t+1}}{K_{t+1}} + 1 - \delta) \quad (7\text{-}12)$$

$$C_t + K_{t+1} - (1-\delta)K_t + G_t = A_t K_t^\alpha L_t^{1-\alpha} = Y_t \quad (7\text{-}13)$$

Substituting Equation (7-10) and Equation (7-12) into Equation (7-11), we obtain Equation (7-14), the Euler's equation of intertemporal consumption; substituting Equation (7-10) into Equation (7-11), we obtain the Euler's equation of consumption and leisure:

$$C_t^{*-\theta} L_t^{1+\sigma} - \beta\phi C_{t+1}^{*-\theta} L_{t+1}^{1+\sigma} = \beta(C_{t+1}^{*-\theta} L_{t+1}^{1+\sigma} - \beta\phi C_{t+2}^{*-\theta} L_{t+2}^{1+\sigma})R_{t+1} \quad (7\text{-}14)$$

$$R_{t+1} = \alpha \frac{Y_{t+1}}{K_{t+1}} + 1 - \delta \quad (7\text{-}15)$$

$$\lim_{j \to \infty} E_t \beta^{t+j} \lambda_{t+j} K_{t+j} = 0 \quad (7\text{-}16)$$

Equation (7-16) is the transverse condition of the model. Equation (7-4), Equation (7-7), Equation (7-10)~Equation (7-13) constitute a non-linear difference equation system. Normally, such equation system does not have an analytic solution, so we need to obtain the numerical solution through numerical simulation.

7.2 Numerical Simulation and Dynamic Analysis

7.2.1 Steady State of Model and Log-Linearization

To solve the model equilibrium through numerical simulation, we need to log-linearize the model when it is near its steady state. Thus we have to solve the steady state of the model. When the economy is at its steady state, there is no technological shock and the proportion of government purchase in the GDP is fixed, which implies all the variables do not vary over time. We calculate the steady-state value based on the first-order condition of the model. The steady-state value is represented by the variable with a line drawn above it.

$$\frac{\bar{K}}{\bar{Y}} = \frac{\alpha\beta}{1-\beta(1-\delta)} \tag{7-17}$$

$$\frac{\bar{I}}{\bar{Y}} = \delta\frac{\bar{K}}{\bar{Y}} = \frac{\delta\alpha\beta}{1-\beta(1-\delta)} \tag{7-18}$$

$$\frac{\bar{C}}{\bar{Y}} = \frac{(1-\alpha)(\theta-1)(1-\beta\phi)}{(1+\sigma)(1-\phi)} \tag{7-19}$$

$$\frac{\bar{L}}{\bar{Y}} = \left[\frac{\alpha\beta}{1-\beta(1-\delta)}\right]^{\frac{\alpha}{1-\alpha}} \tag{7-20}$$

The variable in lowercase letters with a tilde above it denotes the percentage of the variable's deviation from its value of steady-state equilibrium. x=y, c*, l, g, c, a. $\tilde{x}_t = (X_t-\bar{X})/\bar{X}$, which can also be approximated as: $\tilde{x}_t = \ln X_t - \ln \bar{X}$, or $X_t = \bar{X}e^{\tilde{x}_t} \approx \bar{X}(1+\tilde{x}_t)$. Log-linearizing Equation (7-4), Equation (7-7), Equation (7-10) ~Equation (7-13) near the steady state, we obtain:

$$\tilde{c}_i^* = \frac{\tilde{c}_t - \phi\tilde{c}_{t-1}}{1-\phi} \tag{7-21}$$

$$\frac{1}{1-\beta\phi}\left[-\theta\tilde{c}_t + (1+\sigma)\tilde{l}_i\right] - \frac{\beta\phi}{1-\beta\phi}\left[-\theta\tilde{c}_i + (1+\sigma)\tilde{l}_{t+1}\right] = \lambda_t \tag{7-22}$$

$$(1-\theta)\tilde{c}_t + \sigma\tilde{l}_t = \lambda_t + \alpha\tilde{k}_{t+1} - \alpha\tilde{l}_t + \tilde{a}_t \tag{7-23}$$

$$(1-\theta)\tilde{c}_t + \sigma\tilde{l}_t = \lambda_t + \alpha\tilde{k}_{t+1} - \alpha\tilde{l}_t + \tilde{a}_t \tag{7-24}$$

$$\lambda_t = E_t\left\{\lambda_{t+1} + [1-\beta(1-\delta)]\left[\tilde{a}_t + (1-\alpha)\tilde{l}_{t+1} - (1-\alpha)\tilde{k}_{t+1}\right]\right\} \tag{7-25}$$

$$\frac{\bar{C}}{\bar{Y}}\tilde{c}_t + \frac{\bar{K}}{\bar{Y}}\tilde{k}_{t+1} - (1-\delta)\frac{\bar{K}}{\bar{Y}}\tilde{k}_t + \frac{\bar{G}}{\bar{Y}}\tilde{g}_t = \alpha\tilde{k}_t + (1-a)\tilde{l}_t + \tilde{a}_t \tag{7-26}$$

$$\tilde{a}_t = \rho_A \tilde{a}_{t-1} + \varepsilon_t^A, \varepsilon_t^A \sim N(0, \sigma_A^2) \tag{7-27}$$

$$\tilde{g}_t = \rho_A \tilde{g}_{t-1} + \varepsilon_t^G, \varepsilon_t^G \sim N(0, \sigma_G^2) \tag{7-28}$$

Equation (7-21)-Equation (7-27) constitute a dynamic difference equation system. When the relevant parameters are determined through methods such as calibration or Bayesian estimator, the equation system can be solved with Matlab/Dynare programme (Uhlig, 1995)[12].

7.2.2 Parameter Calibration

According to the settings of the model, the parameters that need to be calibrated include the coefficient of relative risk aversion θ, discount factor β, depreciation rate δ, labour preference elasticity σ, labour supply L, output-capital elasticity α, coefficient of consumption habit ϕ, scale of Government purchase G/Y, parameter of technological shock ρ_A and σ_A, parameter of government consumption shock ρ_G and σ_G and parameter of technological level A.

As for output-capital elasticity α, based on the conclusions in Chapter 3 and the relevant literature, the benchmark value is set as: α=0.65.

As for discount factor β, in the empirical research carried out by domestic and foreign scholars, the reasonable range of discount factor is [0.95, 0.99]. Based on China's statistics of consumer price index during 1978–2016, we obtain that the price level rose by 4.95 percent annually on average during 1978–2016. Accordingly, the benchmark value of discount factor β is set as 0.95.

As for depreciation rate, its reasonable range adopted internationally is [0.05, 0.08]. For instance, Perkins (1988)[13], Wang and Yao (2001)[14] assume the depreciation rate to be 5 percent; Hall and Jones (1999)[15] and Young (2003)[16] assume it to be 6 percent. To accord with the previous analysis, we set it as: δ=9.6 percent.

As for the coefficient of relative risk aversion θ, Gu and Xiao (2004)[17] calculate China's coefficient of relative risk aversion of consumers during 1985–2002 with Keynes-Ramsey-Rule and Arrow-Pratt measure of absolute risk aversion. The results are, respectively, 3.169 and 3.916 on average. Gu et al. (2013)[18] improve the model of intertemporal substitution elasticity of consumption as well as the method, and further estimate China's household coefficient of relative risk aversion to be 3.2 on average during 2000–2008 with chronological recursion. Yao (2010)[19] calculates the coefficient of relative risk aversion of Hebei Province to be 2.32 through building an autoregressive distributed lag dynamic model. Considering the study object is the whole country, we assume the number to be 3.5 which is the median value of the calculation results in the study.

As for the coefficient of consumption habit ϕ, Ireland (2011)[20] estimates it to be 0.39 while Wu and Chao (2014)[21] estimate it to be 0.45. Liu (2008)[22] and Li (2012)[23] calibrate the result to be 0.65. We also set it as 0.65 in this book.

As for the parameter of technological shock ρ_A and σ_A, we carry out growth accounting with Cobb-Douglas production function to obtain the total factor productivity. In addition, we obtain the autoregressive coefficient ρ_A and the standard deviation σ_A. Li (2012), respectively, calibrates ρ_A and σ_A to be 0.71 and 0.042, while Huang (2005)[24] calibrates them to be 0.727 and 0.0246. We take 0.71 and 0.042 in this book.

As for the parameter of government consumption shock ρ_G and σ_G, we take the logarithm of the data of government purchase and use the Hodrick-Prescott filter or the band-pass filter to remove trend components from the raw data. Moreover, we obtain the autoregressive coefficient ρ_G and the standard deviation σ_G through first-order autoregression on cyclical components. Based on the analysis made by Li (2012), we calibrate ρ_G and σ_G to be 0.696 and 0.085.

As for scale of Government purchase G/Y, according to China's statistics during 1978–2016, the proportion of government consumption in the GDP was 15 percent on average. Thus we set G/Y as 0.15.

As for labour supply L, the time endowment of labourers is standardized to be 1 in the model. The study on the U.S. labour market carried out by Hansen (1985) shows that non-market activities occupy twice the time of market activities and labour takes up 1/3 of the total time. Additionally, according to China's actual situation, the eight-hour working time occupies 1/3 of the 24-hour total time endowment. Therefore, we calibrate labour supply to be: L=1/3.

As for labour preference elasticity σ, based on the above-mentioned calibration of parameters, labour preference elasticity can be obtained from Equation (7-19). Here we calibrate it to be 1.22.

As for the parameter of technological level A, we calibrate it to be 1 based on the existing literature.

Table 7-1 Benchmark Values of Parameter Calibration in the Model

Parameter	α	β	δ	θ	σ	φ	L	G/Y	A	ρ_A	ρ_G	σ_A	σ_G
Benchmark	0.65	0.95	0.096	3.5	1.22	0.65	1/3	0.15	1	0.71	0.696	0.042	0.085

7.2.3 Numerical Simulation and Dynamic Analysis

7.2.3.1. Steady-State Consumption Rate

We conduct the numerical simulation based on the calibrated parameters in Table 7-1 and then obtain the steady-state consumption rate ((C+G)/Y) as 58.02 percent, which is the final consumption rate consisting of the household consumption rate and the calibrated government consumption rate (15 percent). Thus the household consumption rate is 43.02 percent. Such a result is close to China's actual consumption rate. During 1978–2016, China's average final consumption rate was

58.7 percent. Since all the parameters are calibrated based on China's economic statistics, the simulation on the evolution of China's consumption rate achieves good results.

7.2.3.2. Dynamic Effect of Final Consumption Rate and Other Variables Responding to Technological Shocks and Government Expenditure Shocks

Figure 7-1 shows the impulse response of final consumption rate and other variables to technology shocks. The result indicates output and investment respond in an extremely similar way, only differing in the degree. In response to a positive 1 percent technology shock, output and investment immediately deviate from the steady-state value with a respective maximum deviation range of 0.0916 percent and 0.0727 percent in the current period, after which both slowly return to the steady-state value. Both output and investment have a positive and relatively long-lasting response to a technology shock.

Given a positive 1 percent technology shock, final consumption shows a hump-shaped response, with 0.049 percent of immediate positive deviation from the steady-state value in the current period. It then continues to rise in the second and third period and reaches the maximum deviation range of 0.0243 percent in the third period, followed by the slow return to the steady-state value. Final consumption has a positive and relatively long-lasting response to a technology shock.

In response to a positive 1 percent technology shock, final consumption deviates negatively from the steady-state value in the current period with the maximum deviation range of 0.0073 percent and reaches the minimum negative deviation in the eighth period, followed by a gradual return to the steady-state value. Such response may result from the improvement in output level caused by the rise of rate of technological progress. A large proportion of the incremented output will be used for capital accumulation, which further leads to the decrease of consumption rate. Figure 7-1 demonstrates that final consumption has a negative and relatively long-lasting response to a technology shock.

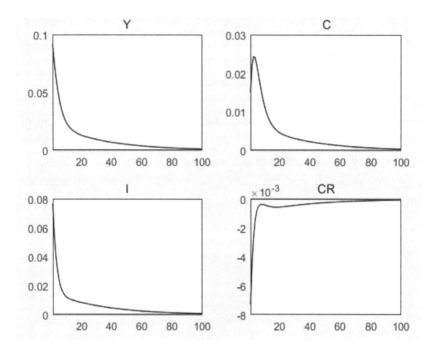

Figure 7-1 Impulse Response of Economic Variables to Technology Shocks

Figure 7-2 shows the impulse response of final consumption rate and other variables to government consumption shocks. In response to a positive 1 percent government consumption shock, output immediately achieves the maximum positive deviation of 0.005 percent from the steady-state value in the current period, after which progressively returns to the steady-state value. In the eighth period, it starts to negatively deviate from the steady-state value, achieving the maximum negative deviation of 0.001 percent in the thirteenth period. Since then it keeps negatively deviating with the deviation range gradually decreasing.

Given a positive 1 percent government consumption shock, final consumption shows a hump-shaped response with 0.00088 percent of immediate positive deviation from the steady-state value in the current period. It then reaches the maximum deviation of 0.0012 percent in the second and third period, followed by the gradual return to the steady-state value. In the eleventh period, it starts to negatively deviate, achieving the maximum negative deviation of 0.0003 percent in the twentieth period. Since then it keeps negatively deviating with the deviation range gradually decreasing.

In response to a positive 1 percent government consumption shock, investment immediately shows a negative deviation from the steady-state value in the current period with the maximum deviation range of 0.0037 percent. Since then it starts to negatively deviate with the deviation range progressively decreasing and eventually returns to the steady-state value. Investment has a positive and relatively long-lasting response to a technology shock.

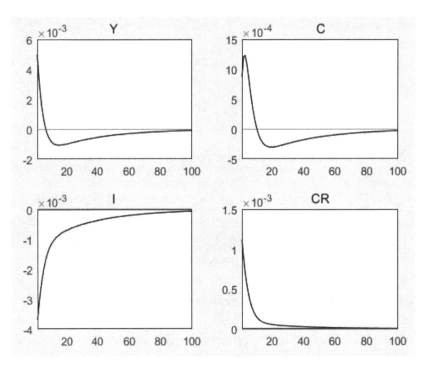

Figure 7-2 Impulse Response of Economic Variables to Government Consumption Shocks

Given a positive 1 percent government consumption shock, final consumption rate immediately shows a positive deviation from the steady-state value in the current period, reaching the maximum deviation range of 0.0011 percent. Since then it keeps positively deviating with the deviation range gradually decreasing and eventually returning to the steady-state value.

7.2.3.3. Sensitivity Analysis of Steady-State Consumption Rate to Parameters

To study on the sensitivity of steady-state value to various parameters in the DSGE model, we obtain the steady-state value in the Dynare programme by taking different values of the parameters. Table 7-2 demonstrates the sensitivity data of the steady-state consumption rate to the three parameters including output-capital elasticity, depreciation rate and discount factor.

Table 7-2 Sensitivity Analysis of Steady-State Consumption Rate to Parameters

Output-capital Elasticity	Steady-state Consumption Rate (%)	Changes of Steady-state Consumption Rate (percentage point)	Depreciation Rate	Steady-state Consumption Rate (%)	Changes of Steady-state Consumption Rate (percentage point)	Discount Factor	Steady-state Consumption Rate (%)	Changes of Steady-state Consumption Rate (percentage point)
0.30	80.62	—	0.026	78.51	—	0.88	73.15	—
0.35	77.39	-3.23	0.036	73.6	-4.91	0.89	71.58	1.57
0.40	74.16	-3.23	0.046	69.69	-3.91	0.90	69.87	1.71
0.45	70.93	-3.23	0.056	66.49	-3.2	0.91	67.98	1.89
0.50	67.71	-3.22	0.066	63.84	-2.65	0.92	65.89	2.09
0.55	64.48	-3.23	0.076	61.6	-2.24	0.93	63.57	2.32
0.60	61.25	-3.23	0.086	59.68	-1.92	0.94	60.96	2.61
0.65*	58.02	-3.23	0.096*	58.02	-1.66	0.95*	58.02	2.94
0.70	54.79	-3.23	0.106	56.57	-1.45	0.96	54.67	3.35
0.75	51.56	-3.23	0.116	55.29	-1.28	0.97	50.84	3.83
0.80	48.33	-3.23	0.126	54.15	-1.14	0.98	46.4	4.44

Notes: The steady-state consumption here only represents the corresponding steady-state consumption rate with the relevant parameter varying, while all other parameters are taken as the benchmark values. *denotes the benchmark values of parameters taken in the model.

Output-capital elasticity is inversely proportional to the steady-state consumption rate. Higher output-capital elasticity indicates a lower steady-state consumption rate, which is consistent with the analysis result of the Ramsey model. When the output-capital elasticity is 0.30, the corresponding steady-state consumption rate is 80.62 percent. Such a result is consistent with the statistics of the developed countries. For every 5 percentage-point increase in output-capital elasticity, the steady-state consumption rate of the economy decreases by 3.23 percentage points.

Depreciation rate is also inversely proportional to the steady-state consumption rate. A higher depreciation rate implies a lower steady-state consumption rate, which is consistent with the analysis result of the Ramsey model. When the depreciation rate is 10 percent, the corresponding steady-state consumption rate is 58.02 percent. Such a result is consistent with China's economic statistics. Additionally, as depreciation rate rises, its marginal impact on steady-state consumption rate weakens.

Discount factor is inversely proportional to the steady-state consumption rate. A higher discount factor indicates a lower steady-state consumption rate. The relationship between discount factor and steady-state consumption rate is straightforward. Discount factor in fact indicates the extent of patience of consumers[25]. Greater patience of consumers implies greater possibility to postpone consumption, which causes a lower consumption rate in the current period. For example, in the period of hyperinflation, less patience of consumer (lower discount factor) indicates more willingness to consume in the current period, resulting in a higher consumption rate. Furthermore, the relationship between discount rate and discount factor can be demonstrated as $\beta=1/(1+\rho)$. Here ρ represents discount rate, and β stands for discount factor. They are inversely proportional to each other. Accordingly, the conclusions made in this chapter are consistent with the study result of the relationship between discount rate and optimal consumption rate in the Ramsey model in Chapter 5.

7.3 Summary

In Chapter 7, we build a DSGE model to look into consumption rate. Considering that the DSGE model is based on the optimization of economic agents, we define the consumption rate in a steady-state economy as the optimal consumption rate for convenience to further analyse how optimal consumption rate and economic output respond to various exogenous shocks. The conclusions are as follows:

First, we conduct the numerical simulation based on the calibrated parameters and then obtain the steady-state consumption rate as 58.02 percent, which is the final consumption rate consisting of the household consumption rate and the calibrated government consumption rate (15 percent). Thus the household consumption rate is 43.02 percent. Such a result is close to China's actual consumption rate. During 1978–2016, China's average final consumption rate was 58.7 percent.

Next, in response to a positive 1 percent technology shock, final consumption deviates negatively from the steady-state value in the current period with the maximum deviation range of 0.0073 percent and reaches the minimum negative deviation in the eighth period, followed by a gradual return to the steady-state value. Such response may result from the improvement in output level caused by the rise of rate of technological progress. A large proportion of the incremented output will be used for capital accumulation, which further leads to the decrease of consumption rate. Final consumption rate has a negative and relatively long-lasting response to a technology shock.

Furthermore, given a positive 1 percent government consumption shock, final consumption rate immediately shows a positive deviation from the steady-state value in the current period, reaching the maximum deviation range of 0.0011 percent. Since then it keeps deviating positively with the deviation range gradually decreasing and eventually returns to the steady-state value.

Finally, the sensitivity analysis of steady-state consumption rate to various parameters in the DSGE model indicates as follows: output-capital elasticity, depreciation rate and discount factor are all inversely proportional to the steady-state consumption rate. The impact of the variation of these parameters on the optimal consumption rate is in line with expectations.

Notes

1 Huang Zelin, "A Study on Business Cycle and the Effects of Fiscal Policy in China: An Empirical Study on a RBC Model with Three Sections," *Economic Research Journal* 6 (2005).
2 Jia Junxue and Guo Qingwang, "Types of Fiscal Expenditure, Fiscal Policy Action Mechanism and Optimal Monetary and Fiscal Rules," *World Economy* 11 (2012).
3 Wang Yufeng and Xiao Hongwei, "Fiscal Expenditure, Residents' Consumption and Economic Fluctuation: Based on the Analysis of Dynamic Stochastic General Equilibrium Mod-els," *Scientific Decision Making* 2 (2015).
4 Mao Yanjun, Wang Xiaofang, and Xu Wencheng, "Consumption Constraints and Macroeconomic Effects of Monetary Policy --Based on the Analysis of Dynamic Stochastic General Equilibrium Model," *Nankai Economic Studies* 1 (2013).
5 Gong Min and Li Wenpu, "High Capital Share and Low Consumption Ratio in China—An Explanation Based on Dynamic General Equilibrium Model and Calibration," *Academic Monthly* 9 (2013).
6 Wu Xiaoli and Chao Jiangfeng, "On the Effect of Fiscal Expenditure Structure on Household Consumption Rate and Transmission Mechanisms: Simulation Analysis Based on Three-sector DSGE Model," *Journal of Finance and Economics* 6 (2014).
7 Wu Xiaoli, Gong Min, and Chao Jiangfeng, "Uncertainty, Credit Constraints, Habit Formation and Real Business Cycle in China: Base on the DSGE Model by the Bayes Estimation Method," *On Economic Problems* 6 (2014).
8 Linnemann L., "The Effect of Government Spending on Private Consumption: A Puzzle?" *Journal of Money Credit & Banking* 38, no. 7 (2006): 1715–1735.
9 Li Jianqiang, "Empirical Study on the Impact of Fiscal Expenditure on Household Consumption in China," Doctoral Thesis, Soochou University, 2012.
10 In fact, if $\phi=1$, then the consumption function is $C_t^*=C_t-C_{t-1}$. According to the modern consumption theory, rational consumers smooth their lifetime consumption level, which is further extended that rational consumers also smooth the variation of their lifetime consumption.
11 $\beta=1/(1+\rho)$. Here β represents discount rate.
12 Uhlig H., "A Toolkit for Analyzing Nonlinear Dynamic Stochastic Models Easily," Discussion Paper, 1995, 1995–97: 30–62.
13 Perkins D.H., "Reforming China's Economic System," *Journal of Economic Literature* 26, no. 2 (1988): 601–645.

14 Wang Yang and Yao Yudong Yao, "Sources of China's Economic Growth 1952–1999: Incorporating Human Capital Accumulation," *World Bank Working Paper*, 2001.
15 Hall Robert E. and Jones Charles I., "Why do Some Countries Produce So Much More Output per Worker than Others?" *Quarterly Journal of Economics* 114, no. 1 (1999): 83–116.
16 Young Alwyn, "Gold into Base Metals: Productivity Growth in the People's Republic of China during the Reform Period," *Journal of Political Economy* 111, no. 6 (2003): 1220–1260.
17 Gu Liubao and Xiao Hongye, "Two Statistical Methods to Estimate Intertemporal Substitution Elasticity of Consumption of China," *Statistical Research* 9 (2004).
18 Gu Liubao, Yao Hailiang, and Chen Bofei, " Research on the Estimation of China's Household Intertemporal Substitution Elasticity of Consumption with Chronological Recursion," *China Economic Quarterly* 4 (2013).
19 Yao Hailiang, "A Research on Econometric Models of Consumer Behavior of Residents in Hebei Province," Thesis for the Master Degree, Hebei University, 2010.
20 Ireland P., "A New Keynesian Perspective on the Great Recession," *Journal of Money, Credit and Banking* 43, no. 1 (2011): 31–54.
21 Wu Xiaoli and Chao Jiangfeng, "On the Effect of Fiscal Expenditure Structure on Household Consumption Rate and Transmission Mechanisms: Simulation Analysis Based on Three-sector DSGE Model," *Journal of Finance and Economics* 6 (2014).
22 Liu Bin, "Development and Application of the DSGE Model for Monetary Policy Analysis in China," *Journal of Financial Research* 10 (2008).
23 Li Jianqiang, "Empirical Study on the Impact of Fiscal Expenditure on Household Consumption in China," Doctoral Thesis, Soochou University, 2012.
24 Huang Zelin, "A Study on Business Cycle and the Effects of Fiscal Policy in China: An Empirical Study on a RBC Model with Three Sections," *Economic Research Journal* 6 (2005).

Chapter 8

Evaluation of the Steadiness of China's Economic Growth and Analysis of the Factors Affecting It

Since 1978, the fluctuating range of China's economic growth rate has been narrowing (see Figure 8-1), implying an improvement in the steadiness of the economic growth. But under the impact of various factors, the steadiness of China's economic growth rate is far from its ideal state. The economic growth and its steadiness greatly influence the national economic welfare: on one hand, a low economic growth rate indicates the national income and even the national welfare level grow at a low rate; on the other hand, if the economic growth rate is highly volatile, then the volatility in the national income will cause loss in the economic welfare (Chen, 2006)[1]. Therefore, the evaluation of the steadiness of China's economic growth rate and the analysis of the factors affecting it which are of great theoretical and practical significance contributes to the steadiness of China's economic growth.

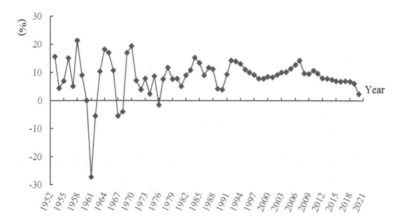

Figure 8-1 Variation of China's Economic Growth Rate
Source: Database of National Bureau of Statistics of China

In fact, stable economic growth has major significance to the improvement in the national economic welfare of an economy. Generally speaking, the stability of economic growth can be measured from the following two aspects: on one hand, a stable growth rate indicates low volatility in economic growth rate. Dramatic increases or decreases in economic growth rate can lead to the decline of the steadiness; on the other hand, low volatility in economic growth rate, or, to be more precise, the long economic cycle, implies that the economy keeps growing for a long time.

Generally speaking, traditional analysis of economic volatility illustrates the factors that affect the stability of economic growth from the perspectives of aggregate supply and aggregate demand and holds a view that all the factors (supply shocks and demand shocks) that affect the curves of aggregate supply and demand can result in the economic volatility, which further weakens the stability of economic growth. In this book, we study the factors affecting the stability of economic growth from a new perspective, looking into the influence of changes in economic structures (demand structure, industry structure, factor structure and ownership structure) on the stability of economic growth. Structuralism believes that the adjustment in economic structures is a major drive for economic growth, which means that economic structure can affect the growth of an economy. Such argument is verified by the empirical research carried out by many scholars. Accordingly, as the factors affecting economic growth, economic structures (demand structure, industry structure, factor structure and ownership structure) certainly influence the stability of economic growth. The outline of this chapter is as follows: first, we analyse how the four factors including demand structure, industry structure, factor structure and ownership structure affect the stability of economic growth; next, we construct an econometric model within an analytical framework to further quantitatively analyse the extent of impact of various factors on the stability of economic growth; finally, we put forward the suggestion for policies to improve the steadiness of China's economic growth based on the study conclusions.

8.1 Demand Structure and Economic Growth Stability

8.1.1 Foreword

The demand structure refers to the proportional relation among consumption, investment, government purchase and demand of net exports as well as the internal proportional relation among various demands. In different stages of economic development, the evolution of demand structure shows the regularity. The most famous research on such a topic is carried out by Chenery and Syrquin[2]. With empirical analysis based on the statistics of countries at different development stages and also the statistics of the same country at different development stages, they point out that the evolution of the demand structure follows a law: the consumption rate and the investment rate of industrialization were, respectively, 85 percent and 15 percent at the early stage; 80 percent and 20 percent at the middle stage; and 77 percent and 23 percent at the late stage. The law shows that as economy develops, consumption rate declines while investment rate rises. If the stability of consumption and investment is not improved during the economic development, then the changes in the structure will damage the stability of economic growth.

There is little literature that directly analyses the impact of demand structure on the stability of economic growth. Eggers and Ioannides (2006)[3] decompose the variance of America's economic growth rate into structure effect, volatility effect and coupling effect. Their empirical analysis shows that the adjustment in demand structure in America since 1947 has a positive impact on its economic growth stability (the structure effect coefficient is 23.4 percent), which implies that the adjustments of the structure can explain 23.4 percent decrease of America's GDP growth rate. Ji and Liu (2014)[4] set up indicators of advanced and rationalized demand structure to analyse the impact of demand structure on economic volatility. Their study shows that the improvement in the level of advanced and rationalized demand structure effectively inhibits the economic volatility and thus increases the stability of economic growth. Learning from Eggers and Ioannides, Yang and Liu (2011)[5] decompose China's economic growth rate into structure effect, volatility effect and coupling effect, finding out that the adjustment in China's demand structure has no positive impact on its economic growth stability (the structure effect coefficient is -3.48 percent).

In this chapter, we first make descriptive statistical analysis of the relationship between demand structure and the stability of economic growth; next, we conduct impulse response function analysis of the fluctuating components in the GDP[6] and the proportions of the three demands to study the time course and the dynamic trajectory of the impact of changes in demand structure on economic volatility; and finally, we decompose China's economic growth rate into structure effect, volatility effect and coupling effect with the method developed by Eggers and Ioannides to look into the impact of the evolution of demand structure on the steadiness of China's economic growth.

8.1.2 Descriptive Statistical Analysis of the Relationship between Demand Structure and the Stability of Economic Growth

Final Consumption, investment and net export constitute the aggregate demand of national economy. According to the macroeconomic theories, the stability of the three demands differs: the stability of consumption demand is relatively better. Since the marginal propensity to consume and the average propensity to consume are both below 1, the growth rate of consumption is lower than that of the GDP in an economic boom while the decreasing rate of consumption is lower than that of the GDP growth in an economic downturn. Thus the stability of consumption demand is better than that of the economic growth, and the stability of investment demand is relatively poorer. According to the Keynesian theory, investment tends to be influenced by the "animal spirits" as well as the multiplier-acceleration mechanism. As a result, the stability of investment demand is normally poorer than that of the GDP growth. The stability of net export demand is generally the worst due to the many factors affecting it. With surplus and deficit alternately appearing, the stability of net export demand is normally poorer than that of the economic growth. Demand structure which denotes the variation of the proportions of final consumption, investment and net export is a major factor affecting the stability of economic growth. A larger proportion of final consumption demand indicates smaller proportions of investment and net export, implying a better stability of economic growth. On the contrary, a smaller proportion of final consumption demand indicates larger proportions of investment and net export, implying a poorer stability of economic growth.

8.1.2.1. Analysis of the Coefficient of Rolling Standard Deviation Based on Growth Rates

In terms of demand, as final consumption, gross capital formation and net export constitute the GDP, economic fluctuation can be regarded as the result of the fluctuation of the three demands. With the calculation method used in Equation (1-1), we obtain the coefficients of the rolling standard deviation of China's annual GDP and the growth rates of the demands (see Figure 8-2). Figure 8-2 shows that the steadiness of China's economic growth of the demand side has three features: First, the stability of the growth of China's GDP, final consumption and gross capital formation has been overall improved since the reform and opening-up. Second, the stability of the growth of gross capital formation and net export is poorer than that of the growth of GDP and final consumption. Third, the stability of the growth of final consumption has been close to that of GDP growth in most years since 1978, but the former was poorer than the latter during 2003–2014.

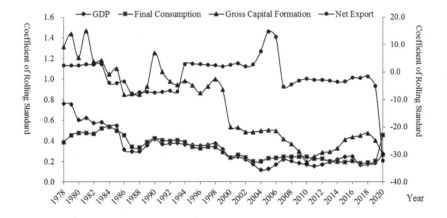

Figure 8-2 Variation of the Stability of the Growth of China's GDP, Consumption, Investment and Net Export since the Reform and Opening-Up
Notes: The left axis represents the coefficients of the standard deviation of China's GDP, final consumption and gross capital formation, and the right axis represents the coefficient of the standard deviation of China's net export.
Source: *National Bureau of Statistics of China* and Author's Calculation

Additionally, the average value, standard deviation and the coefficients of standard deviation of the growth rates of China's GDP and the three demands since the reform and opening-up are obtained based on the statistics during 1978–2020 as a whole (see Table 8-1). The annual growth rate of China's GDP is 9.19 percent with the standard deviation of 2.89 percent, and the coefficient of the standard deviation is 0.311. Generally speaking, the change in demand structure is a major cause for the fluctuation of economic growth. The annual growth rate of final consumption during 1978–2020 is 8.97 percent with the lowest coefficient of the standard deviation of 0.344 among the three demands, and the standard deviation is 2.98 percent. The annual growth rate of the gross capital formation is 9.65 percent, with the coefficient of the standard deviation of 0.677 and the standard deviation is 6.53 percent. Overall, the gross net export is the most volatile with the coefficient of the standard deviation of -16.664 and the standard deviation of 1534.38 percent. Yet since the proportion of net export in the GDP by expenditure is relatively small, it has less influence on the stability of the GDP growth.

Table 8-1 Average Value, Standard Deviation and Coefficients of Standard Deviation of the Growth Rates of China's GDP and the Three Demands since the Reform and Opening-Up

	Average (%)	Standard Deviation (%)	Coefficient of Standard Deviation
GDP	9.19	2.89	0.311
Final Consumption	8.97	2.98	0.332
Gross Capital Formation	11.49	4.39	0.677
Net Export	-92.08	1534.38	-16.664

Source: *National Bureau of Statistics of China* and author's calculation

8.1.2.2. Analysis of the Variation Range of Growth Rates

Table 8-2 demonstrates the growth rates of China's GDP and the three demands as well as their variation range during 1978–2014. In terms of the three demands, there are, respectively, 6 years, 18 years and 38 years where the variation range of the growth rates of final consumption, gross capital formation and net export are above ±50 percent. During 1993–2020, among the variation range of the growth rates of China's three demands, there are two years where the variation range of the growth rate of final consumption is over ±50 percent, while there are five years where the variation range of the growth rate of gross capital formation is over ±50 percent. Accordingly, the stability of the growth of China's GDP and demands has been improved since the reform and opening-up. Conducting the stationarity test of the econometrics on the series of the variation range of the growth rates of China's GDP and the three demands, we find out that the four series are all integrated of order zero. In other words, the series are overall stationary, implying that China's economic growth since the reform and opening-up has been relatively steady.

Table 8-2 Growth Rates and the Variation of China's GDP and the Three Demands during 1978–2020

Unit: %

Year	GDP Growth Rate	Variation Range of GDP Growth	Growth Rate of Final Consumption	Variation Range of Final Consumption Growth Rate	Growth Rate of Gross Capital Formation	Variation Range of Gross Capital Formation Growth Rate	Growth Rate of Net Export	Variation Range of Net Export Growth Rate
1978	11.7	53.9	7.3	101.8	20.3	114.0	189.8	20985.4
1979	7.6	-35.0	10.0	38.3	4.1	-79.9	40.5	-78.7
1980	7.8	2.6	9.3	-7.1	4.6	12.2	-30.9	-176.3
1981	5.1	-34.6	6.9	-26.0	-0.3	-106.6	172.7	-659.1
1982	9.0	76.5	7.7	11.2	6.3	-2171.5	112.3	-34.9
1983	10.8	20.0	12.0	56.7	11.3	80.3	-106.9	-195.2
1984	15.2	40.7	16.0	32.9	18.4	62.4	-8972.4	8292.9
1985	13.4	-11.8	14.9	-6.7	27.4	49.4	171.2	-101.9
1986	8.9	-33.6	6.9	-53.4	3.7	-86.4	-126.2	-173.7
1987	11.7	31.5	7.7	10.3	8.1	116.7	4291.9	-3500.5
1988	11.2	-4.3	7.9	3.2	15.9	97.4	-10.1	-100.2
1989	4.2	-62.5	5.2	-34.8	0.1	-99.5	-83.7	732.0
1990	3.9	-7.1	5.5	7.2	-7.9	-9913.5	119.0	-242.1
1991	9.3	138.5	9.2	66.5	9.6	-221.4	7.1	-94.0
1992	14.2	52.7	13.5	47.1	18.9	96.0	-128.0	-1897.2
1993	13.9	-2.1	13.8	2.3	17.5	-7.4	99.5	-177.7
1994	13.0	-6.5	7.9	-43.2	10.9	-37.6	313.0	214.7
1995	11.0	-15.4	8.6	9.2	12.8	17.2	48.9	-84.4
1996	9.9	-10.0	10.3	19.7	9.0	-29.6	19.6	-59.9
1997	9.2	-7.1	6.5	-36.7	3.6	-59.6	89.5	356.3
1998	7.8	-15.2	8.4	28.9	6.3	72.5	11.7	-86.9
1999	7.7	-1.3	10.8	28.8	4.7	-25.8	-28.4	-343.2
2000	8.5	10.4	10.5	-3.0	5.3	14.3	0.8	-102.9
2001	8.3	-2.4	6.8	-35.6	14.8	178.3	-52.2	-6336.2
2002	9.1	9.6	8.7	28.3	10.2	-31.3	7.8	-115.0
2003	10.0	9.9	6.2	-28.5	17.4	70.4	-23.1	-394.9
2004	10.1	1.0	7.8	25.3	15.0	-13.6	-19.0	-17.6
2005	11.4	12.9	12.0	54.3	9.4	-37.1	20.2	-206.2
2006	12.7	11.4	10.5	-12.6	13.5	43.5	23.7	17.4
2007	14.2	11.8	13.4	27.6	15.6	15.1	12.7	-46.5
2008	9.7	-31.7	8.4	-37.0	12.0	-22.9	3.9	-69.0
2009	9.4	-3.1	10.8	27.9	17.6	46.4	-92.5	-2448.0
2010	10.6	12.8	10.1	-5.8	14.3	-18.9	-29.8	-67.7
2011	9.6	-9.4	12.5	23.0	8.3	-41.9	-24.9	-16.7

Table 8-2 Continued

Year	GDP Growth Rate	Variation Range of GDP Growth	Growth Rate of Final Consumption	Variation Range of Final Consumption Growth Rate	Growth Rate of Gross Capital Formation	Variation Range of Gross Capital Formation Growth Rate	Growth Rate of Net Export	Variation Range of Net Export Growth Rate
2012	7.9	-17.7	8.6	-30.9	7.1	-13.8	7.4	-129.6
2013	7.8	-1.3	7.6	-11.9	8.9	24.4	-12.3	-266.9
2014	7.4	-5.1	8.0	5.9	7.2	-18.6	-4.8	-61.4
2015	7.0	-5.4	9.1	13.5	3.7	-48.6	18.6	-491.2
2016	6.8	-2.9	8.2	-10.4	7.3	95.5	-35.2	-289.2
2017	6.9	1.5	7.1	-13.3	6.3	-13.9	17.1	-148.5
2018	6.7	-2.9	7.8	9.9	6.6	5.5	-64.9	-480.5
2019	6.0	-10.4	6.3	-19.4	3.9	-40.2	60.8	-193.7
2020	2.3	-61.7	-0.9	-114.7	5.1	29.2	27.1	-55.5

Source: *National Bureau of Statistics of China* and author's calculation

8.1.3 Variance Decomposition Model

The variance of the GDP growth rate is decomposed with the method developed by Eggers and Ioannides (2006)[7]. g_t denotes the growth rate in Period t; n denotes the amount of sectors in the economy; g_t^i represents the growth rate of Sector i in Period t; s_t^i represents the proportion of Sector i in the GDP. In this way, the GDP growth rate can be denoted as the weighted sum of the growth rate and the proportion in the GDP of each sector:

$$g_t = \sum_i^n s_t^i g_t^i \tag{8-1}$$

Generally speaking, the variation range of each sector's proportion in the GDP in national economy is far smaller than the fluctuating range of each sector's growth rate. Thus supposing every sector's growth rate remains stable in adjacent periods, we have $s_t^i = s^i$. Based on Equation (8-1), we obtain the variance of the GDP growth rate in Period t and the variance fluctuation:

$$Var(g_t) = \sum_i^n s^i Var(g_t^i) + 2\sum_i^n \sum_j^n s^i s^j Cov(g_t^i, g_t^j) \qquad (8\text{-}2)$$

$$\Delta Var(g) = Var(g_2) - Var(g_1) = \Delta Var(g)_C + \Delta Var(g)_V + \Delta Var(g)_I \qquad (8\text{-}3)$$

$$\Delta Var(g)_C = \sum_i^n \Delta(s^i)^2 Var(g_1^i) + 2\sum_i^n \sum_j^n \Delta(s^i s^i) Cov(g_1^i, g_1^j) \qquad (8\text{-}4)$$

$$\Delta Var(g)_V = \sum_i^n (s_1^i)^2 \Delta Var(g^i) + 2\sum_i^n \sum_j^n s_1^i s_1^i \Delta Cov(g^i, g^j) \qquad (8\text{-}5)$$

$$\Delta Var(g)_I = \sum_i^n \Delta(s^i)^2 \Delta Var(g^i) + 2\sum_i^n \sum_j^n \Delta(s^i s^i) \Delta Cov(g^i, g^j) \qquad (8\text{-}6)$$

Here Equation (8-3) shows the variation range of the variance of the GDP growth in Period 1 and Period 2, which can be composed into structure effect, volatility effect and coupling effect based on Equation (8-4), Equation (8-5) and Equation (8-6).

Equation (8-4) demonstrates the structure effect which refers to the variation range of the variance of the GDP growth rate caused by the changes in each sector's proportion in the GDP. The variance and covariance of each sector are calculated as weights. In national economy, the stability of each sector differs. If the evolution or adjustment of structure leads to the increase of the proportion of the relatively stable sectors in the GDP and the decrease of the proportion of the relatively volatile sectors in the GDP, then such adjustment will improve the stability of economic growth.

Equation (8-4) shows the volatility effect which refers to the variation range of the variance of the GDP growth rate caused by the fluctuation range of each sector's growth rate. Each sector's proportion in the GDP is calculated as weights. As the factors including economic policy-making and policy system are progressively improved, each sector's stability will generally increase, which will further result in the gradual improvement of the stability of economic growth.

Equation (8-6) displays the coupling effect which refers to the residual value after deducting structure effect and volatility effect, representing the combined influence of the changes in each sector's structure and fluctuation range on the variance of the GDP growth rate.

8.1.4 Contribution of Demand Structure to the Steadiness of China's Economic Growth

Based on China's accounting statistics by expenditure approach during 1978–2014, we let final consumption, gross capital formation and net export be the three components of the GDP in the variance decomposition model and denote demand structure with the proportional relation among them. GDP, final consumption, gross capital formation and net export are converted into actual variables, respectively, based on GDP deflator, CPI, fixed assets price indices and GDP deflator to obtain the growth rates of the variables. The material comes from *National Bureau of Statistics of China*.

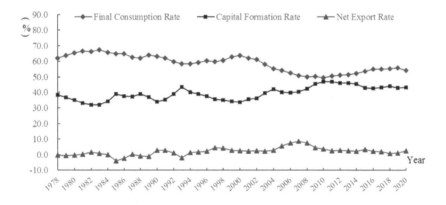

Figure 8-3 Evolution of China's Demand Structure during 1978–2020
Source: *National Bureau of Statistics of China*

Judging from the evolution of China's demand structure during 1978–2020, the proportion of final consumption which is relatively stable continued to slowly decline by 7.66 percentage points from 61.9 percent in 1978 to 54.3 percent in 2020 while the proportion of gross capital formation which is relatively unstable rose by 4.8 percentage points from 38.4 percent in 1978 to 43.1 percent in 2020. Though the proportion of net export in the GDP was low, it was positive in most years, reaching

2.6 percent in 2020. Therefore, according to the preliminary analysis of the evolution of demand structure, the adjustment or change in China's demand structure fails to enhance the stability of economic growth (see Figure 8-3).

Judging from the stability of each component of the GDP (see Figure 8-4), the fluctuation range of final consumption growth rate is narrowing while that of growth rates of gross capital formation and net export shows no such sign.

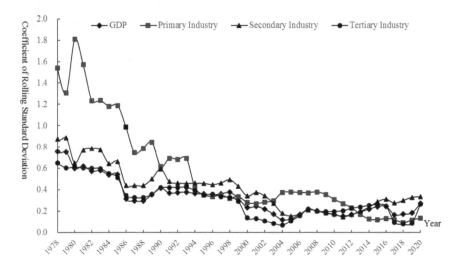

Figure 8-4 Growth Rates of China's GDP and the Three Demands
Notes: The growth rate of net export is not shown in the figure due to its high volatility and low proportion in the GDP.

The structure effect, volatility effect and coupling effect of the variance of the GDP growth are calculated based on the variance decomposition model. According to the result shown in Table 8-3, the structure effect is -7.2 percent, which indicates that around 7.2 percent increase of the GDP volatility is caused by the variation of demand structure. Such variation weakens the stability of economic growth, showing a low structure effect; the volatility effect is 110.6 percent, which implies that the further increase in the stability of demands contributes to the improvement of the economic growth stability; the coupling effect is -3.4 percent, showing that the interaction among the components of aggregate demand increases the economic volatility.

According to the result of the variance decomposition, the variation of demand structure and the coupling effect among demands undermine the stability of economic growth. On the contrary, the decrease in the volatility of the components of demand is a main reason for the decline of the volatility of China's economic growth, which further helps strengthen the stability. To achieve that, we first need to raise the final consumption rate, especially the household consumption rate, and focus on stable consumption when we try to increase the growth rate of consumption; second, we need to enhance the control of gross capital formation to optimize its scale and structure and lower the volatility of investment growth; third, we should accelerate the adjustment of industry structure to make China's demand match its supply, which eventually reduces the imbalance in China's net exports.

Table 8-3 Result of the Variance Decomposition of the GDP Volatility (Demand Structure)

	Ratio (%)
Structure Effect	-7.2
Volatility Effect	110.6
Coupling Effect	-3.4

Source: *National Bureau of Statistics of China* and author's calculation

8.2 Industry Structure and Economic Growth Stability

8.2.1 Foreword

With given technological level, the existing pattern of specialization and division of labour determines the industry structure of an economy which further influences the economic growth. Thus the variation of industry structure is closely correlated with economic growth. On one hand, industry structure has an impact on economic growth. That is, industry structure varies with economic growth. On the other hand, economic growth pattern (transformation) also depends on industry structure (adjustment). Generally speaking, the impact of industry structure on economic growth can be analysed from the following two aspects: first, from the static aspect, supposing that the proportional relation among all industries remains unchanged during the investigated periods, industry structure will eventually vary as time changes due to the different growth rates of industries resulting from their different properties and features; second, from the dynamic aspect, supposing that the proportions of industries change in a certain investigated period, industry structure will change at the end of the investigated periods.

Issues around the influencing mechanism of industry structure on the stability of economic growth and its approach have gathered attention from scholars home and abroad. Foreign scholars have not reached a consensus on such a topic. A few of them believe that the transformation of industry structure fails to help decrease economic volatility (Blanchard & Simon, 2001)[8]. Yet an increasing number of scholars carry out their studies from different perspectives, finding out that the transformation of industry structure does reduce economic volatility. Specifically, if the proportion of the industries that are relatively stable in the economy increases, then economic volatility decreases. Peneder (2003)[9] investigates the impact of changes of industry structure on economic volatility with dynamic panel based on the statistics of OECD member countries. The result shows that the changes of industry structure can explain 30 percent decrease in economic volatility. Eggers and Ioannides (2006)[10] hold a view that the existing literature underestimates the role of industry structure adjustment plays in stabilizing the economy. With an empirical study on the variance analysis model, they conclude that 32.4 percent decrease in America's economic volatility since 1947 can be explained by the transformation of industry structure.

Domestic scholars make similar conclusions that the transformation of industry structure helps stabilize the economy. They look into the issue from two different perspectives: one is to verify whether industry structure can stabilize economic volatility (Fang & Zhan, 2011[11]; Gan et al., 2011[12]); the other is to calculate the contribution rate of industry structure adjustment to the decline of economic volatility based on the variance decomposition model developed by Eggers and Ioannides (2006) (Yang & Liu, 2011[13]; Li, 2012[14]; Li, 2011[15]).

We first make a descriptive statistical analysis of the relationship between demand structure and the stability of economic growth; next, we conduct impulse response function analysis of the fluctuating components in the GDP[16] and the proportions of the three demands to study the time course and the dynamic trajectory of the impact of changes in demand structure on economic volatility; and finally, we decompose China's economic growth rate into structure effect, volatility effect and coupling effect with the method developed by Eggers and Ioannides[17] to further investigate the impact of the evolution of demand structure on the steadiness of China's economic growth.

8.2.2 Descriptive Statistical Analysis of the Relationship between Industry Structure and the Stability of economic growth

According to economic theories, the progressive optimization is the premise of stable economic growth. To keep the sustained and stable economic growth, we should improve the structure while the economic aggregate grows. The different stability of the three industries in national economy and the industry structure determine the overall steadiness of the economic growth: the stability of the primary industry which is restricted by natural conditions and other uncertain factors is more volatile than that of the second industry and the tertiary industry; the stability of the second industry, mainly influenced by factors such as industrialization strategy and investment, is the second volatile industry; and the volatility of the tertiary industry which provides service for the primary industry and the secondary industry is affected by the volatility of the rest two industries. Due to their different stability, the industry structure acts as a major variable when we look into the factors affecting the overall economic growth. The larger the proportion of the relatively stable industry is, the better the economic steadiness is; also, the larger the proportion of the relatively volatile industry is, the poorer the economic steadiness is.

8.2.2.1. Analysis of the Coefficient of Rolling Standard Deviation Based on Growth Rate

In terms of the supply side, since the GDP is the sum of the output of the three industries, the economic fluctuation can be regarded as the combined result from the fluctuations of the three industries. Based on the calculation method in Equation (1-1), we obtain the coefficients of rolling standard deviation of China's annual GDP and the industries' growth rates (see Figure 8-5). Figure 8-5 demonstrates the three features of China's economic growth stability: first, overall, the stability of the GDP and the three industries has been gradually improved since the reform and opening-up; second, as for industries, the stability of the tertiary industry, close to the GDP growth stability, is better than that of the primary industry and the secondary industry; and third, the growth of the tertiary industry is the most stable. Since 2000, China's primary industry has been the most volatile while the secondary industry and the tertiary industry share similar stability with the GDP.

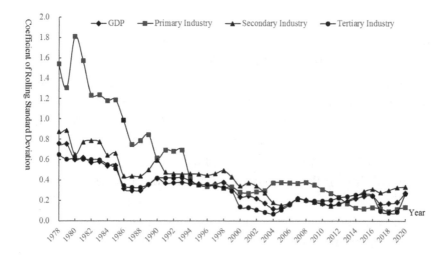

Figure 8-5 Variation of the Stability of China's GDP and the Three Industries since the Reform and Opening-Up
Source: *National Bureau of Statistics of China* and Author's Calculation

In addition, the average value, standard deviation and the coefficients of standard deviation of the growth rates of China's GDP and the three industries since the reform and opening-up are obtained based on the statistics during 1978–2020 as a whole (see Table 8-4). The annual growth rate of China's GDP is 9.19 percent with 2.89 percent standard deviation and the coefficient of the standard deviation is 0.311.

Generally, the fluctuation of industry structure is a major cause for the fluctuation of economic growth. The coefficient of the standard deviation of the primary industry is 0.551, which is the highest among the three industries. Yet its standard deviation is the lowest (2.39 percent). Such a result illustrates that the growth rate of the primary industry is relatively low with high volatility, which can be explained by the restriction of natural conditions on the primary industry. In the years where natural disaster happens, its growth tends to dramatically fall. The coefficient of the standard deviation of the secondary industry is 0.435 with 4.54 percent standard deviation, which is higher than that of the tertiary industry. Overall, the tertiary industry is the least volatile. Its coefficient of the standard deviation is only 0.333 with 3.42 percent standard deviation. Judging from that, the volatility of China's economic growth primarily results from the imbalance in the growth of the industry sectors. In other words, the structural volatility leads to the volatility of the economic aggregate.

Table 8-4 Average Value, Standard Deviation and Coefficients of Standard Deviation of the Growth Rates of China's GDP and the Three Industries since the Reform and Opening-Up

	Average (%)	Standard Deviation (%)	Coefficient of Standard Deviation
GDP	9.19	2.89	0.311
Primary Industry	4.34	2.39	0.551
Secondary Industry	10.44	4.54	0.435
Tertiary Industry	10.29	3.42	0.333

Notes: The data in Table 8-4 is calculated based on the statistics during 1978–2020.

Source: *National Bureau of Statistics of China* and Author's Calculation

8.2.2.2. Analysis of the Variation Range of Growth Rates

Table 8-5 demonstrates the growth rates of China's GDP and the three industries as well as their variation range during 1978–2020. In terms of the variation range of the GDP growth rate, there are six years where the variation range is above ±50 percent. Particularly, there is one year (1991) where the range is over 100 percent. Since the reform and opening-up entered in the second stage in 1992, the national macro-control policies and the orientation have been transformed with a focus on the stability of economic growth. During 1993–2020, the variation range of China's economic growth never exceeded ±50 percent. Moreover, it had been controlled within ±30 percent (except for the 2008 financial crisis and the impact of COVID-19 in 2020, the economic growth rates were -31.7 percent and -61.7 percent, respectively). Overall, China's economic growth has kept a steady and relatively high growth. In terms of the industries, there are, respectively, 11 years, 7 years and 5 years where the variation range of the primary, secondary and tertiary industry is above ±50 percent. Only a few years during 1993–2020 have witnessed an excess of ±50 percent in the variation range of the growth of China's three industries.

Table 8-5 Growth Rates and the Variation of China's GDP and the Three Industries during 1978–2020

Unit: %

Year	GDP Growth Rate	Variation Range of GDP Growth Rate	Growth Rate of the Tertiary Industry	Variation Range of the Tertiary Industry Growth Rate	Growth Rate of the Secondary Industry	Variation Range of the Secondary Industry Growth Rate	Growth Rate of the Primary Industry	Variation Range of the Primary Industry Growth Rate
1978	11.7	53.9	4.1	-286.4	15.0	13.6	13.6	46.2
1979	7.6	-35.0	6.1	48.8	8.2	-45.3	7.8	-42.6
1980	7.8	2.6	-1.5	-124.6	13.5	64.6	6.1	-21.8
1981	5.1	-34.6	7.0	-566.7	1.9	-85.9	9.6	57.4
1982	9.0	76.5	11.5	64.3	5.6	194.7	12.7	32.3
1983	10.8	20.0	8.3	-27.8	10.4	85.7	14.6	15.0
1984	15.2	40.7	12.9	55.4	14.4	38.5	19.4	32.9
1985	13.4	-11.8	1.8	-86.0	18.4	27.8	18.1	-6.7
1986	8.9	-33.6	3.3	83.3	10.2	-44.6	12.3	-32.0
1987	11.7	31.5	4.7	42.4	13.6	33.3	14.7	19.5
1988	11.2	-4.3	2.5	-46.8	14.3	5.1	13.2	-10.2
1989	4.2	-62.5	3.1	24.0	3.7	-74.1	5.8	-56.1
1990	3.9	-7.1	7.3	135.5	3.2	-13.5	2.7	-53.4
1991	9.3	138.5	2.4	-67.1	13.8	331.3	9.2	240.7
1992	14.2	52.7	4.7	95.8	21.0	52.2	12.6	37.0
1993	13.9	-2.1	4.6	-2.1	19.7	-6.2	12.2	-3.2
1994	13.0	-6.5	3.9	-15.2	18.1	-8.1	11.4	-6.6

Table 8-5 Continued

Year	GDP Growth Rate	Variation Range of GDP Growth Rate	Growth Rate of the Tertiary Industry	Variation Range of the Tertiary Industry Growth Rate	Growth Rate of the Secondary Industry	Variation Range of the Secondary Industry Growth Rate	Growth Rate of the Primary Industry	Variation Range of the Primary Industry Growth Rate
1995	11.0	-15.4	4.9	25.6	13.8	-23.8	10.1	-11.4
1996	9.9	-10.0	5.0	2.0	12.1	-12.3	9.2	-8.9
1997	9.2	-7.1	3.4	-32.0	10.5	-13.2	10.4	13.0
1998	7.8	-15.2	3.4	0.0	8.9	-15.2	8.4	-19.2
1999	7.7	-1.3	2.7	-20.6	8.2	-7.9	9.2	9.5
2000	8.5	10.4	2.3	-14.8	9.5	15.9	9.8	6.5
2001	8.3	-2.4	2.6	13.0	8.5	-10.5	10.3	5.1
2002	9.1	9.6	2.7	3.8	9.9	16.5	10.5	1.9
2003	10.0	9.9	2.4	-11.1	12.7	28.3	9.5	-9.5
2004	10.1	1.0	6.1	154.2	11.1	-12.6	10.1	6.3
2005	11.4	12.9	5.1	-16.4	12.1	9.0	12.4	22.8
2006	12.7	11.4	4.8	-5.9	13.5	11.6	14.1	13.7
2007	14.2	11.8	3.5	-27.1	15.1	11.9	16.1	14.2
2008	9.7	-31.7	5.2	48.6	9.8	-35.1	10.5	-34.8
2009	9.4	-3.1	4.0	-23.1	10.3	5.1	9.6	-8.6
2010	10.6	12.8	4.3	7.5	12.7	23.3	9.7	1.0
2011	9.6	-9.4	4.2	-2.3	10.7	-15.7	9.5	-2.1
2012	7.9	-17.7	4.5	7.1	8.4	-21.5	8.0	-15.8
2013	7.8	-1.3	3.8	-15.6	8.0	-4.8	8.3	3.7
2014	7.4	-5.1	4.1	7.9	7.2	-10.0	8.3	0.0
2015	7.0	-5.4	3.9	-4.9	5.9	-18.1	8.8	6.0
2016	6.8	-2.9	3.3	-15.4	6.0	1.7	8.1	-8.0
2017	6.9	1.5	4.0	21.2	5.9	-1.7	8.3	2.5
2018	6.7	-2.9	3.5	-12.5	5.8	-1.7	8.0	-3.6
2019	6.0	-10.4	3.1	-11.4	4.9	-15.5	7.2	-10.0
2020	2.3	-61.7	3.0	-3.2	2.6	-46.9	2.1	-70.8

Source: *China Statistical Yearbook-2015* and Author's Calculation

8.2.3 Contribution of Demand Structure to the Steadiness of China's Economic Growth

Based on China's accounting statistics by production approach during 1978–2020, we let the primary industry, the secondary industry and the tertiary industry be the three components of the GDP in the variance analysis model and denote industry structure with the proportional relation among them. GDP, the primary industry, the secondary industry and the tertiary industry are converted into actual variables, respectively, based on GDP deflator, the primary industry deflator, the secondary industry deflator and the tertiary industry deflator to obtain the growth rates of the variables. The material comes from *National Bureau of Statistics of China*.

Judging from the evolution of China's industry structure during 1978–2020, the proportion of the tertiary industry which is relatively stable continued to slowly rise by 29.9 percentage points from 24.6 percent in 1978 to 54.5 percent in 2020 while the proportion of the secondary industry which is relatively unstable kept fluctuating, declining by 9.9 percentage points from 47.7 percent in 1978 to 37.8 percent in 2020. The proportion of the primary industry in the GDP kept dropping, from 27.7 percent in 1978 to 7.7 percent in 2020. Therefore, according to the preliminary analysis of the evolution of industry structure, the adjustment or change in China's industry structure helps enhance the stability of economic growth to some extent.

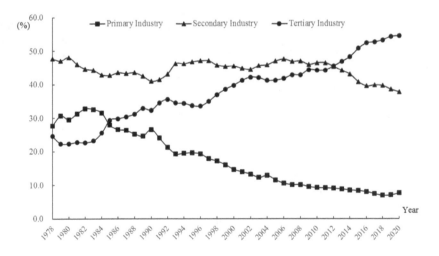

Figure 8-6 Evolution of China's Industry Structure during 1978–2020

Judging from the stability of each component of the GDP (see Figure 8-7), the fluctuation range of the growth rates of the primary industry and the tertiary industry is narrowing while that of the growth rate of the secondary industry shows no such sign.

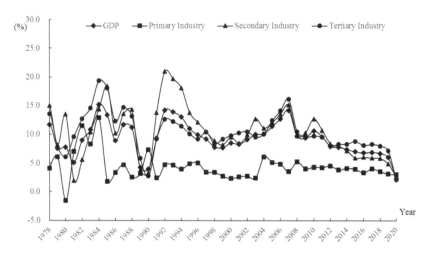

Figure 8-7 Growth Rates of China's GDP and the Three Industries
Source: *National Bureau of Statistics of China* and Author's Calculation

The structure effect, volatility effect and coupling effect of the variance of the GDP growth are calculated based on the variance decomposition model. According to the result shown in Table 8-6, the structure effect is 28.5 percent, which indicates that around 28.5 percent decrease of the GDP volatility is caused by the variation of industry structure. Such variation enhances the stability of economic growth, mainly because the proportion of the tertiary industry which is relatively stable rises with the drop of the proportion of the primary industry while that of the secondary industry which is relatively unstable slightly varies. The volatility effect is 82.7 percent, implying that the further increase in the stability of industries contributes to the improvement of the economic growth stability and the decline of the volatility in GDP results from the increase in the stability of the three industries. The coupling effect is -11.2 percent, showing that the interaction among the three industries increases the economic volatility. Judging from the result of the variance decomposition, the variation of industry structure helps stabilize the economic volatility. Specifically, the decrease in the volatility of the industries contributes mostly to the economic stabilization whereas the coupling effect strengthens the economic volatility.

Table 8-6 Result of the Variance Decomposition of the GDP Volatility (Industry Structure)

	Ratio (%)
Structure Effect	28.5
Volatility Effect	82.7
Coupling Effect	-11.2

Source: *National Bureau of Statistics of China* and Author's Calculation

8.3 Factor Structure and Economic Growth Stability

The theories of economic growth illustrate that factor input and production technology constitute economic output. Generally speaking, the most important input factors are capital, labour and technology, and capital can be further divided into human capital, material capital, and social capital. When the factor inputs fluctuate, output also fluctuates. Thus the variation of factor structure affects the stability of economic growth.

In 8.3, we calculate the income shares of capital, labour and other factor inputs (factor elasticity of output) based on the relationship between factor and growth to analyse the factor input of China's long-term economic growth and its structure features. In addition, we look into the impact of factor structure on the steadiness of China's economic growth with growth accounting model.

8.3.1 *Perspective of Growth Accounting: Factor Structure and Economic Growth Stability*

8.3.1.1. Factor Input of China's Long-Term Economic Growth and Its Structure Features

Since it is relatively difficult to measure the factors other than labour force and material capital, we refer to all the factors excluding these two as total factor, whose contribution to economic growth is measured by total factor productivity.

(1) Variation Trend of Factor Input Structure

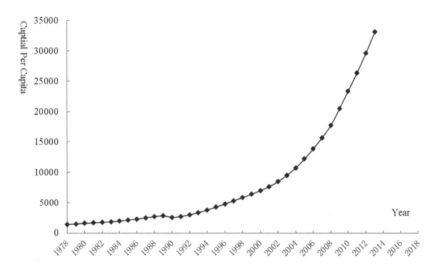

Figure 8-8 China's Capital-labour Ratio during 1978–2013

During 1978–2013, the features of the structure variation of China's labour force input and material capital input are as follows: (i) Over this period, the growth rate of China's capital accumulation was far higher than that of the labour input. Specifically, the capital stock increased by a factor of 44.9 times from 568.66 billion yuan in 1978 (constant price in 1978) to 25546.84 billion yuan in 2013; (ii) The labour force input grew by a factor of 1.92 times from 401.52 million in 1978 to 769.77 million in 2013. Figure 8-8 illustrates China's capital-labour ratio during 1978–2013 (constant price in 1978; Unit: Yuan per capita), showing that China's capital stock per capita has gone through three stages of variation: in the first stage (1978–1990), China's capital stock per capita kept fluctuating around 2,500 yuan per capita; in the second stage (1991–2000), its growth rate began to rise; and in the third stage (2000–2013), its growth rate dramatically rose.

In terms of the growth rates of capital input and labour input, the average annual growth rate of China's capital input was 11.50 percent, close to that of the economy which was 9.80 percent. On the contrary, the average annual growth rate of the labour input was 1.88 percent, much lower than that of the capital input. The variation of China's factor inputs has also experienced three stages (see Table 8-7): (i) In the first stage (1978–1990), China's capital growth rate was lower than the labour growth rate. The economic growth mainly depended on the improvement in the efficiency of factor inputs; (ii) In the second stage (1991–2000), the growth rate of China's capital input dramatically increased to 12.24 percent while that of the labour input decreased to 1.07 percent resulting from the one-child policy. The feature that the economic growth is driven by investment began to show; (iii) In the third stage (2000–2013), the capital input remained a high growth rate of 13.53 percent whereas the growth rate of the labour input fell to 0.47 percent. After entering the third stage, the above-mentioned feature has become more obvious and the efficiency of capital input has been going down because of continuous investment. Therefore, the most serious economic problem faced by China is how to raise the utility efficiency of capital and labour in order to achieve the transition from factor-input-driven economic growth to innovation-driven economic growth.

Table 8-7 Average Growth Rates of China's Factor Inputs in Various Periods
Unit: %

Period	Economic Growth Rate	Capital Growth Rate	Labour Growth Rate
1978–2013	9.80	11.50	1.88
1978–1990	9.04	9.31	4.06
1991–2000	10.55	12.24	1.07
2000–2013	10.12	13.53	0.47

8.3.1.2. Prediction about the Variation Trend of Future Factor Structure
In terms of labour force supply, though the natural growth rate of China's population will fall in the future 10 years, the employed population will

remain an average annual growth rate of 1.6 percent due to the implement of the "Selective Two-Child Policy" (for couples where either the husband or the wife is from a single-child family) and the "Universal Two-Child Policy". In terms of capital input, the growth rate of China's capital stock will drop in the coming 10 years because of the transition in the economic growth, structural adjustment and other factors. Given the feature of China's investment-driven economic growth, the capital input is able to maintain a growth rate of over 10 percent.

8.3.1.3. Contributions of Factor Input and Total Factor Productivity to China's Economic Growth

(1) Growth Accounting Model

The sources of economic growth are the increase in factor input and the improvement in total factor productivity. Abramowitz (1956)[18] and Solow (1957)[19] developed the growth accounting theory together to solve the issue around the source of economic growth. In their model, the impact of labour force input, capital input and technological progress on economic growth is mainly investigated. The aggregate production function is considered as follows:

$$Y(t) = F(K(t), A(t)L(t))$$

Taking derivative of aggregate output Y (t) with respect to time (t), we obtain:

$$\dot{Y}(t) = \frac{\partial Y}{\partial K}\dot{K}(t) + \frac{\partial Y}{\partial L}\dot{L}(t) + \frac{\partial Y}{\partial A}\dot{A}(t) \qquad (8\text{-}7)$$

Here $\frac{\partial Y}{\partial K}$, $\frac{\partial Y}{\partial L}$ respectively denote the marginal output of capital and labour.

Dividing both sides of Equation (8-7) by Y (t), we have:

$$\frac{\dot{Y}(t)}{Y(t)} = \frac{K(t)}{Y(t)}\frac{\partial Y(t)}{\partial K(t)}\frac{\dot{K}(t)}{K(t)} + \frac{L(t)}{Y(t)}\frac{\partial Y(t)}{\partial L(t)}\frac{\dot{L}(t)}{L(t)} + \frac{A(t)}{Y(t)}\frac{\partial Y(t)}{\partial A(t)}\frac{\dot{A}(t)}{A(t)}$$

$$= \alpha_K(t)\frac{\dot{K}(t)}{K(t)} + \alpha_L(t)\frac{\dot{L}(t)}{L(t)} + B(t) \qquad (8\text{-}8)$$

Here $\alpha_K(t)$ and $\alpha_L(t)$, respectively, represent the output elasticity of capital and labour at time (t).

$B(t) = \dfrac{\partial Y(t)}{\partial A(t)}\dfrac{A(t)}{Y(t)}\dfrac{\dot{A}(t)}{A(t)}$ is referred as Solow Residual or Total Factor Productivity, which is caused by technological progress, efficiency improvement and system transformation. The items in Equation (8-8) reflect the respective contribution of the growth of the factors to output: The left side shows the output growth and the first, second and third items on the right side show the respective contribution of capital, labour and human

capital to output. In the empirical research on the factors of economic growth, the Cobbs-Douglas production function is generally adopted:

$$Y(t) = F(K(t), A(t)L(t)) = K(t)^{\alpha} \left[A(t)L(t)\right]^{\beta}, 0 < \alpha < 1 \qquad (8\text{-}9)$$

(2) Data Source

Before conducting regression analysis of Equation (8-9) to further look into the contribution of the factors to economic growth, we need to collect the data of Y (t), K (t), A (t) and L (t). The following data comes from Table 4-1 in 4.2.

In our model, besides the mentioned factor inputs in Equation (8-9), we also have to take into consideration other factors that contribute to China's continuous economic growth: oth (t) =$e^{\mu t}$. Substituting oth (t) =$e^{\mu t}$ into Equation (8-9) and taking the log of both sides of Equation (8-9), we obtain:

$$\ln Y = \alpha_0 + \alpha \ln K + \beta \ln L + \mu_t \qquad (8\text{-}10)$$

Here $\alpha_0=\beta\ln A$. We make an estimation on Equation (8-10) based on the data in Table 4-1 and then obtain:

$$\ln Y = -5.4846 + 0.7535\ln K + 0.6765\ln L \qquad (8\text{-}11)$$

$$(10.17)\ (70.27)\ (11.71)$$

$$R^2 = 0.9991 \quad AdjR^2 = 0.9991 \quad F = 17776.30$$

The estimation result shows a high goodness of fit and also high coefficients of all the input factors. According to the growth accounting theory and Equation (8-8), with the other conditions given and fixed, for every 1 percent increase in labour input, output will rise by 0.6765 percent; with the other conditions given and fixed, for every 1 percent increase in capital invest, output will rise by 0.7535 percent.

8.3.1.4. Impact of Factor Structure on China's Economic Growth Stability

Equation (8-11) shows the result of empirical analysis that the fluctuation of the growth rates of China's factors of production can directly cause the fluctuation of the economic growth: for every 1 percent fluctuation of labour input, the economy fluctuates by 0.6765 percent; for every 1 percent fluctuation of capital input, the economy fluctuates by 0.7535 percent. Judging from the volatility of every factor, it can be stated as follows: the labour factor is less volatile due to the restraint of the law of population evolution; the capital factor is much more volatile because it is formed from the accumulation of investment which often fluctuates greatly with the economic cycles; and the fluctuation of total factor productivity is a major source of economic fluctuation (Li, 2010)[20].

8.3.2 Economic Fluctuation Caused by Factor Input Fluctuation and Structural Variation

The aggregate production function indicates that factor input along with production technology generates economic output. Accordingly, factor input and variation of factor structure can lead to output fluctuation. Among the studies carried out by domestic scholars on the relationship between factor input and economic volatility (economic steadiness) from the perspective of factor input, the most representative ones are as follows: Guo and Jia (2004)[21], respectively, measure the volatility of output, investment and total factor productivity based on the gap of output, investment and total factor productivity, and analyse the impact of the shocks (volatility) of investment and total factor productivity on economic volatility. The study finding shows that the shocks (volatility) of investment and total factor productivity are the major causes for economic volatility. Specifically, the impact of total factor productivity is larger and longer-lasting. Chen (2010)[22] looks into the impact of exogenous shocks and variation of factor input on the fluctuation of China's output based on provincial panel data, concluding that the investment fluctuation greatly strengthens the economic fluctuation while the labour input fluctuation has no such impact. Ran, Cao and Zhong (2008)[23] investigates the impact of factor input, currency supply and technological progress on China's economic fluctuation. They point out that among the three variables, the fluctuation of capital input has the largest impact on China's economic fluctuation, followed by currency fluctuation, while the fluctuation of technological progress has the smallest but the longest lasting impact. Fang and Zhan (2011)[24] analyse the impact of capital shocks, labour shocks and the upgrade of industry structure on China's fluctuation. Such impact evolves in various stages: prior to 1992, capital shocks, labour shocks and the upgrade of industry structure are all violent; since 1992, capital has the biggest shocks on the economy, followed by labour while the shocks of the upgrade of industry structure have been negative all the time.

In 8.3, we analyse the impact of the variation of labour, capital and factor structure on China's economic volatility (steadiness) through building a state-space model based on the traditional aggregate production function.

8.3.2.1. Theoretical Model

Based on the model built by Fang and Zhan (2011)[25], we add indicators including labour, capital, factor structure and technology into the aggregate production function:

$$Y_t = F(K_t, L_t, S_t, A_t) \tag{8-12}$$

Here Y_t denotes level of output; K_t denotes capital input; L_t represents labour input; S_t represents factor structure. Since only two factors of production are considered in the model, we measure S_t with capital-labour ratio; A_t represents level of technology (denoted by Constant c in the short term). Taking the log of both sides of Equation (8-12), we obtain the linear production function:

$$\ln Y = c + \alpha \ln K + \beta \ln L + \gamma \ln S + \mu_t \tag{8-13}$$

As we are looking into the impact of the fluctuation of factor input on output fluctuation, we make the following assumption: $\ln Y = \ln \bar{Y} + \varepsilon_{Y,t}$. Here $\bar{Y}$ represents potential output and $\varepsilon_{Y,t}$ denotes the difference between the log of actual output and the log of potential output, which reflects the percentage of the deviation of the economic growth from its potential output and measures the economic volatility. We also assume that $\ln K = \ln \bar{K} + \varepsilon_{K,t}, \ln L = \ln \bar{L} + \varepsilon_{L,t}, \ln S = \ln \bar{LS} + \varepsilon_{S,t}$. Here $\varepsilon_{K,t}$, $\varepsilon_{L,t}$ and $\varepsilon_{S,t}$, respectively, measure capital fluctuation, labour fluctuation and the variation of factor structure. Detrending Equation (8-13), we obtain:

$$\varepsilon_{Y,t} = c + \alpha \varepsilon_{K,t} + \beta \varepsilon_{L,t} + \gamma \varepsilon_{S,t} + \mu_t \tag{8-14}$$

Equation (8-14) shows how capital fluctuation, labour fluctuation and the variation of factor structure affect output fluctuation. We assume: $\tilde{Y} = \varepsilon_{Y,t}, \tilde{K}_t = \varepsilon_{K,t}, \tilde{L}_t = \varepsilon_{L,t}$ and $\tilde{U}_t = \varepsilon_{S,t}$. Then Equation (8-14) transforms into:

$$\tilde{Y}_t = c + \alpha \tilde{K}_t + \beta \tilde{K}_t + \gamma \tilde{S}_t + \mu_t \tag{8-15}$$

Equation (8-15) is a significant model to measure the impact of capital fluctuation, labour fluctuation and the variation of factor structure on economic fluctuation.

8.3.2.2. State-Space Model

We make analysis based on China's macroeconomic statistics which fall into the category of time series during 1978–2013. Given the massive transformation of China's economic structure and system since the reform and opening-up, it would be difficult to observe the impact of the variation of factor structure on the economic volatility if we use the traditional model with fixed parameters. Thus we build a model with time-varying parameters based on the state-space model of the econometrics:

$$\boxed{\text{Measurement Equation:}} \tilde{Y}_t = c + sv_{1t}\tilde{k}_t + sv_{2t}\tilde{k}_t + sv_{3t}\tilde{S}_t + \mu_t$$

$$\boxed{\text{Equation of Stata:}} sv_{1t} = \gamma_1 sv_{1t-1} + \eta_{1t}, sv_{2t} = \gamma_2 sv_{2t-1} + \eta_{2t}, sv_{3t} = \gamma_3 sv_{3t-1} + \eta_{3t}$$

Here the average values of μ_t and η_{it} are both 0 and mutually independent. That is, $\begin{bmatrix} \mu_t \\ \eta_{it} \end{bmatrix} \sim N\left(\begin{bmatrix} 0 \\ 0 \end{bmatrix}, \begin{bmatrix} \sigma_1^2 & 0 \\ 0 & \rho_i^2 \end{bmatrix}\right), i = 1,2,3; t = 1,2,\cdots,T$.

8.3.2.3. Data Processing and Empirical Analysis

(1) Source of Basic Data

Table 8-8 shows the relevant basic data. The data on output (Y), capital stock (K) and labour force (L) in Equation (8-13) come from Table 4-3 in section 4.3, and the data on factor structure (S) are obtained through dividing K by L.

Table 8-8 Relevant Economic Statistics of China during 1978–2013

Year	Y (100 Million yuan)	K (100 Million yuan)	L (10 Thousand People)	S (yuan Per Capita)
1978	3650.20	5686.64	40152.00	1416.28
1979	3927.62	6172.43	41024.00	1504.59
1980	4237.90	6764.69	42361.00	1596.91
1981	4454.03	7288.02	43725.00	1666.79
1982	4854.89	7888.10	45295.00	1741.49
1983	5379.22	8583.07	46436.00	1848.37
1984	6196.86	9492.84	48197.00	1969.59
1985	7033.44	10573.31	49873.00	2120.05
1986	7659.41	11749.37	51282.00	2291.13
1987	8555.57	13156.38	52783.00	2492.54
1988	9522.34	14648.96	54334.00	2696.09
1989	9922.28	15589.55	55329.00	2817.61
1990	10309.25	16554.65	64749.00	2556.74
1991	11268.01	17821.41	65491.00	2721.20
1992	12879.34	19672.07	66152.00	2973.77
1993	14669.57	22253.56	66808.00	3330.97
1994	16591.28	25404.51	67455.00	3766.14
1995	18416.32	28986.17	68065.00	4258.60
1996	20239.54	32973.63	68950.00	4782.25
1997	22101.57	36978.99	69820.00	5296.33
1998	23825.50	41202.28	70637.00	5832.96
1999	25636.23	45612.82	71394.00	6388.89
2000	27789.68	50386.80	72085.00	6989.92
2001	30096.22	55710.39	72797.00	7652.84
2002	32834.98	62089.77	73280.00	8472.95
2003	36118.48	70274.78	73736.00	9530.59
2004	39766.44	79723.63	74264.00	10735.16
2005	44260.05	90985.67	74647.00	12188.79
2006	49881.08	103908.45	74978.00	13858.52
2007	56964.19	118048.12	75321.00	15672.67
2008	62432.75	133948.34	75564.00	17726.48
2009	68176.56	155492.69	75828.00	20505.97
2010	75403.28	177905.51	76105.00	23376.32
2011	82566.59	201660.40	76420.00	26388.43
2012	88924.22	227430.10	76704.00	29650.36
2013	95771.38	255468.44	76977.00	33187.63

Source: *China Statistical Yearbook (2015)* and Author's Calculation

(2) Data Processing on Volatility Components

According to the domestic and foreign studies, there are three methods to decompose the volatility components and trend components of economic variables: detrending (HP filter, BP filter and Kalman filter, etc.) production function and Phillips Curve. Most of the existing literature on economic volatility applies HP filter to obtain the volatility components of Y, K, L and S. The working principle of HP filter is as follows: filtering (detrending) is applied on the time series of the log of economic variables $(y_t)_{t=1}^T$, and the trend components (g_t) of economic variables are calculated by minimizing the value of the following expression:

$$\min_{gt,t=1,\cdots,T} \sum_{t=1}^{T}(y_t-g_t)^2 + \lambda \sum_{t=1}^{T}[(g_{t+1}-g_t)-(g_t-g_{t+1})]^2$$

Here y_t denotes the log of the economic variables, g_t denotes the trend components of the economic variables, and λ represents a parameter selected by the observer. As for the annual data, we assume λ to be 100. Filtering the log of the economic variables, we obtain the fluctuating components of the economic variables: $\tilde{Y}$, $\tilde{K}$, $\tilde{L}$ and $\tilde{S}$ (see Figure 8-9).

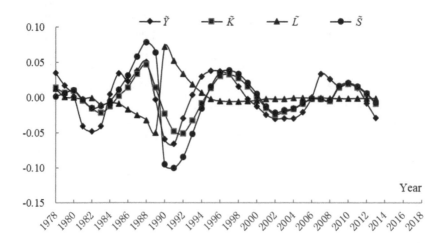

Figure 8-9 Volatility Components of Output (Y), Capital stock (K), Labour force (L) and Factor Structure (S)

Considering the 1990s is a turning point for China's market-oriented reform, we divide the time series between 1978 and 2013 into two stages, taking 1992 as the boundary: the first stage starts from 1978 to 1991, and the second stage starts from 1992 to 2013. Table 8-9 demonstrates the features of economic fluctuation, factor shocks and structural variation. Overall, the volatility of all the factors in the first stage during the reform and opening-up is higher than that in the second stage. Such a result can be explained by the great shocks to the factor of production caused by the impact of the reforms of social security and investment system on the planned economy system prior to the reform and opening-up. Judging from the volatility, in the first stage (1978–1991), factor structural variation was the most volatile, followed by economic fluctuation. The volatility of capital shock[26] was close to that of factor shock; in the second stage (1992–2013), the volatility of economic fluctuation, factors and their structures dropped to different extent. Specifically, factor structural variation was the most volatile, followed by economic fluctuation and capital shock, while labour shock was the least volatile. In terms of the cyclicity of factors and their structures, both capital and factor structure show the feature of pro-cyclicality whereas labour presents the feature of counter-cyclicality[27].

Table 8-9 Descriptive Statistics on Economic Fluctuation, Factor Shocks and Structural Variation

	Standard Deviation (%)			Relevant Coefficients of the Economic Fluctuation		
	1978–2013	1978–1991	1992–2013	1978–2013	1978–1991	1992–2013
$\tilde{Y}$	3.1141	3.9800	2.4908	1	1	1
$\tilde{K}$	2.2151	2.4381	2.1166	0.7572	0.8691	0.6709
$\tilde{L}$	2.0351	3.1357	0.8961	-0.4961	-0.6177	-0.2297
$\tilde{S}$	3.8292	5.1386	2.8338	0.7017	0.7893	0.5737

8.3.2.4. Analysis of the State-Space Model with Time-Varying Parameters

With both the equation of state and the measurement equation passing the test, we obtain the estimated parameters of the equation of state through estimating Equation (8-16) based on China's statistics during

1978–2013, as shown in Figure 8-10. If the relationship between shocks of capital, labour and structural variation and economic volatility is relatively stable[28], then the parameters including sv_1, sv_2 and sv_3 should be fixed in Figure 8-10 and their variation trend with time should all be linear. But according to the estimation of the parameters of the state-space model, the trend is obviously curvy, which indicates that the impact of shocks of capital, labour and factor structural variation on economic volatility is dynamic. Such situation is a result of the transformation of China's economic system, the adjustment in the economic structure and the changes of development approach. Figure 8-10 shows that the variation of sv_1, sv_2 and sv_3 can be divided into two stages: in the first stage (1978–1991), sv_1, sv_2 and sv_3 fluctuate dramatically; in the second stage (1992–2013), sv_1, sv_2 and sv_3 vary regularly.

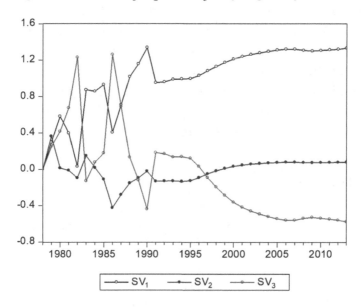

Figure 8-10 Estimated Time-Varying Parameters of the State-Space Model

The two stages of the impact of shocks of capital, labour and factor structural variation on economic volatility are bounded by year 1992. In 1992, Deng Xiaoping's remarks in his tour to China's southern provinces indicate that China's market-oriented reform had entered a new stage. In the first stage (1978–1991), China's economic factor allocation featured insufficient capital factor and relatively sufficient labour factor. Therefore, the labour share of output was higher than capital share. Judging from the impact of the factor shocks on the economic volatility, the shocks of capital, labour and factor structural variation had great impacts. Specifically, the contribution of capital shock to the economic volatility was the biggest among the three and showed a rising trend in fluctuation; the contribution of labour shock to the economic volatility fluctuated around 0; and the contribution of shock of factor structural variation ranked the second and showed a decreasing trend in fluctuation. It can be told that the progressive adjustment in factor structure helps weaken the economic volatility, though the effect is subtle. The violent fluctuation of all the factors may result from the fluctuation of the factor allocation caused by the immature market-oriented reform, the lack of experience in market economy operation and the transformation of various systems and mechanisms.

Since 1992, China's market-oriented reform entered the next stage. As the reform of China's economic system has deepened, capital factor has been gradually supplemented. As previously analysed, before and after the financial crisis in 2008, China's capital stock was close to the golden-rule capital stock. As a result, the capital share of output over this period was higher than that over the last period. In terms of labour factor, the labour share of output declined to some extent due to factors such as the waning of demographic dividend. The shocks of capital, labour and factor structural variation all present certain regularity. Specifically, the contribution of capital shock was the greatest and also positive, showing a gradually rising trend, which was corresponding with its highest volatility of investment in demand structure to some extent; the contribution of labour shock was close to 0, implying that China's labour supply was relatively sufficient over this period; and the contribution of shock of factor structural variation shows a gradually decreasing trend, contrary to the trend of capital shocks, and it has turned negative since 1998. Such fact indicates that shock of factor structural variation has weakened the economic volatility since 1998. Moreover, as the capital stock per capita gets closer to the golden-rule capital stock, the stabilization effect of factor structure on the economic volatility has progressively appeared.

8.3.2.5. Impulse Response Analysis of Factor Shocks

Though the model with time-varying parameters shows the variation trend of the contribution of shocks of factors and the variation of factor structure to economic volatility, it fails to reflect the dynamic response process of economic volatility to factor shocks. Since capital shocks, labour shocks, shocks of the variation of factor structure and economic volatility are all stationary series, impulse response analysis can be carried out. Figure 8-11, Figure 8-12 and Figure 8-13, respectively, demonstrate the impulse response of economic volatility to labour shocks and shocks of the variation of factor structure.

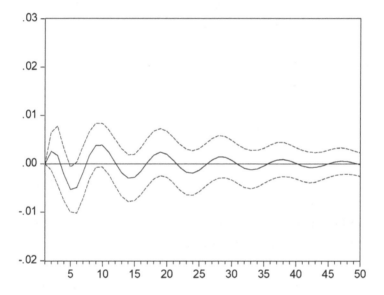

Figure 8-11 Impulse Response of $\tilde{Y}$ to Shocks of $\tilde{K}$

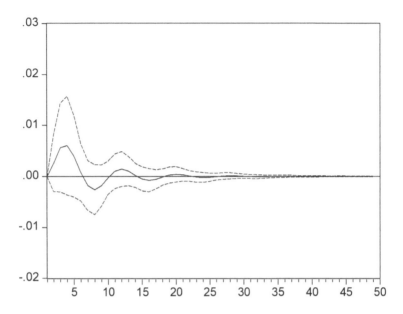

Figure 8-12 Impulse Response of $\tilde{Y}$ to Shocks of $\tilde{L}$

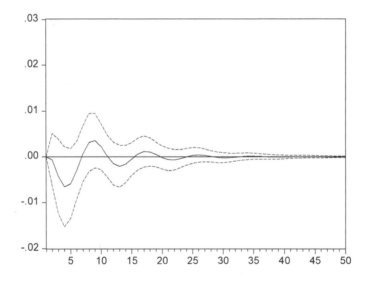

Figure 8-13 Impulse Response of $\tilde{Y}$ to Shocks of $\tilde{S}$

When capital gives a positive shock to economic volatility, the volatility is strengthened after the first and the second period. From the third to the eighth period, the shocks turn negative and reach the peak in the fifth period, easing the volatility. Yet since the eighth period, the shocks have turned positive again. Such pattern is in a five-year cycle, but its influencing range gradually narrows and the shocks to the economy almost disappear in the fiftieth period, which can be explained by the capital formation cycle. After the investment decision is made, it normally takes five years to generate productivity. Therefore, in the short term, capital shock increases economic volatility; in the medium term, it eases the volatility; in the long term, its influence nearly disappears.

When labour gives a positive shock to economic volatility, the volatility is enhanced from the first to the seventh period, reaching the peak in the fifth period. From the eighth to the tenth period, the shocks turn negative and reach the peak in the ninth period. The pattern of shocks from the eleventh to the twentieth period is the same as that from the first to the tenth period, though the amplitude weakens. Accordingly, we can tell that the impact of labour shocks on economic volatility can last about 20 years, which coincides with the reproduction cycle of this human generation.

When the variation of factor structure gives a positive shock to economic volatility, the volatility is eased from the first to the seventh period and the peak of the negative shock is reached in the fourth period. From the eighth to the eleventh period, the shocks turn positive and reach the peak in the ninth period. The pattern of shocks from the twelfth to the twentieth period is the same as that from the first to the tenth period. It can be told that the impact of the variation of factor structure on economic volatility can last about 25 years. Such a result is related to the adoption of capital stock per capita in our study to measure factor structure, as the variation of factor structure can reflect the changes in the levels of both capital and labour.

8.4 Ownership Structure and Economic Growth Stability

8.4.1 Impact of Ownership Structure on Economic Growth Stability

The co-existing of diverse forms of ownership is a prominent feature of China's economy. Thus ownership structure can also affect the steadiness of China's economic growth. Currently domestic scholars (Wu & Zhang, 2015)[29] believe that there are two paths for ownership structure to affect China's economic growth and its economic volatility: (1) the path of production. The non-state-owned economy focuses more on innovation and the improvement of efficiency to strengthen the total factor productivity, which further accelerates the potential economic growth rate[30]; (2) the path of price. The non-state-owned economy is more sensitive and adaptive to the changes of price, while the state-owned economy is less sensitive and adaptive due to factors such as soft budget constraints. The analysis made by Gao (2000)[31] based on China's provincial statistics shows that for every 1 percentage-point increase in the proportion of the non-state-owned economy, the economic growth rate will rise by 0.64 percentage points. Through analysing the impact of ownership structure on factor inputs (labour and capital), Li et al. (2001)[32] point out that when the proportion of the non-state-owned economy reaches over 53 percent, China's economic growth will enter a virtuous circle due to the function of economies of scale. Adding ownership structure into the aggregate production function and carrying out empirical analysis based on China's economic statistics, Tian (2012) finds out China's optimal ownership structure during 1978–2006, where the proportion of the state-owned economy is 25.05 percent[33]. Liu and Shi (2010) hold the view that the dual efficiency loss exists in the state-owned enterprises. Specifically, both the self loss and other efficiency loss caused by the self loss lower the overall economic growth rate[34]. Wang (2011) investigates the impact of diverse forms of ownership in various stages of the economic cycle, finding out that the state-owned economy has a positive impact on the steadiness of economic growth[35]. Wu and Zhang (2015)[36] analyse the impact of the state-owned economy on China's economic operation based on the provincial industrial statistics. Their study shows that the decrease in the proportion of the state-owned economy helps improve capital utility efficiency, economic growth and export-oriented level, which further contributes to stabilizing the economy.

8.4.2 Correlation Analysis of Ownership Structure and Economic Growth Stability

In the macroeconomic analysis, the volatility of different forms of ownership varies. In section 8.4, we categorize the enterprises based on the forms of ownership into state-owned enterprises and non-state-owned enterprises. Due to the huge gap between the volatility of these two enterprises, the variation of ownership structure can also affect the stability of economic growth. It is generally believed that the volatility of investment and production in the state-owned enterprises is higher than that of investment and production in the non-state-owned enterprises. A special principal–agent relationship where there is a great number of principals (owners) exists in the public enterprises. But the agents cannot be properly supervised. In addition, as the manager of the agents, his economic income and social status are decided by the scale of his enterprises. Thus he has great "desire for expansion". Moreover, to promote the economic growth, the government will first scale up the investment in the state-owned economy. Affected by the above two factors, the investment in the state-owned enterprises often grows too fast, resulting in the economic overheating. When the economy is overheated, the national policy to control the economy will first function on the state-owned enterprises, causing their investment scale to shrink sharply. As for non-state-owned enterprises, their production and investment are greatly constrained by the market. Additionally, the external environment has a relatively smaller impact on them. Therefore, the volatility of the non-state-owned enterprises is relatively lower.

The total investment in fixed assets in China's non-state-owned economy has grown fast since 2000. It reached 38701.55 billion yuan in 2014, which was 23.58 times of the 1641.325 billion yuan in 2000. The proportion of the investment in fixed assets in the non-state-owned economy in the total investment in fixed assets rose from 49.86 percent in 1990 to 75.59 percent in 2014 (see Figure 8-14). Due to the lack of statistics on the non-state-owned economy and state-owned economy, we simply illustrate the relationship between ownership structure and the stability of economic growth based on the relationship between the standard deviation of the GDP growth rate and the proportion of the investment in fixed assets in the non-state-owned economy as follows (see Figure 8-15): as the proportion of the investment in fixed assets in the non-state-owned (state-owned) economy gradually rises (falls), the stability of economic growth progressively increases (decreases). They are positively (negatively) correlated.

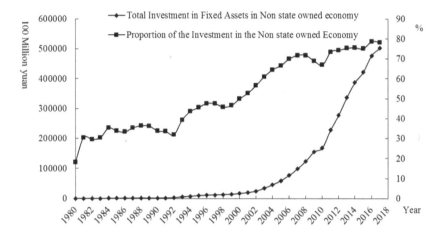

Figure 8-14 Total Investment in Fixed Assets in China's Non-state-owned Economy and Its Proportion

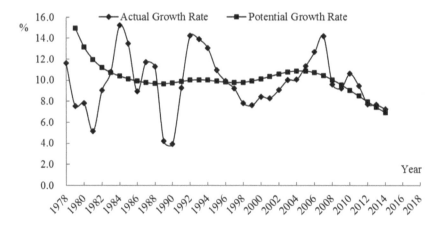

Figure 8-15 Proportion of the Investment in Fixed Assets in the Non-state-Owned Economy and the Steadiness of the Economic Growth
Notes: Calculated based on the statistics of the 10 years prior to this year (including this year), the standard deviation of the GDP growth here is the rolling standard deviation, which means every standard deviation is calculated for each year.
Source: *China Statistical Yearbook-2020* and Author's Calculation

8.5 Empirical Analysis of the Factors Affecting the Steadiness of China's Economic Growth

In section 8.5, we first construct the stability index of economic growth which acts as an indicator to measure the stability of economic growth. Then we use the econometric model to quantitatively analyse how deeply the factors including demand structure, industry structure, ownership structure and output gap affect the stability of economic growth[37].

8.5.1 Construction of the Stability Index of Economic Growth

8.5.1.1. Potential Output and Potential Growth Rate

Since the end of the twentieth century, the HP filter developed by Hodrick and Prescott (1980)[38] has been increasingly widely applied in various areas. Its fundamental principle is to regard the tendency value of sample points as the potential GDP and further estimate the potential GDP by minimizing the actual GDP and the tendency value of sample points. Based on the time series of China's actual GDP during 1978–2014, we first obtain China's potential output with HP filter and then calculate China's potential economic growth rate and the actual growth rate based on the series of both the potential output and the actual GDP (see Figure 8-16).

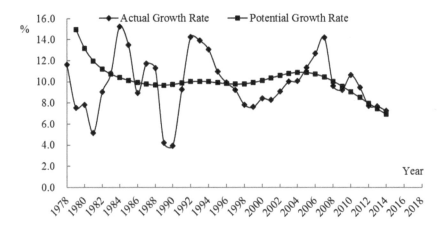

Figure 8-16 China's Actual Growth Rate and Potential Growth Rate

8.5.1.2. Stability Index of Economic Growth

We calculate the stability index of economic growth (W) based on Formula (1-3). As Figure 8-17 shows, since 1978, though there have been fluctuations: the stability index of China's economic growth has remained positive without the appearance of the classical fluctuation (decline in the economic aggregate) or the extremely unstable phenomenon that there is a two-fold difference between the actual growth rate and the potential growth rate.

8.5.2 Economic Growth Stability and Output Gap

In fact, output gap is correlated with the stability of economic growth: the closer the actual economic growth rate is to the potential growth rate (i.e., the smaller the output gap is), the steadier the economic growth is; the more the actual economic growth rate deviates from the potential growth rate (i.e., the larger the output gap is), the unsteadier the economic growth is. Such analysis is properly indicated in Figure 8-18. The relationship between the stability index of the economic growth during 1978–2014 and the actual economic growth rate can be demonstrated with an inverted U-shaped curve. When the actual economic growth rate reaches 10 percent (the potential growth rate), the stability index of the economic growth touches its peak. When the actual economic growth rate is lower or higher than 10 percent, the stability index of the economic growth falls.

Figure 8-17 China's Economic Growth Rate and Stability Index of Its Economic Growth

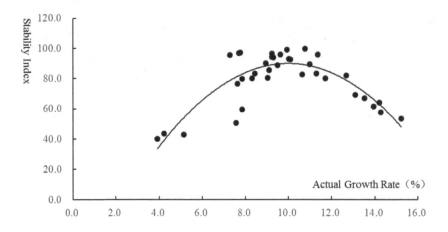

Figure 8-18 Stability Index and the Actual Growth Rate of Output

8.5.3 Empirical Analysis of the Factors Affecting Economic Growth Stability

8.5.3.1. Model and Data Source

Based on the previous analysis, the factors affecting economic growth stability include industry structure, demand structure, output gap and ownership structure of investors. Thus we can construct a model to quantitatively analyse the impact of these factors on economic growth stability. Supposing the impact of all these factors is linear, we have the following model:

$$Y = \beta_0 + \beta_1 OG + \beta_2 DS + \beta_3 IS + \beta_4 OS + \mu \qquad (8\text{-}17)$$

Here Y denotes stability index of economic growth; OG denotes output gap; DS represents demand structure; IS represents industry structure; and OS represents ownership structure.

The stability index of economic growth is obtained by the method introduced previously (see Table 8-10). But considering the convenience for data processing, we select five new series of the stability index of economic growth as the dependent variables of the regression model by moving average method; OG is the absolute value of the deviation between the actual economic growth rate and the potential economic growth rate; DS is represented by the proportion of consumption in the GDP, that is, the consumption rate; IS is represented by the proportion of the added value of the secondary industry in the GDP; OS is denoted by the proportion of the fixed investment in the state-owned economy in the national aggregate fixed investment.

Table 8-10 Relevant Data of the Empirical Analysis of China's Economic Growth Stability

Year	Stability Index	DS (%)	IS (%)	OG (%)	OS (%)
1981	71.02	66.72	45.8	3.80	69.46
1982	69.11	66.48	44.5	5.67	70.42
1983	68.57	67.43	44.1	1.44	69.54
1984	76.99	65.77	42.8	0.60	64.66
1985	75.87	65.02	42.6	5.08	66.08
1986	73.66	64.76	43.4	3.52	66.63
1987	72.14	62.58	43.2	0.96	64.58
1988	67.08	61.85	43.4	1.88	63.53
1989	67.55	63.94	42.4	1.63	63.67
1990	63.08	63.32	40.9	5.60	66.11
1991	58.81	61.91	41.4	5.92	66.38
1992	64.43	59.71	43.0	0.74	68.05
1993	74.70	58.26	46.1	4.19	60.63
1994	75.99	58.19	46.1	3.86	56.42
1995	83.17	59.07	46.7	3.01	54.44
1996	86.63	60.00	47.0	0.93	52.40
1997	87.82	59.64	47.0	0.10	52.49
1998	86.24	60.48	45.7	0.58	54.11
1999	82.40	62.67	45.3	2.07	53.42
2000	80.71	63.68	45.4	2.39	50.14
2001	83.55	62.01	44.7	1.76	47.31
2002	87.01	61.01	44.3	2.10	43.40
2003	89.37	57.94	45.5	1.51	38.98
2004	89.32	55.21	45.8	0.72	35.51
2005	84.37	54.11	46.9	0.71	33.42
2006	85.52	52.36	47.4	0.58	29.97
2007	86.80	50.63	46.7	2.15	28.19
2008	83.68	49.74	46.8	0.35	28.18
2009	84.69	49.96	45.7	1.56	31.03
2010	91.67	49.07	46.2	0.96	33.10
2011	88.68	50.24	46.1	0.23	26.48
2012	97.15	50.81	45.0	0.24	25.68
2013	96.79	51.04	43.7	0.32	24.61
2014	95.41	51.42	42.7	0.35	24.41

8.5.3.2. Data Stationarity and Cointegration Test

Due to the non-stationarity of the statistics, spurious regression tends to occur when time-series data are used. Thus we test for the data stationarity before regression. Table 8-11 shows the result of an ADF test for the data stationarity. Conducting an ADF test on the level value and the first-order difference of five variables including stability index of economic growth, OG, DS, IS and OS, we see that at the significance level of 1 percent, the level values of the five variables are non-stationary; at the significance level of 1 percent, the first-order difference series of the five variables are stationary. In other words, the five variables series are integrated of order one.

Table 8-11 Result of Unit Root Test (ADF Test)

Variable	ADF	Critical Value at 10%	Critical Value at 5%	Critical Value at 1%	Condition (G,T,N)	Result
Y	-1.341348	-2.625121	-2.971853	-3.689194	(G,0,1)	Non-stationary
△Y	-3.775704	-2.625121	-2.971853	-3.689194	(C,0,1)	Stationary
OG	-2.403275	-1.610011	-1.952910	-2.647120	(0,0,0)	Non-stationary
△OG	-7.286159	-2.627420	-2.976263	-3.699871	(G,0,2)	Stationary
DS	-2.155654	-3.225334	-3.580623	-4.323979	(C,T,1)	Non-stationary
△DS	-2.781760	-1.609798	-1.953381	-2.650145	(0,0,1)	Stationary
IS	-1.889437	-2.625121	-2.971853	-3.689194	(G,0,1)	Non-stationary
△IS	-3.979278	-1.609798	-1.953381	-2.650145	(0,0,1)	Stationary
OS	-1.799918	-3.221728	-3.574244	-4.309824	(G,T,0)	Non-stationary
△OS	-4.439568	-2.625121	-2.971853	-3.689194	(G,0,1)	Stationary

Notes: C, T and N, respectively, represent "with constant term", "with time trend" and "with difference lag order". The Schwarz Information Criterion (SIC) is used in the selection of lag order.

Though non-stationary, the five variables including stability index of economic growth, OG, DS, IS and OS are all integrated of order one and meet the premises of a cointegration test. We carry out the Johansen Cointegration test to testify whether these exists a long-term equilibrium relation. As Table 8-12 shows, at the significance level of 5 percent, there exists cointegration relation among the five variables.

Table 8-12 Result of Johansen Cointegration Test

Null Hypothesis	Characteristic Value	Trace Statistic	Critical Value at 5%	Probability	Maximum Characteristic Value	5% Critical Value	Value of P
None	0.861916	119.0357	69.81889	0.0000	55.43692	33.87687	0.0000
At most 1	0.580613	63.59878	47.85613	0.0009	24.33093	27.58434	0.1236
At most 2	0.555355	39.26785	29.79707	0.0030	22.69339	21.13162	0.0299
At most 3	0.445539	16.57446	15.49471	0.0343	16.51322	14.26460	0.0217
At most 4	0.002185	0.061238	3.841466	0.8045	0.061238	3.841466	0.8045

8.5.3.3. Regression Analysis

Regressing Equation (8-17) based on the sample data in Table 8-10, we obtain the estimated result (see Table 8-13).

The result of regression shows that the t-statistics of the parameters of all the variables are higher than the critical value at the significance level of 5 percent. The goodness of fit after adjustment is higher than 0.80 with the Durbin-Watson (DW) statistic of 1.4197, indicating that the model has no autocorrelation and is well set.

Table 8-13 Result of the Empirical Analysis of the Factors Affecting Steadiness

Explanatory Variable	Estimated Value of Parameters	Standard Deviation	T-Statistic	Value of P
OG	-0.968000	0.463217	-2.089733	0.0466
DS	0.785944	0.308528	2.547402	0.0171
IS	1.471444	0.247986	5.933580	0.0000
OS	-0.624317	0.150958	-4.135693	0.0003
Goodness of Fit (R2)	0.826273	Average Explained Variables		78.39795
Modified Goodness of Fit (R2)	0.806227	Average Standard Deviation of Explained Variables		9.077139
Standard Error of the Regression	3.995721	Akaike Information Criterion (AIC)		5.731891
Residual Sum of Square (RSS)	415.1105	Schwarz Criterion		5.918717
Log-likelihood Ratio	-81.97837	H-Q Information Criterion		5.791658
DW Statistics	1.419702			

Table 8-13 shows that the stability of economic growth is mainly affected by output gap, demand structure, industry structure and ownership structure of investors. Specifically, the impact of demand structure and industry structure is positive, while that of output gap and ownership structure of investors is negative. Such a result is consistent with the previous theoretical analysis. These four factors can explain over 80 percent of the variation of the economic growth stability. In detail, for every 1 percentage-point increase in output gap, the stability index of economic growth declines by 0.97; for every 1 percentage-point increase in demand structure (final consumption rate), the stability index of economic growth rises by 0.79; for every 1 percentage-point increase in industry structure, the stability index of economic growth rises by 1.47; and for every 1 percentage-point increase in ownership structure (proportion of the state-owned economy), the stability index of economic growth declines by 0.62.

8.6 Conclusion and Policy Suggestions

8.6.1 Conclusions of the Study

In Chapter 8, we first sum up the measurement indicators of economic growth stability to further analyse the evolution of China's economic growth stability since the reform and opening-up. Then we investigate the factors affecting China's economic growth stability based on China's actual circumstances. The conclusions are as follows:

First, the stability of the growth of China's GDP, final consumption and gross capital formation has been overall improved since the reform and opening-up: (i) The stability of the growth of gross capital formation and net export is poorer than that of the growth of GDP and final consumption; (ii) The stability of the growth of final consumption has been close to that of GDP growth in most years since 1978. According to the result of the variance decomposition, the structure effect of demand structure is -5.2 percent, which indicates that the variation of demand structure weakens the stability of economic growth. This is mainly because the proportion of final consumption which is relatively more stable in demand decreases while the proportions of capital formation and net export which are relatively less stable increase; (iii) The volatility effect of demand is 108.2 percent, which implies that the further increase in the stability of demands contributes to the improvement of the economic growth stability; (iv) The coupling effect of demand is -2.9 percent, showing that the interaction among the components of demand improves the economic volatility.

Second, overall, the stability of the GDP and the three industries has been gradually improved since the reform and opening-up: (i) As for industries, the stability of the tertiary industry, close to the GDP growth stability, is better than that of the primary industry and the secondary industry; (ii) The growth of the primary industry is the most volatile while the growth of the secondary and tertiary industry is more stable. According to the result of the variance decomposition, the structure effect of industry is 25.6 percent, which indicates that such variation enhances the stability of economic growth, mainly because the proportion of the tertiary industry which is relatively stable rises with the drop of the proportion of the primary industry while that of the secondary industry which is relatively unstable slightly varies; (iii) The volatility effects 81.3 percent, which implies that the further increase in the stability of industries contributes to the improvement of the economic growth stability and the 81.3 percent decline of the volatility in GDP results from the increase in the stability of the three industries; (iv) The coupling effect is -6.9 percent, showing that the interaction among the three industries increases the economic volatility.

Third, judging from the impact of factor structure on China's economic growth stability, the fluctuation of the growth rates of China's factors of production can directly cause the fluctuation of the economic growth: (i) For every 1 percent fluctuation of labour input, the economy fluctuates by 0.6765 percent; (ii) For every 1 percent fluctuation of capital input, the economy fluctuates by 0.7535 percent. Judging from the impact of various factor shocks and the variation of factor structure on the economic volatility, the two stages of the impact of shocks of capital, labour and factor structural variation on the economic volatility are bounded by Year 1992. In 1992, Deng Xiaoping's remarks in his tour to China's southern provinces indicate that China's market-oriented reform had entered a new stage. In the first stage (1978–1991), China's economic factor allocation featured insufficient capital factor and relatively sufficient labour factor. Therefore, the labour share of output was higher than capital shares. Judging from the impact of the factor shocks on the economic volatility, the shocks of capital, labour and factor structural variation affected greatly. Specifically, the contribution of capital shock on the economic volatility was the biggest among the three and showed a rising trend in fluctuation: (1) The contribution of labour shock to the economic volatility fluctuated around 0; (2) The contribution of shock of factor structural variation ranked the second and showed a decreasing trend in fluctuation. It can be told that the progressive adjustment in factor structure helps weaken the economic volatility, though the effect is subtle. The violent fluctuation of all the factors may result from the fluctuation of the factor allocation caused by the immature market-oriented reform, the lack of experience in market economy operation and the transformation of various systems and mechanisms.

Fourth, output gap also affects the stability of economic growth. Generally speaking, the wider the gap is, the poorer the stability of economic growth is.

Fifth, the ownership structure of investment subjects is a factor that affects steadiness as well. The larger the proportion of the state-owned economy is, the poorer the stability of economic growth is.

Finally, the stability of economic growth is mainly affected by output gap, demand structure, industry structure and ownership structure of investors: (i) For every 1 percentage-point increase in output gap, the stability index of economic growth declines by 0.97; (ii) For every 1 percentage-point increase in demand structure (final consumption rate), the stability index of economic growth rises by 0.79; (iii) For every 1 percentage-point increase in industry structure, the stability index of economic growth rises by 1.47; and (iv) For every 1 percentage-point increase in ownership structure (proportion of the state-owned economy), the stability index of economic growth declines by 0.62.

8.6.2 Suggestion for Polices

At the current stage, China's main macroeconomic goal is to maintain a sustained, rapid and steady growth. As great attention is paid to the stability of economic growth, we put forward the following suggestion for policies to help strengthen the steadiness of China's economic growth.

First, household consumption rate should be raised. According to the previous analysis in this chapter, the increase in consumption has a positive impact on the stability index of economic growth, improving the economic growth stability. But China's consumption rate has been in a decreasing trend since the reform and opening-up, going down by 10.7 percentage points over 36 years from 61.4 percent in 1978 to 50.7 percent in 2014. We further conclude that the decline of China's consumption rate is mainly caused by the decrease of China's household consumption rate with the government consumption rate remaining at 15 percent. Therefore, to raise the consumption rate, we first need to increase the household consumption rate, which can be achieved through the following: (i) increasing household income to make the growth of household income keep pace with the GDP growth; (ii) improving the social security system to ward off the worries of residents when they consume; (iii) accelerating the adjustment of income distribution to raise the proportion of labour income in the GDP in the primary distribution; (iv) narrowing the income gap to promote the growth of consumption demand; (v) optimizing the internal structure of the consumption expenditure of urban and rural residents to strongly improve the level of service consumption, which is a premise of the sustainable growth of consumption.

Second, the management of macroeconomic supply should be enhanced to raise the actual economic growth rate to the level of the potential growth rate, which will further improve the steadiness of the economic growth. Regarding the management of supply, it is significant to maximize the potential for supply through the major transformation of production technology and reconstruction of the dynamic mechanism of supply. Meanwhile, industry structure should be reasonably planned and adjusted to make supply structure adapt to demand structure and thus reduce idle resources and stockpiles of supply. Obviously, compared with the management of demand, the management of supply is harder to yield results in the short term and thus requires long-term efforts. However, once the foundation of supply is truly improved, the conflicts between demand and supply can be fundamentally coordinated to lay a solid foundation for enhancing the stability of economic growth.

Third, the adjustment of industry structure should be accelerated. Corresponding with the supply side in the economy, industry structure need to be adjusted with the demand side in the economy (demand structure). In fact, the adjustment of industry structure can be achieved through adjusting demand structure (Shen, 2011)[39]. In addition, in terms of industry structure itself, we can optimize it by increasing the inputs into the agricultural infrastructure to properly adjust the internal structure and further lower the volatility of agricultural output; transforming and upgrading industry structure during the process of promoting industrialization; and keep promoting the traditional industries with focus on fundamental and emerging service industries.

Fourth, factor input structure should be optimized. As the fluctuations of production factors will lead to the fluctuation of economic growth rate, it needs to be ensured that the supply of production factors matches the demand so as to reduce the factor volatility caused by the misallocation of resources. The optimization can be achieved by raising the investment into research and development to increase total factor productivity; increasing the investment into education to improve the quality of labourers; and expanding the effective investment to stabilize the level of capital accumulation.

Fifth, the reform of ownership structure should be promoted. Meanwhile, the ratio of the state-owned economy to the non-state-owned economy ought to be adjusted. Though it is generally believed that the efficiency of the state-owned economy is lower than that of the non-state-owned economy, the state-owned economy is still a major tool for national macroeconomic regulation and also an economic stabilizer. Therefore, it is impossible to lower the proportion of the state-owned economy without restrictions. There must be an optimal scale for the state-owned economy (Tian & Jing, 2008)[40], to which the state-owned economy should converge. Furthermore, the volatility of the state-owned economy can be reduced through reforming the state-owned economy itself, which eventually contributes to improving the stability of economic growth.

Notes

1 Chen Yanbin, "Welfare Cost of China's Business Cycle," *The Journal of World Economy* 2 (2006).
2 Chenery H. and Syrquin M. *Industrialization and Growth*, trans. Wu Qi et al. (Shanghai People's Publishing House, 1995).
3 Eggers A. and Ioannides Y.M., "The Role of Output Composition in the Stabilization of U.S.Output Growth," *Discussion Papers* 28, no. 3 (2006): 585–595.
4 Ji Ming and Liu Zhibiao, "The Impact of the evolution of China's Demand Structure on the Economic Growth and Economic Fluctuation," *Economic Science* 1 (2014).
5 Yang Tianyu and Liu Yunting, "Structural Transformation and Stabilization of Business Cycle," *Economic Theory and Business Management* 7 (2011).
6 The fluctuating component of the GDP obtained from the HP-filtered series represents the percentage of GDP deviation from trend.
7 Eggers A. and Ioannides Y.M., "The Role of Output Composition in the Stabilization of U.S.Output Growth," *Discussion Papers* 28, no. 3 (2006): 585–595.
8 Blanchard O. and Simon J., "The Long and Large Decline in U.S.Output Volatility," *Brookings Papers on Economic Activity* 32, no. 1 (2001): 135–164.
9 Peneder M., "Industrial Structure and Aggregate Growth," *Economic Dynamics* 14, no. 4 (2003): 427–448.
10 Eggers A. and Ioannides Y.M., "The Role of Output Composition in the Stabilization of U.S.Output Growth," *Discussion Papers* 28, no. 3 (2006): 585–595.
11 Fang Fuqian and Zhan Xinyu, "Empirical Analysis of the Stabilizing Effect of Industrial Structure Upgrading on the Economic Fluctuations in China," *Economic Theory and Business Management* 9 (2011).
12 Gan Chunhun, Zhen Ruogu, and Yu Dianfan, "The Impact of China's Industry Structure Transformation on the Economic Growth and Fluctuation," *Economic Research Journal* 5 (2011).
13 Yang Tianyu and Liu Yunting, "Structural Transformation and Stabilization of China's Macroeconomy," *Economic Theory and Business Management* 7 (2011).
14 Li Qiang, "Industrial Structure Changes Aggravate or Restrain Economic Fluctuations?--Based on Analysis of China," *Research on Economics and Management* 7 (2012).
15 Li Meng, "Research on the Correlationship between Industry Structure and Economic Fluctuation," *Economic Review* 6 (2010).
16 The fluctuating component of the GDP obtained from the HP-filtered series represents the percentage of GDP deviation from trend.
17 Eggers A. and Ioannides Y.M., "The Role of Output Composition in the Stabilization of U.S.Output Growth," *Discussion Papers* 28, no. 3 (2006): 585–595.
18 Abramowitz Moses, "Resource and Output Trends in the United States since 1870,"*American Economic Review* 46, no. 2 (1956): 5–23.

19 Solow M. Robert, "Technical Change and the Aggregate Production Function," *Review of Economics and Statistics* 39, no. 3 (1957): 312–320.
20 LI Chunji, "China's Business Cycle from the Shocks to Investment and Technologies: An Analysis Based on the Estimation of RBC Model," *On Economic Problems* 9 (2010).
21 Guo Qingwang and Jia Junxue, "The Spelling out of China's Economic Fluctuation: Impact by Investment and Productivity of All Factors," *Management World* 7 (2004).
22 Chen Liang, "Exogenous Shocks, Variation of Factor Inputs and Output Volatility," Thesis for Master Degree, School of Economics of Fudan University, 2010.
23 Ran Guanghe, Cao Yuequn, and Dehua, "Factor Input, Money Supply and Their Influence on China's Economic Fluctuation," *Management World* 2 (2008).
24 Fang Fuqian and Zhan Xinyu, "Empirical Analysis of the Stabilizing Effect of Industrial Structure Upgrading on the Economic Fluctuations in China," *Economic Theory and Business Management* 9 (2011).
25 Fang Fuqian and Zhan Xinyu, "Empirical Analysis of the Stabilizing Effect of Industrial Structure Upgrading on the Economic Fluctuations in China," *Economic Theory and Business Management* 9 (2011).
26 According to the tradition Keynesian economic theory, the volatility of investment is generally higher than that of the GDP, but it is worth noting that here we refer to the volatility of capital. Since even huge changes in investment merely result in minor changes in capital stock, the conclusion that the volatility of capital stock is lower than that of output is not contrary to the traditional economic theory.
27 Based on Figure 8-9, with the adjustment in the statistical standard, China's employed population in 1989 was 55.29 million and rose by about 100 million to 64.49 million in 1990. On contrary to such a huge number, the annual increase in the near years was only 10 million on average. As there is lack of appropriate ways to adjust the statistics, we keep the statistics original.
28 Corresponding with what the model with fixed parameters demonstrates.
29 Wu Zhenyu and Zhang Wenkui, "An Empirical Study on the Impact of the Proportion of the State-owned Economy on the Macroeconomic Operation During 2000–2012," *Management World* 2 (2015).
30 For instance, in terms of investment behaviour, the investment in the non-state-owned economy pays more attention to efficiency while that in the state-owned economy may involve other purposes (such as to stabilize the economy).
31 Gao Li, "An Empirical Analysis of Investment Slowdown in the Non-state-owned Economy—The Micro Formation Mechanism ofDeflation," *Reform* 6 (2000).
32 Liu Wei and Li Shaorong, "The Ownership Change and the Economic Growth and Upgrading of Factors Efficiency," *Economic Research Journal* 1 (2001).
33 Tian Weimin and Jing Weimin, "Optimal Arrangement of Ownership Structure Based on Economic Growth—Empirical Study on the Relationship Between

China"s Ownership Structure and Economic Growth," *On Economic Problems* 8 (2008).

34 Liu Ruiming and Shi Lei, "The Dual Efficiency Loss of State-Owned Enterprises and Economic Growth," *Economic Research Journal* 1 (2010).

35 Wang Wencheng, "The Influence of Different Ownership on Economic Growth," *China Soft Science Magazine* 6 (2011).

36 Wu Zhenyu and Zhang Wenkui, "An Empirical Study on the Impact of the Proportion of the State-owned Economy on the Macroeconomic Operation During 2000–2012," *Management World* 2 (2015).

37 Due to the lack of reasonable measurement indicators for factor structure, we did not add factor structure into the econometric model for analysis.

38 Hodrick R.J. and Prescott E.C., "Postwar U.S.Business Cycles: An Empirical Investigation," *Journal of Money Credit & Banking* 29, no.1 (1981): 1–16.

39 Shen Lisheng, "How does the Change of Final Demand Structure Affect the Change of Industrial Structure?--Analysis Based on the Input-Output Model," *The Journal of Quantitative & Technical Economics* 12 (2011).

40 Tian Weimin and Jing Weimin, "Optimal Arrangement of Ownership Structure Based on Economic Growth—Empirical Study on the Relationship Between China"s Ownership Structure and Economic Growth," *On Economic Problems* 8 (2008).

Chapter 9

Analysis of the Impact of Final Consumption Rate on Economic Growth and Its Steadiness

Final consumption rate generally affects economic growth and its steadiness in the following two ways: The first is the traditional indirect transmission mechanism of investment. Specifically, as output is segmented into consumption and investment, if consumption rate is too high (investment rate is relatively low)[1], there lacks impetus for economic growth and thus the long-term and steady growth of economy is undermined. On the contrary, if consumption rate is too low (investment rate is relatively high)[2], economy is dynamically inefficient, which also weakens the long-term and steady growth of economy and further causes loss in household welfare. Only when consumption rate reaches its optimal level can economy have sufficient impetus for its growth and achieve dynamic efficiency, which ensures economic growth and its steadiness. The second is consumption which is the most stable variable accounting for the largest proportion in aggregate demand. Though the impact of increase in consumption rate on economic growth is not as remarkable as that of increase in investment rate, it is lasting longer and more stable[3]. In addition, as long as consumption rate is below its optimal level, there won't be any negative effect such as economic dynamic inefficiency. Therefore, the rise of consumption rate is an internal impetus for the long-term and sustained growth of economy. For the economic development, consumption functions as an "automatic stabilizer". When consumption rate remains at a low level resulting from long-term weak consumption, investment and net export from the demand side are unable to keep long-time steady growth even if the impetus for growth from the supply side is strong. Eventually, problems such as overcapacity, low investment efficiency and excessive reliance on external demand arise, which further leads to weak economic growth with the risk of falling into the "middle-income trap".

There is not much literature on the mechanism of how consumption rate affects economic growth as well as its steadiness. Among the existing literature, only Ouyang et al. (2016)[4] carry out relevant research where they sum up the three kinds of mechanism of how consumption rate affects economic growth: First, the increase or decrease in household consumption rate directly results in the acceleration or deceleration of economic growth. But the effect of changes in investment caused by household consumption on economic growth may differ from that of household consumption. Second, changes in household consumption scale affect economic growth by influencing the utility efficiency of factors, which can be achieved through exerting influence on economies of scale and economic structures. Third, changes in household consumption scale may affect technological innovation and thus promote or inhibit economic growth. But the analysis of the impact of consumption rate on economic growth as well as consumption growth merely gives theoretical elaboration, lacking construction of a theoretical model.

According to the above analysis, it is hard to quantitatively analyse the two ways consumption rate affects economic growth and its steadiness. Thus in this chapter, we look into the impact of changes in consumption rate on economic growth and its steadiness through numerical simulation. Considering the availability of data and the necessity to carry out multi-perspective analysis, we investigate the impact from the following three aspects: first, from the aspect of national accounts, with fixed growth rates of consumption, investment and net export, we simulate the impact of changes in final consumption rate on economic growth; second, from the aspect of input and output, with increasing consumption rate as well as decreasing investment rate and net export rate, we analyse such impact; third, based on China's statistics during 1978–2016, we build a VAR model of final consumption rate, investment rate and economic growth rate to investigate the impact of changes in consumption rate on China's economic growth and its steadiness.

9.1 Analysis of the Impact of Increase in Consumption Rate on Economic Growth – from the Perspective of National Accounts

Though the "high investment and growth" pattern of economy contributes to China's rapid economic growth over the past three decades, it also causes severe imbalance in China's demand structure. Specifically, China's capital formation rate keeps rising year by year, reaching 46.8 percent in 2014, while the final consumption rate keeps falling, touching 50.7 percent in 2014. The statistics show that China's capital formation rate (final consumption rate) is far higher (lower) than the level of the countries at the same development stage as well as the world average level. The imbalance in demand structure exerts negative influence on the sustainability and health of economic growth. For instance, the policy for long-term investment eventually results in overcapacity caused by excessive investment in some industries, which inhibits the long-term economic growth.

China promulgated the policy to boost domestic demand back in the 1990s. Since consumption accounts for the largest proportion in domestic demand, it is proposed in the *Outline of the 12th Five-Year Plan* to ease the negative influence of China's low final consumption rate on the sustainability of economic growth with measures that include boosting domestic demand and establishing a long-term mechanism that improves the level of consumption. As for the question of what impact will the increase in final consumption rate have on China's economic growth and its steadiness, only a few scholars within China carried out research in relevant fields. Yet they did not focus on this specific topic.

Among the relevant studies, Shen (2011)[5] points out that if the consumption rate increases by 5 percentage points with the rate of capital formation and exports, respectively, declining by 2.5 percentage points, the structural transformation of final demand barely affects GDP. Lin and Wang (2013)[6] conclude that since the fourth quarter of 1995, China's economy has been out of the boom-bust cycle which refers to the alternating phases of economic growth and decline and has entered the Great Moderation where the waves of the economic cycle are becoming ripples. The stability of economic growth has been dramatically improved ever since. Guo, Wang and Wu (2017)[7] measure the impact of changes in demand structure (with decreasing investment rate and fixed government rate as well as net export rate) on the steadiness of China's economic growth and household consumption rate based on the estimation of the Cobb-Douglas aggregate production function. The result shows that the fall of investment rate leads to the decrease of economic growth rate and increase in household consumption rate.

Based on the above analysis, we investigate the impact of improvement in consumption rate on economic growth and its stability through numerical simulation from the aspect of national accounts. The outline of this chapter is as follows: in the first part, we discuss the influence of final consumption and capital formation on long-term economic growth; in the second part, we analyse the relationship between final consumption rate as well as contribution rate of final consumption and economic growth as well as its steadiness; and in the third part, we look into the impact of the increase in final consumption rate on the stability of economic growth.

9.1.1 Final Consumption's Role in Sustaining Economic Growth

From the aspect of demand, economic growth is primarily driven by the "troika" consisting of consumption, investment and export. Since export is an external demand which mainly relies on the international economic situation, it is unable to promote long-term economic growth. In this way, consumption and investment are the only two driving forces of the long-run demand of economic growth. Consumption growth rate, investment growth rate and demand structure (final consumption rate and capital formation rate) determine the prospect of economic growth. Transforming GDP=C+I+NX, the identity of national accounts, into its incremental: GDP=ΔC+ΔI+ΔNX, and then dividing both sides of the equation by GDP, we obtain:

$$\frac{\Delta GDP}{GDP} = \frac{\Delta C}{GDP} + \frac{\Delta I}{GDP} + \frac{\Delta NX}{GDP}$$

$$= \frac{\Delta C}{C} \times \frac{C}{GDP} + \frac{\Delta I}{I} \times \frac{I}{GDP} + \frac{\Delta NX}{NX} \times \frac{NX}{GDP} \quad (9\text{-}1)$$

Here $\Delta C/C$, $\Delta I/I$ and $\Delta NX/NX$, respectively, represent the growth rates of final consumption rate, gross capital formation and net export; C/GDP, I/GDP and NX/GDP, respectively, denote final consumption rate, capital formation rate and net export rate. Equation (9-1) indicates that economic growth rate is decided by investment growth rate, consumption growth rate, net export growth rate and demand structure. Since the reform and opening-up, China's demand structure has witnessed major changes. Such structural changes, the growth rates of investment and consumption as well as other economic features, are all decisive factors in the evolution of economic growth. To underline the impact of investment and consumption on China's economic growth, we carry out the analysis through building a time-varying state-space model.

We make the analysis based on China's macroeconomic statistics during 1978–2016 which falls under the category of time series. Considering China's economic structure and mechanism have experienced huge changes since the reform and opening-up, it would be difficult to observe the dynamic impact of investment and consumption on economic growth. Therefore, we build a time-varying model based on the econometric state-space model:

$$\boxed{\text{Measurement Equation}}\ GDPg_t = c + sv_{1t}Cg_t + sv_{2t}Ig_t + \mu_t$$

$$sv_{1t} = \gamma_1 sv_{1t-1} + \eta_{1t} \quad (9\text{-}2)$$

$$\boxed{\text{Equation of State}}\ sv_{2t} = \gamma_2 sv_{2t-1} + \eta_{2t}$$

Here both μ_t and η_{it} are 0 on average and they are mutually independent. Then we have: $\begin{bmatrix}\mu_t\\\eta_{it}\end{bmatrix} \sim N\left(\begin{bmatrix}0\\0\end{bmatrix},\begin{bmatrix}\sigma_1^2 & 0\\0 & \rho_i^2\end{bmatrix}\right), i=1,2; t=1,2,\cdots,T.$

In Equation (9-2), $GDPg_t$ represents economic growth rate which is obtained by subtracting 100 from China's GDP index in *China Statistical Yearbook* (the index was 100 last year); Cg_t and Ig_t, respectively, denote the growth rates of final consumption and investment, which can be deduced based on Equation (9-1) and the contribution rates of the three demands to economic growth. In the measurement equation of the model, $GDPg_t$ is an explained variable while Cg_t and Ig_t are explanatory variables. Additionally, sv_1 and sv_2 are regression coefficients. As they are set to be time-varying, their variation with time following the random walk process are unobservable, which reflects the variation process of the sensitivity of economic growth to consumption growth and investment growth.

According to Table 9-1 which demonstrates the result of estimation on Equation (9-2) obtained with the help of a software called Eviews, all variables pass the significance test.

Table 9-1 Estimation Result of the State-Space Model

	Fixed Parameter	Standard Error	Z-Statistic	Probability
C(1)	3.960342	1.083560	3.654935	0.0003
C(2)	0.790069	0.252764	3.125716	0.0018
	Variable Parameter	Root Mean Square	Z-Statistic	Probability
SV1	0.333177	0.054091	6.159543	0.0000
SV2	0.238791	0.043099	5.540477	0.0000

Judging from the regression coefficients of the state-space model, the sensitivity of GDP growth rate to consumption growth rate (0.333177) is higher than that to investment growth rate (0.238791). Figure 9-1 shows the trend of the sensitivity of GDP growth rate to consumption growth rate and investment growth rate during 1978–2016. sv_1 represents the sensitivity of consumption growth rate, and sv_2 denotes the sensitivity of investment growth rate. According to the state-space model, sv_1 (sv_2) represents the change in GDP growth rate caused by every 1 percentage-point change in consumption (investment) growth rate.

First, Figure 9-1 demonstrates that for the long run, the sensitivity of GDP growth to consumption growth is far higher than that to investment growth. Such a result indicates investment is unlikely to replace consumption as the first driving force of sustainable, steady and long-term economic growth.

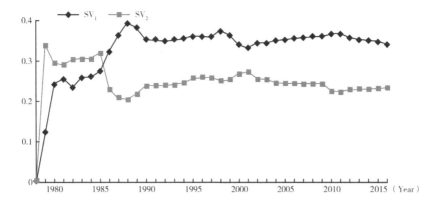

Figure 9-1 Estimated Variable Parameters of the Impact of Consumption and Investment on Economic Growth

Second, the trend of the sensitivity of China's economic growth to consumption growth can be divided into different stages: (i) In the first stage (1978–1988), when the contribution of consumption growth to economic growth gradually increased, economic growth became more sensitive to consumption growth. It is mainly because the demand for consumption of Chinese households was long inhibited prior to the reform and opening-up while such inhibition was eliminated after the reform and opening-up. (ii) In the second stage (1989 till now), the contribution rate of consumption growth to economic growth basically remained stable, fluctuating around 0.35.

Third, the trend of the sensitivity of China's economic growth to investment growth can also be divided into different stages: (i) In the first stage (1978–1988), when the contribution of investment growth to economic growth gradually decreased, economic growth became less sensitive to consumption growth though still more sensitive than it was to consumption growth. It can be explained by the insufficiency of supply after the reform and opening-up. When the long inhibition of demand for investment was eliminated, investment efficiency was improved and meanwhile restricted by the law of diminishing marginal returns. (ii) In the second stage (1989–2001), the contribution of investment growth to economic growth slowly climbed, resulting from the progressive reform of investment structure and mechanism after China entered its new stage of reform. (iii) In the third stage (2002–till now), the sensitivity of economic growth to investment slowly declined. Since the twenty-first century, the feature that China's economy is mainly driven by investment has become more marked, along with the problems it causes such as the decrease in investment efficiency and overcapacity. As a result, the sensitivity of economic growth to investment growth has weakened.

9.1.2 Relationship between Final Consumption Rate and Economic Growth as well as Its Steadiness

9.1.2.1. Final Consumption Rate and the Contribution Rate of Final Consumption[8]

In GDP=CH+I+G+NX, the macroeconomic identity of national accounts, CH represents household consumption; I represents investment; G denotes government purchase; and NX denotes net export. In China's national economic statistics, household consumption and government purchase are combined as final consumption (C); investment is seen as gross capital formation (I); and the meaning of net export is the same as that in the western accounting system. Thus we have GDP=C+I+NX. Dividing both sides of the equation by GDP, we obtain: $\frac{GDP}{GDP} = \frac{C}{GDP} + \frac{I}{GDP} + \frac{NX}{GDP}$. That is: $\frac{C}{GDP} + \frac{I}{GDP} + \frac{NX}{GDP} = 1$. The sum of final consumption rate (CR), capital formation rate (IR) and net export rate (NXR) equals 1. The increment of GDP=C+I+NX is: $\Delta GDP = \Delta C + \Delta I + \Delta NX$. Dividing both sides of the equation by ΔGDP, we have the expression of the contribution rate of final consumption rate, capital formation and net export to economic growth rate: $\frac{\Delta C}{\Delta GDP} + \frac{\Delta I}{\Delta GDP} + \frac{\Delta NX}{\Delta GDP} = 100\%$. Here $\frac{\Delta C}{\Delta GDP}$ represents the contribution rate of final consumption rate; $\dfrac{\Delta I}{\Delta GDP}$ represents the contribution rate of capital formation; and $\dfrac{\Delta NX}{\Delta GDP}$ represents the contribution rate of net export.

The above analysis indicates that the contribution of consumption to economy can be measured from the following two perspectives: the first is the contribution to the GDP; and the second is the contribution to the economic increment (economic growth). The former, reflecting the contribution of consumption to the GDP, is normally measured by final consumption rate which is the proportion of gross final consumption (gross capital formation) in the GDP. The latter, reflecting the contribution of increment of final consumption to economic growth, is the proportion of increment of final consumption in the GDP. Figure 9-2 shows the respective contribution of final consumption to both GDP and economic increment. It can be told that the contribution rate of final consumption is more volatile than final consumption rate, but final consumption rate seems to act as the trend component of the contribution rate of final consumption. Thus the contribution rate of final consumption fluctuates around final consumption rate.

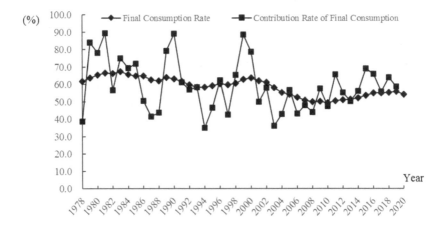

Figure 9-2 China's Final Consumption Rate and Contribution Rate of Final Consumption since 1978

To further analyse the relationship between the incremental contribution of consumption and its aggregate contribution which, in other words, is the relationship between final consumption rate and the contribution rate of final consumption, we decompose the trend components and fluctuation components of final consumption rate and final consumption contribution rate with HP filters (see Figures 9-3 and 9-4).

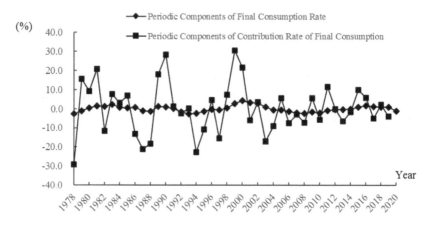

Figure 9-3 Fluctuation Components of China's Final Consumption Rate and Contribution Rate of Final Consumption

Judging from the periodic components of final consumption rate and the contribution rate of final consumption, both final consumption rate and the contribution rate of final consumption fluctuate around 0, but the latter is way more volatile than the former. Judging from the trend components of final consumption rate and the contribution rate of final consumption, both of them show a decreasing trend since 1978. Yet the gap between them is quite small. Moreover, they are highly correlated with the correlation coefficient reaching 0.905. In the regression, the trend component of the contribution rate of final consumption acts as the dependent variable while the trend component of final consumption rate acts as the independent variable, with the coefficient of the independent variable reaching 1.07. Such a result indicates that for every 1 percentage-point increase in the trend components of final consumption rate, the trend components of the contribution rate of final consumption rises by 1.07 percentage points. Therefore, we take the trend component of final consumption rate as an alternative indicator to measure the contribution of consumption to economic growth.

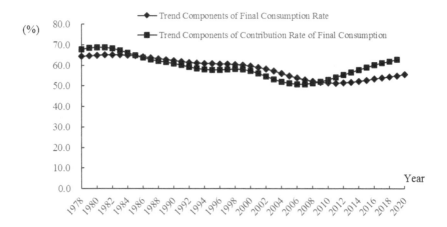

Figure 9-4 Trend Components of China's Final Consumption Rate and the Contribution Rate of Final Consumption

9.1.2.2. Relationship between Final Consumption Rate and Economic Growth

Equation 9-1 demonstrates that GDP growth rate equals the sum of final consumption rate times consumption growth rate, capital formation rate times capital formation rate growth rate and net export rate times net export growth rate. Specifically, the product of final consumption rate and consumption growth rate measures the contribution of consumption to economic growth; the product of capital formation rate and capital formation rate growth rate measures the contribution of capital formation rate to economic growth; and net export rate measures the contribution of net export to economic growth. Table 9-2 shows the growth rates of China's three demands since 1978. Given the growth rates of the three demands, we take the trend components of both final consumption rate and capital formation as the alternative indicators of the contribution rates of final consumption and capital formation. In this way, we are able to simulate the impact of such structural change on economic growth with rising consumption rate, falling capital formation rate and unchanging net export rate.

Table 9-2 Growth Rates of the Three Demands since 1978
Unit: %

Year	Growth Rate of Consumption	Growth Rate of Capital Formation	Growth Rate of Net Export	Year	Growth Rate of Consumption	Growth Rate of Capital Formation	Growth Rate of Net Export
1978	7.3	20.3	189.8	2000	10.5	5.3	0.0
1979	10.0	4.1	40.5	2001	6.8	14.8	-52.2
1980	9.3	4.6	-30.9	2002	8.7	10.2	7.8
1981	6.9	-0.3	172.7	2003	6.2	17.4	-23.1
1982	7.7	6.3	112.3	2004	7.8	15.0	-19.0
1983	12.0	11.3	-106.9	2005	12.0	9.4	20.2
1984	16.0	18.4	-8972.4	2006	10.5	13.5	23.7
1985	14.9	27.4	171.2	2007	13.4	15.6	12.7
1986	6.9	3.7	-126.2	2008	8.4	12.0	3.9
1987	7.7	8.1	4291.9	2009	10.8	17.6	-92.5
1988	7.9	15.9	-10.1	2010	10.1	14.3	-29.8
1989	5.2	0.0	-83.7	2011	12.5	8.3	-24.9
1990	5.5	-7.9	119.0	2012	8.6	7.1	7.4
1991	9.2	9.6	7.1	2013	7.6	8.9	-12.3
1992	13.5	18.9	-128.0	2014	8.0	7.2	-4.8
1993	13.8	17.5	99.5	2015	9.1	3.7	18.6
1994	7.9	10.9	313.0	2016	8.2	7.3	-35.2
1995	8.6	12.8	48.9	2017	7.1	6.3	17.1
1996	10.3	9.0	19.6	2018	7.8	6.6	-64.9
1997	6.5	3.6	89.5	2019	6.3	3.9	60.8
1998	8.4	6.3	11.7	2020	-0.9	5.1	27.1
1999	10.8	4.7	-28.4				

Source: *National Bureau of Statistics of China*

9.1.2.3. Steadiness of China's Economic Growth

The volatility of economic growth is commonly measured by standard deviation or rolling standard deviation of economic growth rate (Blanchard & Simon, 2001[9]; Mankiw, 2006[10]), and a lower standard deviation reflects the lower volatility of economic growth. Standard deviation of economic growth rate measures the amount of variation from the mean over a specific period. For instance, the standard deviation of GDP growth rate is 3.37 percent during 1978–1991 and 2.20 percent during 1992–2014, which are, respectively, calculated based on the GDP growth rates over the two periods. Such a result indicates the economic growth became steadier in the second stage of reform and opening-up, and rolling standard deviation reflects the changes in the volatility of economic growth more directly and dynamically. Annual rolling standard deviations can be calculated over specific rolling time periods, and an increase or decrease in the number more straightforwardly demonstrates the changes in the volatility of economic growth. Since the data are collected on an annual basis, we set the number of rolling period as 10. To obtain the rolling standard deviation of economic growth in Period T, we calculate a standard deviation of Period T based on the economic growth rates from Period T-9 to Period T. Figure 9-5 shows the rolling standard deviation of China's economic growth since 1978, indicating that the steadiness of China's economic growth has been greatly improved. The rolling standard deviation of the economic growth dropped from 6.35 percent in 1978 to its lowest point of 1.09 percent in 2004, and kept fluctuating around 1.81 percent since 2004.

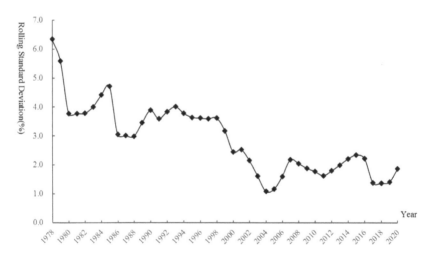

Figure 9-5 Variation Trend of the Steadiness of China's Economic Growth

9.1.3 Analysis of the Impact of the Increase in Final Consumption Rate on China's Economic Growth

To investigate the impact of the increase in consumption rate on China's economic growth and its steadiness, we only look into the impact of changes in final consumption rate and capital formation rate on economic growth rate in the simulation analysis as the proportion of net exports of China's economy is relatively small and stable, with the assumption that the growth rates of final consumption, gross capital formation and net exports remain unchanged in every scenario.

We analyse the following three scenarios illustrating the variation trend of China's GDP growth rate to reflect the impact of changes in final consumption rate on economic growth rate and its steadiness (see Table 9-3).

Benchmark Scenario: Actual final consumption rate, capital formation rate and net export rate since 1978;

Scenario 1: Final consumption rate falls by 5 percentage points; capital formation rate rises by 5 percentage points; and net export rate remains unchanged.

Scenario 2: Final consumption rate rises by 5 percentage points; capital formation rate falls by 5 percentage points; and net export rate remains unchanged.

Scenario 3: Final consumption rate rises by 10 percentage points; capital formation rate falls by 10 percentage points; and net export rate remains unchanged.

Table 9-3 Variation Trend of Final Consumption Rate in Benchmark Scenario and Other Three Scenarios

	Final Consumption Rate	Capital Formation Rate	Net Export Rate
Scenario 1	5 percentage points lower than Benchmark Scenario	5 percentage points higher than Benchmark Scenario	Unchanged
Benchmark Scenario	Actual final consumption rate, capital formation rate and net export rate since 1978		
Scenario 2	5 percentage points higher than Benchmark Scenario	5 percentage points lower than Benchmark Scenario	Unchanged
Scenario 3	10 percentage points higher than Benchmark Scenario	10 percentage points lower than Benchmark Scenario	Unchanged

Given the growth rates of the three demands in Table 9-2 and the demand structure in Table 9-3, we obtain the economic growth rate in every scenario based on Equation (9-1) (see Figure 9-6 and Table 9-4).

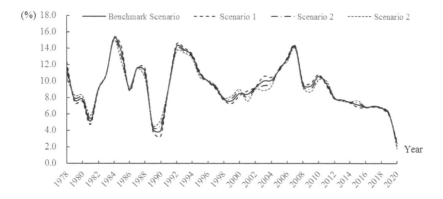

Figure 9-6 GDP Growth Rates in Benchmark Scenario and Other Three Scenarios

As for the impact of changes in final consumption rate on China's GDP growth rate, China's final consumption rates during 1978–2020 and 1992–2020 were lower than the capital formation rate, respectively, by 0.6808 percentage points and 1.1879 percentage points. Accordingly, compared with Benchmark Scenario, the increase of final consumption rate in two scenarios causes the economic growth rate to, respectively, fall by 0.0340 percentage points (Scenario 2, final consumption rate rises by 5 percentage points) and 0.0681 percentage points (Scenario 3, final consumption rate rises by 10 percentage points). According to the data during 1978–2020, China's average GDP growth rate is 9.2837 percent in Benchmark Scenario, 9.3178 percent in Scenario 1 (final consumption rate falls by 5 percentage points, and capital formation rate rises by 5 percentage points), 9.2497 percent in Scenario 2 (final consumption rate rises by 5 percentage points, and capital formation rate falls by 5 percentage points) and 9.2156 percent in Scenario 3 (final consumption rate rises by 10 percentage points, and capital formation rate falls by 10 percentage points).

Table 9-4 GDP Growth Rates in Benchmark Scenario and Other Three Scenarios
Unit: %

Year	Benchmark Scenario	Scenario 1	Scenario 2	Scenario 3	Year	Benchmark Scenario	Scenario 1	Scenario 2	Scenario 3
1978	11.6	12.2	11.0	10.4	1997	9.2	9.0	9.4	9.5
1979	7.6	7.3	7.9	8.2	1998	7.8	7.7	7.9	8.0
1980	7.8	7.6	8.0	8.3	1999	7.6	7.3	7.9	8.2
1981	5.1	4.7	5.5	5.8	2000	8.4	8.1	8.7	8.9
1982	9.0	8.9	9.1	9.1	2001	8.2	8.6	7.8	7.4
1983	10.8	10.8	10.8	10.9	2002	9.0	9.0	9.0	8.9
1984	15.2	15.3	15.1	15.0	2003	10.1	10.7	9.5	9.0
1985	13.5	14.1	12.9	12.2	2004	10.1	10.4	9.8	9.4
1986	8.9	8.7	9.1	9.2	2005	11.3	11.2	11.4	11.5
1987	11.7	11.7	11.7	11.6	2006	12.7	12.9	12.5	12.4
1988	11.3	11.7	10.9	10.5	2007	14.2	14.3	14.1	14.0
1989	4.2	3.8	4.6	4.9	2008	9.6	9.8	9.4	9.3
1990	3.9	3.3	4.5	5.0	2009	9.2	9.5	8.9	8.5
1991	9.3	9.3	9.3	9.2	2010	10.6	10.8	10.4	10.1
1992	14.3	14.6	14.0	13.7	2011	9.4	9.2	9.6	9.7
1993	13.9	14.0	13.8	13.6	2012	7.6	7.5	7.7	7.8
1994	13.1	13.3	12.9	12.7	2013	7.7	7.8	7.6	7.5
1995	11.0	11.2	10.8	10.6	2014	7.3	7.3	7.3	7.3
1996	9.9	9.8	10.0	10.0	2015				

During 1978–1991, final consumption rate was higher than gross capital formation growth rate by 0.3697 percentage points. Its increase leads to the rise of the average GDP growth rate, and its decrease results in the fall of the average GDP growth rate. In detail, China's average GDP growth rate is 9.2929 percent in Benchmark Scenario, 9.2744 percent in Scenario 1 (final consumption rate falls by 5 percentage points, and capital formation rate rises by 5 percentage points), 9.3113 percent in Scenario 2 (final consumption rate rises by 5 percentage points, and capital formation rate falls by 5 percentage points) and 9.3298 percent in Scenario 3 (final consumption rate rises by 10 percentage points, and capital formation rate falls by 10 percentage points).

Table 9-5 Standard Deviation and Average Value of GDP Growth Rate in Benchmark Scenario and Other Three Scenarios during Different Periods

Unit: %

Period	Variable	Benchmark	Scenario 1	Scenario 2	Scenario 3
1978–2020	Standard Deviation	2.8799	3.0349	2.7442	2.6310
	Average	9.2837	9.3178	9.2497	9.2156
1978–1991	Standard Deviation	3.3523	3.6562	3.0638	2.7955
	Average	9.2929	9.2744	9.3113	9.3298
1992–2020	Standard Deviation	2.6876	2.7583	2.6335	2.5972
	Average	9.2793	9.3387	9.2199	9.1605

Source: Author's Calculation

9.1.4 Analysis of the Impact of Changes in Final Consumption Rate on Economic Growth Stability

As for the impact of changes in final consumption rate on the stability of China's GDP growth rate, we use the standard deviation of the growth rate of variables to reflect their stability. The smaller is standard deviation of the growth rate of variable, the higher is its stability; the larger is the standard deviation of the growth rate of variable, the poorer is its stability. First, we analyse the difference among the stability of the three demands in various periods (Table 9-6). The stability of final consumption, gross capital formation and net export during 1978–1991, 1992–2020 and 1978–2020 all presents a feature. Measuring the stability of the three demands by the standard deviation of their growth rates, we find out that final consumption is the most stable, followed by gross capital formation, whereas net export is the least stable. During 1992–2020, the standard deviation of the growth rate of final consumption was 2.8977 percent; that of gross capital formation was 4.7418 percent; and that of net export was 75.4009 percent.

Table 9-6 Standard Deviation and Average of the Growth Rates of China's Three Demands during Different Periods

Unit: %

Period	Variable	Final Consumption	Gross Capital Formation	Net Export
1978–2020	Standard Deviation	2.9793	6.5302	1534.3752
	Average	8.9667	9.6475	-92.0780
1978–1991	Standard Deviation	3.2532	9.3712	2742.9397
	Average	9.0407	8.6711	-301.8404
1992–2020	Standard Deviation	2.8977	4.7418	75.4009
	Average	8.9310	10.1189	9.1865

Source: Author's Calculation

The interrelation among the stability of different demands during all periods remains stable. Specifically, final consumption is the most stable, followed by gross capital formation, while net export is the least stable. Thus we can speculate that the increase in final consumption rate with decreasing capital formation rate and invariant net export will weaken the stability of GDP growth rate. Table 9-5 proves such speculation to be true. Compared with Benchmark Scenario, during 1978–1991, 1992–2020 and 1978–2020, the standard deviation of GDP growth rate, respectively, rose by -0.0185 percentage points, 0.0594 percentage points and 0.0341 percentage points in Scenario 1 (final consumption rate falls by 5 percentage points, and capital formation rate rises by 5 percentage points); it fell by -0.0184 percentage points, 0.0594 percentage points and 0.0340 percentage points in Scenario 2 (final consumption rate rises by 5 percentage points, and capital formation rate falls by 5 percentage points); and it declined by 0.0369 percentage points, 0.1188 percentage points and 0.0681 percentage points in Scenario 3 (final consumption rate rises by 10 percentage points, and capital formation rate falls by 10 percentage points). According to the analysis of the impact of 5-percentage-point and 10-percentage-point increase in final consumption rate on the standard deviation of GDP growth rate, final consumption rate is in positive correlation with the stability of GDP growth rate.

Judging from the rolling standard deviation of GDP growth rate, the increase of final consumption rate has the largest impact on the stability of GDP growth rate. The final consumption rates in different scenarios and Benchmark Scenario are sequenced as: Scenario 1<Benchmark Scenario<Scenario 2<Scenario 3. Figure 9-7 where the line representing the trend of rolling standard deviation of Scenario 1 is at the top with the line of Scenario 3 at the bottom shows that the sequence of the rolling standard deviation of GDP growth rates in different scenarios is consistent with the above sequence. Accordingly, the increase in final consumption rate contributes greatly to improving the stability of economic growth.

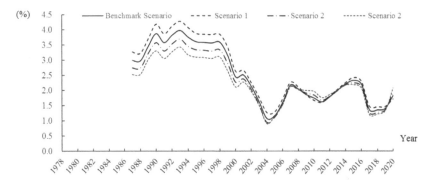

Figure 9-7 Trend of the Rolling Standard Deviation of GDP Growth Rates in Benchmark Scenario and Other Three Scenarios

Notes: Since the data in Benchmark Scenario and other three Scenarios are collected from 1978 with 10 rolling periods of rolling standard deviation, we calculate the rolling standard deviation from 1978.

9.1.5 Conclusion

Table 9-2 demonstrates that the impact of the increase in final consumption rate on GDP growth rate depends on the relationship between the average growth rate of final consumption and the average growth rate of gross capital formation in investigated periods. Such impact is relatively small: if the average growth rate of final consumption is higher than that of gross capital formation, then the increase in final consumption rate, the decrease in capital formation rate and the invariance of net export rate will raise economic growth rate. On the contrary, if the average growth rate of final consumption is lower than the average growth rate of gross capital formation, then the increase in final consumption rate, the decrease in capital formation rate and the invariance of net export rate will bring down economic growth rate.

Generally speaking, the respective stability of final consumption rate, gross capital formation and net export is sequenced as: final consumption>gross capital formation>net export. Therefore, the increase in final consumption rate, the decrease in capital formation rate and the invariance of net export rate will improve the stability of economic growth.

9.2 Impact of Variation in Consumption Rate on Economic Growth – Based on Input-Output Table

In section 9.2, we analyse the impact of the variation in final consumption rate on economic growth through scenario simulation based on China's 2012 input-output table[11]. Our study shows that raising final consumption rate has a relatively small impact on economic growth rate.

9.2.1 Input-Output Model

The input-output table combining both production process and ultimate demand is an appropriate tool for analysing the contribution of final consumption, capital formation, import and export to economic growth from the aspect of demand. Compared with national accounts, it can further reveal the roles of various demands. With the help of input-output table, many domestic scholars obtain satisfactory results in their study on the contribution of export to economic growth. Shen (2009[12], 2011[13]) quantitatively measures the contribution of "troika" which is constituted by consumption, investment and export to China's economy with input-output model. According to the model, the basic calculation formula of input-output is as follows:

$$X = (I - A)^{-1}(Y - M) \qquad (9\text{-}3)$$

According to the input-output table released by the National Bureau of Statistics, in Equation (9-3), X represents gross output; A represents direct

IMPACT OF FINAL CONSUMPTION RATE ON ECONOMIC GROWTH

consumption coefficient matrix; Y denotes final product; and M denotes import. These vectors or matrices are obtained based on the competitive input-output table which refers to the competition resulting from the different sources of products that are not distinguished during calculation. The intermediate input and ultimate input in the input-output flow may come from domestic products, overseas products or both. Thus the competitive input-output table cannot be directly used for calculation and analysis. To solve that problem, we compile a non-competitive input-output table (Table 9-7) where domestic products and overseas products are distinguished. In Table 9-7, the superscript d denotes domestic products; the superscript m denotes imports; the lowercase letters represent annual flow; and the uppercase letters represent total value. In this way, domestic products and overseas products are clearly distinguished in terms of intermediate input and use, yet the transfer value of overseas products is contained in final products. Therefore, it needs to be deducted in the subsequent calculation of the contribution of investment, consumption and export to economic growth.

Table 9-7 Non-competitive Input-Output Table

		Intermediate Use	Ultimate Use					
	Department	1,2,...,n	Consumption	Capital Formation	Export	Total	Import	Gross Output
Chinese Input in Domestic Products	1 2 . . . n	x_{ij}^d	c_i^d	in_i^d	ex_i^d	Y_i^d		X_i
Chinese Input in Imports	1 2 . . . n	x_{ij}^m	c_i^m	in_i^m	ex_i^m	Y_i^m	M_i	
Value Added		V_j						
Gross Input		X_j						

Given the equilibrium in the input-output table and letting the direct consumption coefficient be $a_{ij}^d = \dfrac{x_{ij}}{X_j}$, we obtain:

$$\sum_{j=1}^{n} a_{ij}^d X_j + Y_i^d = X_i, \quad i = 1, 2, \ldots, n \qquad (9\text{-}4)$$

Transforming it into the matrix form $A^d X + Y^d = X$, we obtain:

$$X = (I - A^d)^{-1} Y^d \qquad (9\text{-}5)$$

$(I-A^d)^{-1} = B^d$ in Equation (9-5) denotes the Leontief Inverse Matrix of domestic products. Here b_{ji}^d denotes the total consumption (total demand) of one-unit domestic final product in Sector j to Sector i and I represents identity matrix.

Y^d represents direct consumption matrix excluding the input-output model of import as well as column vector of local final demand. Letting C, IN and EX denoting consumption, investment and export, we have:

$$Y^d = C^d + IN^d + EX^d \qquad (9\text{-}6)$$

We let $r_j = \dfrac{V_j}{X_j}$, j=1, 2 ... n, meaning the rate of increased value equals the value increased by total input per unit in Sector j. The sum of the increased value of each sector equals GDP. Here R denotes the row vector of 1 × n, and X denotes the column vector of total output. Then we substitute the Equation (9-5) and Equation (9-6) into the equation:

$$GDP = \sum_{i=1}^{n} V_j = \sum_{i=1}^{n} r_j X_j = RX = R(I - A^d)^{-1} Y^d$$

$$= R(I - A^d)^{-1}(C^d + IN^d + EX^d)$$

$$= R(I - A^d)^{-1}C^d + R(I - A^d)^{-1}IN^d + R(I - A^d)EX^d$$

$$= GDP^C + GDP^{IN} + GDP^{EX} \qquad (9\text{-}7)$$

GDP^C, GDP^{IN} and GDP^{EX} in Equation (9-7), respectively, represent the increased economic growth driven by consumption (C^d), investment (IN^d) and export (EX^d).

Moreover, the above analysis is based on the split non-competitive input-output table[14]. Assuming the domestic and foreign products of the same sector are homogeneous, we obtain:

$$y_i^m = M_i \frac{y_i}{\sum_{j=1}^{n} x_{ij} + \sum_{j=1}^{k} y_j}, \quad x_{ij}^m = M_i \frac{x_{ij}}{\sum_{j=1}^{n} x_{ij} + \sum_{j=1}^{k} y_j} \qquad (9\text{-}8)$$

Here y^i represents the final consumption of Item I in the original competitive input-output table, and xij represents the consumption in Sector I during the producing process of Sector j in the original competitive input-output table. Then we obtain China's non-competitive input-output table based on the above equation.

9.2.2 Contribution of Consumption, Investment and Export to China's Economic Growth

The input-output table is released by the National Bureau of Statistics every five years. Currently, China's latest input-output table was released in 2012. In 9.2.2, we carry out analysis based on the input-output table of 42 sectors. Since the original table is competitive, we split it into a non-competitive one based on Equation (9-8). The result that distinguishes intermediate products and final products is shown in Table 9-8. Judging from the flow of all final products, 41.37 percent of China's final products is used for consumption, 37.82 percent for investment and 20.81 percent for export. Judging from domestic final products, 42.09 percent is used for consumption, 38.07 percent for investment and 19.51 percent for export.

Table 9-8 Split Non-competitive Input-Output Table of 2012

Unit: 100 Million Yuan

	Gross Output	Intermediate Products	final products	Consumption	Capital Formation	Export	Others
Gross Products	1601627.10	1064826.9	656774.32	271718.58	248389.90	136665.85	2052.83
Domestic Products	1479600.10	976083.11	625543.97	263307.13	238127.13	122056.89	2052.83
Imports	122026.98	88743.80	31230.35	8411.45	10262.77	14608.96	
	Proportion in Gross Output (%)			Proportion in Final Products (%)			
Gross Products		66.48	41.01	41.37	37.82	20.81	0.31
Domestic Products		65.97	42.28	42.09	38.07	19.51	0.33
Imports		72.72	25.59	41.07	37.73	20.81	

Based on Equation (9-7), we obtain the increased economic growth driven by of the "troika" consisting of consumption, investment and export (see Table 9-9). Table 9-9 shows that in 2012, consumption, investment and export, respectively, account for 42.09 percent, 38.07 percent and 19.51 percent in domestic final products. The proportion of the increased economic growth driven by them in GDP is, respectively, 44.24 percent, 37.01 percent and 18.39 percent, which is exactly the contribution of the "troika" to economic growth in 2012. Though such contribution is not comparable with the final consumption rate, capital formation rate and net export rate (50.8 percent, 46.5 percent and -2.7 percent) calculated by the expenditure method, it can still be told that export makes great contrbution. Compared with 2007 (Shen, 2011)[15], the respective driving structure of consumption, capital formation and export changed from 41.78 percent, 31.15 percent and 26.26 percent in 2007 to 44.24 percent, 37.01 percent and 18.39 percent in 2012. The proportion of the increased economic growth driven by consumption rose by 2.46 percentage points in 2012; that driven by capital formation increased by 5.86 percentage points; and that driven by export fell by 7.87 percentage points. Such statistics indicate that the demand-driven structure of China's economic growth has transformed after the financial crisis: the increased value driven by consumption and capital formation has increased whereas that driven by export has decreased.

Meanwhile, the increased value driven by each domestic final product is lower than its own value, which means the increased value driven by one-unit final product is below 1. The driving coefficients of consumption, capital formation, export and others are, respectively, 0.959, 0.861, 0.778 and 0.932. As the driving coefficient of consumer goods and other products is higher than that of investment goods and export products, the proportion of the increased value driven by consumption and others is higher than that of consumption and others in final products, while the proportion of the increased value driven by capital formation and export is lower than that of capital formation and export in final products.

Table 9-9 Final Products in China and the Increased Value Driven by Them in 2012

Unit: 100 Million Yuan

	Domestic Final Products				Increased Value Driven by Final Products			
GDP	Consumption	Capital Formation	Export	Others	Consumption	Capital Formation	Export	Others
536800.2	263307.13	238127.13	122056.89	2052.83	237478.97	198682.79	98725.31	1913.16
Ratio (%)	42.09	38.07	19.51	0.33	44.24	37.01	18.39	0.36
Increased Value Driven by Final Product Per Unit					0.9588	0.8609	0.7775	0.9320

9.2.3 Simulation Analysis of the Variation of Final Consumption Rate on Economic Growth

To investigate the impact of the changes in consumption rate on economic growth, we carry out scenario simulation analysis. Assuming the total amount of domestic final products is given, through changing the proportion of consumption, capital formation and export in final demand, we calculate the increased value in the three industries driven by various domestic final products based on Equation (9-7) to obtain the variation trend of GDP: see Table 9-10 for the Benchmark Scenario and Simulation Scenario.

Table 9-10 Domestic Final Products and the Structure in Benchmark Scenario and Simulation Scenario

	Consumption	Capital Formation	Export	Others	Total
Benchmark Scenario (100 Million yuan)	263307.13	238127.13	122056.89	2052.83	625543.97
Structure (%)	42.09	38.07	19.51	0.33	100
Benchmark Scenario (100 Million yuan)	294584.33	222488.53	106418.29	2052.83	625543.97
Structure (%)	47.09	35.57	17.01	0.33	100

Benchmark Scenario: Structure of domestic final products shown in the input-output table in 2012.

Benchmark Scenario: The final consumption, capital formation and export respectively account for 42.09 percent, 38.07 percent and 19.51 percent in the structure of final product.

Simulation Scenario: In the structure of final product, the proportion of final consumption rises by 5 percentage points while that of both capital formation and export declines by 2.5 percentage points. The proportion of others remains the same.

Table 9-11 demonstrates the final demand structure in Benchmark Scenario and Simulation Scenario after adding import products (the import products of each sector remain unchanged). With imports taken into consideration, the final consumption rate, capital formation rate and net export rate in Benchmark Scenario are 52.29 percent, 47.29 percent and 0.01 percent, respectively. Judging from the changes in final demand structure, the final consumption rate in Simulation Scenario rises by 6.22 percentage points with capital formation rate and net export, respectively, falling by 3.11 percentage points and 3.11 percentage points, compared to Benchmark Scenario.

Table 9-11 Demand Structure in Benchmark Scenario and Simulation Scenario with Final Demand Ratio of Imports Taken into Consideration

	Consumption	Capital Formation	Net Export	Others
Benchmark Scenario	263307.13	238127.13	29.91	2052.83
Structure (%)	52.29	47.29	0.01	0.41
Benchmark Scenario	294584.33	222488.53	-15608.68	2052.83
Structure (%)	58.51	44.19	-3.10	0.41

According to Equation (9-7), Table 9-8 and the non-competitive input-output table, we obtain the increased value driven by consumption, capital formation, export and others in the two scenarios (see Table 9-12). Table (9-12) shows the simulated impact of the increase in final consumption rate on economic growth based on the input-output table. The final consumption rate in Simulation Scenario increases by 6.22 percentage points (capital formation rate decreases by 3.11 percentage points and net export decreases by 3.11 percentage points). As a result, GDP increases by 251.179 billion yuan, an increase of 0.47 percent compared with Benchmark Scenario. Compared with the GDP in 2011, final consumption rate increases by 6.22 percentage points, resulting in the growth rate in 2012 climbing from 7.7 percent to 8.205 percent[16]. Therefore, it can be told that the increase of 6.22 percentage points in final consumption rate leads to the increase of 0.505 percentage points in economic growth rate, which can be further concluded that the increase in final consumption rate has a relatively small impact on economic growth.

Table 9-12 GDP and Its Structure in Benchmark Scenario and Simulation Scenario

		Final Consumption	Capital Formation	Export	Others	GDP	Variation of GDP (100 as the benchmark)
Benchmark Scenario	Increase in GDP (100 million yuan)	237478.97	198682.79	98725.31	1913.16	536800.23	—
	Contribution Rate to GDP (%)	44.2397296	37.0124264	18.391443	0.3564007	100	—
Simulation Scenario	Increase in GDP (100 million yuan)	265688.15	185634.63	86076.08	1913.16	539312.02	2511.79
	Contribution Rate to GDP (%)	49.26	34.42	15.96	0.35	100.00	0.47

9.3 Dynamic Analysis of the Impact of the Increase in Consumption Rate on China's Economic Growth

9.3.1 Consumption Rate, Investment Rate and China's Economic Growth

9.3.1.1. Descriptive Analysis of Consumption Rate, Investment Rate and China's Economic Growth

To make it equal GDP which is the sum of final consumption, gross capital formation and net export, we need to deduct export from the sum of consumption, investment and export which are known as the "troika" driving economic growth from the aspect of demand. Based on China's economic reality, its net export is positive in most years and relatively small, fluctuating around 3 percent (its maximum is 8.7 percent in 2007). Figure 9-8 demonstrates China's GDP growth rate, final consumption rate and capital formation rate during 1953–2020. The trends of GDP growth rate and capital formation rate are roughly the same. Since investment is a leading pro-cyclical variable, capital formation rate reaches its peak and trough one year ahead of GDP. But such stable relationship changed during 2007–2011 with GDP growth rate decreasing from 14.2 percent in 2007 to 9.6 percent in 2011. Meanwhile, capital formation rate increased from 40.4 percent to 47.0 percent in 2011, due to China's 4-trillion investment stimulus policy which leads to the continuous rise of investment rate in 2008, 2009, 2010 and 2011. On the contrary, GDP growth rate gradually fell because of the decrease in export and investment efficiency. Since 2012, the relationship between GDP growth rate and capital formation rate has progressively gone back to where it was. The inverse co-relationship between GDP growth rate and capital formation rate implies that the feature of China's investment-driven economic growth is quite marked.

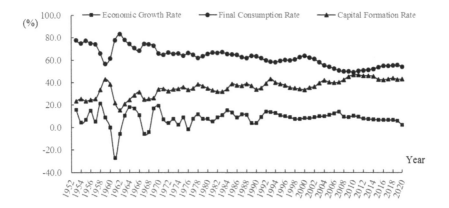

Figure 9-8 China's GDP Growth Rate, Final Consumption Rate and Capital Formation Rate during 1953–2020
Source: *National Bureau of Statistics*.

Judging from the relationship between final consumption rate and economic growth rate, they are inversely correlated with each other to a small extent. For example, during 1992–2007, GDP growth rate fell from 14.2 percent in 1992 to 7.7 percent in 1999 and then bounced back to 14.2 percent. Meanwhile, final consumption rate rose from 59.8 percent in 1993 to its maximum of 63.9 percent in 2000 and then fell to 50.9 percent in 2007. Such inverse correlation reflects the following: first, the change in the proportion of consumption which is the most stable consisting part in GDP causes no fluctuation in GDP; second, since the sum of consumption and investment accounts for about 97 percent in GDP and capital formation rate moves in the same direction as GDP, consumption rate is inevitably in an inverse correlation with GDP.

Figure 9-7 reflects the inverse co-relationship between capital formation rate and final consumption rate. When the proportion of net export remains at around 3 percent, every 1 percentage-point increase in capital formation rate will inevitably lead to 1 percentage-point decrease in final consumption rate. Therefore, final consumption rate is clearly correlated with capital formation rate.

9.3.1.2. Volatility of Consumption Rate, Investment Rate and China's Economic Growth

To further analyse the relation among consumption rate, investment rate and China's economic growth, we obtain the trend components and periodic components of all the variables with HP filters (see Figure 9-9 and Figure 9-10).

Judging from the periodic components of consumption rate, investment rate and China's economic growth, GDP growth rate is in positive correlation with capital formation rate and in inverse correlation with final consumption rate, while final consumption rate is in inverse correlation with capital formation rate.

Judging from the trend components of consumption rate, investment rate and China's economic growth, the potential GDP growth rate remains positive. Though it kept decreasing during 1953–1961, it has been on an increasing trend since 1962. During 1985–2008, GDP growth rate remained roughly at 10 percent. After 2008, it decreased to some extent. The trend components of final consumption rate kept fluctuating, falling from 75.4 percent in 1953 to 55.5 percent in 2020, and the capital formation rate also kept fluctuating, rising from 25.2 percent in 1953 to 43.2 percent in 2020.

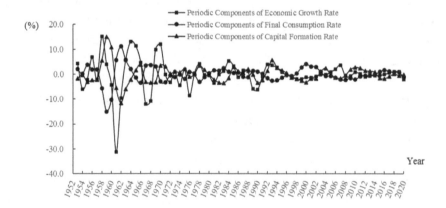

Figure 9-9 Periodic Components of GDP Growth Rate, Final Consumption Rate and Capital Formation Rate

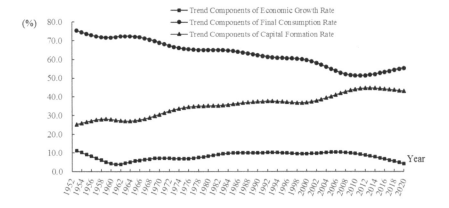

Figure 9-10 Trend Components of GDP Growth Rate, Final Consumption Rate and Capital Formation Rate

In addition, to investigate the correlation among GDP growth rate, final consumption rate and capital formation rate, we calculate the correlation coefficient of all the variables (see Table 9-13). According to the calculation result, GDP growth rate is in weak negative correlation with final consumption rate with the correlation coefficient of -0.2386; GDP growth rate is in weak positive correlation with capital formation rate with the correlation coefficient of 0.2501; and final consumption rate is in high negative correlation with capital formation rate with the correlation coefficient of -0.9677.

Table 9-13 Correlation Coefficient of GDP Growth Rate (GR), Final Consumption Rate (CR) and Capital Formation Rate (IR)

	GR	CR	IR
GR	1.0000	-0.2386	0.2501
CR	-0.2386	1.0000	-0.9677
IR	0.2501	-0.9677	1.0000

9.3.2 Construction of the VAR Model of GDP Growth Rate, Final Consumption Rate and Capital Formation Rate

The vector autoregressive model (VAR) was introduced into economics in 1980 by C.A. Sims, an econometrician and a macroeconomist. In a multivariate regression model called VAR model, the endogenous variables and lag values of the system act as independent variables while the endogenous variables act as dependent variables. Such model can measure the dynamic relation among joint endogenous variables. Thus we construct a VAR model of final consumption rate, capital formation rate and economic growth rate to analyse their dynamic relation. The mathematical expression of VAR (p) is written as:

$$y_t = \alpha + A_1 y_{t-1} + \cdots + A_p y_{t-p} + \varepsilon_t$$

Here y_t represents the column vector of m-dimensional endogenous variables; $A_1, \ldots, A_p$ represent the parameter matrix to be estimated; and p denotes the lag order; and ε_t denotes the m-dimensional disturbance column vector[17].

9.3.2.1. Selection of Variables and Data Source

In this section, we focus on the dynamic relation among final consumption rate, capital formation rate and economic growth rate, taking these three variables as the endogenous variables. We select the data of China's final consumption rate (CR) and capital formation rate (IR) during 1978–2020, and deduct 100 from the GDP index of 100 in the previous year to obtain economic growth rate (GR). The data comes from the database of National Bureau of Statistics.

9.3.2.2. Unit Root Test

In this section, we carry out the ADF unit root test on the stationarity of the logarithm and difference logarithm series of the time series. According to Table 9-14, the three variables including GR, CR and IR are all stationary, which is written in I (0).

Table 9-14 Result of Unit Root Test (ADF Test)

Variable	ADF	Critical Value at 10%	Critical Value at 5%	Critical Value at 1%	Condition (G,T,N)	Result
GR	-6.2495	-2.5906	-2.9062	-3.5332	(C,0,1)	Stationary I (0)
CR	-5.0252	-3.1715	-3.4865	-4.1184	(C,T,7)	Stationary I (0)
IR	-6.5898	-3.1674	-3.4794	-4.1032	(G,T,1)	Stationary I (0)

Note: C, T and N, respectively, represent "with constant term", "with time trend" and "with difference lag order". The Schwarz Information Criterion (SIC) is used in the selection of lag order.

9.3.2.3. Analysis of the VAR Model and Its Stability

Using Eviews, an econometric software, we conclude that the optimum lag order is 2 based on the selecting standard of lag orders including SIC, AC and HQ. After regression, we obtain the following VAR (2) model (see Table 9-15).

Table 9-15 Regression Result of the VAR Model of GR, CR and IR

	GR	CR	IR
GR(-1)	0.505317	-0.221553	0.222443
	(0.19491)	(0.09290)	(0.09361)
	[2.59263]	[-2.38488]	[2.37627]
GR(-2)	-0.244888	0.173327	-0.183454
	(0.12845)	(0.06122)	(0.06169)
	[-1.90648]	[2.83103]	[-2.97368]
CR(-1)	-0.466292	1.207922	-0.286455
	(0.67528)	(0.32186)	(0.32433)
	[-0.69051]	[3.75289]	[-0.88322]
CR(-2)	-0.110469	-0.045406	-0.151018
	(0.67911)	(0.32369)	(0.32617)
	[-0.16267]	[-0.14028]	[-0.46301]
IR(-1)	-0.615104	0.255733	0.688359
	(0.61050)	(0.29099)	(0.29322)
	[-1.00754]	[0.87885]	[2.34762]
IR(-2)	-0.202361	0.056375	-0.320377
	(0.61987)	(0.29545)	(0.29771)
	[-0.32646]	[0.19081]	[-1.07612]
C	0.715440	-0.212731	0.500130
	(0.40537)	(0.19321)	(0.19469)
	[1.76493]	[-1.10102]	[2.56884]
R-squared	0.307268	0.882121	0.845401
Adj. R-squared	0.236821	0.870133	0.829679
F-Statistic	4.361677	73.58533	53.77222

Table 9-15 demonstrates that in the equation of economic growth rate, the coefficients of economic growth rate, final consumption rate and capital formation rate during lag period 1 are, respectively, 0.5053, -0.4663 and -0.6151. Among them, only the coefficient of economic growth rate is significant. The coefficients of economic growth rate, final consumption rate and capital formation rate during lag period 2 are, respectively, -0.2449, -0.1105, and -0.2024. All of the coefficients are not significant. In the equation of final consumption rate, the coefficients of economic growth rate, final consumption rate and capital formation rate during lag period 1 are, respectively, -0.2216, 1.2079, and 0.2557. Among them, the coefficient of economic growth rate and final consumption rate are significant. The coefficients of economic growth rate, final consumption rate and capital formation rate during lag period 2 are, respectively, 0.1733, -0.0454 and 0.0564. Only the coefficient of final consumption rate is significant. In the equation of capital formation rate, the coefficients of economic growth rate, final consumption rate and capital formation rate during lag period 1 are, respectively, 0.2224, -0.2865, and 0.6883. The coefficient of economic growth rate and the capital formation rate are significant. The coefficients of economic growth rate, final consumption rate and capital formation rate during lag period 2 are, respectively, -0.1835, -0.1510 and -0.3204. Only the coefficient of economic growth rate is significant.

The above analysis implies that the three variables including economic growth rate, final consumption rate, and capital formation rate are mainly depended on the changes in their lagged values. Such changes follow a certain law that economic growth rate, final consumption rate and capital formation are fairly sustainable. The further analysis of the dynamic relation among these three variables is based on the following impulse response function and variance decomposition analysis.

According to the steps to carry out the VAR model analysis, the stationarity of the VAR model needs to be tested before we analyse with impulse response function. Only when the reciprocals of the characteristic roots of the model lie inside the unit circle can the impulse response function analysis be carried out because the result indicates the VAR model is stationary. Figure 9-11 shows all of the reciprocals of the roots lie inside the unit circle, revealing a high goodness of fit. Therefore, we carry out the follow-up impulse response function analysis.

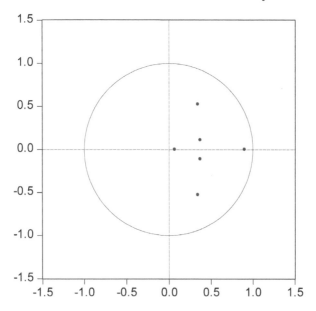

Figure 9-11 Unit Root Test on the VAR Model of Economic Growth Rate, Final Consumption Rate and Capital Formation Rate

9.3.3 Impulse Response Analysis of Final Consumption Rate, Capital Formation Rate and Economic Growth

The impulse response function reflects the dynamic impact of random disturbances on the corresponding variables in the system in response to one standard deviation innovation shock. In a VAR model, the impulse response function can be used to investigate the dynamic response of economic growth rate, final consumption rate, and capital formation rate to various innovation shocks. Assuming that the shocks to final consumption rate and capital formation rate occur during the shocks to economic growth rate, the shock to final consumption rate and capital formation rate will have a long-term (continuous) and short-term (temporary) effect on economic growth. Meanwhile, the shock to economic growth rate will also affect final consumption rate and capital formation rate. During the reform and opening-up, the change in consumption structure and the reform of investment mechanism can be regarded as long-term shocks to final consumption rate and capital formation rate while other shocks in the current period can be regarded as temporary impacts on final consumption rate and investment rate. In Table 9-15 which displays the VAR (2) model of the three variables, taking final consumption rate, capital formation rate, and economic growth rate as dependent variables, we look into the impact of random disturbance from one standard deviation of other variables and the dependent variables themselves as well as the duration of the impact. The dynamic response function of the inter-shocks among final consumption rate, capital formation rate and economic growth is obtained based on the VAR (2) model. The response path of the impulse response function is demonstrated in Figure 9-12, Figure 9-13 and Figure 9-14 where the horizontal axis represents the lag period of shocks (Unit: Year), the horizontal axis represents the degree of response of endogenous variables to shocks and the curve denotes the impulse response function.

9.3.3.1. Analysis of the Impulse Response of Economic Growth Rate to Various Shocks

Figure 9-12 shows the curve of impulse response of economic growth (GR) to shocks of GR, final consumption (CR) and capital formation rate (IR). First of all, we analyse the impulse response function of GR to shocks of GR. When GR is given a shock of positive standard deviation of GR in the current period, the response degree of GR sharply declines from 5.97 percent to -1.64 percent in the following four periods before rising to 0.11 percent in the eighth period, and gradually disappears in the tenth period. The result indicates that with the deepening of China's market-oriented reform, the steadiness of China's economic growth has been progressively improved and the economy is not constantly volatile. The shock of standard deviation of economic growth merely has a short-term impact on economic growth. In this way, when it comes to policy-making in the future, the emphasis should be put on the supply side to strengthen the sustainability of economic growth.

IMPACT OF FINAL CONSUMPTION RATE ON ECONOMIC GROWTH

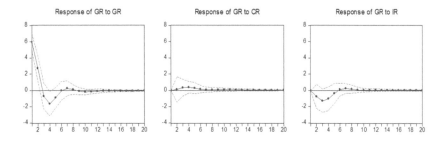

Figure 9-12 Curve of Impulse Response of Economic Growth (GR) to Shocks of Itself, Final Consumption Rate (CR) and Capital Formation Rate (IR)

Next, we investigate the impact of final consumption rate (CR) shocks on economic growth rate (GR). When GR is given a shock of positive standard deviation of CR in the current period, the response of GR reaches its maximum of 0.38 percent in the fourth period and falls to 0.03 percent in the twentieth period. Judging from the degree of response of GR to CR shocks, the variation of GR is relatively slight, which accords with the conclusion made from the perspective of national income accounting. When final consumption rate rises by 1 percentage point, economic growth rate is barely affected. In conclusion, final consumption rate has a larger impact on the steadiness and sustainability of economic growth.

Finally, we look into the impact of capital formation rate (IR) shocks on economic growth rate (GR). When GR is given a shock of positive standard deviation of IR in the current period, the response degree of GR remains negative from the first period to the fifth period, reaching its negative maximum of -1.28 percent in the third period. It turns positive since the sixth period though the degree is relatively small and then gradually disappears. Judging from the degree of response of GR to IR shocks, the variation of GR is relatively slight, which accords with the conclusion made from the perspective of national income accounting. When capital formation rate rises by 1 percentage point, economic growth rate is barely affected, remaining at its potential level.

9.3.3.2. Analysis of the Impulse Response of Final Consumption Rate to Various Shocks

Figure 9-13 shows the curve of impulse response of final consumption rate (CR) to shocks of economic growth (GR), CR and capital formation rate (IR). First of all, we analyse the impulse response function of CR to shocks of GR. When CR is given a shock of positive standard deviation of GR in the current period, the response of CR remains negative and keeps decreasing. In the twentieth period, the impact of GR shocks on CR almost disappears. Judging from the response function of CR to GR shocks, the negative impact of GR shocks on CR keeps lasting until the twentieth period. Given China's economic reality, to raise the economic growth rate in the short run, the most direct and effective way is to increase investment. But the increase in investment will lead to the crowding-out effect causing the decrease in final consumption, which eventually results in the rise of GDP as well as the decline of final consumption (final consumption rate). Since China's reform and opening-up, the economy has been growing at a high rate. Its typical investment-driven feature contributes to the decrease in consumption rate to some extent.

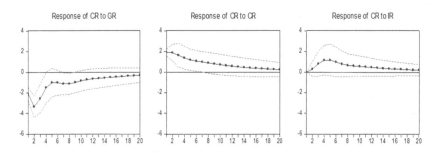

Figure 9-13 Curve of Impulse Response of Final Consumption Rate (CR) to Shocks of Economic Growth (GR), Itself and Capital Formation Rate (IR)

Next, we investigate the impulse response function of final consumption rate (CR) to CR shocks. When CR is given a shock of positive standard deviation of CR in the current period, the response of CR reaches its maximum of 0.1.97 percent in the first period and falls to 0.26 percent in the twentieth period. The result implies that final consumption itself is remarkably stable. For instance, when the variation of consumption structure causes final consumption to change, such influence will keep lasting until the next variation of consumption structure happens.

Finally, we look into the dynamic impact of capital formation rate (IR) shocks on final consumption rate (CR). When CR is given a shock of positive standard deviation of IR in the current period, the response degree of CR keeps increasing from 0.00 % in the first period to 1.18 percent in the fifth period. Since the eighth period, it gradually decreases, reaching 0.20 percent in the twentieth period. Judging from the dynamic impact of IR shocks on CR, the short-term changes in investment will result in the adjustment of final consumption rate. But since investment is both the current demand and the future productivity, capital has progressively played the role of productivity as time goes by, demonstrating its influence on consumption.

9.3.3.3. Analysis of the Impulse Response of Capital Formation Rate to Various Shocks

Figure 9-14 displays the curve of impulse response of capital formation rate (IR) to shocks of economic growth (GR), final consumption rate (CR) and IR. First of all, we analyse the impact of GR shocks on IR. When IR is given a shock of positive standard deviation of GR in the current period, the response of IR remains positive. It reaches its maximum of 3.31 percent in the second period and falls to 0.24 percent in the twentieth period. It can be told that the response function of IR to GR shocks is opposite to that of CR, though their response degree is similar. Given China's economic reality, to raise the economic growth rate in the short run, the most direct and effective way is to increase investment. For every 1 percentage-point increase in GDP, capital formation rate needs to rise by more than 1 percentage point with fixed investment growth rate.

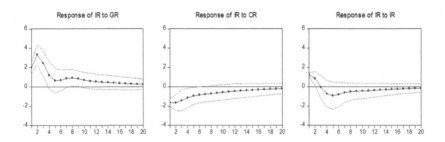

Figure 9-14 Curve of Impulse Response of Capital Formation Rate (IR) to Shocks of Economic Growth (GR), Final Consumption Rate (CR) and Itself

Next, we investigate the impact of final consumption rate (CR) shocks on capital formation rate (IR). When IR is given a shock of positive standard deviation of CR in the current period, the response of IR remains negative, keeping increasing from -1.64 percent in the first period to -0.21 percent in the twentieth period. Since the reform and opening-up, China's average net export rate is 3 percent. Thus when net export rate is fixed, the increase in final consumption rate will inevitably lead to the decrease in capital formation rate. As the consumption habits of consumers are relatively stable in general, final consumption remains stable and the impact of its shocks on capital formation rate is long-lasting.

Finally, we look into the impulse response function of capital formation rate (IR) shocks to IR shocks. When IR is given a shock of positive standard deviation of IR in the current period, the response degree of IR keeps falling from 1.21 percent in the first period to -0.07 percent in the third period, reaching its negative maximum of -0.94 percent in the fifth period. Since the sixth period, the degree of negative response begins to decline, reaching -0.16 percent in the twentieth period. Given China's economic reality, investment has the strongest response to shocks of itself in the first three periods with a clear investment cycle, which indicates that the contraction and expansion of China's investment policy have strong cyclical influence on investment.

9.3.4 Analysis of the Variance Decomposition of Final Consumption Rate, Capital Formation Rate and Economic Growth Rate

Variance decomposition shows that when a certain variable in the VAR model is given a shock of one-unit standard deviation, the percentage of predicted error variance of the variable reflects the interaction among variables. Specifically, the error variance of time series is the result of its own disturbance terms as well as other disturbance terms in the system. The purpose of variance decomposition is to decompose the Mean Square Error of the system into the contribution made by the shocks of every variable. Table 9-16, Table 9-17 and Table 9-18 demonstrate the variance decomposition result of final consumption rate, capital formation rate and economic growth.

According to Table 9-16, judging from the impact of shocks of variables on economic growth rate, economic growth rate is mainly affected by itself. After the first period where it is only influenced by itself, such impact slowly declines and basically remains at 92.40 percent in the fifteenth period; the contribution rate of final consumption rate to economic growth is relatively small. In conclusion, on one hand, the impact of change in final consumption rate on economic growth rate is relatively small. On the other hand, its impact on the volatility of economic growth is also small, which indicates the increase in final consumption rate helps stabilize economic growth; the contribution rate of capital formation rate to the volatility of economic growth rises from 0 percent in the first period to 6.15 percent in the fifteenth period and eventually remains at 6.77 percent, which accords with the previous conclusion that gross capital formation affects economic growth more directly than final consumption.

Table 9-16 Variance Decomposition of GR

Period	S.E.	GR	CR	IR
1	5.966400	100.000000	0.000000	0.000000
2	6.617370	98.694270	0.032363	1.273363
3	6.786466	94.950560	0.271463	4.777974
4	7.064314	93.003460	0.544835	6.451705
5	7.134892	92.735050	0.689749	6.575205
6	7.137683	92.664710	0.737757	6.597529
7	7.146975	92.548550	0.752000	6.699452
8	7.150226	92.487260	0.764027	6.748711
9	7.151829	92.465690	0.779573	6.754742
10	7.154814	92.453460	0.795879	6.750661
11	7.156983	92.441300	0.809520	6.749182
12	7.158111	92.427710	0.819560	6.752734
13	7.158831	92.414950	0.826949	6.758106
14	7.159403	92.404970	0.832810	6.762220
15	7.159916	92.397660	0.837717	6.764625
16	7.160375	92.392070	0.841837	6.766091
17	7.160753	92.387520	0.845219	6.767263
18	7.161050	92.383700	0.847943	6.768357
19	7.161283	92.380530	0.850128	6.769341
20	7.161470	92.377960	0.851892	6.770152

According to Table 9-17, judging from the impact of shocks of variables on final consumption rate, the contribution rate of economic growth to final consumption rate falls from 68.14 percent in the second period to 55.28 percent which is its stable level; the contribution rate of final consumption rate to itself fall from 45.20 percent in the first period to 32.27 percent which is its stable level; the contribution rate of capital formation rate to final consumption rate increases from 0 percent in the first period to 12.45 percent which is its stable level. Therefore, final consumption rate has a much larger impact on itself than capital formation rate and economic growth rate do, which implies that consumption is sustainable.

Table 9-17 Variance Decomposition of CR

Period	S.E.	GR	CR	IR
1	2.843800	54.797680	45.202320	0.000000
2	4.793849	68.140550	31.440050	0.419403
3	5.741830	67.510950	30.144280	2.344766
4	6.206145	63.661330	30.816250	5.522426
5	6.509957	60.312540	31.410000	8.277465
6	6.750830	58.381570	31.775800	9.842629
7	6.961764	57.531280	31.919350	10.549370
8	7.141511	57.136140	31.955850	10.908010
9	7.283553	56.810450	31.994450	11.195090
10	7.392362	56.477100	32.051690	11.471210
11	7.477070	56.178780	32.108460	11.712760
12	7.544918	55.947070	32.152790	11.900140
13	7.600169	55.778360	32.183860	12.037780
14	7.645183	55.653040	32.206020	12.140940
15	7.681609	55.554190	32.223370	12.222430
16	7.710951	55.473230	32.237830	12.288940
17	7.734601	55.406880	32.249860	12.343260
18	7.753722	55.353340	32.259600	12.387050
19	7.769220	55.310580	32.267350	12.422060
20	7.781793	55.276410	32.273520	12.450070

According to Table 9-18, judging from the impact of shocks of variables on capital formation rate, the contribution rate of economic growth to capital formation rate rises from 49.18 percent in the first period to 68.24 percent in the third period before falling to 58.07 percent which is its stable level. The contribution rate of final consumption rate to capital formation rate fall from 32.87 percent in the first period to 28.93 percent which is its stable level. The contribution of capital formation rate to itself decreases from 17.95 percent in the first period to 12.99 percent which is its stable level. Overall, capital formation rate is mainly affected by itself and final consumption rate.

Table 9-18 Variance Decomposition of IR

Period	S.E.	GR	CR	IR
1	2.865576	49.181170	32.871400	17.947430
2	4.765206	66.138070	24.296320	9.565606
3	5.539870	68.243290	24.663860	7.092844
4	5.830347	65.780280	26.180230	8.039495
5	6.015070	62.882600	27.131060	9.986342
6	6.165791	61.028330	27.726710	11.244960
7	6.307015	60.204560	28.056060	11.739380
8	6.435681	59.867700	28.217550	11.914750
9	6.538807	59.591120	28.344180	12.064700
10	6.616515	59.277870	28.470060	12.252070
11	6.676112	58.981440	28.581430	12.437130
12	6.723733	58.746710	28.669460	12.583840
13	6.762773	58.576220	28.735410	12.688370
14	6.794822	58.450790	28.785250	12.763970
15	6.820843	58.352090	28.824650	12.823270
16	6.841792	58.270700	28.856810	12.872490
17	6.858653	58.203480	28.883110	12.913400
18	6.872280	58.148980	28.904390	12.946630
19	6.883333	58.105400	28.921450	12.973150
20	6.892309	58.070580	28.935130	12.994300

Judging from the variance decomposition result of economic growth rate and final consumption rate, economic growth rate has a much larger impact on itself than final consumption rate. Final consumption rate is majorly affected by itself. Such a result accords with the previous analysis of the impulse response function.

9.3.5 Conclusion

In section 9.3.5, we construct a VAR model based on the data of China's final consumption rate, capital formation rate and economic growth rate during 1978–2020 to carry out empirical analysis of the relation among these three variables. The conclusions are as follows:

There is a long-term stable relation of equilibrium among China's final consumption rate, capital formation rate and economic growth rate. The VAR model we construct is stationary. Moreover, the variables and the lagged values mutually affect each other.

Based on the impulse response function analysis, we conclude the following: First, When GR is given a shock of positive standard deviation of GR in the current period, the response degree of GR sharply declines from 5.97 percent to -1.64 percent in the following four periods before rising to 0.11 percent in the eighth period, and gradually disappears in the tenth period. The result indicates that with the deepening of China's market-oriented reform, the steadiness of China's economic growth has been progressively improved and the economy is not constantly volatile. The shock of standard deviation of economic growth merely has a short-term impact on economic growth. When GR is given a shock of positive standard deviation of CR in the current period, the response of GR reaches its maximum of 0.38 percent in the fourth period and falls to 0.03 percent in the twentieth period. In terms of the response degree of GR to IR shocks, the response degree of GR remains negative from the first period to the fifth period, reaching its negative maximum of -1.28 percent in the third period. It turns positive from the sixth period though the degree is relatively small and then gradually disappears.

Second, in terms of the response degree of CR to shocks of GR, IR and CR, the response of CR to both IR and CR shocks remains positive until it disappears in the twentieth period; the impulse response of CR to GR shocks remains negative. To raise the economic growth rate in the short run, the most direct and effective way is to increase investment. But the increase in investment will lead to the crowding-out effect causing the decrease in final consumption, which eventually results in the rise of GDP as well as the decline of final consumption (final consumption rate).

Third, in terms of the impulse response degree of IR to GR, CR and IR, the response of IR remains positive. It reaches its maximum of 3.31 percent in the second period and falls to 0.24 percent in the twentieth period. The response of IR remains negative, and keeps increasing from -1.64 percent in the first period to -0.21 percent in the twentieth period. The response degree of IR keeps falling from 1.21 percent in the first period to -0.07 percent in the third period, reaching its negative maximum of -0.94 percent in the fifth period. Since the sixth period, the degree of negative response begins to decline, reaching -0.16 percent in the twentieth period.

Judging from the variance decomposition result of economic growth rate and final consumption rate, economic growth rate has a much larger impact on itself than final consumption rate. Final consumption rate is mainly affected by itself.

Notes

1 Excessive consumption (insufficient investment) causes consumption rate to exceed optimal consumption rate. Based on such circumstance, further raising final consumption rate will lead to the insufficiency of impetus for economic growth, which accords with the US economic reality.
2 Insufficient consumption (excessive investment) causes consumption rate to be lower than optimal consumption rate. Based on such circumstance, further raising final consumption rate will increase the impetus for economic growth, which accords with China's economic reality.
3 Consumption functions as an "automatic stabilizer" in economic development: in the long run, consumption and GDP grow at roughly the same rate; in the short term, consumption is less volatile than GDP. During an economic downturn, when the GDP growth rate falls, the growth rate of consumption also decreases though not as sharply as GDP. It is consumption that slows down the further economic downturn. During an economic upturn, when the GDP growth rate rises, the growth rate of consumption also increases though not as dramatically as GDP. It is consumption that inhibits the further economic upturn.
4 Ouyang Yao, Fu Yuanhai, and Wang Song, "The Scale Effect and Evolution Mechanism about Household Consumption Demand," *Economic Research Journal* 2 (2016).
5 Shen Lisheng, "How does the Change of Final Demand Structure Affect the Change of Industrial Structure?--Analysis Based on the Input-Output Model," *The Journal of Quantitative & Technical Economics* 12 (2011).
6 Lin Jianhao and Wang Meijin, "The Great Moderation of China's Macroeconomic Fluctuations: An InvestigationTiming and Potential Explanations," *China Economic Quarterly* 2 (2013).
7 Guo Shouting, Wang Yuhua, and Wu Zhenqiu, "Study of the Expansion of Chinese Resident's Consumption and the Macroeconomic Steadiness," *Economic Survey* 2 (2017).

8 The contribution rate of final consumption is the proportion of the increment of final consumption in the increment of GDP.
9 Blanchard O. and Simon J., "The Long and Large Decline in U.S.Output Volatility," *Brookings Papers on Economic Activity* 32, no. 1 (2001): 135–164.
10 Mankiw, N. G., *Macroeconomics (the 6th version)*, trans. Zhang Fan (China Renmin University Press, 2006).
11 The input-output table is released by the National Bureau of Statistics every five years. Currently, China's latest input-output table was released in 2012.
12 Shen Lisheng, "Evaluating the Contribution of Three Components of GDP," *The Journal of Quantitative & Technical Economics* 4 (2009).
13 Shen Lisheng, "How does the Change of Final Demand Structure Affect the Change of Industrial Structure?" *The Journal of Quantitative & Technical Economics* 12 (2011).
14 Li Shantong and Wu Sanmang, "Measurement of the Driving Effect of the 'Four Carriages' Driving China's Regional Economic Growth--An Empirical Analysis Based on Provincial Input-Output Tables," Proceedings of International Conference on Sustainable Development and Policy Decision of Mineral Regions & the 3rd Annual Meeting of the Regional Science Association International, Beijing 3 (2012).
15 Shen Lisheng, "How does the Change of Final Demand Structure Affect the Change of Industrial Structure?" *The Journal of Quantitative & Technical Economics* 12 (2011).
16 The calculation process is as follows: deflating the GDP Deflator in 2012 calculated by the expenditure method in *China Statistical Yearbook-2015*, we have the GDP in Simulation Scenario. Then we compare it with the GDP in 2011 to obtain the GDP growth rate in Simulation Scenario.
17 Gao Tiemei, "Econometric Analysis Method and Modeling-Eviews Application and Examples(2nd Edition)," Tsinghua University, 2009.

Chapter 10

Conclusion and Outlook

10.1 Research Conclusions

Given the fact that China's final consumption rate has been falling year by year and the economy has been experiencing structural deceleration, the improvement of consumption plays a significant role in achieving China's sustained and stable economic growth in the long run, which is reflected in *The 13th Five-Year Plan*. Accordingly, in this book, we first observe the stylized fact about China's final consumption rate and the stability of economic growth and clarify the problems that need to be explained and solved to further carry out the research. Next, we discuss the determination of optimal consumption rate under the condition that the economy achieves its optimal growth and the relationship between optimal consumption rate and economic growth stability. Furthermore, we analyse the factors affecting China's economic growth stability with relevant indicators. Finally, based on China's economic statistics, we look into the impact of final consumption rate on China's economic growth and its steadiness through numerical simulation, input-output model and VAR model. The result indicates that though raising final consumption rate barely affects economic growth rate, it has a large impact on the stability of economic growth. Therefore, the convergence of final consumption rate towards its optimal value is important for achieving China's stable economic growth. Specifically, the following conclusions are obtained based on the study in the previous nine chapters:

First, the stylized fact about China's final consumption rate and the stability of economic growth illustrates implies: China's final consumption rate has been decreasing year by year. But according to China's economic data, the stability of economic growth has been gradually improved. Labour income share and income gap are the major factors affecting final consumption rate. We hold the view that the increase in economic growth stability which is the combined result of marketization reform, economic structure and policies is not directly correlated with the decrease in final consumption rate. In fact, the subsequent empirical research shows that the imbalance (decrease in final consumption rate and increase in capital formation rate) in China's demand structure intensifies economic volatility to some extent.

Second, we investigate the dynamic efficiency and optimal consumption rate within the framework of dynamic efficiency where the optimal consumption rate is defined as the consumption rate reached at the point where the economy achieves golden-rule growth. In that sense, the dynamic efficiency of economy helps illustrate the relationship between the actual consumption rate and the optimal consumption rate: The consumption rate in a dynamically inefficient economy is lower than the optimal consumption rate while it is higher in a dynamically efficient economy than the optimal consumption rate. The empirical analysis based on China's economic statistics during 1992–2016 shows:

(1) During 1992–2007, 2011–2012 and 2016, China's economy is dynamically efficient with its final consumption rate higher than the optimal value; during 2008–2010, 2013–2015, China's economy is dynamically inefficient with its final consumption rate lower than the optimal value; and during 1992–2016, China's optimal consumption rate is about 55 percent. Though the number is far

smaller than the average rate of the world as well as that of the middle-income countries during the corresponding period, the author believes it could be the best performance of the economic entity under the economic conditions during 1992–2016. Thus China's final consumption rate is just relatively low. In this way, such optimal consumption rate (55 percent) could be a short-term goal of demand structure adjustment in *The 13th Five-Year Plan*. The convergence from 50.7 percent in 2014 towards its optimal value (55 percent) helps motivate the consumption which is a driving force of economic growth and meanwhile strengthens the stability of economic growth to some extent.

(2) The decomposition of final consumption rate indicates that final consumption rate depends on labour income ratio and average household propensity. How these two variables vary basically explains the evolution trend of China's final consumption rate during 1992–2016. Based on VAR model, we analyse the relationship between final consumption rate and labour income ratio. It turns out there exists a one-way causality between them. Labour income ratio is the Granger-cause for final consumption rate while final consumption rate is not the Granger-cause for labour income ratio. The increase of labour income ratio greatly contributes to the rise of final consumption rate.

(3) Judging from the final consumption rate at the provincial level, we see that China's final consumption rate was negatively correlated with economic development level during 1993–2016. Among the three regions, the eastern region with the highest level of economic development has the lowest final consumption rate. The central region with the moderate level of economic development has the moderate final consumption rate. The western region with the lowest level of economic development has the highest final consumption rate; judging from the dynamic efficiency at the provincial level, we obtain the contrary conclusion to the existing findings: Overall, the economy is dynamically inefficient in the eastern region while it is dynamically efficient in the central and western regions; judging from the relationship between final consumption rate and optimal consumption

rate, the final consumption rate in the eastern region is overall lower than optimal consumption rate, reflecting the under-consumption in the region. The final consumption rate in the central and western regions is overall higher than the optimal consumption rate, reflecting the over-consumption in the regions.

Third, we look into China's optimal consumption rate based on the Solow model from the following two perspectives: (i) The golden-rule capital stock. It is deduced that optimal consumption rate equals labour flexibility of output. According to the empirical research, China's optimal consumption rate is 67.7 percent; (ii) The capital-output ratio. We calculate China's average optimal consumption rate from 1978 to 2013 since the reform and opening-up to be 64.9 percent. Accordingly, based on the Solow model, the reasonable range of China's optimal consumption rate is [64.9 percent, 67.7 percent], the median of which is about 66 percent, 11 percentage points higher than the optimal consumption rate (55 percent) calculated in the framework of the economic dynamic efficiency. Such difference can be explained by the fact that the Solow–Swan model emphasizes the long-term optimal economic growth while the economic dynamic efficiency stresses both the medium- and short-term growth and economic reality. Judging from the point of view of long-run growth, the reasonable range of optimal consumption rate is [62.75 percent, 67.7 percent], which could be a long-term goal of China's demand structure adjustment subsequent to *The 13th Five-Year Plan*.

Fourth, we obtain the explicit solution of optimal consumption rate within the framework of the Ramsey model with endogenous saving-consumption under the condition that optimal consumption rate is defined as the consumption rate achieved when the economy reaches the steady state. Based on parameter calibration, we calculate China's optimal consumption rate as 62.75 percent and discuss how the changes of exogenous parameters affect optimal consumption rate and simulate the extent of impact of various parameters. Specifically, (i) optimal consumption rate depends on discount rate (ρ), the coefficient of relative risk aversion (θ), technological progress (g), capital flexibility of output (α), population growth rate (n), depreciation rate (δ) and other exogenous parameters. Through calibrating the parameters based on China's actual economic situation and the previous research carried out by domestic and foreign scholars, we conclude that China's optimal consumption rate is 62.75% since the reform and opening-up. (ii) According to the explicit solution of optimal consumption rate, discount rate (ρ), the coefficient of relative risk aversion (θ) and technological progress (g) have a positive impact on optimal consumption rate; technological progress (g) has an uncertain impact; and capital flexibility of output (α), population growth rate (n) and depreciation rate (δ) have a negative impact. (iii) The numerical simulation result shows that capital flexibility of output (α), population growth rate (n) and depreciation rate (δ) all have a constant marginal effect on optimal consumption rate. When capital flexibility of output (α) rises by 5 percentage points, optimal consumption rate falls by 2.48 percentage points. Also, when population growth rate (n) and depreciation rate (δ) increases by 1 percentage point, optimal consumption rate decreases by 1.59 percentage points. Since the condition that $\rho<\theta$ (n+δ) is met, the rise of rate of technological progress will result in the increase of optimal consumption rate and discount rate (ρ), the coefficient of relative risk aversion (θ), and technological progress (g) have a decreasing marginal effect on optimal consumption rate. (iv) Among the six exogenous parameters including discount rate (ρ), the coefficient of relative risk aversion (θ), technological progress (g), capital flexibility of output (α), population growth rate (n) and depreciation rate (δ), the coefficient of relative risk aversion (θ) has the largest impact on optimal consumption rate. The impact of one-unit change of θ is ten times larger than that of other parameters. Given the fact that China's consumption rate is relatively low compared to the world level, we believe that we can make consumption rate converge towards its optimal value through adjusting the above exogenous parameters. Since the optimal consumption rate calculated in Ramsey model is close to that calculated in Solow model, we regard the calculation result obtained in Ramsey model as a long-term goal for economic adjustment from the inductive perspective.

Fifth, we build a model of intertemporal general equilibrium. With calibration of parameters in the model, we discuss the determination and factors affecting optimal consumption rate in an open economy through numerical simulation and make the following conclusions: (i)

The equilibrium model of open economy can explain China's consumption behaviour. Comparing with China's actual economic circumstance and the evolution path of the optimal consumption rate, we find out that in the Solow model, the Ramsey model and the model of open economy, China's final consumption rates are all much lower than its optimal consumption rate. The result implies that China's economic development deviates from its optimal development path. (ii) The range of optimal consumption rate in an open economy with different parameters is [51.1 percent, 80.8 percent]. With all parameters in line with actual economic conditions, we take the median of 66.0 percent. In other words, the optimal consumption rate in an open economy is determined to be 66.0 percent. Such a result is close to that of the Solow model and the Ramsey model. (iii) The impact of the two parameters which reflect household consumption behaviour on equilibrium consumption is as follows: (i) When other parameters are given, discount factor is inversely proportional to equilibrium consumption rate. In other words, a higher discount factor implies greater patience consumers have to postpone consumption in the future, thus causing a lower equilibrium consumption rate. (ii) When other parameters are given, elasticity of substitution is in negative correlation with equilibrium consumption rate. Higher elasticity of intertemporal substitution indicates a lower equilibrium consumption rate, which means consumers are more willing to substitute current consumption between future periods.

Sixth, we discuss consumption rate within the framework of the DSGE model. As the DSGE model is to analyse the optimization of an economic entity, this chapter defines the consumption rate reached at the point where the economy is at the steady state as the optimal consumption rate and investigates the response of optimal consumption rate and economic output to exogenous shocks. The conclusions are made as follows: (i) We conduct the numerical simulation based on the calibrated parameters and then obtain the steady-state consumption rate as 58.02 percent, which is the final consumption rate consisting of the household consumption rate and the calibrated government consumption rate (15 percent). Thus the household consumption rate is 43.02 percent. Such a result is close to China's actual consumption rate. During 1978–2016, China's average final consumption rate was 55.8 percent. (ii) In response to a positive 1 percent technology shock, final consumption deviates negatively from the steady-state value in the current period with the maximum deviation range of 0.0073 percent and reaches the minimum negative deviation in the eighth period, followed by a gradual return to the steady-state value. Such response may result from the improvement in output level caused by the rise of rate of technological progress. A large proportion of the incremented output will be used for capital accumulation, which further leads to the decrease of consumption rate. Final consumption rate has a negative and relatively long-lasting response to a technology shock. (iii) Given a positive 1 percent government consumption shock, final consumption rate immediately shows a positive deviation from the steady-state value in the current period, reaching the maximum deviation range of 0.0011 percent. Since then it keeps positively deviating with the deviation range gradually decreasing and eventually returns to the steady-state value. (iv) The sensitivity analysis of steady-state consumption rate to various parameters in the DSGE model indicates that output-capital elasticity, depreciation rate and discount factor are all inversely proportional to the steady-state consumption rate. The impact of the variation of these parameters on the optimal consumption rate is in line with expectations.

We first sum up the measurement indicators of economic growth stability to further analyse the evolution of China's economic growth stability since the reform and opening-up. Then we investigate the factors affecting China's economic growth stability based on China's actual circumstance. The conclusions are as follows:

(i) The stability of the growth of China's GDP, final consumption and gross capital formation has been overall improved since the reform and opening-up. The stability of the growth of gross capital formation and net export is poorer than that of the growth of GDP and final consumption. The stability of the growth of final consumption has been close to that of GDP growth in most years since 1978. According to the result of the variance decomposition, the structure effect of demand structure is -7.2 percent, which indicates that the variation of demand structure weakens the stability of economic growth. This is mainly because the proportion of final consumption which is relatively more stable in demand decreases while the proportion of capital formation and net export which are relatively less stable increases. The volatility effect of demand is 110.6 percent, which implies that the further increase in the stability of demands contributes to the improvement of the economic growth stability. The coupling effect of demand is -3.4 percent, showing that the interaction among the components of demand improves the economic volatility.

(ii) Overall, the stability of the GDP and the three industries has been gradually improved since the reform and opening-up. As for industries, the stability of the tertiary industry, close to the GDP growth stability, is better than that of the primary industry and the secondary industry. The growth of the primary industry is the most volatile, while the growth of the secondary and tertiary industry is more stable. According to the result of the variance decomposition, the structure effect of industry is 28.5 percent, which indicates that such variation enhances the stability of economic growth, mainly because the proportion of the tertiary industry which is relatively stable rises with the drop of the proportion of the primary industry while that of the secondary industry which is relatively unstable slightly varies. The volatility effect is 82.7 percent, which implies that the further increase in the stability of industries contributes to the improvement of the economic growth stability and the 82.7 percent decline of the volatility in GDP results from the increase in the stability of the three industries. The coupling effect is -11.2 percent, showing that the interaction among the three industries increases the economic volatility.

(iii) Judging from the impact of factor structure on China's economic growth stability, the fluctuation of the growth rates of China's factors of production can directly cause the fluctuation of the economic growth: for every 1 percent fluctuation of labour input, the economy fluctuates by 0.6765 percent; and for every 1 percent fluctuation of capital input, the economy fluctuates by 0.7535 percent. Judging from the impact of various factor shocks and the variation of factor structure on the economic volatility, the two stages of the impact of shocks of capital, labour and factor structural variation on the economic volatility are bounded by year 1992. In 1992, Deng Xiaoping's remarks in his tour to China's southern provinces indicate that China's market-oriented reform had entered a new stage. In the first stage (1978–1991), China's economic factor allocation featured insufficient capital factor and relatively sufficient labour factor. Therefore, the labour share of output was higher than capital shares. Judging from the impact of the factor shocks on the economic volatility, the shocks of capital, labour and factor structural variation affected greatly. Specifically, the contribution of capital shock on the economic volatility was the biggest among the three and showed a rising trend in fluctuation; the contribution of labour shock to the economic volatility fluctuated around 0; and the contribution of shock of factor structural variation ranked the second and showed a decreasing trend in fluctuation. It can be told that the progressive adjustment in factor structure helps weaken the economic volatility, though the effect is subtle. The violent fluctuation of all the factors may result from the fluctuation of the factor allocation caused by the immature market-oriented reform, the lack of experience in market economy operation and the transformation of various systems and mechanisms.

(iv) Output gap also affects the stability of economic growth. Generally speaking, the wider is the gap, the poorer is the stability of economic growth.

(v) The ownership structure of investment subjects is a factor that affects the steadiness as well. The larger is the proportion of the state-owned economy, the poorer is the stability of economic growth.

(vi) The stability of economic growth is mainly affected by output gap, demand structure, industry structure and ownership structure of investors: (i) for every 1-percentage-point increase in output gap, the stability index of economic growth declines by 0.97; (ii) for every 1-percentage-point increase in demand structure (final consumption rate), the stability index of economic growth rise by 0.79; (iii) for every 1-percentage-point increase in industry structure, the stability index of economic growth rise by 1.47; and (iv) for every 1-percentage-point increase in ownership structure (proportion of the state-owned economy), the stability index of economic growth declines by 0.62.

Eighth, we analyse the impact of the variation of final consumption rate on economic growth and its steadiness from the aspects of national accounts, input-output model and VAR model: First, from the aspect of national accounts. Supposing the growth rate of consumption, investment and net export remain the same along with an increased consumption rate, a decreased investment rate and an unvarying net export rate, this book simulates the impact of changing final consumption rate on economic growth and its steadiness. The result shows a rise in consumption rate has much smaller impact on economic growth rate than it does on the stability of economic growth rate. Second, from the aspect of input and output. Supposing consumption rate goes up with a declining investment and a dropping net export rate, a rise in final consumption rate affects economic growth rate slightly. Finally, from the aspect of vector autoregression (VAR) model. The VAR model of final consumption rate, investment rate and economic growth rate based on the statistics in China from 1978 to 2020 is used to analyse the impact of varying consumption rate on economic growth and its steadiness. It can be concluded as follows: Economic growth rate varies slightly to respond to a shock of final consumption rate. According to the result of the variance decomposition of economic growth rate and final consumption rate, the volatility of economic growth rate mainly comes from itself, which indicates variation in final consumption rate has minor impact on economic growth rate.

10.2 Policy Suggestions

Our study indicates that though increasing consumption rate has a relatively subtle impact on economic growth rate, it contributes greatly to the improvement of economic growth stability. Therefore, raising final consumption rate towards its mod-term and short-term optimal value (55 percent and 66 percent) is vital to China's long-term steady growth and the improvement of consumer's welfare level. Based on the previous conclusions, we put forward the following suggestion:

First, a long-term mechanism for increasing consumption should be established to further raise as well as stabilize China's consumption rate.

(i) Improving household income level to enable residents to afford consumption. First, the household income should be raised in many ways, including helping the unemployed in urban and the rural-to-urban migrant workers find jobs and providing employment training for college students. According to the classic theory of consumption, consumption is a function of income. That is to say, an increase of income will lead to a rise of consumption, which further causes a rise of final consumption rate at the macro level. Second, the income distribution system of China should be further reformed through raising the income share of labourers in primary distribution and redistribution, because the rise of income share will directly increase the final consumption rate at the macro level. Third, the establishment of the social security system that combines individual accounts with social pooling should be speeded up to solve the problems for residents in housing, education, medical care, pension and unemployment relief. Thus the average household propensity can progressively go up, eventually resulting in the rise of final consumption rate. Fourth, the construction of capital market should be promoted to change household income structure, which can increase the proportion of investment income (asset income) in household income. In this way, household income is no longer restricted by household labour income.

(ii) Improving the environment for consumption to provide security for consumers. First, the infrastructure of consumption in the process of production, supply and trade flows needs to be optimized so as to reduce the costs for the circulation of commodities and improve the quality of service for consumers. Second, the rule of law related to consumption, including Consumer Protection Law, Deposit Insurance Law and Environmental Protection Law, should be further developed to make consumers less vulnerable. Thus the rights of consumers can be guaranteed and the safety of consumption can be ensured. Third, the social credit system needs to be optimized. Meanwhile, public service systems including the traceability system of product quality and the system of market supervision and management ought to be established to reduce dishonest conduct and encourage honest business operation.

(iii) Stabilizing consumption expectation to make residents more willing to consume. Household consumption is mainly affected by the three factors of expectation including income expectation, expenditure expectation and price expectation. First, policies can be made to stabilize household income expectation. Meanwhile, a stable mechanism for pay rise needs to be established to make household income grow at the same rate as economy. Second, the building of social security system should be further promoted to stabilize household expenditure expectation and increase national expenditure in social security. In this way, the expected expenditure of residents facing uncertainty can be lowered. Third, the national supervision on price ought to be optimized to stabilize price. Especially, the regulation on commodity price that concerns people's livelihood should be enhanced.

(iv) Developing consumption hot spots to unleash consumption potential. With the adjustment of China's economic structure and the gradual upgrade of the consumption structure, new industries, businesses and consumption keep emerging, during which great attention needs to be paid on the transition and conversion to avoid economic growth volatility caused by the decline in consumption impetus. First, the guidance on the development of industries should be strengthened, including information consumption, tourism consumption, housekeeping services, experience consumption, cultural consumption as well as health and elderly care consumption. In addition, relevant policies and regulations need to be promoted. Second, consumer group can be expanded to broaden consumption areas. Generally speaking, urban residents consist of the major consumption group. With the promotion of China's urbanization process, more rural residents will become urban residents, which further provides support for new consumption hot spots. Third, the supply-side structural reform ought to be speeded up to offer effective supply for new consumption demand.

(v) Exploring rural consumption to stimulate the vitality of rural consumption. The previous analysis shows that since 2002, the decrease of China's consumption rate mainly results from the decline of rural household consumption rate. Thus increasing rural household consumption rate helps inhibit the decrease of China's final consumption rate. Measures include the following: First, the income of farmers should be increased to narrow the urban-rural income gap, such as enhancing the training for migrant workers, improving rural infrastructure, promoting the integrated development of agriculture with the secondary and tertiary industries, and effectively raising the agricultural and non-agricultural income of farmers. Second, the equalization process of urban-rural public services should be accelerated to ensure that rural residents have the access to the same public services with urban residents. In this way, rural residents have more income for consumption. Third, more policies can be made to enhance market circulation, which helps solve the problems in the flow of rural products into market to guarantee the income of farmers and meanwhile opens up the channels between commodity market and demand of farmers.

Second, various policies and measures should be made to secure China's stable economic growth.

(i) Dependence on capital should be reduced to lower the capital elasticity of output. On contrary to the continuous decrease in China's final consumption rate, capital formation rate increases year by year. Such increase leads to the year-by-year rise of China's capital accumulation, which further causes capital accumulation to exceed its optimal level (golden-rule capital stock). Since the reform and opening-up, due to the relatively fast growth speed of investment, capital makes the greatest contribution to China's economic growth compared with other factors, which further enhances China's capital deepening and rapidly increases the capital-output ratio. Yet such growth pattern driven by high investment is unsustainable in the long run. Accordingly, there is little probability to drive China's economic growth with investment in a certain period in the future. We have to improve investment efficiency through adjusting the investment structure and eliminating ineffective capacity to weaken capital deepening and lower the capital-output ratio, which finally helps the final consumption rate converge towards the optimal consumption rate. High capital flexibility of output will cause the following problems: (i) On one hand, high capital flexibility of output indicates low output elasticity of labour and also low labour income share. Relevant studies show that marginal propensity to consume of labour income is far greater than that of capital income and low labour income share is bad for the continuous increase of consumption. (ii) On the other hand, high capital flexibility of output results in continuous high investment, eventually leading to capital overaccumulation and dynamic inefficiency of the economy.

(ii) Continuity and coherence of the economic policies should be ensured to reduce the economic volatility because high volatility in inflation rate, economic growth rate and interest rate will affect the preference of consumers, especially the discount rate and the coefficient of relative risk aversion: (i) When inflation rate and interest rate are high, the discount rate of consumers will be accordingly raised. Though such rise helps increase the optimal consumption rate, a high consumption rate is not necessarily good for economy. It should adapt to the current economic development stage. (ii) When inflation rate, economic growth rate and interest rate are highly volatile, the uncertainty faced by consumers are increased, which leads to the deviation of consumption rate from its optimal level. Raising the actual economic growth rate to the level of the potential growth rate will further improve the steadiness of the economic growth. Regarding the management of supply, it is significant to maximize the potential for supply through the major transformation of production technology and reconstruction of the dynamic mechanism of supply. Meanwhile, industry structure should be reasonably planned and adjusted to make supply structure adapt to demand structure and thus reduce idle resources and stockpiles of supply. Obviously, compared with the management of demand, the management of supply is harder to yield results in the short term and thus requires long-term efforts. However, once the foundation of supply is truly improved, the conflicts between demand and supply can be fundamentally coordinated to lay a solid foundation for enhancing the stability of economic growth.

(iii) The supply-side structural reform should be promoted. Corresponding with the supply side in the economy, industry structure needs to be adjusted with the demand side in the economy (demand structure). In fact, the adjustment of industry structure can be achieved through adjusting demand structure. In addition, in terms of industry structure itself, we can optimize it through: increasing the inputs into the agricultural infrastructure to properly adjust the internal structure and further lower the volatility of agricultural output; transforming and upgrading industry structure during the process of promoting industrialization; and keeping promoting the traditional industries with focuses on fundamental and emerging service industries. Judging from the factor structure, as the fluctuations of production factors will lead to the fluctuation of economic growth rate, it needs to be ensured that the supply of production factors matches the demand so as to reduce the factor volatility caused by the misallocation of resources. The optimization can be achieved through the following: raising the investment into research and development to increase total factor productivity; increasing the investment into education to improve the quality of labourers; and expanding the effective investment to stabilize the level of capital accumulation. Moreover, the reform of ownership structure should be promoted. Meanwhile, the ratio of the state-owned economy to the non-state-owned economy ought to be adjusted. Though it is generally believed that the efficiency of the state-owned economy is lower than that of the non-state-owned economy, the state-owned economy is still a major tool for national macroeconomic regulation and also an economic stabilizer. Therefore, it is impossible to lower the proportion of the state-owned economy without restrictions. There must be an optimal scale for the state-owned economy, to which the state-owned economy should converge. Furthermore, the volatility of the state-owned economy can be reduced through reforming the state-owned economy itself, which eventually contributes to improving the stability of economic growth.

(iv) Effective investment needs to be constantly expanded to moderately lower capital formation rate. On contrary to the continuous decrease in China's final consumption rate, capital formation rate increases year by year. Such increase leads to the year-by-year rise of China's capital accumulation, which further causes capital accumulation to exceed its optimal level (golden-rule capital stock). Specific measures include adjusting investment structure to reduce the investment in the industries presenting overcapacity; expanding the investment in emerging industries and technologies.

(v) The input into research and development should be increased. Our numerical simulation result shows that the rise of rate of technological progress will cause the increase of optimal consumption rate. Therefore, accelerating technology progress helps consumption rate converge towards its optimal value. After 30 years of development, the gap between the technology level of China and that of developed countries keeps narrowing. Since there is little room for improving the level of production technology through technology introduction, we should level up the input into independent research and development.

(vi) Population should grow at a moderate rate. According to the simulation result, as population growth rate goes up, optimal consumption rate goes down. Though population growth contributes to the economic growth, it takes long time to achieve such effect and will lead to the constant negative effect – aging of population.

(vii) Actions need to be taken to reduce the volatility of final consumption and gross capital formation. The stability of economic growth depends on the stability of final consumption, gross capital formation and net export. As net export accounts for a relatively small proportion and is largely affected by the international market, it barely affects the stability of economic growth. Accordingly, the stability of final consumption and gross capital formation plays a decisive role in stabilizing economic growth. Specific measures include avoiding the simulation policies that helps stabilizing economic growth in the short run but causes potential problems in the long run; improving the sustainability of policies of consumption and investment and meanwhile increasing the coordination between the new policies and the previous ones.

(viii) Capital depreciation in some fields should be reduced to raise consumption rate to its optimal level. Research based on Ramsey model and DSGE model shows that a low depreciation rate helps maintain a relatively high consumption rate, which further contributes to the stabilization of economic growth. The reduced part of capital depreciation can be used for consumption to raise consumption rate. Many buildings in China are demolished shortly after they were built, which is a great waste of capital. Though the GDP rises, national welfare is not much improved. Thus proper plans should be made before capital investment to raise the efficiency of capital use.

10.3 Deficiency and Outlook

In this book, we focus on the relationship between optimal consumption rate and China's stable economic growth. Judging from the conclusions we make, deficiencies are reflected in the following two aspects:

First, in terms of research methods, the research paradigm in current macroeconomic research is based on the Dynamic Stochastic General Equilibrium (DSGE) model for the analysis of macroeconomic issues. Thus we follow such paradigm, adopting methods such as scenario analysis, numerical simulation, parameter calibration and DSGE model. But few factors are considered during the construction of model. For instance, there lacks factors such as open economy, financial market and labour market.

Second, in terms of the research on optimal consumption rate and economic growth stability in this book, there lacks a logically rigorous framework to organize the content of each chapter. Especially in the research on optimal consumption rate, we expound, respectively, based on various models of economic growth. Due to the large difference in the assumption and equilibrium of each growth model, the conclusions are sometimes difficult to harmonize.

Third, in terms of the impact of optimal consumption rate on the stability of economic growth, due to the lack of relevant literature on theoretical analysis, we mainly discuss from the aspect of empirical analysis.

Considering the above-mentioned deficiencies, the future research can take the following aspects into consideration:

First, a DSGE model that accords more with economic reality can be constructed to analyse the issue on optimal consumption rate and China's stable economic growth, in which factors including open economy, financial market and labour market are considered. In this way, more detailed explanation based on the model can be provided.

Second, based on the Unified Growth Theory and the latest literature on economic growth, a more logically rigorous framework can be established to organize the study on optimal consumption rate and economic growth stability.

Appendix

Appendix 1 1993–2016 Relationship between Dynamic Efficiency and Optimal Consumption Rate of Beijing

Year	Final Consumption Expenditure (100 million yuan)	Labour Income (100 million yuan)	Difference between Aggregate Consumption and Labour Income (100 million yuan)	Dynamic Efficiency	Final Consumption Rate (%)	Labour Income Ratio (%)	Ratio of Difference in GDP (%)	Comparison between Actual Consumption Rate and Optimal Consumption Rate
1993	310.28	407.13	-96.85	Dynamically Inefficient	30.43	39.93	-9.50	Consumption Rate<Optimal Consumption Rate
1994	396.29	533.46	-137.17	Dynamically Inefficient	30.05	40.46	-10.40	Consumption Rate<Optimal Consumption Rate
1995	506.58	680.33	-173.75	Dynamically Inefficient	29.89	40.14	-10.25	Consumption Rate<Optimal Consumption Rate
1996	617.85	798.98	-181.13	Dynamically Inefficient	36.81	47.60	-10.79	Consumption Rate<Optimal Consumption Rate
1997	703.36	924.15	-220.79	Dynamically Inefficient	37.59	49.40	-11.80	Consumption Rate<Optimal Consumption Rate

1998	809.80	1058.90	−249.10	Dynamically Inefficient	39.57	51.75	−12.17	Consumption Rate<Optimal Consumption Rate
1999	954.14	1192.05	−237.91	Dynamically Inefficient	43.88	54.82	−10.94	Consumption Rate<Optimal Consumption Rate
2000	1687.96	1394.06	293.90	Dynamically Efficient	53.39	44.09	9.30	Consumption Rate>Optimal Consumption Rate
2001	1911.65	1615.58	296.07	Dynamically Efficient	51.56	43.57	7.98	Consumption Rate>Optimal Consumption Rate
2002	2300.26	1901.15	399.11	Dynamically Efficient	53.31	44.06	9.25	Consumption Rate>Optimal Consumption Rate
2003	2636.50	2225.71	410.79	Dynamically Efficient	52.65	44.45	8.20	Consumption Rate>Optimal Consumption Rate
2004	3085.28	2725.25	360.03	Dynamically Efficient	51.14	45.17	5.97	Consumption Rate>Optimal Consumption Rate
2005	3486.51	3338.91	147.60	Dynamically Efficient	50.03	47.91	2.12	Consumption Rate>Optimal Consumption Rate

(*Continued*)

Appendix 1 Continued

Year	Final Consumption Expenditure (100 million yuan)	Labour Income (100 million yuan)	Difference between Aggregate Consumption and Labour Income (100 million yuan)	Dynamic Efficiency	Final Consumption Rate (%)	Labour Income Ratio (%)	Ratio of Difference in GDP (%)	Comparison between Actual Consumption Rate and Optimal Consumption Rate
2006	4138.53	3840.14	298.39	Dynamically Efficient	50.98	47.31	3.68	Consumption Rate>Optimal Consumption Rate
2007	5108.67	4626.11	482.56	Dynamically Efficient	51.88	46.98	4.90	Consumption Rate>Optimal Consumption Rate
2008	6026.41	5896.59	129.82	Dynamically Efficient	54.22	53.05	1.17	Consumption Rate>Optimal Consumption Rate
2009	6930.41	6448.68	481.73	Dynamically Efficient	57.03	53.06	3.96	Consumption Rate>Optimal Consumption Rate
2010	8032.80	7265.99	766.81	Dynamically Efficient	56.92	51.48	5.43	Consumption Rate>Optimal Consumption Rate
2011	9488.19	8392.00	1096.19	Dynamically Efficient	58.38	51.64	6.74	Consumption Rate>Optimal Consumption Rate

2012	10655.05	9557.77	1097.28	Dynamically Efficient	59.59	53.46	6.14	Consumption Rate>Optimal Consumption Rate
2013	11946.10	10728.86	1217.24	Dynamically Efficient	61.26	55.02	6.24	Consumption Rate>Optimal Consumption Rate
2014	13329.20	11674.30	1654.90	Dynamically Efficient	62.49	54.73	7.76	Consumption Rate>Optimal Consumption Rate
2015	14503.60	13332.17	1171.44	Dynamically Efficient	63.02	57.93	5.09	Consumption Rate>Optimal Consumption Rate
2016	15406.53	14157.87	1248.66	Dynamically Efficient	60.02	55.16	4.86	Consumption Rate>Optimal Consumption Rate

Appendix 2 1993–2016 Relationship between Dynamic Efficiency and Optimal Consumption Rate of Tianjin

Year	Final Consumption Expenditure (100 million yuan)	Labour Income (100 million yuan)	Difference between Aggregate Consumption and Labour Income (100 million yuan)	Dynamic Efficiency	Final Consumption Rate (%)	Labour Income Ratio (%)	Ratio of Difference in GDP (%)	Comparison between Actual Consumption Rate and Optimal Consumption Rate
1993	244.85	234.91	9.94	Dynamically efficient	45.67	43.82	1.85	Consumption Rate>Optimal Consumption Rate
1994	323.76	335.98	-12.22	Dynamically Inefficient	44.65	46.33	-1.69	Consumption Rate<Optimal Consumption Rate
1995	402.95	437.87	-34.92	Dynamically Inefficient	43.91	47.72	-3.81	Consumption Rate<Optimal Consumption Rate
1996	513.32	561.20	-47.88	Dynamically Inefficient	46.69	51.04	-4.36	Consumption Rate<Optimal Consumption Rate
1997	575.77	666.50	-90.73	Dynamically Inefficient	46.61	53.96	-7.34	Consumption Rate<Optimal Consumption Rate

1998	622.70	734.84	-112.14	Dynamically Inefficient	46.60	54.99	-8.39	Consumption Rate<Optimal Consumption Rate
1999	716.80	785.45	-68.65	Dynamically Inefficient	49.43	54.17	-4.73	Consumption Rate<Optimal Consumption Rate
2000	843.89	750.87	93.02	Dynamically efficient	49.59	44.12	5.47	Consumption Rate>Optimal Consumption Rate
2001	948.42	813.18	135.24	Dynamically efficient	49.42	42.37	7.05	Consumption Rate>Optimal Consumption Rate
2002	1040.49	876.99	163.50	Dynamically efficient	48.38	40.78	7.60	Consumption Rate>Optimal Consumption Rate
2003	1193.05	936.83	256.22	Dynamically efficient	46.28	36.34	9.94	Consumption Rate>Optimal Consumption Rate
2004	1343.65	1102.65	241.00	Dynamically efficient	43.19	35.44	7.75	Consumption Rate>Optimal Consumption Rate
2005	1509.06	1289.45	219.61	Dynamically efficient	38.64	33.02	5.62	Consumption Rate>Optimal Consumption Rate

(Continued)

Appendix 2 Continued

Year	Final Consumption Expenditure (100 million yuan)	Labour Income (100 million yuan)	Difference between Aggregate Consumption and Labour Income (100 million yuan)	Dynamic Efficiency	Final Consumption Rate (%)	Labour Income Ratio (%)	Ratio of Difference in GDP (%)	Comparison between Actual Consumption Rate and Optimal Consumption Rate
2006	1767.99	1493.56	274.43	Dynamically efficient	39.62	33.47	6.15	Consumption Rate>Optimal Consumption Rate
2007	2072.90	1743.93	328.97	Dynamically efficient	39.46	33.20	6.26	Consumption Rate>Optimal Consumption Rate
2008	2534.01	2631.91	-97.90	Dynamically Inefficient	37.71	39.17	-1.46	Consumption Rate<Optimal Consumption Rate
2009	2879.25	2978.82	-99.57	Dynamically Inefficient	38.28	39.60	-1.32	Consumption Rate<Optimal Consumption Rate
2010	3538.18	3733.98	-195.80	Dynamically Inefficient	38.36	40.48	-2.12	Consumption Rate<Optimal Consumption Rate

2011	4286.34	4597.05	-310.71	Dynamically Inefficient	37.91	40.66	-2.75	Consumption Rate<Optimal Consumption Rate
2012	4879.39	5292.39	-413.00	Dynamically Inefficient	37.84	41.05	-3.20	Consumption Rate<Optimal Consumption Rate
2013	5634.80	6043.35	-408.55	Dynamically Inefficient	39.21	42.05	-2.84	Consumption Rate<Optimal Consumption Rate
2014	6253.61	6615.33	-361.72	Dynamically Inefficient	39.76	42.06	-2.30	Consumption Rate<Optimal Consumption Rate
2015	7155.66	7060.19	95.47	Dynamically efficient	43.27	42.69	0.58	Consumption Rate>Optimal Consumption Rate
2016	8012.04	7550.29	461.75	Dynamically efficient	44.80	42.21	2.58	Consumption Rate>Optimal Consumption Rate

Appendix 3 1993–2016 Relationship between Dynamic Efficiency and Optimal Consumption Rate of Hebei

Year	Final Consumption Expenditure (100 million yuan)	Labour Income (100 million yuan)	Difference between Aggregate Consumption and Labour Income (100 million yuan)	Dynamic Efficiency	Final Consumption Rate (%)	Labour Income Ratio (%)	Ratio of Difference in GDP (%)	Comparison between Actual Consumption Rate and Optimal Consumption Rate
1993	870.45	874.39	-3.94	Dynamically Inefficient	51.48	51.71	-0.23	Consumption Rate<Optimal Consumption Rate
1994	1059.29	1258.39	-199.10	Dynamically Inefficient	48.42	57.53	-9.10	Consumption Rate<Optimal Consumption Rate
1995	1348.75	1725.31	-376.56	Dynamically Inefficient	47.33	60.55	-13.21	Consumption Rate<Optimal Consumption Rate
1996	1553.79	1969.74	-415.95	Dynamically Inefficient	45.00	57.04	-12.05	Consumption Rate<Optimal Consumption Rate
1997	1740.18	2212.69	-472.51	Dynamically Inefficient	44.01	55.96	-11.95	Consumption Rate<Optimal Consumption Rate
1998	1819.20	2366.64	-547.44	Dynamically Inefficient	42.74	55.61	-12.86	Consumption Rate<Optimal Consumption Rate

1999	1983.79	2576.81	-593.02	Dynamically Inefficient	43.42	56.40	-12.98	Consumption Rate<Optimal Consumption Rate
2000	2240.68	2810.22	-569.54	Dynamically Inefficient	44.42	55.71	-11.29	Consumption Rate<Optimal Consumption Rate
2001	2490.38	3045.85	-555.47	Dynamically Inefficient	45.14	55.21	-10.07	Consumption Rate<Optimal Consumption Rate
2002	2838.41	3160.57	-322.16	Dynamically Inefficient	47.16	52.52	-5.35	Consumption Rate<Optimal Consumption Rate
2003	3029.25	3520.77	-491.52	Dynamically Inefficient	43.77	50.87	-7.10	Consumption Rate<Optimal Consumption Rate
2004	3677.23	3656.49	20.74	Dynamically efficient	43.38	43.13	0.24	Consumption Rate>Optimal Consumption Rate
2005	4273.61	4514.70	-241.09	Dynamically Inefficient	42.68	45.09	-2.41	Consumption Rate<Optimal Consumption Rate
2006	4966.60	5438.52	-471.92	Dynamically Inefficient	43.31	47.43	-4.12	Consumption Rate<Optimal Consumption Rate

(*Continued*)

Appendix 3 Continued

Year	Final Consumption Expenditure (100 million yuan)	Labour Income (100 million yuan)	Difference between Aggregate Consumption and Labour Income (100 million yuan)	Dynamic Efficiency	Final Consumption Rate (%)	Labour Income Ratio (%)	Ratio of Difference in GDP (%)	Comparison between Actual Consumption Rate and Optimal Consumption Rate
2007	5871.11	6893.85	-1022.74	Dynamically Inefficient	43.15	50.66	-7.52	Consumption Rate<Optimal Consumption Rate
2008	6695.14	9037.30	-2342.16	Dynamically Inefficient	41.81	56.44	-14.63	Consumption Rate<Optimal Consumption Rate
2009	7220.83	10009.72	-2788.89	Dynamically Inefficient	41.90	58.08	-16.18	Consumption Rate<Optimal Consumption Rate
2010	8326.02	11844.63	-3518.61	Dynamically Inefficient	40.83	58.08	-17.25	Consumption Rate<Optimal Consumption Rate
2011	9633.82	13121.83	-3488.01	Dynamically Inefficient	39.30	53.52	-14.23	Consumption Rate<Optimal Consumption Rate

APPENDIX

2012	11081.10	14339.51	-3258.41	Dynamically Inefficient	41.70	53.96	-12.26	Consumption Rate<Optimal Consumption Rate
2013	11886.59	15034.90	-3148.31	Dynamically Inefficient	42.00	53.12	-11.12	Consumption Rate<Optimal Consumption Rate
2014	12538.97	15582.79	-3043.82	Dynamically Inefficient	42.62	52.96	-10.35	Consumption Rate<Optimal Consumption Rate
2015	13197.78	16168.48	-2970.70	Dynamically Inefficient	44.28	54.25	-9.97	Consumption Rate<Optimal Consumption Rate
2016	14536.13	17107.98	-2571.85	Dynamically Inefficient	45.33	53.34	-8.02	Consumption Rate<Optimal Consumption Rate

Appendix 4 1993–2016 Relationship between Dynamic Efficiency and Optimal Consumption Rate of Shanxi

Year	Final Consumption Expenditure (100 million yuan)	Labour Income (100 million yuan)	Difference between Aggregate Consumption and Labour Income (100 million yuan)	Dynamic Efficiency	Final Consumption Rate (%)	Labour Income Ratio (%)	Ratio of Difference in GDP (%)	Comparison between Actual Consumption Rate and Optimal Consumption Rate
1993	418.60	300.02	118.58	Dynamically efficient	59.41	42.58	16.83	Consumption Rate>Optimal Consumption Rate
1994	494.90	372.67	122.23	Dynamically efficient	57.96	43.65	14.32	Consumption Rate>Optimal Consumption Rate
1995	627.20	478.26	148.94	Dynamically efficient	57.41	43.78	13.63	Consumption Rate>Optimal Consumption Rate
1996	754.50	580.90	173.60	Dynamically efficient	57.68	44.41	13.27	Consumption Rate>Optimal Consumption Rate
1997	852.50	650.11	202.39	Dynamically efficient	57.60	43.92	13.67	Consumption Rate>Optimal Consumption Rate

APPENDIX

1998	791.30	710.83	80.47	Dynamically efficient	49.58	44.54	5.04	Consumption Rate>Optimal Consumption Rate
1999	857.14	719.53	137.61	Dynamically efficient	57.09	47.93	9.17	Consumption Rate>Optimal Consumption Rate
2000	946.04	798.24	147.80	Dynamically efficient	51.77	43.68	8.09	Consumption Rate>Optimal Consumption Rate
2001	1046.43	869.96	176.47	Dynamically efficient	52.97	44.04	8.93	Consumption Rate>Optimal Consumption Rate
2002	1236.00	999.39	236.61	Dynamically efficient	53.17	42.99	10.18	Consumption Rate>Optimal Consumption Rate
2003	1399.60	1135.37	264.24	Dynamically efficient	50.27	40.78	9.49	Consumption Rate>Optimal Consumption Rate
2004	1702.10	1345.02	357.08	Dynamically efficient	48.92	38.66	10.26	Consumption Rate>Optimal Consumption Rate
2005	1979.05	1597.28	381.77	Dynamically efficient	47.65	38.46	9.19	Consumption Rate>Optimal Consumption Rate

(*Continued*)

Appendix 4 Continued

Year	Final Consumption Expenditure (100 million yuan)	Labour Income (100 million yuan)	Difference between Aggregate Consumption and Labour Income (100 million yuan)	Dynamic Efficiency	Final Consumption Rate (%)	Labour Income Ratio (%)	Ratio of Difference in GDP (%)	Comparison between Actual Consumption Rate and Optimal Consumption Rate
2006	2330.01	1863.68	466.33	Dynamically efficient	47.05	37.63	9.42	Consumption Rate>Optimal Consumption Rate
2007	2717.89	2143.46	574.43	Dynamically efficient	45.13	35.59	9.54	Consumption Rate>Optimal Consumption Rate
2008	3208.86	3095.53	113.33	Dynamically efficient	43.78	42.23	1.55	Consumption Rate>Optimal Consumption Rate
2009	3385.33	3543.36	-158.03	Dynamically Inefficient	45.51	47.64	-2.12	Consumption Rate<Optimal Consumption Rate
2010	4130.68	3820.25	310.43	Dynamically efficient	44.89	41.52	3.37	Consumption Rate>Optimal Consumption Rate

2011	4868.11	4909.21	-41.10	Dynamically Inefficient	43.32	43.69	-0.37	Consumption Rate<Optimal Consumption Rate
2012	5506.09	5585.14	-79.05	Dynamically Inefficient	45.46	46.11	-0.65	Consumption Rate<Optimal Consumption Rate
2013	6182.79	6051.64	131.15	Dynamically efficient	49.06	48.02	1.04	Consumption Rate>Optimal Consumption Rate
2014	6365.56	6290.78	74.78	Dynamically efficient	49.88	49.30	0.59	Consumption Rate>Optimal Consumption Rate
2015	7134.70	6381.50	753.20	Dynamically efficient	55.89	49.99	5.90	Consumption Rate>Optimal Consumption Rate
2016	7451.46	6520.28	931.18	Dynamically efficient	57.10	49.96	7.14	Consumption Rate>Optimal Consumption Rate

Appendix 5 1993–2016 Relationship between Dynamic Efficiency and Optimal Consumption Rate of Inner Mongolia

Year	Final Consumption Expenditure (100 million yuan)	Labour Income (100 million yuan)	Difference between Aggregate Consumption and Labour Income (100 million yuan)	Dynamic Efficiency	Final Consumption Rate (%)	Labour Income Ratio (%)	Ratio of Difference in GDP (%)	Comparison between Actual Consumption Rate and Optimal Consumption Rate
1993	320.92	344.75	-23.83	Dynamically Inefficient	60.24	64.72	-4.47	Consumption Rate<Optimal Consumption Rate
1994	406.88	440.87	-33.99	Dynamically Inefficient	59.67	64.65	-4.99	Consumption Rate<Optimal Consumption Rate
1995	505.84	530.62	-24.78	Dynamically Inefficient	60.73	63.71	-2.97	Consumption Rate<Optimal Consumption Rate
1996	573.13	615.90	-42.77	Dynamically Inefficient	58.20	62.54	-4.34	Consumption Rate<Optimal Consumption Rate
1997	639.84	682.99	-43.15	Dynamically Inefficient	58.18	62.10	-3.92	Consumption Rate<Optimal Consumption Rate

1998	664.00	746.52	-82.52	Dynamically Inefficient	56.80	63.85	-7.06	Consumption Rate<Optimal Consumption Rate
1999	724.54	770.55	-46.01	Dynamically Inefficient	57.74	61.41	-3.67	Consumption Rate<Optimal Consumption Rate
2000	873.65	801.10	72.55	Dynamically efficient	56.76	52.05	4.71	Consumption Rate>Optimal Consumption Rate
2001	974.99	863.14	111.85	Dynamically efficient	56.89	50.36	6.53	Consumption Rate>Optimal Consumption Rate
2002	1137.21	959.82	177.39	Dynamically efficient	58.59	49.45	9.14	Consumption Rate>Optimal Consumption Rate
2003	1259.57	1173.89	85.68	Dynamically efficient	52.74	49.15	3.59	Consumption Rate>Optimal Consumption Rate
2004	1495.19	1373.80	121.39	Dynamically efficient	49.17	45.17	3.99	Consumption Rate>Optimal Consumption Rate
2005	1802.84	1684.03	118.81	Dynamically efficient	46.17	43.12	3.04	Consumption Rate>Optimal Consumption Rate

(*Continued*)

Appendix 5 Continued

Year	Final Consumption Expenditure (100 million yuan)	Labour Income (100 million yuan)	Difference between Aggregate Consumption and Labour Income (100 million yuan)	Dynamic Efficiency	Final Consumption Rate (%)	Labour Income Ratio (%)	Ratio of Difference in GDP (%)	Comparison between Actual Consumption Rate and Optimal Consumption Rate
2006	2129.59	1897.75	231.84	Dynamically efficient	43.07	38.38	4.69	Consumption Rate>Optimal Consumption Rate
2007	2630.87	2311.60	319.27	Dynamically efficient	40.96	35.99	4.97	Consumption Rate>Optimal Consumption Rate
2008	3278.65	3566.09	-287.44	Dynamically Inefficient	38.59	41.97	-3.38	Consumption Rate<Optimal Consumption Rate
2009	3941.11	4746.64	-805.53	Dynamically Inefficient	40.46	48.73	-8.27	Consumption Rate<Optimal Consumption Rate
2010	4588.14	5340.59	-752.45	Dynamically Inefficient	39.31	45.76	-6.45	Consumption Rate<Optimal Consumption Rate

2011	5526.64	6552.47	-1025.83	Dynamically Inefficient	38.49	45.63	-7.14	Consumption Rate<Optimal Consumption Rate
2012	6244.16	7308.81	-1064.65	Dynamically Inefficient	39.32	46.02	-6.70	Consumption Rate<Optimal Consumption Rate
2013	6889.61	8011.24	-1121.63	Dynamically Inefficient	40.93	47.59	-6.66	Consumption Rate<Optimal Consumption Rate
2014	7158.23	9195.08	-2036.85	Dynamically Inefficient	40.28	51.75	-11.46	Consumption Rate<Optimal Consumption Rate
2015	7452.82	9237.38	-1784.56	Dynamically Inefficient	41.80	51.80	-10.01	Consumption Rate<Optimal Consumption Rate
2016	8030.92	9424.67	-1393.75	Dynamically Inefficient	44.30	51.99	-7.69	Consumption Rate<Optimal Consumption Rate

Appendix 6 1993–2016 Relationship between Dynamic Efficiency and Optimal Consumption Rate of Liaoning

Year	Final Consumption Expenditure (100 million yuan)	Labour Income (100 million yuan)	Difference between Aggregate Consumption and Labour Income (100 million yuan)	Dynamic Efficiency	Final Consumption Rate (%)	Labour Income Ratio (%)	Ratio of Difference in GDP (%)	Comparison between Actual Consumption Rate and Optimal Consumption Rate
1993	962.51	939.63	22.88	Dynamically efficient	47.87	46.73	1.14	Consumption Rate>Optimal Consumption Rate
1994	1239.61	1178.72	60.89	Dynamically efficient	50.35	47.88	2.47	Consumption Rate>Optimal Consumption Rate
1995	1501.84	1389.43	112.41	Dynamically efficient	53.76	49.74	4.02	Consumption Rate>Optimal Consumption Rate
1996	1728.74	1647.61	81.13	Dynamically efficient	54.91	52.33	2.58	Consumption Rate>Optimal Consumption Rate
1997	1877.85	1902.56	-24.71	Dynamically Inefficient	53.80	54.51	-0.71	Consumption Rate<Optimal Consumption Rate

1998	2128.10	2072.96	55.14	Dynamically efficient	54.82	53.40	1.42	Consumption Rate>Optimal Consumption Rate
1999	2330.53	2125.47	205.06	Dynamically efficient	55.87	50.95	4.92	Consumption Rate>Optimal Consumption Rate
2000	2587.52	2204.13	383.39	Dynamically efficient	55.42	47.21	8.21	Consumption Rate>Optimal Consumption Rate
2001	2828.09	2323.66	504.43	Dynamically efficient	56.19	46.17	10.02	Consumption Rate>Optimal Consumption Rate
2002	3031.47	2559.22	472.25	Dynamically efficient	55.54	46.89	8.65	Consumption Rate>Optimal Consumption Rate
2003	3102.51	2802.81	299.70	Dynamically efficient	51.69	46.69	4.99	Consumption Rate>Optimal Consumption Rate
2004	3248.30	3039.27	209.03	Dynamically efficient	48.69	45.55	3.13	Consumption Rate>Optimal Consumption Rate
2005	3688.94	4524.42	-835.48	Dynamically Inefficient	45.84	56.22	-10.38	Consumption Rate<Optimal Consumption Rate

(*Continued*)

Appendix 6 Continued

Year	Final Consumption Expenditure (100 million yuan)	Labour Income (100 million yuan)	Difference between Aggregate Consumption and Labour Income (100 million yuan)	Dynamic Efficiency	Final Consumption Rate (%)	Labour Income Ratio (%)	Ratio of Difference in GDP (%)	Comparison between Actual Consumption Rate and Optimal Consumption Rate
2006	4054.93	5128.57	-1073.64	Dynamically Inefficient	43.58	55.12	-11.54	Consumption Rate<Optimal Consumption Rate
2007	4717.14	6067.11	-1349.97	Dynamically Inefficient	42.25	54.34	-12.09	Consumption Rate<Optimal Consumption Rate
2008	5595.95	7297.91	-1701.96	Dynamically Inefficient	40.94	53.39	-12.45	Consumption Rate<Optimal Consumption Rate
2009	6311.05	7868.25	-1557.20	Dynamically Inefficient	41.49	51.72	-10.24	Consumption Rate<Optimal Consumption Rate
2010	7374.14	9431.14	-2057.00	Dynamically Inefficient	39.95	51.10	-11.14	Consumption Rate<Optimal Consumption Rate

2011	8867.21	10782.35	-1915.14	Dynamically Inefficient	39.89	48.51	-8.62	Consumption Rate<Optimal Consumption Rate
2012	10073.24	12137.58	-2064.34	Dynamically Inefficient	40.54	48.85	-8.31	Consumption Rate<Optimal Consumption Rate
2013	11214.85	12283.51	-1068.66	Dynamically Inefficient	41.42	45.36	-3.95	Consumption Rate<Optimal Consumption Rate
2014	12192.71	13926.97	-1734.26	Dynamically Inefficient	42.59	48.65	-6.06	Consumption Rate<Optimal Consumption Rate
2015	13019.49	13446.80	-427.31	Dynamically Inefficient	45.41	46.90	-1.49	Consumption Rate<Optimal Consumption Rate
2016	13149.51	10388.89	2760.62	Dynamically efficient	59.11	46.70	12.41	Consumption Rate>Optimal Consumption Rate

Appendix 7 1993–2016 Relationship between Dynamic Efficiency and Optimal Consumption Rate of Jilin

Year	Final Consumption Expenditure (100 million yuan)	Labour Income (100 million yuan)	Difference between Aggregate Consumption and Labour Income (100 million yuan)	Dynamic Efficiency	Final Consumption Rate (%)	Labour Income Ratio (%)	Ratio of Difference in GDP (%)	Comparison between Actual Consumption Rate and Optimal Consumption Rate
1993	436.06	408.84	27.22	Dynamically efficient	60.74	56.95	3.79	Consumption Rate>Optimal Consumption Rate
1994	577.59	601.30	-23.71	Dynamically Inefficient	59.62	62.07	-2.45	Consumption Rate<Optimal Consumption Rate
1995	703.38	715.41	-12.03	Dynamically Inefficient	61.73	62.79	-1.06	Consumption Rate<Optimal Consumption Rate
1996	811.44	870.01	-58.57	Dynamically Inefficient	60.02	64.35	-4.33	Consumption Rate<Optimal Consumption Rate
1997	928.35	949.12	-20.77	Dynamically Inefficient	63.23	64.64	-1.41	Consumption Rate<Optimal Consumption Rate

APPENDIX 349

1998	969.20	1040.39	-71.19	Dynamically Inefficient	61.69	66.22	-4.53	Consumption Rate<Optimal Consumption Rate
1999	1030.43	1087.25	-56.82	Dynamically Inefficient	61.33	64.72	-3.38	Consumption Rate<Optimal Consumption Rate
2000	1185.61	1224.48	-38.87	Dynamically Inefficient	63.56	65.64	-2.08	Consumption Rate<Optimal Consumption Rate
2001	1331.32	1474.40	-143.08	Dynamically Inefficient	63.76	70.62	-6.85	Consumption Rate<Optimal Consumption Rate
2002	1444.68	1604.46	-159.78	Dynamically Inefficient	62.33	69.23	-6.89	Consumption Rate<Optimal Consumption Rate
2003	1678.60	1818.66	-140.06	Dynamically Inefficient	64.59	69.98	-5.39	Consumption Rate<Optimal Consumption Rate
2004	1693.27	1481.51	211.76	Dynamically efficient	56.21	49.18	7.03	Consumption Rate>Optimal Consumption Rate
2005	1921.64	1699.59	222.05	Dynamically efficient	51.09	45.18	5.90	Consumption Rate>Optimal Consumption Rate

(*Continued*)

Appendix 7 Continued

Year	Final Consumption Expenditure (100 million yuan)	Labour Income (100 million yuan)	Difference between Aggregate Consumption and Labour Income (100 million yuan)	Dynamic Efficiency	Final Consumption Rate (%)	Labour Income Ratio (%)	Ratio of Difference in GDP (%)	Comparison between Actual Consumption Rate and Optimal Consumption Rate
2006	2137.57	1941.82	195.75	Dynamically efficient	43.05	39.11	3.94	Consumption Rate>Optimal Consumption Rate
2007	2588.42	2278.79	309.63	Dynamically efficient	46.21	40.68	5.53	Consumption Rate>Optimal Consumption Rate
2008	3057.70	2731.33	326.37	Dynamically efficient	45.02	40.22	4.81	Consumption Rate>Optimal Consumption Rate
2009	3416.95	3070.80	346.15	Dynamically efficient	44.57	40.06	4.52	Consumption Rate>Optimal Consumption Rate
2010	3778.84	3538.93	239.91	Dynamically efficient	40.40	37.84	2.57	Consumption Rate>Optimal Consumption Rate

2011	4423.67	4290.24	133.43	Dynamically efficient	39.63	38.44	1.20	Consumption Rate>Optimal Consumption Rate
2012	4942.04	4818.66	123.38	Dynamically efficient	38.95	37.98	0.97	Consumption Rate>Optimal Consumption Rate
2013	5500.45	5270.48	229.97	Dynamically efficient	39.44	37.79	1.65	Consumption Rate>Optimal Consumption Rate
2014	5407.99	5966.36	-558.37	Dynamically Inefficient	39.18	43.22	-4.05	Consumption Rate<Optimal Consumption Rate
2015	5593.22	6430.99	-837.77	Dynamically Inefficient	39.77	45.73	-5.96	Consumption Rate<Optimal Consumption Rate
2016	5567.07	6744.56	-1177.49	Dynamically Inefficient	37.67	45.64	-7.97	Consumption Rate<Optimal Consumption Rate

Appendix 8 1993–2016 Relationship between Dynamic Efficiency and Optimal Consumption Rate of Heilongjiang

Year	Final Consumption Expenditure (100 million yuan)	Labour Income (100 million yuan)	Difference between Aggregate Consumption and Labour Income (100 million yuan)	Dynamic Efficiency	Final Consumption Rate (%)	Labour Income Ratio (%)	Ratio of Difference in GDP (%)	Comparison between Actual Consumption Rate and Optimal Consumption Rate
1993	603.90	517.44	86.46	Dynamically efficient	50.39	43.18	7.21	Consumption Rate>Optimal Consumption Rate
1994	805.40	692.16	113.24	Dynamically efficient	50.18	43.13	7.06	Consumption Rate>Optimal Consumption Rate
1995	1081.30	994.35	86.95	Dynamically efficient	54.30	49.93	4.37	Consumption Rate>Optimal Consumption Rate
1996	1245.40	1196.16	49.24	Dynamically efficient	52.54	50.46	2.08	Consumption Rate>Optimal Consumption Rate
1997	1313.60	1326.57	-12.97	Dynamically Inefficient	49.24	49.73	-0.49	Consumption Rate<Optimal Consumption Rate

1998	1364.10	1380.75	-16.65	Dynamically Inefficient	49.17	49.77	-0.60	Consumption Rate<Optimal Consumption Rate
1999	1431.20	1405.95	25.25	Dynamically efficient	49.93	49.05	0.88	Consumption Rate>Optimal Consumption Rate
2000	1580.00	1448.16	131.84	Dynamically efficient	50.14	45.95	4.18	Consumption Rate>Optimal Consumption Rate
2001	1752.30	1645.04	107.27	Dynamically efficient	51.69	48.52	3.16	Consumption Rate>Optimal Consumption Rate
2002	1872.30	1804.22	68.09	Dynamically efficient	51.48	49.60	1.87	Consumption Rate>Optimal Consumption Rate
2003	2076.30	1992.06	84.24	Dynamically efficient	51.17	49.10	2.08	Consumption Rate>Optimal Consumption Rate
2004	2304.10	1805.49	498.61	Dynamically efficient	48.50	38.01	10.50	Consumption Rate>Optimal Consumption Rate

(*Continued*)

Appendix 8 Continued

Year	Final Consumption Expenditure (100 million yuan)	Labour Income (100 million yuan)	Difference between Aggregate Consumption and Labour Income (100 million yuan)	Dynamic Efficiency	Final Consumption Rate (%)	Labour Income Ratio (%)	Ratio of Difference in GDP (%)	Comparison between Actual Consumption Rate and Optimal Consumption Rate
2005	2660.75	2061.55	599.20	Dynamically efficient	48.28	37.40	10.87	Consumption Rate>Optimal Consumption Rate
2006	2961.21	2342.29	618.92	Dynamically efficient	47.85	37.85	10.00	Consumption Rate>Optimal Consumption Rate
2007	3514.30	2722.39	791.91	Dynamically efficient	49.47	38.32	11.15	Consumption Rate>Optimal Consumption Rate
2008	4297.71	3292.52	1005.19	Dynamically efficient	51.69	39.60	12.09	Consumption Rate>Optimal Consumption Rate
2009	4850.25	3661.86	1188.39	Dynamically efficient	56.48	42.64	13.84	Consumption Rate>Optimal Consumption Rate

2010	5585.71	4031.76	1553.95	Dynamically efficient	53.87	38.88	14.99	Consumption Rate>Optimal Consumption Rate
2011	6586.71	4884.78	1701.93	Dynamically efficient	52.35	38.82	13.53	Consumption Rate>Optimal Consumption Rate
2012	7260.45	5688.82	1571.63	Dynamically efficient	53.03	41.55	11.48	Consumption Rate>Optimal Consumption Rate
2013	7963.60	6360.86	1602.74	Dynamically efficient	55.37	44.23	11.14	Consumption Rate>Optimal Consumption Rate
2014	8877.27	6878.57	1998.70	Dynamically efficient	58.12	45.03	13.08	Consumption Rate>Optimal Consumption Rate
2015	8986.69	7444.74	1541.95	Dynamically efficient	59.58	49.36	10.22	Consumption Rate>Optimal Consumption Rate
2016	9579.97	7772.82	1807.15	Dynamically efficient	62.26	50.52	11.75	Consumption Rate>Optimal Consumption Rate

Appendix 9 1993–2016 Relationship between Dynamic Efficiency and Optimal Consumption Rate of Shanghai

Year	Final Consumption Expenditure (100 million yuan)	Labour Income (100 million yuan)	Difference between Aggregate Consumption and Labour Income (100 million yuan)	Dynamic Efficiency	Final Consumption Rate (%)	Labour Income Ratio (%)	Ratio of Difference in GDP (%)	Comparison between Actual Consumption Rate and Optimal Consumption Rate
1993	679.35	591.77	87.58	Dynamically Inefficient	44.94	39.15	5.79	Consumption Rate<Optimal Consumption Rate
1994	873.89	727.02	146.87	Dynamically Inefficient	44.32	36.87	7.45	Consumption Rate<Optimal Consumption Rate
1995	1085.33	946.92	138.41	Dynamically Inefficient	44.07	38.45	5.62	Consumption Rate<Optimal Consumption Rate
1996	1252.33	1119.14	133.19	Dynamically Inefficient	43.15	38.56	4.59	Consumption Rate<Optimal Consumption Rate
1997	1423.63	1255.41	168.22	Dynamically Inefficient	42.37	37.36	5.01	Consumption Rate<Optimal Consumption Rate

1998	1526.30	1408.28	118.02	Dynamically Inefficient	41.38	38.18	3.20	Consumption Rate<Optimal Consumption Rate
1999	1719.48	1594.17	125.31	Dynamically Inefficient	42.61	39.51	3.11	Consumption Rate<Optimal Consumption Rate
2000	2244.52	1810.50	434.02	Dynamically efficient	47.04	37.95	9.10	Consumption Rate>Optimal Consumption Rate
2001	2476.20	2030.98	445.22	Dynamically efficient	47.53	38.98	8.55	Consumption Rate>Optimal Consumption Rate
2002	2791.06	2316.08	474.98	Dynamically efficient	48.62	40.34	8.27	Consumption Rate>Optimal Consumption Rate
2003	3217.59	2574.94	642.65	Dynamically efficient	48.07	38.47	9.60	Consumption Rate>Optimal Consumption Rate
2004	3832.59	2910.36	922.23	Dynamically efficient	47.48	36.05	11.42	Consumption Rate>Optimal Consumption Rate
2005	4480.34	3477.93	1002.41	Dynamically efficient	48.45	37.61	10.84	Consumption Rate>Optimal Consumption Rate

(*Continued*)

Appendix 9 Continued

Year	Final Consumption Expenditure (100 million yuan)	Labour Income (100 million yuan)	Difference between Aggregate Consumption and Labour Income (100 million yuan)	Dynamic Efficiency	Final Consumption Rate (%)	Labour Income Ratio (%)	Ratio of Difference in GDP (%)	Comparison between Actual Consumption Rate and Optimal Consumption Rate
2006	5175.15	4038.36	1136.79	Dynamically efficient	48.95	38.20	10.75	Consumption Rate>Optimal Consumption Rate
2007	6170.38	4706.01	1464.37	Dynamically efficient	49.39	37.67	11.72	Consumption Rate>Optimal Consumption Rate
2008	7172.67	5688.83	1483.84	Dynamically efficient	50.98	40.43	10.55	Consumption Rate>Optimal Consumption Rate
2009	7868.64	6196.93	1671.71	Dynamically efficient	52.30	41.19	11.11	Consumption Rate>Optimal Consumption Rate
2010	9424.29	7079.15	2345.14	Dynamically efficient	54.90	41.24	13.66	Consumption Rate>Optimal Consumption Rate

2011	10821.18	8095.10	2726.08	Dynamically efficient	56.37	42.17	14.20	Consumption Rate>Optimal Consumption Rate
2012	11528.58	8808.60	2719.98	Dynamically efficient	57.12	43.65	13.48	Consumption Rate>Optimal Consumption Rate
2013	12516.27	9782.19	2734.08	Dynamically efficient	57.94	45.28	12.66	Consumption Rate>Optimal Consumption Rate
2014	13858.14	10811.27	3046.87	Dynamically efficient	58.80	45.87	12.93	Consumption Rate>Optimal Consumption Rate
2015	14854.50	11639.67	3214.83	Dynamically efficient	59.13	46.33	12.80	Consumption Rate>Optimal Consumption Rate
2016	16177.04	12850.06	3326.98	Dynamically efficient	57.41	45.60	11.81	Consumption Rate>Optimal Consumption Rate

Appendix 10 1993–2016 Relationship between Dynamic Efficiency and Optimal Consumption Rate of Jiangsu

Year	Final Consumption Expenditure (100 million yuan)	Labour Income (100 million yuan)	Difference between Aggregate Consumption and Labour Income (100 million yuan)	Dynamic Efficiency	Final Consumption Rate (%)	Labour Income Ratio (%)	Ratio of Difference in GDP (%)	Comparison between Actual Consumption Rate and Optimal Consumption Rate
1993	1251.08	1352.49	-101.41	Dynamically Inefficient	41.73	45.11	-3.38	Consumption Rate<Optimal Consumption Rate
1994	1721.45	1919.36	-197.91	Dynamically Inefficient	42.43	47.31	-4.88	Consumption Rate<Optimal Consumption Rate
1995	2250.66	2549.06	-298.40	Dynamically Inefficient	43.66	49.45	-5.79	Consumption Rate<Optimal Consumption Rate
1996	2721.84	2982.20	-260.36	Dynamically Inefficient	45.33	49.67	-4.34	Consumption Rate<Optimal Consumption Rate
1997	3020.94	3320.30	-299.36	Dynamically Inefficient	45.22	49.70	-4.48	Consumption Rate<Optimal Consumption Rate
1998	3161.90	3541.23	-379.33	Dynamically Inefficient	44.08	49.37	-5.29	Consumption Rate<Optimal Consumption Rate

APPENDIX

1999	3339.79	3707.78	-367.99	Dynamically Inefficient	43.83	48.66	-4.83	Consumption Rate<Optimal Consumption Rate
2000	3710.72	4110.16	-399.44	Dynamically Inefficient	43.38	48.05	-4.67	Consumption Rate<Optimal Consumption Rate
2001	4141.92	4549.56	-407.64	Dynamically Inefficient	43.80	48.11	-4.31	Consumption Rate<Optimal Consumption Rate
2002	4801.91	5070.44	-268.53	Dynamically Inefficient	45.27	47.80	-2.53	Consumption Rate<Optimal Consumption Rate
2003	5484.04	5910.92	-426.88	Dynamically Inefficient	44.07	47.50	-3.43	Consumption Rate<Optimal Consumption Rate
2004	6227.21	6359.81	-132.60	Dynamically Inefficient	41.50	42.39	-0.88	Consumption Rate<Optimal Consumption Rate
2005	7658.70	7977.81	-319.11	Dynamically Inefficient	41.18	42.89	-1.72	Consumption Rate<Optimal Consumption Rate
2006	9045.95	9292.84	-246.89	Dynamically Inefficient	41.61	42.74	-1.14	Consumption Rate<Optimal Consumption Rate

(*Continued*)

Appendix 10 Continued

Year	Final Consumption Expenditure (100 million yuan)	Labour Income (100 million yuan)	Difference between Aggregate Consumption and Labour Income (100 million yuan)	Dynamic Efficiency	Final Consumption Rate (%)	Labour Income Ratio (%)	Ratio of Difference in GDP (%)	Comparison between Actual Consumption Rate and Optimal Consumption Rate
2007	10933.68	10168.98	764.70	Dynamically efficient	42.02	39.08	2.94	Consumption Rate<Optimal Consumption Rate
2008	12843.37	13146.64	-303.27	Dynamically Inefficient	41.45	42.43	-0.98	Consumption Rate<Optimal Consumption Rate
2009	14375.40	15770.06	-1394.66	Dynamically Inefficient	41.72	45.77	-4.05	Consumption Rate<Optimal Consumption Rate
2010	17238.08	17998.71	-760.63	Dynamically Inefficient	41.61	43.45	-1.84	Consumption Rate<Optimal Consumption Rate
2011	20649.28	21549.29	-900.01	Dynamically Inefficient	42.05	43.88	-1.83	Consumption Rate<Optimal Consumption Rate

Year							
2012	22714.57	24011.04	-1296.47	Dynamically Inefficient	42.02	44.42	-2.40	Consumption Rate<Optimal Consumption Rate
2013	26422.79	27074.93	-652.14	Dynamically Inefficient	44.66	45.76	-1.10	Consumption Rate<Optimal Consumption Rate
2014	31067.33	30093.22	974.11	Dynamically efficient	47.73	46.23	1.50	Consumption Rate>Optimal Consumption Rate
2015	35041.42	32722.13	2319.29	Dynamically efficient	49.98	46.67	3.31	Consumption Rate>Optimal Consumption Rate
2016	39499.88	35382.10	4117.78	Dynamically Inefficient	51.04	45.72	5.32	Consumption Rate>Optimal Consumption Rate

Appendix 11 1993–2016 Relationship between Dynamic Efficiency and Optimal Consumption Rate of Zhejiang

Year	Final Consumption Expenditure (100 million yuan)	Labour Income (100 million yuan)	Difference between Aggregate Consumption and Labour Income (100 million yuan)	Dynamic Efficiency	Final Consumption Rate (%)	Labour Income Ratio (%)	Ratio of Difference in GDP (%)	Comparison between Actual Consumption Rate and Optimal Consumption Rate
1993	849.96	851.96	-2.00	Dynamically Inefficient	44.51	44.62	-0.10	Consumption Rate<Optimal Consumption Rate
1994	1173.68	1221.42	-47.74	Dynamically Inefficient	44.01	45.80	-1.79	Consumption Rate<Optimal Consumption Rate
1995	1495.24	1600.94	-105.70	Dynamically Inefficient	41.89	44.85	-2.96	Consumption Rate<Optimal Consumption Rate
1996	1806.91	1812.51	-5.60	Dynamically Inefficient	43.39	43.53	-0.13	Consumption Rate<Optimal Consumption Rate
1997	2004.31	2082.95	-78.64	Dynamically Inefficient	43.39	45.09	-1.70	Consumption Rate<Optimal Consumption Rate

1998	2172.30	2204.71	-32.41	Dynamically Inefficient	43.65	44.31	-0.65	Consumption Rate<Optimal Consumption Rate
1999	2355.39	2348.82	6.57	Dynamically efficient	43.86	43.74	0.12	Consumption Rate>Optimal Consumption Rate
2000	3150.88	2781.41	369.47	Dynamically efficient	51.31	45.29	6.02	Consumption Rate>Optimal Consumption Rate
2001	3579.14	3025.68	553.46	Dynamically efficient	51.88	43.86	8.02	Consumption Rate>Optimal Consumption Rate
2002	4062.46	3381.30	681.16	Dynamically efficient	50.76	42.25	8.51	Consumption Rate>Optimal Consumption Rate
2003	4623.26	4074.86	548.40	Dynamically efficient	47.64	41.99	5.65	Consumption Rate>Optimal Consumption Rate
2004	5416.73	4926.23	490.50	Dynamically efficient	46.50	42.29	4.21	Consumption Rate>Optimal Consumption Rate

(Continued)

Appendix 11 Continued

Year	Final Consumption Expenditure (100 million yuan)	Labour Income (100 million yuan)	Difference between Aggregate Consumption and Labour Income (100 million yuan)	Dynamic Efficiency	Final Consumption Rate (%)	Labour Income Ratio (%)	Ratio of Difference in GDP (%)	Comparison between Actual Consumption Rate and Optimal Consumption Rate
2005	6347.60	5596.34	751.26	Dynamically efficient	47.31	41.71	5.60	Consumption Rate>Optimal Consumption Rate
2006	7499.76	6658.50	841.26	Dynamically efficient	47.71	42.36	5.35	Consumption Rate>Optimal Consumption Rate
2007	8620.50	7814.04	806.46	Dynamically efficient	45.97	41.67	4.30	Consumption Rate>Optimal Consumption Rate
2008	9828.95	9295.10	533.85	Dynamically efficient	45.80	43.31	2.49	Consumption Rate>Optimal Consumption Rate
2009	10864.59	9560.64	1303.95	Dynamically efficient	47.26	41.59	5.67	Consumption Rate>Optimal Consumption Rate

Year							
2010	12765.63	11328.31	1437.32	Dynamically efficient	46.05	40.86	5.18	Consumption Rate>Optimal Consumption Rate
2011	15041.98	13844.83	1197.15	Dynamically efficient	46.54	42.84	3.70	Consumption Rate>Optimal Consumption Rate
2012	16509.40	15312.87	1196.53	Dynamically efficient	47.63	44.17	3.45	Consumption Rate>Optimal Consumption Rate
2013	17737.24	18793.69	-1056.45	Dynamically Inefficient	47.21	50.03	-2.81	Consumption Rate<Optimal Consumption Rate
2014	19365.42	19460.97	-95.55	Dynamically Inefficient	48.21	48.44	-0.24	Consumption Rate<Optimal Consumption Rate
2015	20936.30	21601.92	-665.62	Dynamically efficient	48.82	50.37	-1.55	Consumption Rate<Optimal Consumption Rate
2016	22751.65	23290.76	-539.11	Dynamically efficient	48.15	49.29	-1.14	Consumption Rate<Optimal Consumption Rate

Appendix 12 1993–2016 Relationship between Dynamic Efficiency and Optimal Consumption Rate of Anhui

Year	Final Consumption Expenditure (100 million yuan)	Labour Income (100 million yuan)	Difference between Aggregate Consumption and Labour Income (100 million yuan)	Dynamic Efficiency	Final Consumption Rate (%)	Labour Income Ratio (%)	Ratio of Difference in GDP (%)	Comparison between Actual Consumption Rate and Optimal Consumption Rate
1993	664.74	658.60	6.14	Dynamically efficient	62.13	61.56	0.57	Consumption Rate>Optimal Consumption Rate
1994	882.64	785.69	96.95	Dynamically efficient	59.30	52.79	6.51	Consumption Rate>Optimal Consumption Rate
1995	1174.65	1089.72	84.93	Dynamically efficient	58.63	54.39	4.24	Consumption Rate>Optimal Consumption Rate
1996	1368.54	1244.58	123.96	Dynamically efficient	58.50	53.20	5.30	Consumption Rate>Optimal Consumption Rate
1997	1612.22	1414.58	197.64	Dynamically efficient	60.38	52.98	7.40	Consumption Rate>Optimal Consumption Rate
1998	1690.40	1467.34	223.06	Dynamically efficient	60.25	52.30	7.95	Consumption Rate>Optimal Consumption Rate

1999	1861.17	1484.45	376.72	Dynamically efficient	63.99	51.04	12.95	Consumption Rate>Optimal Consumption Rate
2000	1947.78	1517.59	430.19	Dynamically efficient	64.05	49.90	14.15	Consumption Rate>Optimal Consumption Rate
2001	2108.09	1604.48	503.61	Dynamically efficient	64.07	48.77	15.31	Consumption Rate>Optimal Consumption Rate
2002	2262.95	1752.09	510.86	Dynamically efficient	63.68	49.31	14.38	Consumption Rate>Optimal Consumption Rate
2003	2520.31	1776.35	743.96	Dynamically efficient	63.44	44.71	18.73	Consumption Rate>Optimal Consumption Rate
2004	2835.44	2230.66	604.78	Dynamically efficient	58.89	46.33	12.56	Consumption Rate>Optimal Consumption Rate
2005	3006.70	2556.88	449.82	Dynamically efficient	56.20	47.79	8.41	Consumption Rate>Optimal Consumption Rate
2006	3374.70	2872.20	502.50	Dynamically efficient	55.21	46.99	8.22	Consumption Rate>Optimal Consumption Rate

(*Continued*)

Appendix 12 Continued

Year	Final Consumption Expenditure (100 million yuan)	Labour Income (100 million yuan)	Difference between Aggregate Consumption and Labour Income (100 million yuan)	Dynamic Efficiency	Final Consumption Rate (%)	Labour Income Ratio (%)	Ratio of Difference in GDP (%)	Comparison between Actual Consumption Rate and Optimal Consumption Rate
2007	3979.71	3413.77	565.94	Dynamically efficient	54.07	46.38	7.69	Consumption Rate>Optimal Consumption Rate
2008	4571.97	4943.41	-371.44	Dynamically Inefficient	51.65	55.85	-4.20	Consumption Rate<Optimal Consumption Rate
2009	5179.08	5291.13	-112.05	Dynamically Inefficient	51.47	52.58	-1.11	Consumption Rate<Optimal Consumption Rate
2010	6213.15	6361.47	-148.32	Dynamically Inefficient	50.27	51.47	-1.20	Consumption Rate<Optimal Consumption Rate
2011	7604.30	7807.07	-202.77	Dynamically Inefficient	49.70	51.02	-1.33	Consumption Rate<Optimal Consumption Rate

Year						
2012	8439.01	8867.45	-428.44	Dynamically Inefficient	49.03	51.52	-2.49	Consumption Rate<Optimal Consumption Rate
2013	9189.29	9231.52	-42.23	Dynamically Inefficient	53.39	53.63	-0.25	Consumption Rate<Optimal Consumption Rate
2014	10136.81	10089.36	47.45	Dynamically efficient	48.62	48.39	0.23	Consumption Rate>Optimal Consumption Rate
2015	10970.50	10789.77	180.73	Dynamically Inefficient	49.85	49.03	0.82	Consumption Rate>Optimal Consumption Rate
2016	12112.78	11761.93	350.85	Dynamically efficient	49.63	48.19	1.44	Consumption Rate>Optimal Consumption Rate

Appendix 13 1993–2016 Relationship between Dynamic Efficiency and Optimal Consumption Rate of Fujian

Year	Final Consumption Expenditure (100 million yuan)	Labour Income (100 million yuan)	Difference between Aggregate Consumption and Labour Income (100 million yuan)	Dynamic Efficiency	Final Consumption Rate (%)	Labour Income Ratio (%)	Ratio of Difference in GDP (%)	Comparison between Actual Consumption Rate and Optimal Consumption Rate
1993	682.09	654.17	27.92	Dynamically efficient	61.22	58.71	2.51	Consumption Rate>Optimal Consumption Rate
1994	946.94	873.69	73.25	Dynamically efficient	57.59	53.13	4.45	Consumption Rate>Optimal Consumption Rate
1995	1174.13	1156.77	17.36	Dynamically efficient	56.05	55.22	0.83	Consumption Rate>Optimal Consumption Rate
1996	1406.39	1355.60	50.79	Dynamically efficient	56.61	54.57	2.04	Consumption Rate>Optimal Consumption Rate
1997	1630.58	1573.62	56.96	Dynamically efficient	56.80	54.81	1.98	Consumption Rate>Optimal Consumption Rate

Year						
1998	1723.93	1732.77	-8.84	Dynamically Inefficient	54.56	54.84	-0.28	Consumption Rate<Optimal Consumption Rate
1999	1831.55	1858.08	-26.53	Dynamically Inefficient	53.65	54.42	-0.78	Consumption Rate<Optimal Consumption Rate
2000	2049.66	1916.03	133.63	Dynamically efficient	54.45	50.90	3.55	Consumption Rate>Optimal Consumption Rate
2001	2214.11	2058.83	155.28	Dynamically efficient	54.36	50.55	3.81	Consumption Rate>Optimal Consumption Rate
2002	2412.57	2280.92	131.66	Dynamically efficient	54.00	51.06	2.95	Consumption Rate>Optimal Consumption Rate
2003	2651.77	2532.79	118.98	Dynamically efficient	53.21	50.82	2.39	Consumption Rate>Optimal Consumption Rate
2004	2975.97	2666.42	309.55	Dynamically efficient	51.64	46.27	5.37	Consumption Rate>Optimal Consumption Rate
2005	3295.55	3035.33	260.22	Dynamically efficient	50.17	46.21	3.96	Consumption Rate>Optimal Consumption Rate

(*Continued*)

Appendix 13 Continued

Year	Final Consumption Expenditure (100 million yuan)	Labour Income (100 million yuan)	Difference between Aggregate Consumption and Labour Income (100 million yuan)	Dynamic Efficiency	Final Consumption Rate (%)	Labour Income Ratio (%)	Ratio of Difference in GDP (%)	Comparison between Actual Consumption Rate and Optimal Consumption Rate
2006	3837.08	3501.02	336.07	Dynamically efficient	49.06	44.77	4.30	Consumption Rate>Optimal Consumption Rate
2007	4356.31	4197.02	159.29	Dynamically efficient	46.21	44.52	1.69	Consumption Rate>Optimal Consumption Rate
2008	5191.28	6014.43	-823.15	Dynamically Inefficient	44.87	51.99	-7.12	Consumption Rate<Optimal Consumption Rate
2009	5576.66	6835.55	-1258.89	Dynamically Inefficient	43.65	53.50	-9.85	Consumption Rate<Optimal Consumption Rate
2010	6440.40	7770.03	-1329.63	Dynamically Inefficient	43.13	52.04	-8.90	Consumption Rate<Optimal Consumption Rate

2011	7300.48	9178.86	-1878.38	Dynamically Inefficient	40.71	51.18	-10.47	Consumption Rate<Optimal Consumption Rate
2012	7882.88	10478.07	-2595.19	Dynamically Inefficient	40.01	53.18	-13.17	Consumption Rate<Optimal Consumption Rate
2013	8389.94	11841.45	-3451.51	Dynamically Inefficient	38.56	54.42	-15.86	Consumption Rate<Optimal Consumption Rate
2014	9299.33	13129.78	-3830.45	Dynamically Inefficient	38.66	54.58	-15.92	Consumption Rate<Optimal Consumption Rate
2015	10328.90	14537.64	-4208.74	Dynamically Inefficient	39.76	55.96	-16.20	Consumption Rate<Optimal Consumption Rate
2016	11614.37	16116.75	-4502.38	Dynamically Inefficient	40.31	55.94	-15.63	Consumption Rate<Optimal Consumption Rate

Appendix 14 1993–2016 Relationship between Dynamic Efficiency and Optimal Consumption Rate of Jiangxi

Year	Final Consumption Expenditure (100 million yuan)	Labour Income (100 million yuan)	Difference between Aggregate Consumption and Labour Income (100 million yuan)	Dynamic Efficiency	Final Consumption Rate (%)	Labour Income Ratio (%)	Ratio of Difference in GDP (%)	Comparison between Actual Consumption Rate and Optimal Consumption Rate
1993	460.22	486.03	-25.81	Dynamically Inefficient	63.65	67.22	-3.57	Consumption Rate<Optimal Consumption Rate
1994	597.07	644.56	-47.49	Dynamically Inefficient	63.20	68.23	-5.03	Consumption Rate<Optimal Consumption Rate
1995	790.36	754.47	35.89	Dynamically efficient	64.94	61.99	2.95	Consumption Rate<Optimal Consumption Rate
1996	953.63	943.87	9.76	Dynamically efficient	64.89	64.23	0.66	Consumption Rate>Optimal Consumption Rate
1997	1030.36	1096.91	-66.55	Dynamically Inefficient	61.90	65.90	-4.00	Consumption Rate<Optimal Consumption Rate
1998	1102.40	1135.92	-33.52	Dynamically Inefficient	61.33	63.20	-1.86	Consumption Rate<Optimal Consumption Rate

APPENDIX

Year							
1999	1171.61	1208.88	-37.27	Dynamically Inefficient	61.28	63.23	-1.95	Consumption Rate<Optimal Consumption Rate
2000	1269.58	1279.64	-10.06	Dynamically Inefficient	64.05	64.56	-0.51	Consumption Rate<Optimal Consumption Rate
2001	1357.47	1337.85	19.62	Dynamically efficient	62.79	61.89	0.91	Consumption Rate>Optimal Consumption Rate
2002	1459.65	1469.71	-10.06	Dynamically Inefficient	59.32	59.73	-0.41	Consumption Rate<Optimal Consumption Rate
2003	1525.90	1633.22	-107.32	Dynamically Inefficient	54.20	58.01	-3.81	Consumption Rate<Optimal Consumption Rate
2004	1822.14	2029.63	-207.49	Dynamically Inefficient	52.59	58.58	-5.99	Consumption Rate<Optimal Consumption Rate
2005	2117.30	1937.95	179.35	Dynamically efficient	52.13	47.71	4.42	Consumption Rate>Optimal Consumption Rate
2006	2348.66	2247.25	101.41	Dynamically efficient	49.03	46.91	2.12	Consumption Rate>Optimal Consumption Rate

(Continued)

Appendix 14 Continued

Year	Final Consumption Expenditure (100 million yuan)	Labour Income (100 million yuan)	Difference between Aggregate Consumption and Labour Income (100 million yuan)	Dynamic Efficiency	Final Consumption Rate (%)	Labour Income Ratio (%)	Ratio of Difference in GDP (%)	Comparison between Actual Consumption Rate and Optimal Consumption Rate
2007	2782.34	2671.50	110.84	Dynamically efficient	48.11	46.19	1.92	Consumption Rate>Optimal Consumption Rate
2008	3302.78	3156.64	146.14	Dynamically efficient	47.22	45.13	2.09	Consumption Rate>Optimal Consumption Rate
2009	3538.42	3273.98	264.44	Dynamically efficient	46.27	42.81	3.46	Consumption Rate>Optimal Consumption Rate
2010	4496.69	4471.65	25.04	Dynamically efficient	47.54	47.28	0.26	Consumption Rate>Optimal Consumption Rate
2011	5593.93	5401.18	192.75	Dynamically efficient	47.80	46.15	1.65	Consumption Rate>Optimal Consumption Rate

2012	6314.31	5805.46	508.85	Dynamically efficient	48.76	44.83	3.93	Consumption Rate>Optimal Consumption Rate
2013	7042.13	6521.66	520.47	Dynamically efficient	49.11	45.48	3.63	Consumption Rate>Optimal Consumption Rate
2014	7082.56	6703.43	379.13	Dynamically efficient	45.07	42.66	2.41	Consumption Rate>Optimal Consumption Rate
2015	8418.28	7421.27	997.01	Dynamically efficient	50.34	44.38	5.96	Consumption Rate>Optimal Consumption Rate
2016	9362.73	8141.99	1220.74	Dynamically efficient	50.61	44.01	6.60	Consumption Rate>Optimal Consumption Rate

Appendix 15 1993–2016 Relationship between Dynamic Efficiency and Optimal Consumption Rate of Shandong

Year	Final Consumption Expenditure (100 million yuan)	Labour Income (100 million yuan)	Difference between Aggregate Consumption and Labour Income (100 million yuan)	Dynamic Efficiency	Final Consumption Rate (%)	Labour Income Ratio (%)	Ratio of Difference in GDP (%)	Comparison between Actual Consumption Rate and Optimal Consumption Rate
1993	1263.34	1338.68	−75.34	Dynamically Inefficient	46.18	48.93	−2.75	Consumption Rate<Optimal Consumption Rate
1994	1889.34	1831.84	57.50	Dynamically efficient	49.59	48.08	1.51	Consumption Rate>Optimal Consumption Rate
1995	2479.05	2393.45	85.60	Dynamically efficient	50.64	48.89	1.75	Consumption Rate>Optimal Consumption Rate
1996	2997.89	2763.02	234.87	Dynamically efficient	50.86	46.87	3.98	Consumption Rate>Optimal Consumption Rate
1997	3293.88	3128.37	165.51	Dynamically efficient	49.72	47.22	2.50	Consumption Rate>Optimal Consumption Rate
1998	3533.30	3381.17	152.13	Dynamically efficient	49.33	47.21	2.12	Consumption Rate>Optimal Consumption Rate

1999	3809.13	3643.49	165.64	Dynamically efficient	49.71	47.55	2.16	Consumption Rate>Optimal Consumption Rate
2000	4021.46	4189.11	-167.65	Dynamically Inefficient	48.23	50.24	-2.01	Consumption Rate<Optimal Consumption Rate
2001	4479.42	4620.65	-141.23	Dynamically Inefficient	48.72	50.25	-1.54	Consumption Rate<Optimal Consumption Rate
2002	4887.40	5100.18	-212.78	Dynamically Inefficient	47.56	49.63	-2.07	Consumption Rate<Optimal Consumption Rate
2003	5608.60	5914.16	-305.56	Dynamically Inefficient	46.44	48.97	-2.53	Consumption Rate<Optimal Consumption Rate
2004	6568.66	5562.59	1006.08	Dynamically efficient	43.73	37.03	6.70	Consumption Rate>Optimal Consumption Rate
2005	7478.35	7242.82	235.53	Dynamically efficient	40.72	39.43	1.28	Consumption Rate>Optimal Consumption Rate
2006	8888.17	8993.33	-105.16	Dynamically Inefficient	40.58	41.07	-0.48	Consumption Rate<Optimal Consumption Rate

(Continued)

Appendix 15 Continued

Year	Final Consumption Expenditure (100 million yuan)	Labour Income (100 million yuan)	Difference between Aggregate Consumption and Labour Income (100 million yuan)	Dynamic Efficiency	Final Consumption Rate (%)	Labour Income Ratio (%)	Ratio of Difference in GDP (%)	Comparison between Actual Consumption Rate and Optimal Consumption Rate
2007	10352.82	11448.09	-1095.27	Dynamically Inefficient	40.16	44.41	-4.25	Consumption Rate<Optimal Consumption Rate
2008	12368.40	14452.76	-2084.36	Dynamically Inefficient	39.98	46.72	-6.74	Consumption Rate<Optimal Consumption Rate
2009	13574.79	15960.42	-2385.63	Dynamically Inefficient	40.05	47.09	-7.04	Consumption Rate<Optimal Consumption Rate
2010	15331.20	16229.86	-898.66	Dynamically Inefficient	39.14	41.43	-2.29	Consumption Rate<Optimal Consumption Rate
2011	18095.43	18315.86	-220.43	Dynamically Inefficient	39.89	40.38	-0.49	Consumption Rate<Optimal Consumption Rate

APPENDIX

Year							
2012	20543.68	20197.11	346.57	Dynamically efficient	41.08	40.38	0.69	Consumption Rate>Optimal Consumption Rate
2013	22601.63	23202.69	-601.06	Dynamically Inefficient	41.33	42.43	-1.10	Consumption Rate<Optimal Consumption Rate
2014	24193.05	25001.06	-808.01	Dynamically Inefficient	40.71	42.07	-1.36	Consumption Rate<Optimal Consumption Rate
2015	26144.42	29400.57	-3256.15	Dynamically Inefficient	41.50	46.67	-5.17	Consumption Rate<Optimal Consumption Rate
2016	32149.67	31013.15	1136.52	Dynamically efficient	47.26	45.59	1.67	Consumption Rate>Optimal Consumption Rate

Appendix 16 1993–2016 Relationship between Dynamic Efficiency and Optimal Consumption Rate of Henan

Year	Final Consumption Expenditure (100 million yuan)	Labour Income (100 million yuan)	Difference between Aggregate Consumption and Labour Income (100 million yuan)	Dynamic Efficiency	Final Consumption Rate (%)	Labour Income Ratio (%)	Ratio of Difference in GDP (%)	Comparison between Actual Consumption Rate and Optimal Consumption Rate
1993	879.25	936.44	-57.19	Dynamically Inefficient	52.88	56.32	-3.44	Consumption Rate<Optimal Consumption Rate
1994	1198.86	1421.36	-222.50	Dynamically Inefficient	53.90	63.90	-10.00	Consumption Rate<Optimal Consumption Rate
1995	1595.23	1913.96	-318.73	Dynamically Inefficient	53.13	63.74	-10.61	Consumption Rate<Optimal Consumption Rate
1996	1944.97	2243.00	-298.03	Dynamically Inefficient	53.12	61.26	-8.14	Consumption Rate<Optimal Consumption Rate
1997	2154.98	2377.75	-222.77	Dynamically Inefficient	52.83	58.29	-5.46	Consumption Rate<Optimal Consumption Rate
1998	2235.10	2387.18	-152.08	Dynamically Inefficient	51.30	54.79	-3.49	Consumption Rate<Optimal Consumption Rate

1999	2358.34	2434.99	−76.65	Dynamically Inefficient	51.54	53.21	−1.68	Consumption Rate<Optimal Consumption Rate
2000	2745.80	2623.78	122.02	Dynamically efficient	54.34	51.93	2.41	Consumption Rate>Optimal Consumption Rate
2001	3086.15	2839.19	246.96	Dynamically efficient	55.78	51.31	4.46	Consumption Rate>Optimal Consumption Rate
2002	3386.68	2970.03	416.65	Dynamically efficient	56.11	49.21	6.90	Consumption Rate>Optimal Consumption Rate
2003	3891.70	3145.73	745.97	Dynamically efficient	56.67	45.80	10.86	Consumption Rate>Optimal Consumption Rate
2004	4568.52	4022.06	546.46	Dynamically efficient	53.41	47.02	6.39	Consumption Rate>Optimal Consumption Rate
2005	5353.67	4925.67	428.00	Dynamically efficient	50.57	46.52	4.04	Consumption Rate>Optimal Consumption Rate
2006	6102.27	5355.72	746.55	Dynamically efficient	49.36	43.32	6.04	Consumption Rate>Optimal Consumption Rate

(*Continued*)

Appendix 16 Continued

Year	Final Consumption Expenditure (100 million yuan)	Labour Income (100 million yuan)	Difference between Aggregate Consumption and Labour Income (100 million yuan)	Dynamic Efficiency	Final Consumption Rate (%)	Labour Income Ratio (%)	Ratio of Difference in GDP (%)	Comparison between Actual Consumption Rate and Optimal Consumption Rate
2007	6831.27	6475.97	355.30	Dynamically efficient	45.50	43.14	2.37	Consumption Rate>Optimal Consumption Rate
2008	7759.33	8886.47	-1127.14	Dynamically Inefficient	43.06	49.32	-6.26	Consumption Rate<Optimal Consumption Rate
2009	8742.69	10044.55	-1301.86	Dynamically Inefficient	44.88	51.56	-6.68	Consumption Rate<Optimal Consumption Rate
2010	10209.83	12078.38	-1868.55	Dynamically Inefficient	44.21	52.30	-8.09	Consumption Rate<Optimal Consumption Rate
2011	11783.07	14111.40	-2328.33	Dynamically Inefficient	43.75	52.40	-8.65	Consumption Rate<Optimal Consumption Rate

2012	13338.44	15576.26	-2237.82	Dynamically Inefficient	45.06	52.62	-7.56	Consumption Rate<Optimal Consumption Rate
2013	15287.41	16985.58	-1698.17	Dynamically Inefficient	47.54	52.82	-5.28	Consumption Rate<Optimal Consumption Rate
2014	16850.13	18342.47	-1492.34	Dynamically Inefficient	48.23	52.50	-4.27	Consumption Rate<Optimal Consumption Rate
2015	18722.62	19671.95	-949.33	Dynamically Inefficient	50.60	53.16	-2.57	Consumption Rate<Optimal Consumption Rate
2016	20777.02	21547.46	-770.44	Dynamically Inefficient	51.34	53.24	-1.90	Consumption Rate<Optimal Consumption Rate

Appendix 17 1993–2016 Relationship between Dynamic Efficiency and Optimal Consumption Rate of Hubei

Year	Final Consumption Expenditure (100 million yuan)	Labour Income (100 million yuan)	Difference between Aggregate Consumption and Labour Income (100 million yuan)	Dynamic Efficiency	Final Consumption Rate (%)	Labour Income Ratio (%)	Ratio of Difference in GDP (%)	Comparison between Actual Consumption Rate and Optimal Consumption Rate
1993	870.27	716.75	153.52	Dynamically efficient	60.52	49.85	10.68	Consumption Rate>Optimal Consumption Rate
1994	1058.13	953.28	104.85	Dynamically efficient	55.82	50.29	5.53	Consumption Rate>Optimal Consumption Rate
1995	1333.82	1288.39	45.43	Dynamically efficient	54.78	52.91	1.87	Consumption Rate>Optimal Consumption Rate
1996	1646.74	1682.57	-35.83	Dynamically Inefficient	56.14	57.36	-1.22	Consumption Rate<Optimal Consumption Rate
1997	1783.40	1929.21	-145.81	Dynamically Inefficient	52.93	57.26	-4.33	Consumption Rate<Optimal Consumption Rate
1998	1941.20	2062.84	-121.64	Dynamically Inefficient	53.60	56.96	-3.36	Consumption Rate<Optimal Consumption Rate

1999	1983.14	2052.30	−69.16	Dynamically Inefficient	52.10	53.92	−1.82	Consumption Rate<Optimal Consumption Rate
2000	2030.07	2278.35	−248.28	Dynamically Inefficient	53.98	60.59	−6.60	Consumption Rate<Optimal Consumption Rate
2001	2262.67	2457.00	−194.33	Dynamically Inefficient	55.16	59.90	−4.74	Consumption Rate<Optimal Consumption Rate
2002	2499.95	2691.17	−191.22	Dynamically Inefficient	56.60	60.93	−4.33	Consumption Rate<Optimal Consumption Rate
2003	2819.24	2794.93	24.31	Dynamically efficient	57.41	56.92	0.50	Consumption Rate>Optimal Consumption Rate
2004	3174.18	2644.12	530.06	Dynamically efficient	56.35	46.94	9.41	Consumption Rate>Optimal Consumption Rate
2005	3645.71	3111.05	534.67	Dynamically efficient	55.91	47.71	8.20	Consumption Rate>Optimal Consumption Rate
2006	4245.68	3360.84	884.84	Dynamically efficient	53.26	42.16	11.10	Consumption Rate>Optimal Consumption Rate

(*Continued*)

Appendix 17 Continued

Year	Final Consumption Expenditure (100 million yuan)	Labour Income (100 million yuan)	Difference between Aggregate Consumption and Labour Income (100 million yuan)	Dynamic Efficiency	Final Consumption Rate (%)	Labour Income Ratio (%)	Ratio of Difference in GDP (%)	Comparison between Actual Consumption Rate and Optimal Consumption Rate
2007	4999.66	4031.02	968.64	Dynamically efficient	52.35	42.21	10.14	Consumption Rate>Optimal Consumption Rate
2008	5892.03	6084.66	-192.63	Dynamically Inefficient	50.24	51.88	-1.64	Consumption Rate<Optimal Consumption Rate
2009	6325.15	6509.12	-183.97	Dynamically Inefficient	47.77	49.16	-1.39	Consumption Rate<Optimal Consumption Rate
2010	7389.80	7127.26	262.54	Dynamically Inefficient	45.67	44.04	1.62	Consumption Rate<Optimal Consumption Rate
2011	8931.48	9904.20	-972.72	Dynamically Inefficient	44.29	49.11	-4.82	Consumption Rate<Optimal Consumption Rate

2012	9982.79	11354.86	-1372.07	Dynamically Inefficient	44.06	50.11	-6.06	Consumption Rate<Optimal Consumption Rate
2013	11161.21	12679.72	-1518.51	Dynamically Inefficient	43.89	49.86	-5.97	Consumption Rate<Optimal Consumption Rate
2014	12562.76	14013.86	-1451.10	Dynamically Inefficient	43.73	48.78	-5.05	Consumption Rate<Optimal Consumption Rate
2015	13799.70	15137.98	-1338.28	Dynamically Inefficient	46.70	51.23	-4.53	Consumption Rate<Optimal Consumption Rate
2016	15254.99	16665.54	-1410.55	Dynamically Inefficient	46.70	51.02	-4.32	Consumption Rate<Optimal Consumption Rate

Appendix 18 1993–2016 Relationship between Dynamic Efficiency and Optimal Consumption Rate of Hunan

Year	Final Consumption Expenditure (100 million yuan)	Labour Income (100 million yuan)	Difference between Aggregate Consumption and Labour Income (100 million yuan)	Dynamic Efficiency	Final Consumption Rate (%)	Labour Income Ratio (%)	Ratio of Difference in GDP (%)	Comparison between Actual Consumption Rate and Optimal Consumption Rate
1993	885.05	745.35	139.70	Dynamically efficient	69.24	58.31	10.93	Consumption Rate>Optimal Consumption Rate
1994	1113.62	1079.62	34.00	Dynamically efficient	65.72	63.72	2.01	Consumption Rate>Optimal Consumption Rate
1995	1396.88	1488.59	-91.70	Dynamically Inefficient	63.62	67.80	-4.18	Consumption Rate<Optimal Consumption Rate
1996	1753.27	1712.49	40.78	Dynamically efficient	66.23	64.69	1.54	Consumption Rate>Optimal Consumption Rate
1997	1956.22	1914.89	41.33	Dynamically efficient	65.36	63.98	1.38	Consumption Rate>Optimal Consumption Rate

1998	2062.80	1973.11	89.69	Dynamically efficient	64.23	61.44	2.79	Consumption Rate>Optimal Consumption Rate
1999	2212.47	2013.22	199.25	Dynamically efficient	66.51	60.52	5.99	Consumption Rate>Optimal Consumption Rate
2000	2471.77	2192.51	279.27	Dynamically efficient	69.60	61.73	7.86	Consumption Rate>Optimal Consumption Rate
2001	2638.39	2372.36	266.03	Dynamically efficient	68.85	61.91	6.94	Consumption Rate>Optimal Consumption Rate
2002	2754.62	2511.00	243.62	Dynamically efficient	66.35	60.48	5.87	Consumption Rate>Optimal Consumption Rate
2003	3046.50	2720.11	326.39	Dynamically efficient	65.38	58.37	7.00	Consumption Rate>Optimal Consumption Rate
2004	3552.05	2930.52	621.53	Dynamically efficient	62.96	51.94	11.02	Consumption Rate>Optimal Consumption Rate
2005	4026.02	3505.03	520.99	Dynamically efficient	61.04	53.14	7.90	Consumption Rate>Optimal Consumption Rate

(*Continued*)

Appendix 18 Continued

Year	Final Consumption Expenditure (100 million yuan)	Labour Income (100 million yuan)	Difference between Aggregate Consumption and Labour Income (100 million yuan)	Dynamic Efficiency	Final Consumption Rate (%)	Labour Income Ratio (%)	Ratio of Difference in GDP (%)	Comparison between Actual Consumption Rate and Optimal Consumption Rate
2006	4608.61	4127.71	480.90	Dynamically efficient	59.94	53.69	6.25	Consumption Rate>Optimal Consumption Rate
2007	5275.29	5106.62	168.67	Dynamically efficient	55.88	54.10	1.79	Consumption Rate>Optimal Consumption Rate
2008	5988.91	6339.13	-350.22	Dynamically Inefficient	51.83	54.86	-3.03	Consumption Rate<Optimal Consumption Rate
2009	6644.74	6889.60	-244.86	Dynamically Inefficient	50.88	52.75	-1.87	Consumption Rate<Optimal Consumption Rate
2010	7603.53	8442.20	-838.67	Dynamically Inefficient	47.41	52.64	-5.23	Consumption Rate<Optimal Consumption Rate

2011	9088.73	10292.21	-1203.48	Dynamically Inefficient	46.21	52.33	-6.12	Consumption Rate<Optimal Consumption Rate
2012	10166.09	11537.48	-1371.39	Dynamically Inefficient	45.89	52.08	-6.19	Consumption Rate<Optimal Consumption Rate
2013	11281.02	12925.45	-1644.43	Dynamically Inefficient	46.04	52.75	-6.71	Consumption Rate<Optimal Consumption Rate
2014	12463.11	14470.89	-2007.78	Dynamically Inefficient	46.10	53.52	-7.43	Consumption Rate<Optimal Consumption Rate
2015	14755.76	15445.10	-689.34	Dynamically Inefficient	51.05	53.44	-2.39	Consumption Rate<Optimal Consumption Rate
2016	16122.55	16777.64	-655.09	Dynamically Inefficient	51.10	53.18	-2.08	Consumption Rate<Optimal Consumption Rate

Appendix 19 1993–2016 Relationship between Dynamic Efficiency and Optimal Consumption Rate of Guangdong

Year	Final Consumption Expenditure (100 million yuan)	Labour Income (100 million yuan)	Difference between Aggregate Consumption and Labour Income (100 million yuan)	Dynamic Efficiency	Final Consumption Rate (%)	Labour Income Ratio (%)	Ratio of Difference in GDP (%)	Comparison between Actual Consumption Rate and Optimal Consumption Rate
1993	1852.06	1913.86	-61.80	Dynamically Inefficient	53.45	55.23	-1.78	Consumption Rate<Optimal Consumption Rate
1994	2598.57	2573.61	24.96	Dynamically efficient	56.27	55.73	0.54	Consumption Rate>Optimal Consumption Rate
1995	3363.38	3231.75	131.63	Dynamically efficient	56.69	54.47	2.22	Consumption Rate>Optimal Consumption Rate
1996	3859.32	3763.56	95.76	Dynamically efficient	56.46	55.06	1.40	Consumption Rate>Optimal Consumption Rate
1997	4245.18	4256.00	-10.82	Dynamically Inefficient	54.60	54.74	-0.14	Consumption Rate<Optimal Consumption Rate
1998	4582.16	5101.89	-519.73	Dynamically Inefficient	53.71	59.80	-6.09	Consumption Rate<Optimal Consumption Rate

1999	5083.60	5364.52	−280.92	Dynamically Inefficient	54.95	57.99	−3.04	Consumption Rate<Optimal Consumption Rate
2000	5714.46	5880.66	−166.20	Dynamically Inefficient	53.20	54.75	−1.55	Consumption Rate<Optimal Consumption Rate
2001	6255.92	6410.07	−154.15	Dynamically Inefficient	51.96	53.24	−1.28	Consumption Rate<Optimal Consumption Rate
2002	7286.63	7471.81	−185.18	Dynamically Inefficient	53.97	55.34	−1.37	Consumption Rate<Optimal Consumption Rate
2003	8643.44	8338.08	305.36	Dynamically efficient	54.55	52.62	1.93	Consumption Rate>Optimal Consumption Rate
2004	10162.04	9467.30	694.74	Dynamically efficient	53.87	50.19	3.68	Consumption Rate>Optimal Consumption Rate
2005	11450.96	11149.85	301.12	Dynamically efficient	50.76	49.43	1.33	Consumption Rate>Optimal Consumption Rate
2006	12635.59	12679.79	−44.20	Dynamically Inefficient	47.52	47.69	−0.17	Consumption Rate<Optimal Consumption Rate

(*Continued*)

Appendix 19 Continued

Year	Final Consumption Expenditure (100 million yuan)	Labour Income (100 million yuan)	Difference between Aggregate Consumption and Labour Income (100 million yuan)	Dynamic Efficiency	Final Consumption Rate (%)	Labour Income Ratio (%)	Ratio of Difference in GDP (%)	Comparison between Actual Consumption Rate and Optimal Consumption Rate
2007	14842.85	14923.48	−80.63	Dynamically Inefficient	46.71	46.96	−0.25	Consumption Rate<Optimal Consumption Rate
2008	17202.13	17491.30	−289.17	Dynamically Inefficient	46.75	47.53	−0.79	Consumption Rate<Optimal Consumption Rate
2009	19179.39	18789.19	390.20	Dynamically efficient	48.56	47.58	0.99	Consumption Rate>Optimal Consumption Rate
2010	22480.91	21496.52	984.39	Dynamically efficient	48.83	46.69	2.14	Consumption Rate>Optimal Consumption Rate
2011	26074.76	25549.55	525.21	Dynamically efficient	48.97	47.98	0.99	Consumption Rate>Optimal Consumption Rate

2012	29264.26	28660.91	603.36	Dynamically efficient	51.21	50.15	1.06	Consumption Rate>Optimal Consumption Rate
2013	30437.61	31300.08	-862.47	Dynamically Inefficient	48.72	50.10	-1.38	Consumption Rate<Optimal Consumption Rate
2014	33920.56	33979.63	-59.07	Dynamically Inefficient	50.02	50.11	-0.09	Consumption Rate<Optimal Consumption Rate
2015	37211.27	37564.36	-353.09	Dynamically Inefficient	51.11	51.59	-0.48	Consumption Rate<Optimal Consumption Rate
2016	40885.91	41072.22	-186.31	Dynamically Inefficient	50.57	50.80	-0.23	Consumption Rate<Optimal Consumption Rate

Appendix 20 1993–2016 Relationship between Dynamic Efficiency and Optimal Consumption Rate of Guangxi

Year	Final Consumption Expenditure (100 million yuan)	Labour Income (100 million yuan)	Difference between Aggregate Consumption and Labour Income (100 million yuan)	Dynamic Efficiency	Final Consumption Rate (%)	Labour Income Ratio (%)	Ratio of Difference in GDP (%)	Comparison between Actual Consumption Rate and Optimal Consumption Rate
1993	564.25	529.27	34.98	Dynamically efficient	64.73	60.72	4.01	Consumption Rate>Optimal Consumption Rate
1994	778.82	777.01	1.81	Dynamically efficient	64.99	64.84	0.15	Consumption Rate>Optimal Consumption Rate
1995	993.95	1030.59	-36.64	Dynamically Inefficient	66.37	68.82	-2.45	Consumption Rate<Optimal Consumption Rate
1996	1202.63	1097.78	104.86	Dynamically efficient	70.83	64.65	6.18	Consumption Rate>Optimal Consumption Rate
1997	1255.76	1208.47	47.29	Dynamically efficient	69.10	66.50	2.60	Consumption Rate>Optimal Consumption Rate

APPENDIX 401

1998	1308.70	1238.98	69.72	Dynamically efficient	68.77	65.11	3.66	Consumption Rate>Optimal Consumption Rate
1999	1342.88	1250.96	91.92	Dynamically efficient	68.75	64.04	4.71	Consumption Rate>Optimal Consumption Rate
2000	1448.32	1288.89	159.43	Dynamically efficient	69.63	61.96	7.66	Consumption Rate>Optimal Consumption Rate
2001	1595.34	1383.32	212.02	Dynamically efficient	69.99	60.69	9.30	Consumption Rate>Optimal Consumption Rate
2002	1699.73	1507.73	192.00	Dynamically efficient	67.35	59.74	7.61	Consumption Rate>Optimal Consumption Rate
2003	1859.55	1590.72	268.83	Dynamically efficient	65.92	56.39	9.53	Consumption Rate>Optimal Consumption Rate
2004	2097.15	1755.61	341.54	Dynamically efficient	61.08	51.13	9.95	Consumption Rate>Optimal Consumption Rate
2005	2463.52	2504.36	-40.84	Dynamically Inefficient	61.83	62.86	-1.02	Consumption Rate<Optimal Consumption Rate

(*Continued*)

Appendix 20 Continued

Year	Final Consumption Expenditure (100 million yuan)	Labour Income (100 million yuan)	Difference between Aggregate Consumption and Labour Income (100 million yuan)	Dynamic Efficiency	Final Consumption Rate (%)	Labour Income Ratio (%)	Ratio of Difference in GDP (%)	Comparison between Actual Consumption Rate and Optimal Consumption Rate
2006	2779.59	2974.25	-194.66	Dynamically Inefficient	58.57	62.67	-4.10	Consumption Rate<Optimal Consumption Rate
2007	3343.41	3589.52	-246.11	Dynamically Inefficient	57.41	61.64	-4.23	Consumption Rate<Optimal Consumption Rate
2008	3880.17	4567.31	-687.14	Dynamically Inefficient	55.27	65.05	-9.79	Consumption Rate<Optimal Consumption Rate
2009	4375.89	4857.64	-481.75	Dynamically Inefficient	56.40	62.61	-6.21	Consumption Rate<Optimal Consumption Rate
2010	4942.23	5966.34	-1024.11	Dynamically Inefficient	51.64	62.35	-10.70	Consumption Rate<Optimal Consumption Rate

2011	5601.59	7146.77	-1545.18	Dynamically Inefficient	47.79	60.97	-13.18	Consumption Rate<Optimal Consumption Rate
2012	6517.95	7542.53	-1024.58	Dynamically Inefficient	50.00	57.86	-7.86	Consumption Rate<Optimal Consumption Rate
2013	7407.67	7266.00	141.67	Dynamically efficient	51.52	50.54	0.99	Consumption Rate>Optimal Consumption Rate
2014	8187.66	8538.98	-351.32	Dynamically Inefficient	52.24	54.48	-2.24	Consumption Rate>Optimal Consumption Rate
2015	8878.53	9332.05	-453.52	Dynamically Inefficient	52.84	55.54	-2.70	Consumption Rate>Optimal Consumption Rate
2016	9834.45	10279.09	-444.64	Dynamically Inefficient	53.69	56.12	-2.43	Consumption Rate<Optimal Consumption Rate

Appendix 21 1993–2016 Relationship between Dynamic Efficiency and Optimal Consumption Rate of Hainan

Year	Final Consumption Expenditure (100 million yuan)	Labour Income (100 million yuan)	Difference between Aggregate Consumption and Labour Income (100 million yuan)	Dynamic Efficiency	Final Consumption Rate (%)	Labour Income Ratio (%)	Ratio of Difference in GDP (%)	Comparison between Actual Consumption Rate and Optimal Consumption Rate
1993	125.20	123.05	2.15	Dynamically efficient	48.08	47.25	0.83	Consumption Rate>Optimal Consumption Rate
1994	150.30	165.57	-15.27	Dynamically efficient	45.27	49.87	-4.60	Consumption Rate<Optimal Consumption Rate
1995	178.90	186.82	-7.92	Dynamically efficient	49.24	51.42	-2.18	Consumption Rate<Optimal Consumption Rate
1996	212.60	199.67	12.93	Dynamically efficient	54.55	51.24	3.32	Consumption Rate>Optimal Consumption Rate
1997	228.40	212.19	16.21	Dynamically efficient	55.54	51.60	3.94	Consumption Rate>Optimal Consumption Rate

Year						
1998	245.60	225.15	20.45	Dynamically efficient	55.55	50.93	4.63	Consumption Rate>Optimal Consumption Rate
1999	258.70	245.84	12.86	Dynamically efficient	54.27	51.57	2.70	Consumption Rate>Optimal Consumption Rate
2000	290.70	275.48	15.22	Dynamically efficient	55.18	52.29	2.89	Consumption Rate>Optimal Consumption Rate
2001	310.50	294.44	16.06	Dynamically efficient	55.61	52.73	2.88	Consumption Rate>Optimal Consumption Rate
2002	347.60	331.13	16.47	Dynamically efficient	55.88	53.24	2.65	Consumption Rate>Optimal Consumption Rate
2003	378.60	368.87	9.74	Dynamically efficient	54.62	53.21	1.40	Consumption Rate>Optimal Consumption Rate
2004	428.30	422.86	5.44	Dynamically efficient	53.61	52.93	0.68	Consumption Rate>Optimal Consumption Rate
2005	470.46	469.18	1.28	Dynamically efficient	52.39	52.25	0.14	Consumption Rate>Optimal Consumption Rate

(*Continued*)

Appendix 21 Continued

Year	Final Consumption Expenditure (100 million yuan)	Labour Income (100 million yuan)	Difference between Aggregate Consumption and Labour Income (100 million yuan)	Dynamic Efficiency	Final Consumption Rate (%)	Labour Income Ratio (%)	Ratio of Difference in GDP (%)	Comparison between Actual Consumption Rate and Optimal Consumption Rate
2006	554.22	523.03	31.19	Dynamically efficient	53.04	50.05	2.99	Consumption Rate>Optimal Consumption Rate
2007	660.23	554.00	106.23	Dynamically efficient	52.64	44.17	8.47	Consumption Rate>Optimal Consumption Rate
2008	737.49	871.90	-134.41	Dynamically Inefficient	49.07	58.01	-8.94	Consumption Rate<Optimal Consumption Rate
2009	808.72	911.02	-102.30	Dynamically Inefficient	48.89	55.07	-6.18	Consumption Rate<Optimal Consumption Rate
2010	953.19	1091.60	-138.41	Dynamically Inefficient	46.17	52.87	-6.70	Consumption Rate<Optimal Consumption Rate

APPENDIX

Year							
2011	1180.02	1337.04	-157.02	Dynamically Inefficient	46.78	53.00	-6.22	Consumption Rate<Optimal Consumption Rate
2012	1386.25	1519.73	-133.48	Dynamically Inefficient	48.55	53.22	-4.67	Consumption Rate<Optimal Consumption Rate
2013	1590.38	1855.83	-265.45	Dynamically Inefficient	50.05	58.40	-8.35	Consumption Rate<Optimal Consumption Rate
2014	1722.68	2136.54	-413.86	Dynamically Inefficient	49.21	61.03	-11.82	Consumption Rate<Optimal Consumption Rate
2015	2242.65	2158.52	84.13	Dynamically efficient	60.57	58.29	2.27	Consumption Rate>Optimal Consumption Rate
2016	2489.56	2359.36	130.20	Dynamically efficient	61.42	58.21	3.21	Consumption Rate>Optimal Consumption Rate

Appendix 22 1993–2016 Relationship between Dynamic Efficiency and Optimal Consumption Rate of Chongqing

Year	Final Consumption Expenditure (100 million yuan)	Labour Income (100 million yuan)	Difference between Aggregate Consumption and Labour Income (100 million yuan)	Dynamic Efficiency	Final Consumption Rate (%)	Labour Income Ratio (%)	Ratio of Difference in GDP (%)	Comparison between Actual Consumption Rate and Optimal Consumption Rate
1993	365.66	287.41	78.25	Dynamically efficient	66.12	51.97	14.15	Consumption Rate>Optimal Consumption Rate
1994	475.38	378.65	96.73	Dynamically efficient	62.88	50.09	12.80	Consumption Rate>Optimal Consumption Rate
1995	592.57	545.60	46.97	Dynamically efficient	58.31	53.69	4.62	Consumption Rate>Optimal Consumption Rate
1996	739.84	809.94	-70.10	Dynamically Inefficient	62.75	68.69	-5.95	Consumption Rate<Optimal Consumption Rate
1997	827.15	901.32	-74.17	Dynamically Inefficient	61.27	66.76	-5.49	Consumption Rate<Optimal Consumption Rate
1998	862.20	952.61	-90.41	Dynamically Inefficient	60.32	66.65	-6.33	Consumption Rate<Optimal Consumption Rate

1999	924.14	971.93	-47.79	Dynamically Inefficient	62.45	65.68	-3.23	Consumption Rate<Optimal Consumption Rate
2000	997.92	1019.83	-21.91	Dynamically Inefficient	55.72	56.94	-1.22	Consumption Rate<Optimal Consumption Rate
2001	1081.24	1118.23	-36.99	Dynamically Inefficient	54.69	56.57	-1.87	Consumption Rate<Optimal Consumption Rate
2002	1230.77	1246.35	-15.58	Dynamically Inefficient	55.12	55.82	-0.70	Consumption Rate<Optimal Consumption Rate
2003	1387.96	1400.37	-12.41	Dynamically Inefficient	54.31	54.79	-0.49	Consumption Rate<Optimal Consumption Rate
2004	1572.83	1671.63	-98.80	Dynamically Inefficient	51.83	55.09	-3.26	Consumption Rate<Optimal Consumption Rate
2005	1780.96	1929.42	-148.46	Dynamically Inefficient	51.36	55.64	-4.28	Consumption Rate<Optimal Consumption Rate
2006	2020.59	2206.34	-185.75	Dynamically Inefficient	51.71	56.47	-4.75	Consumption Rate<Optimal Consumption Rate

(*Continued*)

Appendix 22 Continued

Year	Final Consumption Expenditure (100 million yuan)	Labour Income (100 million yuan)	Difference between Aggregate Consumption and Labour Income (100 million yuan)	Dynamic Efficiency	Final Consumption Rate (%)	Labour Income Ratio (%)	Ratio of Difference in GDP (%)	Comparison between Actual Consumption Rate and Optimal Consumption Rate
2007	2434.76	2634.09	-199.33	Dynamically Inefficient	52.07	56.33	-4.26	Consumption Rate<Optimal Consumption Rate
2008	2886.31	3149.35	-263.04	Dynamically Inefficient	49.82	54.36	-4.54	Consumption Rate<Optimal Consumption Rate
2009	3237.21	3473.88	-236.67	Dynamically Inefficient	49.57	53.20	-3.62	Consumption Rate<Optimal Consumption Rate
2010	3811.85	4096.77	-284.92	Dynamically Inefficient	48.10	51.69	-3.59	Consumption Rate<Optimal Consumption Rate
2011	4641.64	5176.93	-535.29	Dynamically Inefficient	46.36	51.71	-5.35	Consumption Rate<Optimal Consumption Rate

2012	5393.05	5963.09	-570.04	Dynamically Inefficient	47.27	52.26	-5.00	Consumption Rate<Optimal Consumption Rate
2013	6001.56	5410.65	590.91	Dynamically efficient	47.42	42.75	4.67	Consumption Rate>Optimal Consumption Rate
2014	6764.67	6163.32	601.35	Dynamically efficient	47.43	43.21	4.22	Consumption Rate>Optimal Consumption Rate
2015	7503.21	6919.75	583.46	Dynamically efficient	47.74	44.03	3.71	Consumption Rate>Optimal Consumption Rate
2016	8444.45	7729.64	714.81	Dynamically efficient	47.60	43.57	4.03	Consumption Rate>Optimal Consumption Rate

Appendix 23 1993–2016 Relationship between Dynamic Efficiency and Optimal Consumption Rate of Sichuan

Year	Final Consumption Expenditure (100 million yuan)	Labour Income (100 million yuan)	Difference between Aggregate Consumption and Labour Income (100 million yuan)	Dynamic Efficiency	Final Consumption Rate (%)	Labour Income Ratio (%)	Ratio of Difference in GDP (%)	Comparison between Actual Consumption Rate and Optimal Consumption Rate
1993	971.00	903.85	67.15	Dynamically efficient	65.34	60.82	4.52	Consumption Rate>Optimal Consumption Rate
1994	1290.51	1207.72	82.79	Dynamically efficient	64.48	60.34	4.14	Consumption Rate>Optimal Consumption Rate
1995	1580.62	1455.64	124.98	Dynamically efficient	63.10	58.11	4.99	Consumption Rate>Optimal Consumption Rate
1996	1879.66	1721.88	157.78	Dynamically efficient	62.97	57.68	5.29	Consumption Rate>Optimal Consumption Rate
1997	2065.60	1949.59	116.01	Dynamically efficient	62.21	58.72	3.49	Consumption Rate>Optimal Consumption Rate

1998	2153.80	2081.45	72.35	Dynamically efficient	60.16	58.14	2.02	Consumption Rate>Optimal Consumption Rate
1999	2247.20	2229.35	17.85	Dynamically efficient	60.55	60.06	0.48	Consumption Rate>Optimal Consumption Rate
2000	2545.13	2385.67	159.46	Dynamically efficient	64.79	60.73	4.06	Consumption Rate>Optimal Consumption Rate
2001	2778.76	2589.44	189.32	Dynamically efficient	64.72	60.31	4.41	Consumption Rate>Optimal Consumption Rate
2002	3014.27	2887.38	126.89	Dynamically efficient	63.79	61.11	2.69	Consumption Rate>Optimal Consumption Rate
2003	3330.47	3182.95	147.52	Dynamically efficient	62.45	59.68	2.77	Consumption Rate>Optimal Consumption Rate
2004	3805.64	3312.63	493.01	Dynamically efficient	59.65	51.93	7.73	Consumption Rate>Optimal Consumption Rate
2005	4267.69	3616.23	651.46	Dynamically efficient	57.79	48.97	8.82	Consumption Rate>Optimal Consumption Rate

(Continued)

Appendix 23 Continued

Year	Final Consumption Expenditure (100 million yuan)	Labour Income (100 million yuan)	Difference between Aggregate Consumption and Labour Income (100 million yuan)	Dynamic Efficiency	Final Consumption Rate (%)	Labour Income Ratio (%)	Ratio of Difference in GDP (%)	Comparison between Actual Consumption Rate and Optimal Consumption Rate
2006	4824.88	4182.87	642.01	Dynamically efficient	55.52	48.13	7.39	Consumption Rate>Optimal Consumption Rate
2007	5671.56	5129.84	541.72	Dynamically efficient	53.70	48.57	5.13	Consumption Rate>Optimal Consumption Rate
2008	6540.17	7160.24	-620.07	Dynamically efficient	51.90	56.82	-4.92	Consumption Rate>Optimal Consumption Rate
2009	7212.50	7108.12	104.38	Dynamically efficient	50.97	50.23	0.74	Consumption Rate>Optimal Consumption Rate
2010	8609.53	8493.82	115.71	Dynamically efficient	50.10	49.42	0.67	Consumption Rate>Optimal Consumption Rate

2011	10424.40	9850.90	573.50	Dynamically efficient	49.58	46.85	2.73	Consumption Rate>Optimal Consumption Rate
2012	11926.70	11064.60	862.10	Dynamically efficient	49.96	46.35	3.61	Consumption Rate>Optimal Consumption Rate
2013	13223.08	11916.10	1306.98	Dynamically efficient	50.35	45.38	4.98	Consumption Rate>Optimal Consumption Rate
2014	14529.94	13294.72	1235.22	Dynamically efficient	50.92	46.59	4.33	Consumption Rate>Optimal Consumption Rate
2015	15774.96	15228.86	546.10	Dynamically efficient	52.49	50.67	1.82	Consumption Rate>Optimal Consumption Rate
2016	17237.92	16614.12	623.80	Dynamically efficient	52.34	50.45	1.89	Consumption Rate>Optimal Consumption Rate

Appendix 24 1993–2016 Relationship between Dynamic Efficiency and Optimal Consumption Rate of Guizhou

Year	Final Consumption Expenditure (100 million yuan)	Labour Income (100 million yuan)	Difference between Aggregate Consumption and Labour Income (100 million yuan)	Dynamic Efficiency	Final Consumption Rate (%)	Labour Income Ratio (%)	Ratio of Difference in GDP (%)	Comparison between Actual Consumption Rate and Optimal Consumption Rate
1993	302.10	263.21	38.89	Dynamically efficient	72.61	63.26	9.35	Consumption Rate>Optimal Consumption Rate
1994	388.91	347.05	41.86	Dynamically efficient	74.62	66.59	8.03	Consumption Rate>Optimal Consumption Rate
1995	513.46	433.06	80.40	Dynamically efficient	79.20	66.80	12.40	Consumption Rate>Optimal Consumption Rate
1996	595.59	487.16	108.43	Dynamically efficient	81.82	66.92	14.90	Consumption Rate>Optimal Consumption Rate
1997	652.57	538.27	114.30	Dynamically efficient	80.69	66.55	14.13	Consumption Rate>Optimal Consumption Rate
1998	685.10	592.46	92.64	Dynamically efficient	78.28	67.69	10.58	Consumption Rate>Optimal Consumption Rate

1999	725.77	640.52	85.25	Dynamically efficient	79.59	70.24	9.35	Consumption Rate>Optimal Consumption Rate
2000	920.46	652.76	267.70	Dynamically efficient	89.37	63.38	25.99	Consumption Rate>Optimal Consumption Rate
2001	1000.35	663.42	336.93	Dynamically efficient	88.27	58.54	29.73	Consumption Rate>Optimal Consumption Rate
2002	1085.75	721.47	364.28	Dynamically efficient	87.32	58.02	29.30	Consumption Rate>Optimal Consumption Rate
2003	1169.55	825.75	343.80	Dynamically efficient	82.00	57.89	24.10	Consumption Rate>Optimal Consumption Rate
2004	1367.94	806.70	561.24	Dynamically efficient	81.53	48.08	33.45	Consumption Rate>Optimal Consumption Rate
2005	1640.41	959.60	680.82	Dynamically efficient	81.80	47.85	33.95	Consumption Rate>Optimal Consumption Rate
2006	1854.35	1260.39	593.96	Dynamically efficient	79.28	53.89	25.39	Consumption Rate>Optimal Consumption Rate

(*Continued*)

Appendix 24 Continued

Year	Final Consumption Expenditure (100 million yuan)	Labour Income (100 million yuan)	Difference between Aggregate Consumption and Labour Income (100 million yuan)	Dynamic Efficiency	Final Consumption Rate (%)	Labour Income Ratio (%)	Ratio of Difference in GDP (%)	Comparison between Actual Consumption Rate and Optimal Consumption Rate
2007	2087.54	1584.50	503.04	Dynamically efficient	72.38	54.94	17.44	Consumption Rate>Optimal Consumption Rate
2008	2354.11	1970.92	383.19	Dynamically efficient	66.10	55.34	10.76	Consumption Rate<Optimal Consumption Rate
2009	2603.31	2199.72	403.59	Dynamically efficient	66.54	56.22	10.31	Consumption Rate<Optimal Consumption Rate
2010	2931.13	2566.60	364.53	Dynamically efficient	63.69	55.77	7.92	Consumption Rate>Optimal Consumption Rate
2011	3438.71	3131.57	307.14	Dynamically efficient	60.31	54.92	5.39	Consumption Rate>Optimal Consumption Rate

2012	3950.64	3833.34	117.30	Dynamically efficient	57.66	55.94	1.71	Consumption Rate>Optimal Consumption Rate
2013	4535.82	4543.30	-7.48	Dynamically Inefficient	56.65	56.74	-0.09	Consumption Rate<Optimal Consumption Rate
2014	5288.50	5272.93	15.57	Dynamically efficient	57.07	56.90	0.17	Consumption Rate>Optimal Consumption Rate
2015	5957.73	6138.08	-180.35	Dynamically Inefficient	56.73	58.44	-1.72	Consumption Rate<Optimal Consumption Rate
2016	6745.95	6873.87	-127.92	Dynamically Inefficient	57.28	58.37	-1.09	Consumption Rate<Optimal Consumption Rate

Appendix 25 1993–2016 Relationship between Dynamic Efficiency and Optimal Consumption Rate of Yunnan

Year	Final Consumption Expenditure (100 million yuan)	Labour Income (100 million yuan)	Difference between Aggregate Consumption and Labour Income (100 million yuan)	Dynamic Efficiency	Final Consumption Rate (%)	Labour Income Ratio (%)	Ratio of Difference in GDP (%)	Comparison between Actual Consumption Rate and Optimal Consumption Rate
1993	471.26	377.69	93.58	Dynamically efficient	60.48	48.47	12.01	Consumption Rate>Optimal Consumption Rate
1994	570.45	452.99	117.46	Dynamically efficient	58.57	46.51	12.06	Consumption Rate>Optimal Consumption Rate
1995	689.39	592.60	96.79	Dynamically efficient	57.13	49.11	8.02	Consumption Rate>Optimal Consumption Rate
1996	858.69	753.96	104.73	Dynamically efficient	57.57	50.55	7.02	Consumption Rate>Optimal Consumption Rate
1997	983.77	824.86	158.91	Dynamically efficient	59.83	50.17	9.66	Consumption Rate>Optimal Consumption Rate
1998	1089.90	864.12	225.78	Dynamically efficient	60.76	48.17	12.59	Consumption Rate>Optimal Consumption Rate

1999	1256.46	957.34	299.12	Dynamically efficient	67.71	51.59	16.12	Consumption Rate>Optimal Consumption Rate
2000	1524.48	936.53	587.95	Dynamically efficient	75.80	46.57	29.23	Consumption Rate>Optimal Consumption Rate
2001	1473.30	1050.06	423.24	Dynamically efficient	68.90	49.11	19.79	Consumption Rate>Optimal Consumption Rate
2002	1581.97	1110.15	471.82	Dynamically efficient	68.40	48.00	20.40	Consumption Rate>Optimal Consumption Rate
2003	1656.30	1242.70	413.60	Dynamically efficient	64.80	48.62	16.18	Consumption Rate>Optimal Consumption Rate
2004	2042.43	1433.43	609.00	Dynamically efficient	66.27	46.51	19.76	Consumption Rate>Optimal Consumption Rate
2005	2364.21	1719.74	644.47	Dynamically efficient	68.28	49.66	18.61	Consumption Rate>Optimal Consumption Rate
2006	2659.07	1927.18	731.89	Dynamically efficient	66.67	48.32	18.35	Consumption Rate>Optimal Consumption Rate

(*Continued*)

Appendix 25 Continued

Year	Final Consumption Expenditure (100 million yuan)	Labour Income (100 million yuan)	Difference between Aggregate Consumption and Labour Income (100 million yuan)	Dynamic Efficiency	Final Consumption Rate (%)	Labour Income Ratio (%)	Ratio of Difference in GDP (%)	Comparison between Actual Consumption Rate and Optimal Consumption Rate
2007	2955.03	2394.48	560.55	Dynamically efficient	61.92	50.17	11.75	Consumption Rate>Optimal Consumption Rate
2008	3410.47	2981.75	428.72	Dynamically efficient	59.92	52.38	7.53	Consumption Rate>Optimal Consumption Rate
2009	3768.76	3211.11	557.65	Dynamically efficient	61.08	52.05	9.04	Consumption Rate>Optimal Consumption Rate
2010	4332.64	3511.27	821.37	Dynamically efficient	59.97	48.60	11.37	Consumption Rate>Optimal Consumption Rate
2011	5273.62	4484.91	788.71	Dynamically efficient	59.30	50.43	8.87	Consumption Rate>Optimal Consumption Rate

2012	6306.75	5474.71	832.04	Dynamically efficient	61.17	53.10	8.07	Consumption Rate>Optimal Consumption Rate
2013	7364.18	6293.40	1070.78	Dynamically efficient	62.83	53.69	9.14	Consumption Rate>Optimal Consumption Rate
2014	8207.52	6760.20	1447.32	Dynamically efficient	64.05	52.75	11.29	Consumption Rate>Optimal Consumption Rate
2015	8855.33	7167.22	1688.11	Dynamically efficient	65.02	52.63	12.40	Consumption Rate>Optimal Consumption Rate
2016	9592.74	7984.16	1608.58	Dynamically efficient	64.87	53.99	10.88	Consumption Rate>Optimal Consumption Rate

Appendix 26 1993–2016 Relationship between Dynamic Efficiency and Optimal Consumption Rate of Shaanxi

Year	Final Consumption Expenditure (100 million yuan)	Labour Income (100 million yuan)	Difference between Aggregate Consumption and Labour Income (100 million yuan)	Dynamic Efficiency	Final Consumption Rate (%)	Labour Income Ratio (%)	Ratio of Difference in GDP (%)	Comparison between Actual Consumption Rate and Optimal Consumption Rate
1993	442.73	422.85	19.88	Dynamically efficient	66.94	63.93	3.01	Consumption Rate>Optimal Consumption Rate
1994	570.34	509.25	61.09	Dynamically efficient	69.84	62.36	7.48	Consumption Rate>Optimal Consumption Rate
1995	673.42	658.70	14.72	Dynamically efficient	67.34	65.87	1.47	Consumption Rate>Optimal Consumption Rate
1996	779.37	732.32	47.05	Dynamically efficient	66.28	62.28	4.00	Consumption Rate>Optimal Consumption Rate
1997	884.58	799.65	84.93	Dynamically efficient	68.04	61.51	6.53	Consumption Rate>Optimal Consumption Rate
1998	899.90	813.91	85.99	Dynamically efficient	65.14	58.91	6.22	Consumption Rate>Optimal Consumption Rate

1999	903.79	841.22	62.57	Dynamically efficient	60.75	56.55	4.21	Consumption Rate>Optimal Consumption Rate
2000	1042.94	1037.47	5.47	Dynamically efficient	57.81	57.51	0.30	Consumption Rate>Optimal Consumption Rate
2001	1337.30	1131.89	205.41	Dynamically efficient	66.51	56.30	10.22	Consumption Rate>Optimal Consumption Rate
2002	1475.50	1176.97	298.53	Dynamically efficient	65.48	52.23	13.25	Consumption Rate>Optimal Consumption Rate
2003	1619.30	1241.25	378.05	Dynamically efficient	62.58	47.97	14.61	Consumption Rate>Optimal Consumption Rate
2004	1827.70	1332.18	495.52	Dynamically efficient	57.55	41.95	15.60	Consumption Rate>Optimal Consumption Rate
2005	2112.91	1705.48	407.43	Dynamically efficient	53.71	43.36	10.36	Consumption Rate>Optimal Consumption Rate
2006	2389.24	1984.48	404.76	Dynamically efficient	50.37	41.83	8.53	Consumption Rate>Optimal Consumption Rate

(*Continued*)

Appendix 26 Continued

Year	Final Consumption Expenditure (100 million yuan)	Labour Income (100 million yuan)	Difference between Aggregate Consumption and Labour Income (100 million yuan)	Dynamic Efficiency	Final Consumption Rate (%)	Labour Income Ratio (%)	Ratio of Difference in GDP (%)	Comparison between Actual Consumption Rate and Optimal Consumption Rate
2007	2842.40	2279.87	562.54	Dynamically efficient	49.37	39.60	9.77	Consumption Rate>Optimal Consumption Rate
2008	3461.00	3479.52	-18.52	Dynamically Inefficient	47.32	47.57	-0.25	Consumption Rate<Optimal Consumption Rate
2009	3897.41	3876.06	21.35	Dynamically efficient	47.71	47.44	0.26	Consumption Rate>Optimal Consumption Rate
2010	4640.10	4229.65	410.45	Dynamically efficient	45.84	41.78	4.05	Consumption Rate>Optimal Consumption Rate
2011	5573.25	5157.24	416.01	Dynamically efficient	44.54	41.22	3.32	Consumption Rate>Optimal Consumption Rate

2012	6387.07	5844.83	542.25	Dynamically efficient	44.19	40.44	3.75	Consumption Rate>Optimal Consumption Rate
2013	7051.85	7096.68	-44.83	Dynamically Inefficient	43.95	44.23	-0.28	Consumption Rate<Optimal Consumption Rate
2014	7816.10	7683.56	132.54	Dynamically efficient	44.18	43.43	0.75	Consumption Rate>Optimal Consumption Rate
2015	8199.95	8111.63	88.32	Dynamically efficient	45.50	45.01	0.49	Consumption Rate>Optimal Consumption Rate
2016	8790.91	8895.14	-104.23	Dynamically Inefficient	45.31	45.85	-0.54	Consumption Rate<Optimal Consumption Rate

Appendix 27 1993-2016 Relationship between Dynamic Efficiency and Optimal Consumption Rate of Gansu

Year	Final Consumption Expenditure (100 million yuan)	Labour Income (100 million yuan)	Difference between Aggregate Consumption and Labour Income (100 million yuan)	Dynamic Efficiency	Final Consumption Rate (%)	Labour Income Ratio (%)	Ratio of Difference in GDP (%)	Comparison between Actual Consumption Rate and Optimal Consumption Rate
1993	263.00	201.39	61.61	Dynamically efficient	70.65	54.10	16.55	Consumption Rate>Optimal Consumption Rate
1994	319.11	244.02	75.09	Dynamically efficient	70.65	54.03	16.63	Consumption Rate>Optimal Consumption Rate
1995	376.81	294.69	82.12	Dynamically efficient	68.10	53.26	14.84	Consumption Rate>Optimal Consumption Rate
1996	485.42	416.78	68.64	Dynamically efficient	67.97	58.36	9.61	Consumption Rate>Optimal Consumption Rate
1997	516.84	445.60	71.24	Dynamically efficient	66.15	57.03	9.12	Consumption Rate>Optimal Consumption Rate
1998	528.10	496.24	31.86	Dynamically efficient	60.72	57.05	3.66	Consumption Rate>Optimal Consumption Rate

1999	547.75	537.94	9.81	Dynamically efficient	58.83	57.78	1.05	Consumption Rate>Optimal Consumption Rate
2000	635.71	662.22	-26.51	Dynamically Inefficient	60.38	62.90	-2.52	Consumption Rate<Optimal Consumption Rate
2001	702.29	658.13	44.16	Dynamically efficient	62.41	58.48	3.92	Consumption Rate>Optimal Consumption Rate
2002	770.54	696.34	74.20	Dynamically efficient	62.54	56.52	6.02	Consumption Rate>Optimal Consumption Rate
2003	863.46	748.21	115.25	Dynamically efficient	61.68	53.45	8.23	Consumption Rate>Optimal Consumption Rate
2004	1047.66	894.66	153.00	Dynamically efficient	62.05	52.99	9.06	Consumption Rate>Optimal Consumption Rate
2005	1217.63	933.26	284.37	Dynamically efficient	62.96	48.26	14.70	Consumption Rate>Optimal Consumption Rate
2006	1367.12	1107.90	259.22	Dynamically efficient	60.03	48.65	11.38	Consumption Rate>Optimal Consumption Rate

(Continued)

Appendix 27 Continued

Year	Final Consumption Expenditure (100 million yuan)	Labour Income (100 million yuan)	Difference between Aggregate Consumption and Labour Income (100 million yuan)	Dynamic Efficiency	Final Consumption Rate (%)	Labour Income Ratio (%)	Ratio of Difference in GDP (%)	Comparison between Actual Consumption Rate and Optimal Consumption Rate
2007	1593.89	1240.42	353.47	Dynamically efficient	58.95	45.87	13.07	Consumption Rate>Optimal Consumption Rate
2008	1897.06	1760.27	136.79	Dynamically Inefficient	59.90	55.58	4.32	Consumption Rate<Optimal Consumption Rate
2009	2127.01	1669.92	457.09	Dynamically efficient	62.79	49.30	13.49	Consumption Rate>Optimal Consumption Rate
2010	2462.03	2253.24	208.79	Dynamically efficient	59.75	54.68	5.07	Consumption Rate>Optimal Consumption Rate
2011	2967.02	2422.43	544.59	Dynamically efficient	59.10	48.25	10.85	Consumption Rate>Optimal Consumption Rate

2012	3327.97	2760.30	567.67	Dynamically efficient	58.90	48.85	10.05	Consumption Rate>Optimal Consumption Rate
2013	3682.89	3285.46	397.43	Dynamically Inefficient	58.76	52.42	6.34	Consumption Rate<Optimal Consumption Rate
2014	4035.59	3509.47	526.12	Dynamically efficient	59.03	51.33	7.70	Consumption Rate>Optimal Consumption Rate
2015	4374.19	3646.78	727.41	Dynamically efficient	64.42	53.71	10.71	Consumption Rate>Optimal Consumption Rate
2016	4751.39	3882.97	868.42	Dynamically efficient	65.99	53.93	12.06	Consumption Rate>Optimal Consumption Rate

Appendix 28 1993–2016 Relationship between Dynamic Efficiency and Optimal Consumption Rate of Qinghai

Year	Final Consumption Expenditure (100 million yuan)	Labour Income (100 million yuan)	Difference between Aggregate Consumption and Labour Income (100 million yuan)	Dynamic Efficiency	Final Consumption Rate (%)	Labour Income Ratio (%)	Ratio of Difference in GDP (%)	Comparison between Actual Consumption Rate and Optimal Consumption Rate
1993	72.80	65.71	7.09	Dynamically efficient	66.41	59.94	6.47	Consumption Rate>Optimal Consumption Rate
1994	92.17	79.86	12.31	Dynamically efficient	66.67	57.77	8.90	Consumption Rate>Optimal Consumption Rate
1995	112.24	95.00	17.24	Dynamically efficient	67.69	57.30	10.40	Consumption Rate>Optimal Consumption Rate
1996	131.10	114.59	16.51	Dynamically efficient	69.86	61.06	8.80	Consumption Rate>Optimal Consumption Rate
1997	132.67	125.93	6.74	Dynamically efficient	63.76	60.52	3.24	Consumption Rate>Optimal Consumption Rate
1998	139.30	130.67	8.63	Dynamically efficient	62.08	58.23	3.84	Consumption Rate>Optimal Consumption Rate

1999	151.45	140.91	10.54	Dynamically efficient	62.71	58.35	4.36	Consumption Rate>Optimal Consumption Rate
2000	171.70	146.36	25.34	Dynamically Inefficient	65.12	55.51	9.61	Consumption Rate<Optimal Consumption Rate
2001	202.88	164.61	38.27	Dynamically efficient	67.60	54.85	12.75	Consumption Rate>Optimal Consumption Rate
2002	227.58	180.93	46.65	Dynamically efficient	66.81	53.11	13.70	Consumption Rate>Optimal Consumption Rate
2003	257.75	199.24	58.51	Dynamically efficient	66.06	51.06	15.00	Consumption Rate>Optimal Consumption Rate
2004	309.76	231.32	78.45	Dynamically efficient	66.46	49.63	16.83	Consumption Rate>Optimal Consumption Rate
2005	360.72	271.46	89.26	Dynamically efficient	66.39	49.96	16.43	Consumption Rate>Optimal Consumption Rate
2006	423.49	330.11	93.38	Dynamically efficient	65.30	50.90	14.40	Consumption Rate>Optimal Consumption Rate

(*Continued*)

Appendix 28 Continued

Year	Final Consumption Expenditure (100 million yuan)	Labour Income (100 million yuan)	Difference between Aggregate Consumption and Labour Income (100 million yuan)	Dynamic Efficiency	Final Consumption Rate (%)	Labour Income Ratio (%)	Ratio of Difference in GDP (%)	Comparison between Actual Consumption Rate and Optimal Consumption Rate
2007	509.45	426.23	83.22	Dynamically efficient	63.89	53.46	10.44	Consumption Rate>Optimal Consumption Rate
2008	593.51	563.43	30.08	Dynamically Inefficient	58.27	55.31	2.95	Consumption Rate<Optimal Consumption Rate
2009	616.51	610.77	5.74	Dynamically efficient	57.02	56.49	0.53	Consumption Rate>Optimal Consumption Rate
2010	720.57	667.11	53.46	Dynamically efficient	53.36	49.40	3.96	Consumption Rate>Optimal Consumption Rate
2011	859.75	793.93	65.82	Dynamically efficient	51.47	47.53	3.94	Consumption Rate>Optimal Consumption Rate

2012	997.36	864.76	132.60	Dynamically efficient	52.67	45.67	7.00	Consumption Rate>Optimal Consumption Rate
2013	1048.49	1004.93	43.56	Dynamically Inefficient	49.41	47.36	2.05	Consumption Rate<Optimal Consumption Rate
2014	1154.40	1125.19	29.21	Dynamically efficient	50.12	48.85	1.27	Consumption Rate>Optimal Consumption Rate
2015	1485.98	1181.46	304.52	Dynamically efficient	61.48	48.88	12.60	Consumption Rate>Optimal Consumption Rate
2016	1676.44	1317.49	358.95	Dynamically efficient	65.17	51.21	13.95	Consumption Rate>Optimal Consumption Rate

Appendix 29 1993–2016 Relationship between Dynamic Efficiency and Optimal Consumption Rate of Ningxia

Year	Final Consumption Expenditure (100 million yuan)	Labour Income (100 million yuan)	Difference between Aggregate Consumption and Labour Income (100 million yuan)	Dynamic Efficiency	Final Consumption Rate (%)	Labour Income Ratio (%)	Ratio of Difference in GDP (%)	Comparison between Actual Consumption Rate and Optimal Consumption Rate
1993	72.16	50.72	21.45	Dynamically efficient	69.24	48.66	20.58	Consumption Rate>Optimal Consumption Rate
1994	95.17	71.97	23.20	Dynamically efficient	70.90	53.61	17.29	Consumption Rate>Optimal Consumption Rate
1995	113.31	94.87	18.44	Dynamically efficient	66.75	55.89	10.86	Consumption Rate>Optimal Consumption Rate
1996	124.59	111.16	13.43	Dynamically efficient	64.35	57.41	6.93	Consumption Rate>Optimal Consumption Rate
1997	130.72	119.71	11.01	Dynamically efficient	61.98	56.76	5.22	Consumption Rate>Optimal Consumption Rate
1998	141.50	132.86	8.64	Dynamically efficient	62.17	58.37	3.80	Consumption Rate>Optimal Consumption Rate

1999	153.97	144.19	9.78	Dynamically efficient	63.76	59.71	4.05	Consumption Rate>Optimal Consumption Rate
2000	193.89	159.02	34.87	Dynamically Inefficient	65.72	53.90	11.82	Consumption Rate<Optimal Consumption Rate
2001	231.99	176.49	55.50	Dynamically efficient	68.75	52.30	16.45	Consumption Rate>Optimal Consumption Rate
2002	260.38	197.87	62.51	Dynamically efficient	69.04	52.46	16.57	Consumption Rate>Optimal Consumption Rate
2003	291.69	231.15	60.54	Dynamically efficient	65.50	51.90	13.59	Consumption Rate>Optimal Consumption Rate
2004	338.66	273.15	65.51	Dynamically efficient	63.05	50.85	12.20	Consumption Rate>Optimal Consumption Rate
2005	401.11	320.69	80.42	Dynamically efficient	65.48	52.35	13.13	Consumption Rate>Optimal Consumption Rate
2006	460.41	391.92	68.49	Dynamically efficient	63.43	53.99	9.43	Consumption Rate>Optimal Consumption Rate

(*Continued*)

Appendix 29 Continued

Year	Final Consumption Expenditure (100 million yuan)	Labour Income (100 million yuan)	Difference between Aggregate Consumption and Labour Income (100 million yuan)	Dynamic Efficiency	Final Consumption Rate (%)	Labour Income Ratio (%)	Ratio of Difference in GDP (%)	Comparison between Actual Consumption Rate and Optimal Consumption Rate
2007	538.50	482.77	55.73	Dynamically efficient	58.59	52.53	6.06	Consumption Rate>Optimal Consumption Rate
2008	652.95	677.74	-24.79	Dynamically Inefficient	54.24	56.29	-2.06	Consumption Rate<Optimal Consumption Rate
2009	656.05	756.86	-100.81	Dynamically Inefficient	48.48	55.93	-7.45	Consumption Rate<Optimal Consumption Rate
2010	824.91	967.42	-142.51	Dynamically Inefficient	48.82	57.26	-8.43	Consumption Rate<Optimal Consumption Rate
2011	1020.18	1114.73	-94.55	Dynamically Inefficient	48.53	53.03	-4.50	Consumption Rate<Optimal Consumption Rate

2012	1184.01	1208.39	-24.38	Dynamically Inefficient	50.57	51.61	-1.04	Consumption Rate<Optimal Consumption Rate
2013	1340.08	1348.83	-8.75	Dynamically Inefficient	52.24	52.58	-0.34	Consumption Rate<Optimal Consumption Rate
2014	1468.62	1480.49	-11.87	Dynamically Inefficient	53.36	53.79	-0.43	Consumption Rate<Optimal Consumption Rate
2015	1719.65	1684.50	35.15	Dynamically efficient	59.06	57.85	1.21	Consumption Rate>Optimal Consumption Rate
2016	1891.59	1745.25	146.34	Dynamically efficient	59.70	55.08	4.62	Consumption Rate>Optimal Consumption Rate

Appendix 30 1993–2016 Relationship between Dynamic Efficiency and Optimal Consumption Rate of Xinjiang

Year	Final Consumption Expenditure (100 million yuan)	Labour Income (100 million yuan)	Difference between Aggregate Consumption and Labour Income (100 million yuan)	Dynamic Efficiency	Final Consumption Rate (%)	Labour Income Ratio (%)	Ratio of Difference in GDP (%)	Comparison between Actual Consumption Rate and Optimal Consumption Rate
1993	300.75	281.81	18.94	Dynamically efficient	59.48	55.73	3.75	Consumption Rate>Optimal Consumption Rate
1994	375.20	364.58	10.62	Dynamically efficient	55.69	54.12	1.58	Consumption Rate>Optimal Consumption Rate
1995	497.56	474.73	22.83	Dynamically efficient	60.30	57.53	2.77	Consumption Rate>Optimal Consumption Rate
1996	579.68	532.43	47.25	Dynamically efficient	63.55	58.37	5.18	Consumption Rate>Optimal Consumption Rate
1997	640.26	615.24	25.02	Dynamically efficient	60.97	58.59	2.38	Consumption Rate>Optimal Consumption Rate
1998	677.20	671.01	6.19	Dynamically efficient	60.64	60.09	0.55	Consumption Rate>Optimal Consumption Rate

1999	745.20	681.14	64.06	Dynamically efficient	63.77	58.29	5.48	Consumption Rate>Optimal Consumption Rate
2000	758.05	706.50	51.55	Dynamically efficient	55.59	51.81	3.78	Consumption Rate<Optimal Consumption Rate
2001	854.60	823.76	30.84	Dynamically efficient	57.29	55.23	2.07	Consumption Rate>Optimal Consumption Rate
2002	948.92	863.03	85.89	Dynamically efficient	58.84	53.52	5.33	Consumption Rate>Optimal Consumption Rate
2003	1012.26	1024.17	−11.91	Dynamically Inefficient	53.66	54.29	−0.63	Consumption Rate<Optimal Consumption Rate
2004	1125.12	1250.96	−125.84	Dynamically Inefficient	50.93	56.63	−5.70	Consumption Rate<Optimal Consumption Rate
2005	1260.06	1328.90	−68.84	Dynamically Inefficient	48.39	51.03	−2.64	Consumption Rate<Optimal Consumption Rate
2006	1453.37	1428.01	25.36	Dynamically efficient	47.73	46.89	0.83	Consumption Rate>Optimal Consumption Rate

(*Continued*)

Appendix 30 Continued

Year	Final Consumption Expenditure (100 million yuan)	Labour Income (100 million yuan)	Difference between Aggregate Consumption and Labour Income (100 million yuan)	Dynamic Efficiency	Final Consumption Rate (%)	Labour Income Ratio (%)	Ratio of Difference in GDP (%)	Comparison between Actual Consumption Rate and Optimal Consumption Rate
2007	1728.39	1645.14	83.25	Dynamically efficient	49.06	46.70	2.36	Consumption Rate>Optimal Consumption Rate
2008	2068.55	2190.16	-121.61	Dynamically Inefficient	49.45	52.36	-2.91	Consumption Rate<Optimal Consumption Rate
2009	2256.64	2445.84	-189.20	Dynamically Inefficient	52.76	57.19	-4.42	Consumption Rate<Optimal Consumption Rate
2010	2893.86	2970.52	-76.66	Dynamically Inefficient	53.22	54.63	-1.41	Consumption Rate<Optimal Consumption Rate
2011	3518.82	3512.28	6.54	Dynamically efficient	53.23	53.14	0.10	Consumption Rate>Optimal Consumption Rate

APPENDIX

2012	4262.51	4178.23	84.28	Dynamically efficient	56.79	55.67	1.12	Consumption Rate>Optimal Consumption Rate
2013	4599.24	4809.67	-210.43	Dynamically Inefficient	55.01	57.53	-2.52	Consumption Rate<Optimal Consumption Rate
2014	5024.50	5355.36	-330.86	Dynamically Inefficient	54.18	57.75	-3.57	Consumption Rate<Optimal Consumption Rate
2015	5639.84	5774.08	-134.24	Dynamically Inefficient	60.48	61.92	-1.44	Consumption Rate<Optimal Consumption Rate
2016	6155.26	6003.43	151.83	Dynamically efficient	63.79	62.21	1.57	Consumption Rate>Optimal Consumption Rate

Printed by
CPI books GmbH, Leck